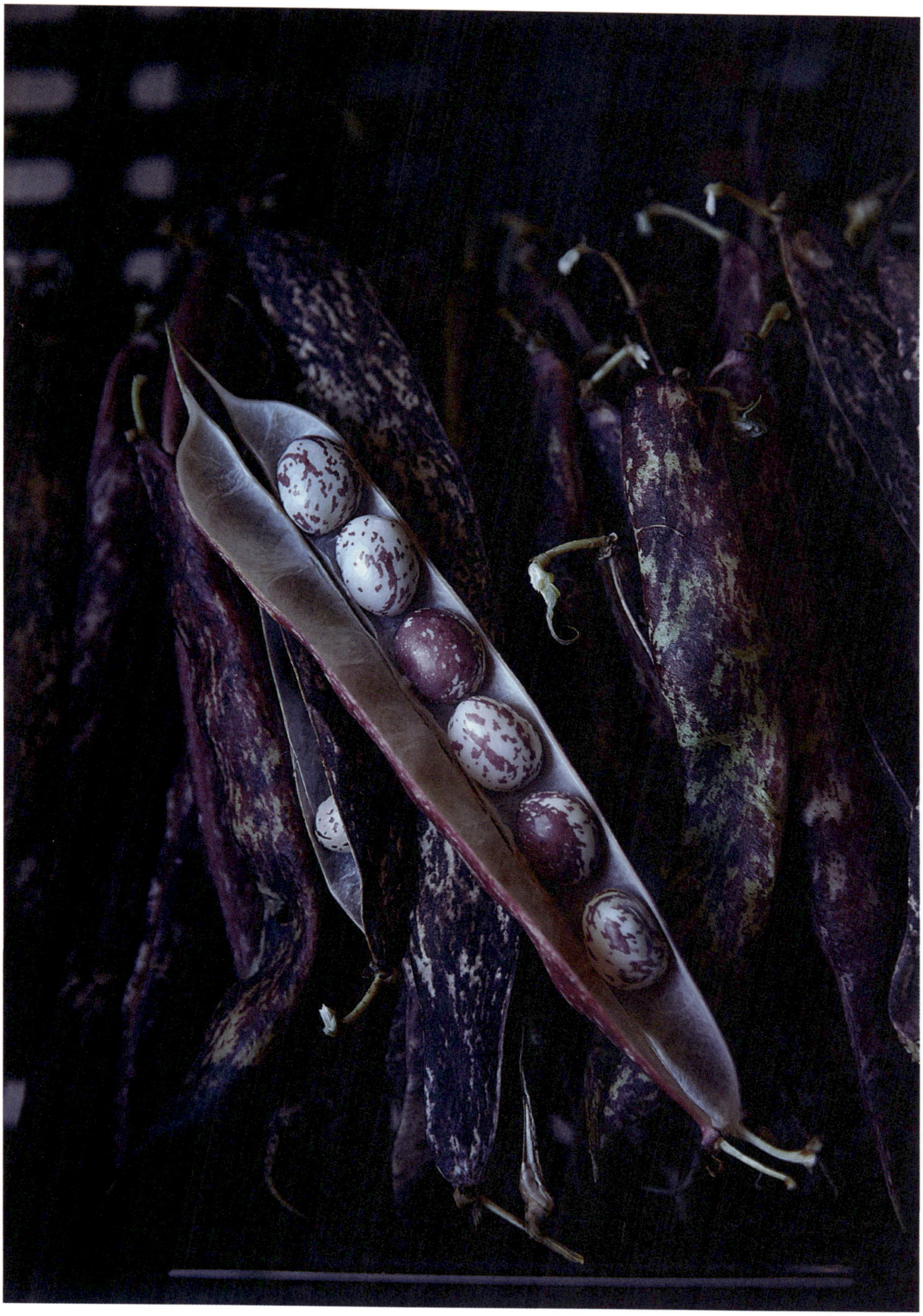

QUADRILLE

FERN VERROW

Jane Scotter and Harry Astley   Photographs by Tessa Traeger

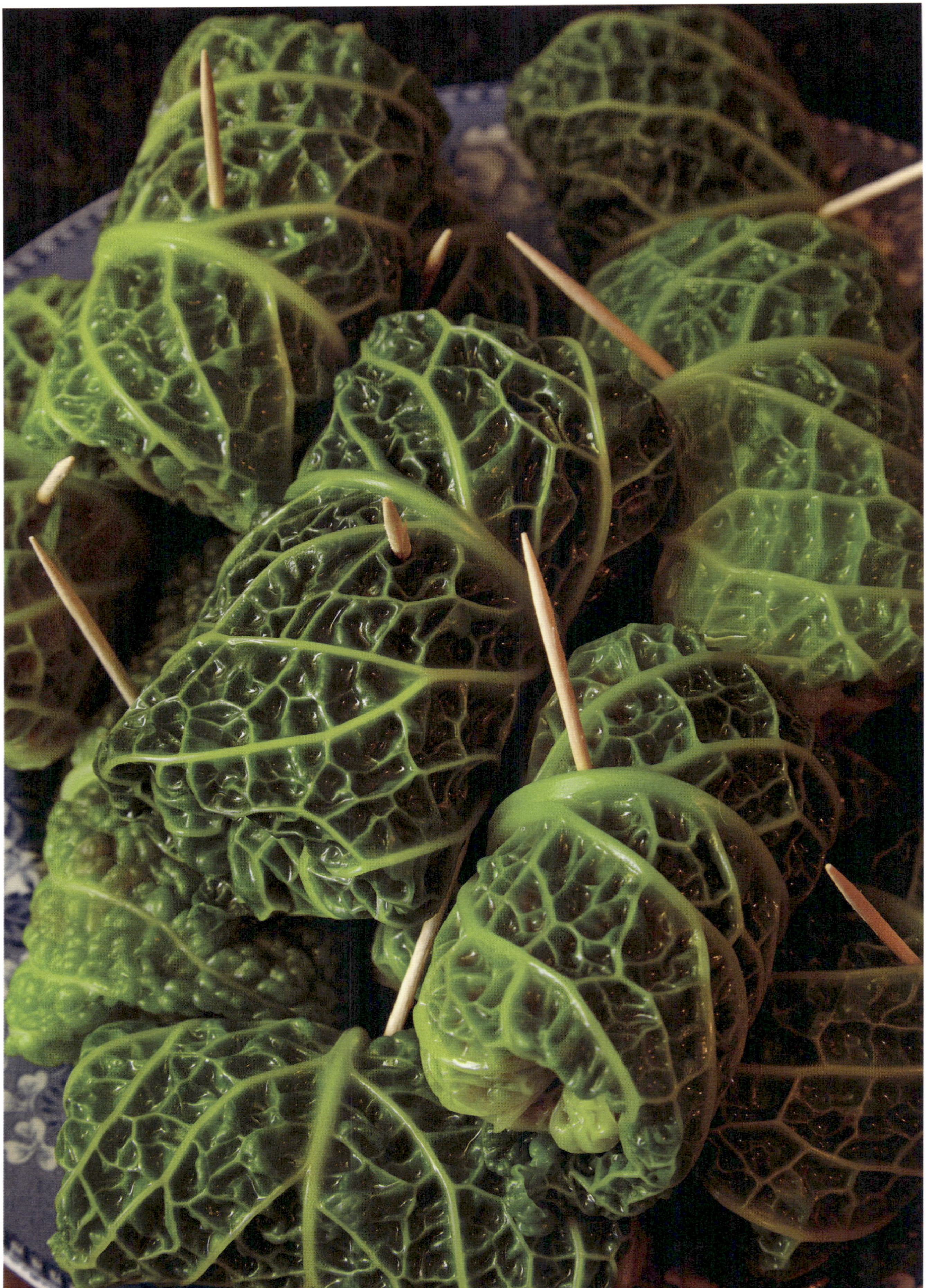

INTRODUCTION 8

EARTH
WINTER 16

WATER
SPRING 72

AIR
SUMMER 136

FIRE
AUTUMN 200

INDEX 266   ACKNOWLEDGEMENTS 270   FURTHER READING 271

FERN

BIODYNAMIC PREPARATIONS

- 500 HORN MANURE
- 501 HORN SILICA
- 502 YARROW
- 503 CHAMOMILE
- 504 NETTLE
- 505 OAK BARK
- 506 DANDELION
- 507 VALERIAN
- 508 EQUISETUM

FERN BREED

HEREFORD

VERROW

TO THE
BLACK MOUNTAINS

MAYA'S FIELD

TO THE
TUMP

SPRING

THE DINGLE

HYDRAM

OAK TREE FIELD

HAY-ON-WYE

Introduction

FERN VERROW IS the name of our farm, a 16-acre smallholding at the foothills of the Black Mountains in Herefordshire, between Hereford and Hay-on-Wye. This beautiful part of England is secluded and unspoiled, with most of the dwellings and farms still occupied by those born and bred here. The area still has many small farms. The air is clean and the farm's water supply comes from our own spring.

When we first came to Fern Verrow in 1996, the land had only ever been used for grazing. This worked in our favour – we were able to begin our cultivation of the land with a blank canvas. We came from London with no experience in farming or horticulture; just the will and desire to grow food, raise some animals and to make a living from it. On our first day our new neighbour, Ernie Price, popped by; his family has lived here for generations. With his twinkly blue eyes, and weathered face he tipped his cap and introduced himself. He was to become an invaluable source of information and knowledge for us; there wasn't a track or mound of land that he did not know. We hit it off straightaway; over many a cup of sugary tea he told us tales of the struggles and triumphs of the land we now called home.

We chose to farm using biodynamic methods, which originated from a series of lectures given in 1924 by the great Austrian thinker, Rudolf Steiner (1861–1925). He had been persistently approached by farmers to give insights into agriculture. Even in the 1920s there was growing concern from farmers about the diminishing fertility of their soil, and the degenerating health of crops and animals, all the result of an increasing use of chemical fertilisers and pesticides. What is interesting to us is that biodynamics was conceived as a way of thinking holistically about food, nutrition and the world of nature as well as a renewal of agricultural practices. It looks not only at the tangible realm of the soil, but also to the unseen forces and energies of life and growth that permeate all living things. It is the oldest consciously organic approach to farming and gardening and has developed over the past 90 years into a worldwide movement, now practised in over 40 countries. Throughout the book we will be describing some of the biodynamic measures we employ.

The honest and challenging nature of growing food is central to why we do it. Our approach to what we grow is based on our enjoyment of cooking and eating. Through our trials and study, we've learned which crops best suit our conditions, which need more thought and expertise, and which are loss leaders. We find that growing vegetables and fruit in good soil, at the right time of year – open to the elements – adds greatly to their character and flavour. Over the years Mother Nature has thrown her best and worst in our direction and we have withstood many a tricky season. She has helped us to understand and respect her. We have learned to adapt and to live with the rhythms and cycles of the year.

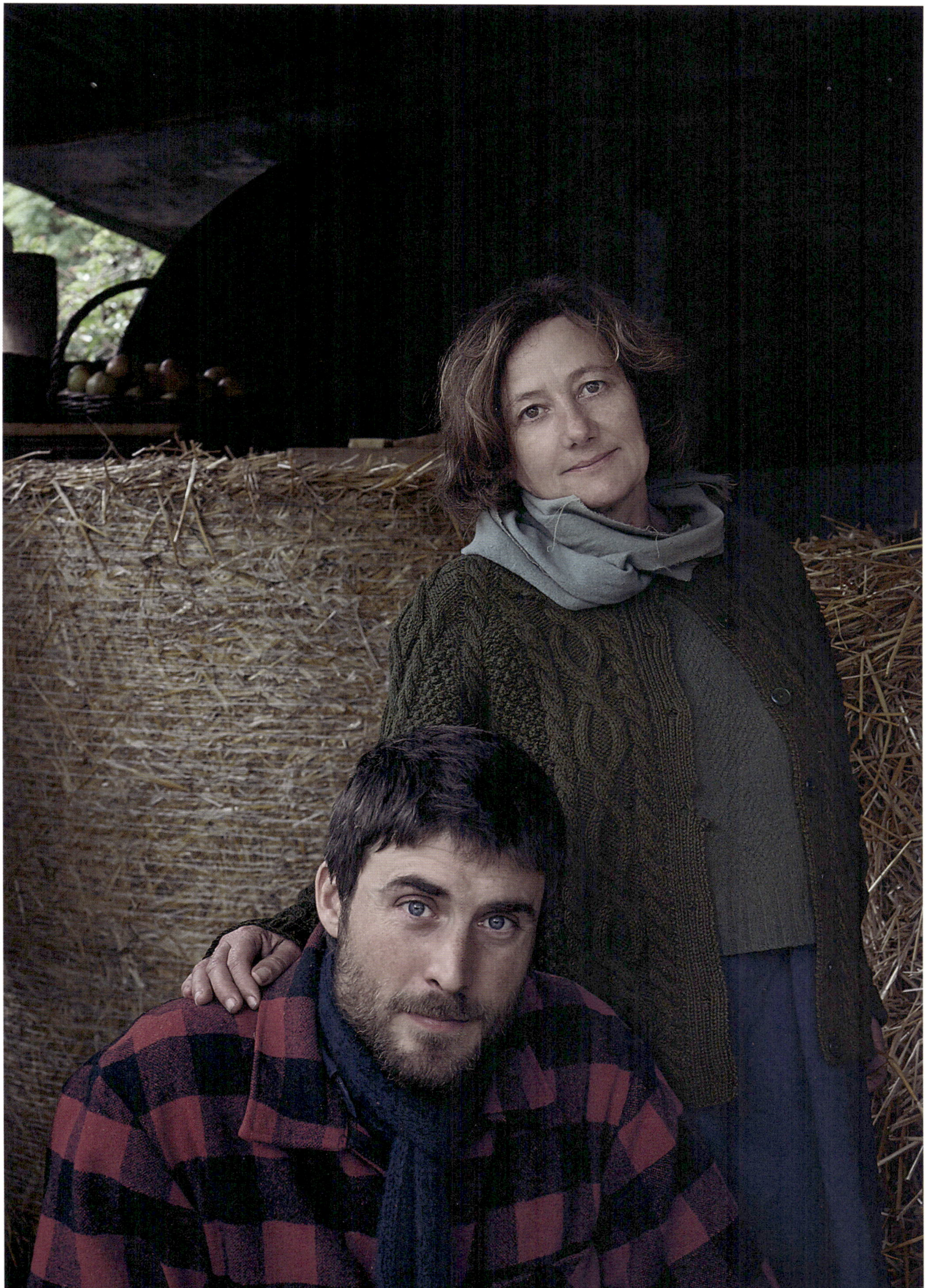

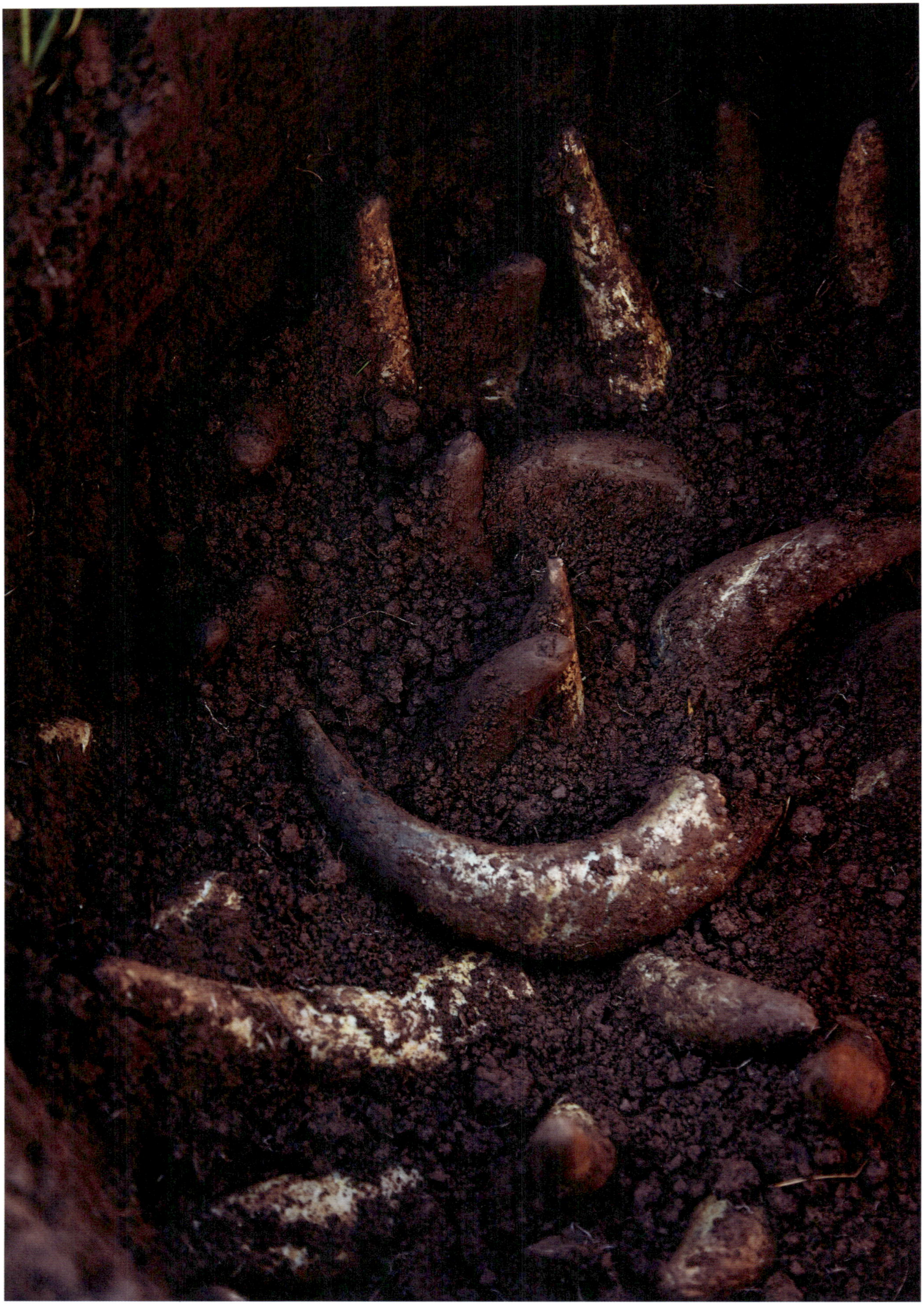

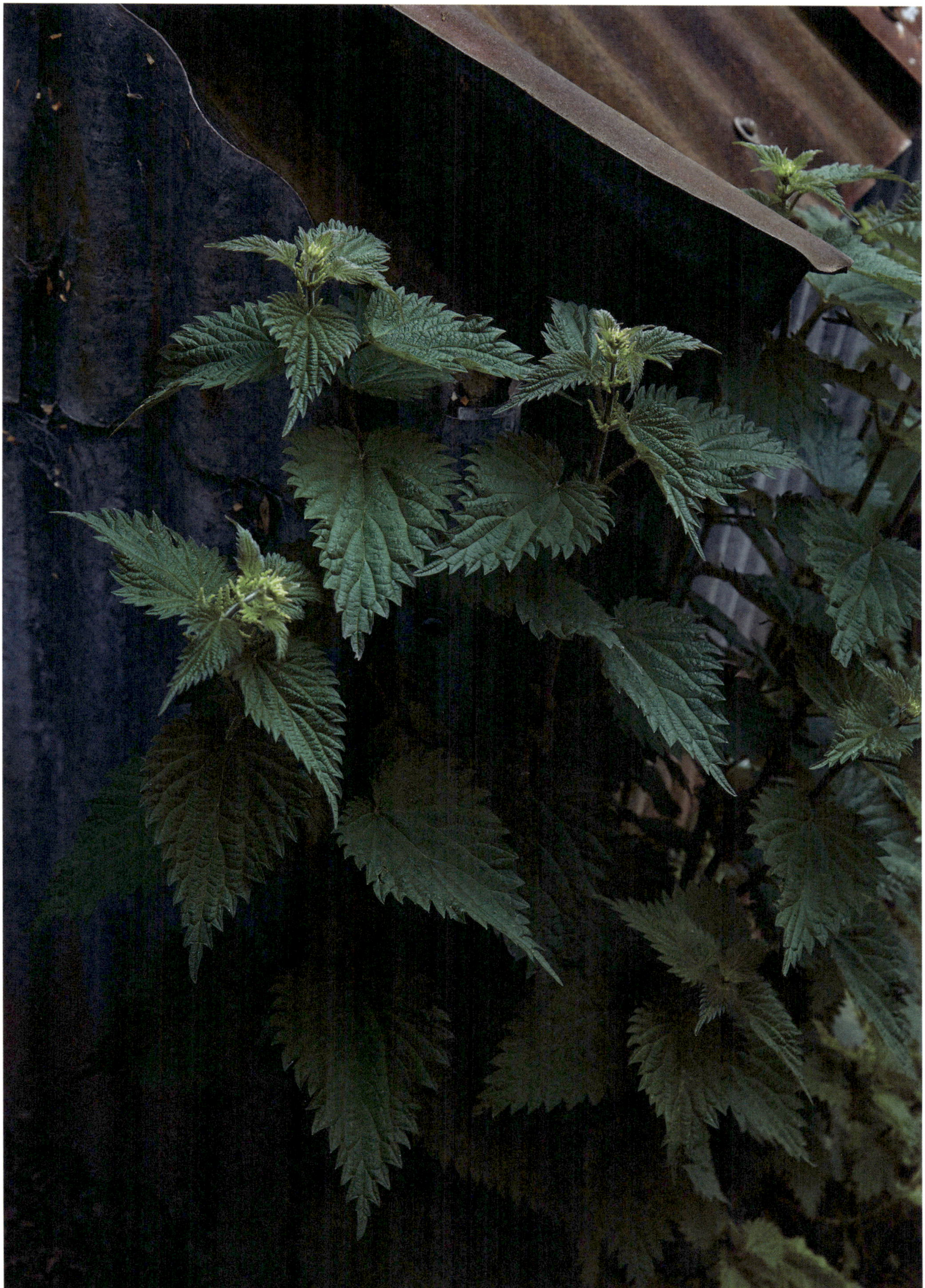

Most people are familiar with the classical elements of earth, water, air and fire. We have structured this book using these four elements to represent the four seasons of the year. The story begins in winter, with the earth, and develops from the ground up, through the spreading and sprouting life in spring (water), to the light and flowering of summer (air), and culminating in the fruiting and transformation of autumn (fire).

At the heart of our story is the Fern Verrow kitchen, the engine room of the farm. It is the place where many ideas are discussed, and decisions made – where our working day begins and ends. No matter how busy we are, cooking is a pleasure we always find time for – often dashing out to a field with a torch to select produce for the evening meal. Seeing the vegetables laid out on our kitchen table, fresh and pleasing to the eye, is still a thrill, and has led to the creation of many of the recipes in this book.

When friends and family have come to stay, some have helped out by taking over the kitchen and cooking for us – and this, too, has led to the creation of what are now considered to be Fern Verrow recipes. And we must not forget the contribution of our customers at the market in London where we have sold our produce once a week for the past fifteen years. Through Saturday morning conversations we've swapped cooking ideas and culinary adventures, old and new.

This book is about how we grow, and how we cook. It is a place to pass on our recipes, as well as the understanding of food and its cultivation that we have developed over the years. It is a celebration of what nature provides. It encourages imagination and consideration in the kitchen, and the pleasures of cooking well, with an appreciation of the different vegetables, fruit and meat as they arrive at our tables throughout the course of the year.

PREVIOUS PAGE: *Horn manure is an essential ingredient in our biodynamic field sprays; nettles are at the heart of our compost preparations.*

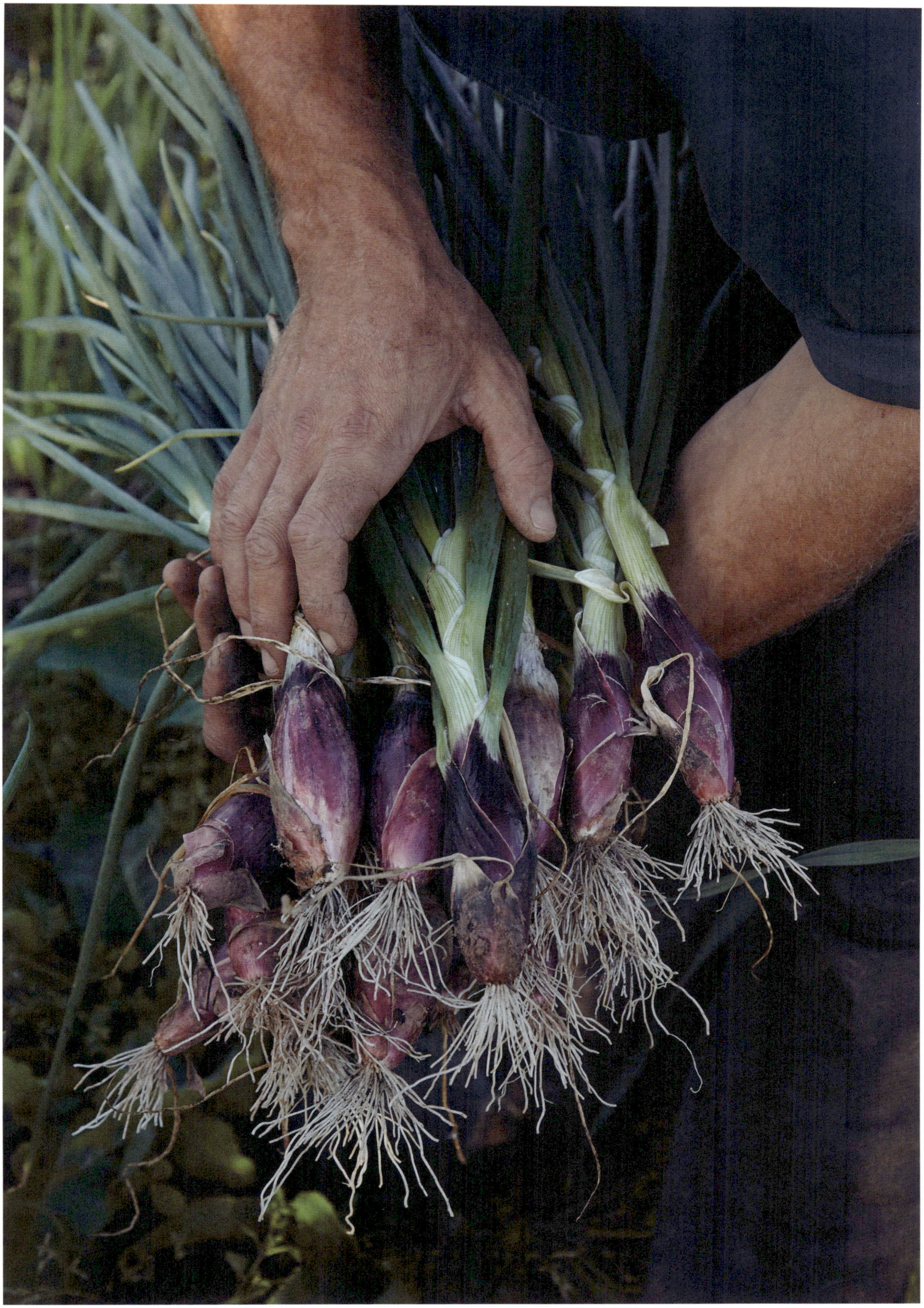

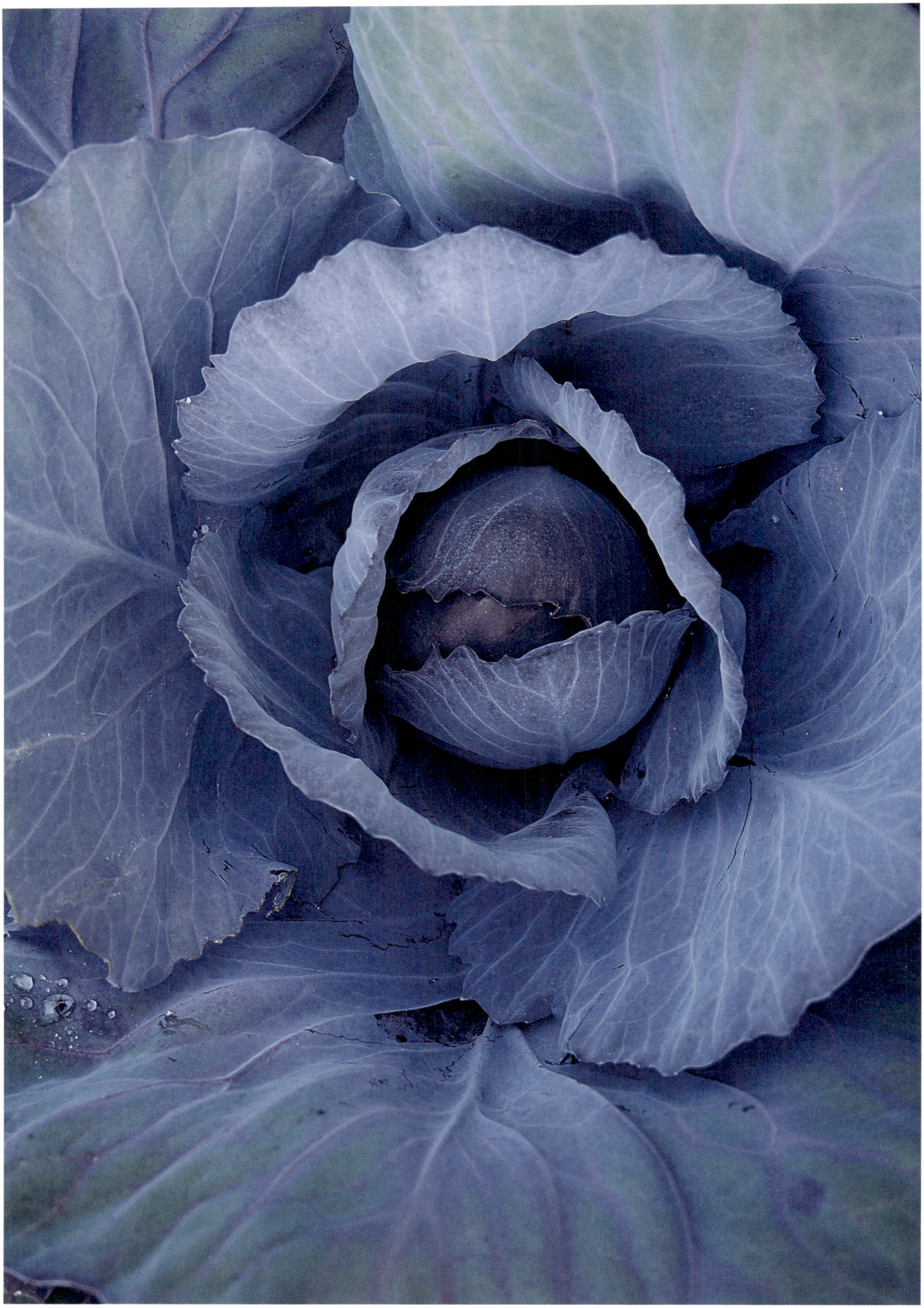

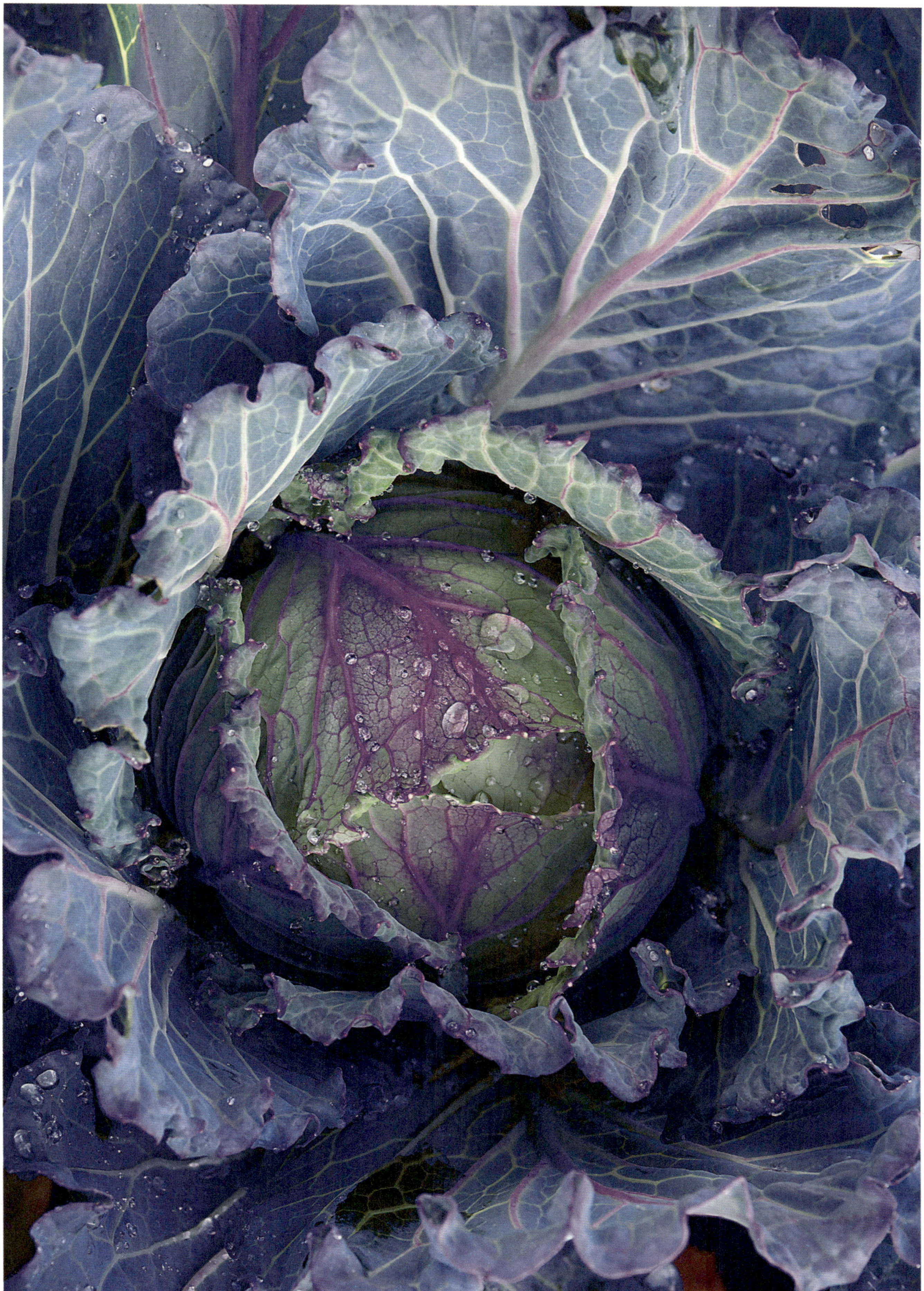

Earth
Winter

WINTER ARRIVES IN its own time: often a little earlier than anticipated, catching us unprepared; in other years later than expected, to our relief. It's not unlike waiting for a guest who plans to settle in. We're pleased to greet him, but feel somewhat unfamiliar with the new regime. As time passes we get reacquainted with each other, then towards the end of the stay we begin to wonder when he'll leave.

The arrival of the first frost, found twinkling on the grass and patterned on the car windscreen, hallmarks a new kind of beginning. The day when we reach for our long johns and thermal vests once again is always a landmark in the year. The daylight hours shrink and darker hours lengthen, as the hibernation period begins.

The wet and cold months before Christmas can be a particular challenge to the spirit. There are weeks when a blanket of cloud envelops the farm. The dank grey fog and mist rarely lift. The rain and the mud, combined with our many layers of clothing, make everything seem heavier, and moving around outside is slow and sometimes frustrating. As we slip and squelch our way around the farm, we vividly remember, and wish for, the ease, lightness and speed of activity we had in the summer. But at the same time we're thankful that the frequent rain swells the streams and brooks with the water that we'll come to rely on during the drier months.

The pace of life slows, and our work activities change. Daily priorities are to keep the animals in as good condition as possible, especially those that are due to have their young at the beginning of spring. So the cows are in the barn, in the dry with clean straw to sleep on, and plenty of hay and fresh water to eat and to drink. The sheep live outside all winter, in their thick coats. Each day they greet us enthusiastically as we arrive in the field with a bale of hay, and sometimes a few vegetables.

During this dormant time we begin pruning the fruit trees and bushes and the roses, forming their shapes and clipping the branches to maximise their fruiting and flowering potential. We're often accompanied by a robin

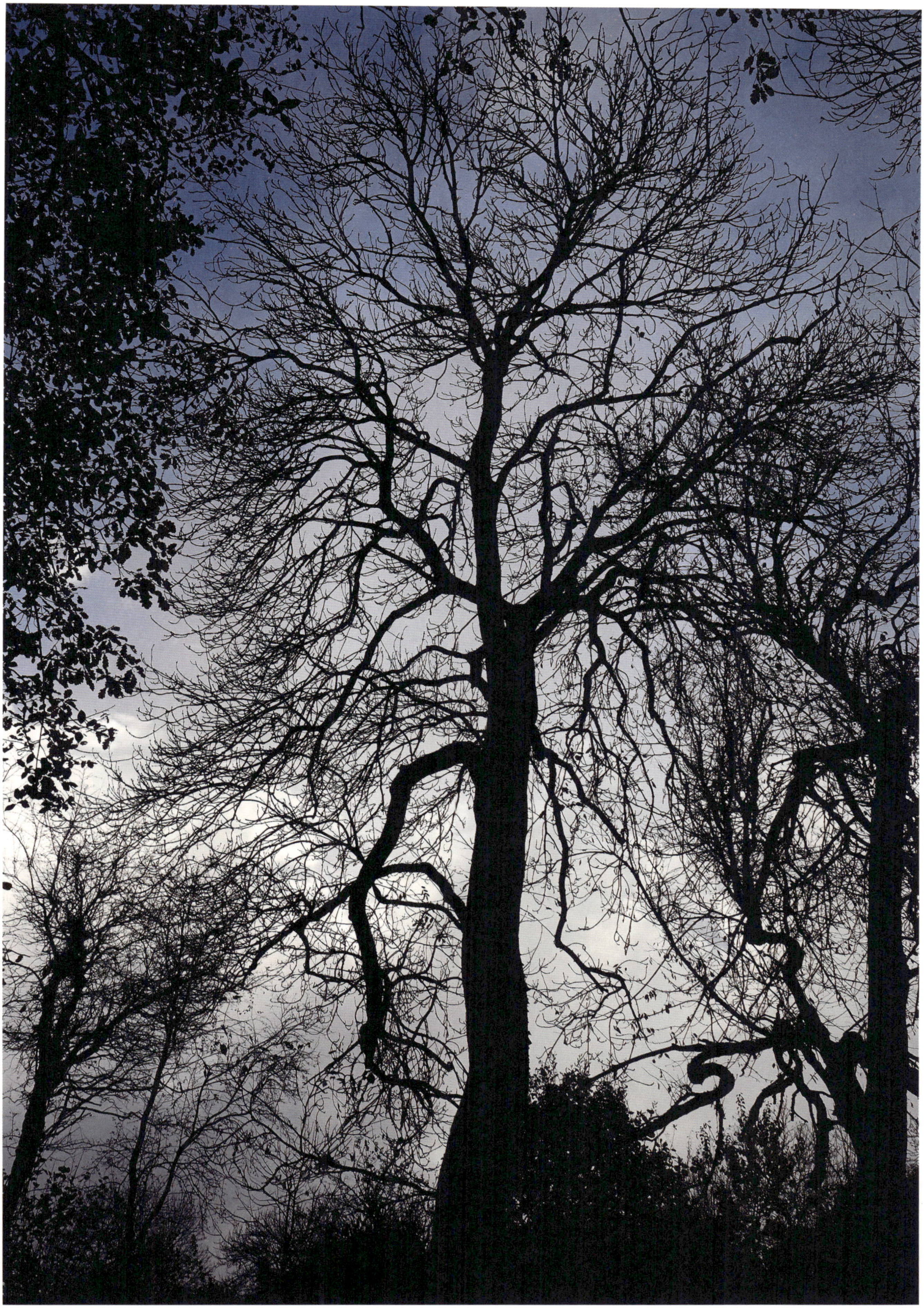

or two – these friendly birds seem to follow us around the farm, watching us carefully. We always stop to say hello and remind them not to steal the newly sown seeds in the greenhouse.

There are new trees and hedges to plant, and old field boundaries to tidy up and repair; stone pathways to build, and ditches that need to be kept clear. The machinery all needs servicing, to ensure the fleet is ready for action in the spring. The weekly trips to market continue.

Harvesting at this time of year can be bleak and hard work in what the locals call 'boss's weather', meaning that you have to work quickly in order to keep warm. We make sure we're thoroughly prepared, thoughtfully suited and booted to keep us from getting too cold and fed up – feet and hands can become unbearably cold. To retreat into the warmth of the kitchen at the end of the day is always very cheering.

On days when it's dry, crisp and bright, usually after Christmas, it's a real pleasure to be outside: the body warm, our cheeks flushed pink as we breathe in the clean, cold air and work amid the beauty that winter offers. Against a backdrop of steely blue skies, the trees fill the landscape, their skeletal limbs stretching out towards the heavens. The frost and occasional snow turn our fields into a winter wonderland. On bright days every tree and blade of grass sparkles. At night the skies are often a clear midnight blue, making this the best time of year to observe the stars.

The earth is at its most self-contained during winter; the re-mineralising, crystallising processes active in the ground are laying the foundations for the life that will rise in the spring. This organising principle is also evident in our own work. At the kitchen table we draw up plans and map out what we'll grow this coming year, discussing ways to improve our methods and browsing through seed catalogues, always choosing a few new things to try out.
We write a wish list of what we hope to achieve on the farm over the next twelve months.

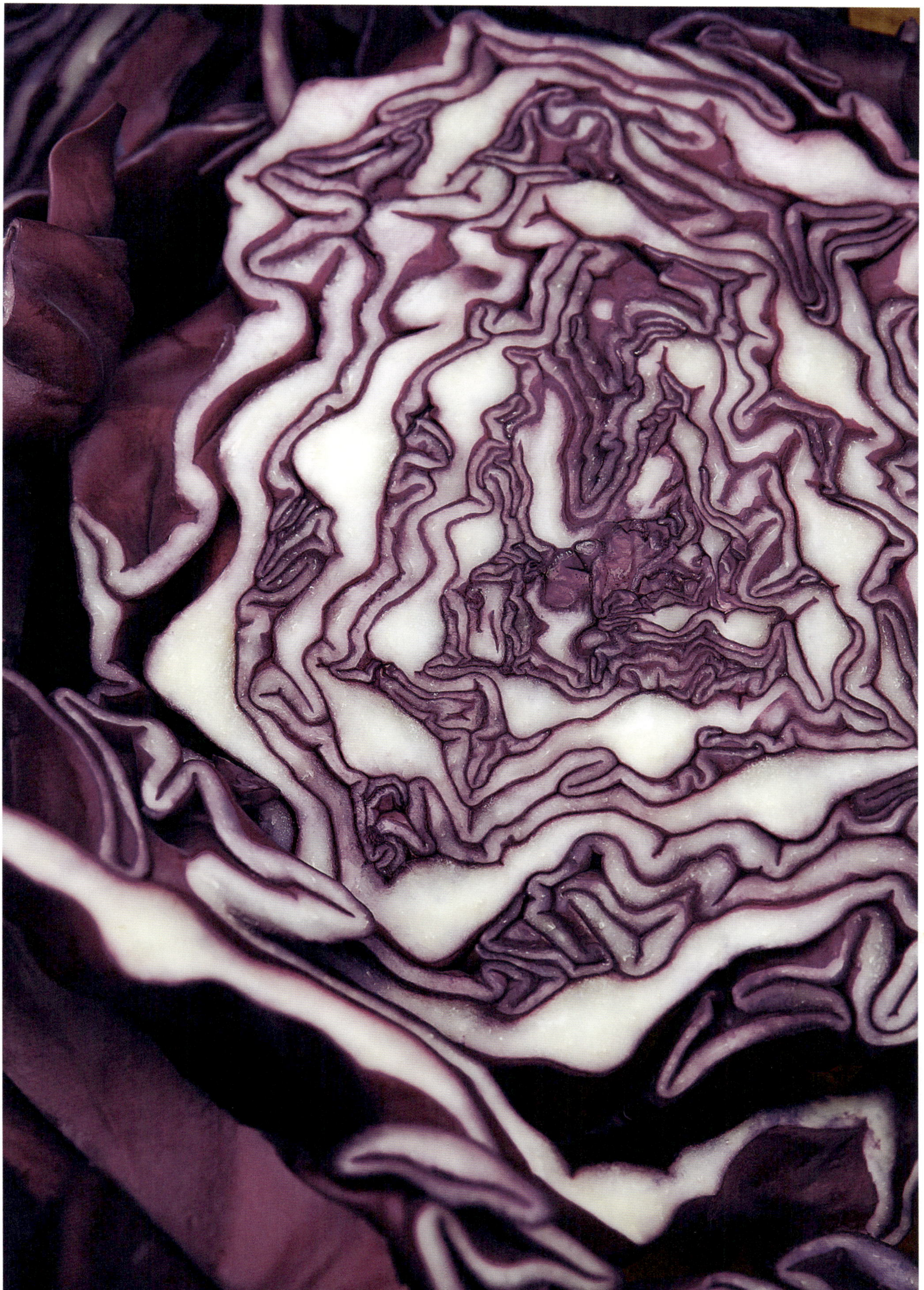

Golden Ball turnip soup

SERVES 6

85g butter
1kg Golden Ball turnips, peeled and cut into cubes
1 teaspoon ground mixed spice
½ teaspoon sea salt
500ml full-fat milk
1 litre vegetable stock
black pepper
Greek yoghurt, to serve

The Golden Ball turnip is less hot and radish-like than other turnips. It has lovely yellow skin and translucent, creamy flesh. Combining it with a little spice makes this a very well-flavoured, pretty-coloured soup. Ordinary turnips won't work as well, but it might be worth trying swede. Serve topped with Greek yoghurt.

Melt the butter in a large pan over a gentle heat. Add the turnips, then cover and sweat for about 20 minutes, until completely soft. Stir in the mixed spice, salt and some pepper, then add the milk and stock. Bring to the boil, turn the heat down to a simmer and cook for 30 minutes.

Remove from the heat and blitz the soup in a food processor or with a stick blender until it is really smooth. Adjust the seasoning if necessary and serve piping hot, with a dollop of Greek yoghurt on top.

Winter vegetable and pearl barley broth

SERVES 8

2 leeks
1 celeriac
1 swede
2 carrots
80g butter
2 bay leaves
3 litres chicken stock
125g pearl barley
a piece of Parmesan rind (optional)
sea salt and black pepper

This makes a wonderfully comforting broth for the depths of winter. We often eat it the day after roasting a chicken, using the chicken carcass to make a stock. It is a favourite lunchtime restorative during the many cold days we spend pruning fruit trees.

If you are a fan of Parmesan cheese, always keep the rind wrapped up in the fridge rather than throwing it away; it is a delicious way to add flavour to broths and soups such as this.

Dice the leeks into cubes about 1cm in size, using as much of the green tops as possible. Place in a colander, rinse and leave to drain. Peel the remaining vegetables and cut them into roughly 1cm cubes.

Put a large pan over a moderate heat and add the butter, followed by the vegetables and bay leaves. Cover and cook gently, stirring occasionally, for 15–20 minutes, until the vegetables are softened but not browned. Pour in the chicken stock, turn up the heat and season with salt and pepper. Add the pearl barley and the Parmesan rind, if using, and cook on a gentle simmer for 30 minutes, until the barley is soft to the bite.

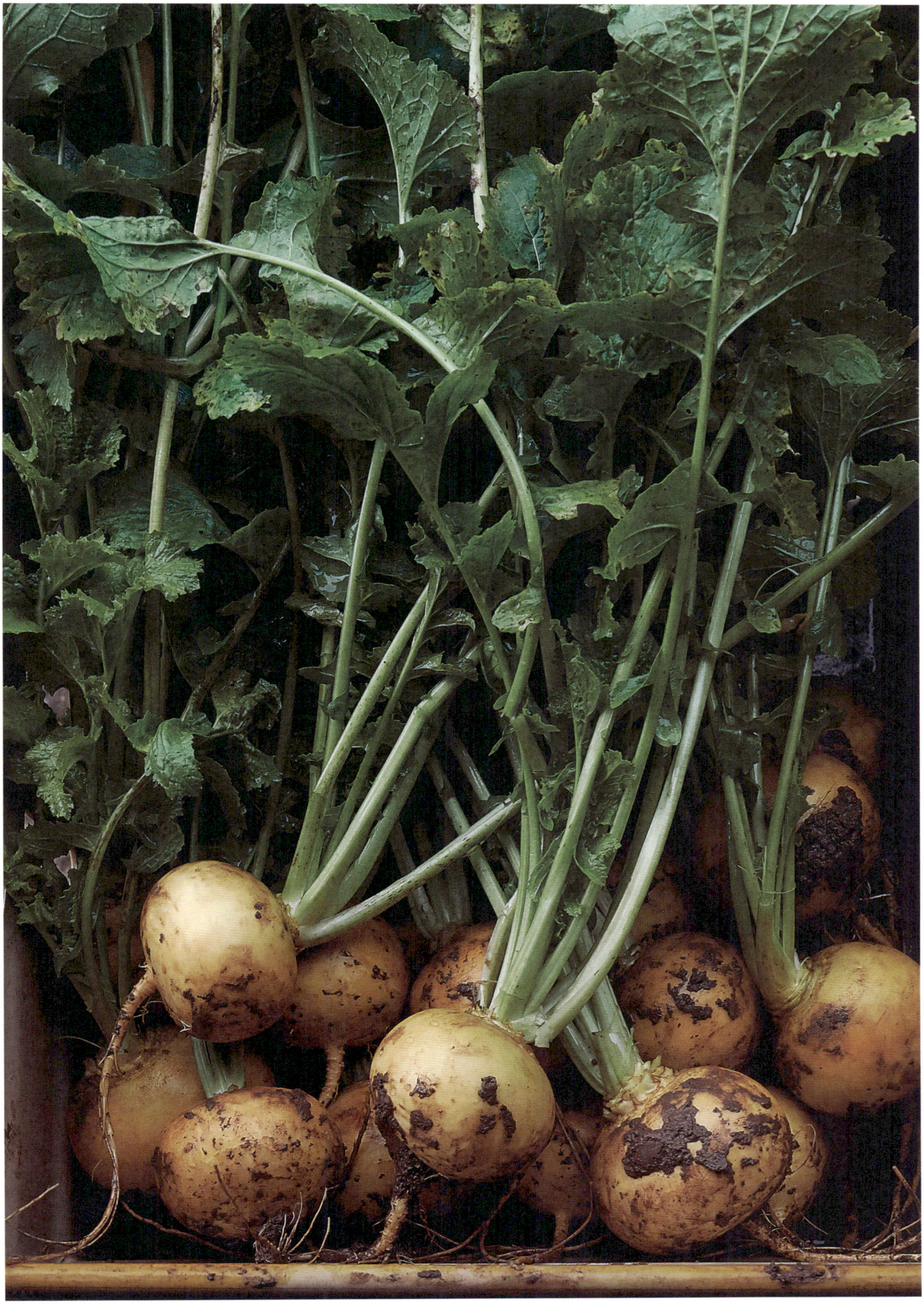

Jerusalem artichoke and parsley soup

SERVES 8

1kg Jerusalem artichokes
80g butter
2 onions, sliced
2 litres chicken stock
300ml milk
2 bay leaves
1 large bunch of parsley (approximately 50g), finely chopped
sea salt and black pepper

To garnish (optional)
vegetable oil for deep-frying
4 Jerusalem artichokes, peeled and cut into matchsticks
a little olive oil

Jerusalem artichokes are definitely in the love-them-or-hate-them category – not as much for their taste as for their unsociable side effects. Undercooking contributes to this problem, so be sure to cook them very well. This means that the soup takes quite a long time to make, but it is well worth it, with a rich flavour and the most fabulous velvety texture.

Do not peel the artichokes, just give them a good scrub with a vegetable brush. Cut them in half lengthways and then slice to just over the thickness of a pound coin.

Melt the butter in a large, heavy-based pan over a low heat and add the artichokes, then the onions. Make a cartouche (a circle of greaseproof paper to cover the contents completely) and pat it down on top of the vegetables so it will envelop the steam that will rise. Put the lid on the pan and leave over a very gentle heat so the artichokes and onions cook very slowly in the butter. This will take about 45 minutes, possibly longer, and will help unearth the artichokes' depth of flavour. Test the centre of the artichoke pieces with a knife; they must be very soft and look translucent. When you are satisfied that they are cooked, remove the cartouche and season the vegetables with a teaspoon of salt and plenty of freshly ground black pepper. Add the stock, milk and bay leaves, stir well and bring to the boil. Reduce the heat and simmer for 45 minutes. Do not worry if the milk appears to have curdled; it will come together again once blended. Remove the bay leaves and blitz the soup in a food processor or with a stick blender until it is smooth, thick and velvety. Stir in the parsley.

To make the garnish, pour some vegetable oil into a deep, heavy-based pan, filling it no more than a third full. Heat until it is hot enough for an artichoke matchstick to sizzle immediately when you drop it in. Add the rest of the artichokes and fry for a minute or so, until golden and crisp. Drain well on kitchen paper and sprinkle with salt. Serve the soup topped with the artichokes and a ribbon of olive oil.

WINTER 25

Roast hake with spinach, bacon and Puy lentils

SERVES 2

150g Puy lentils
1 bay leaf
600ml water
2 hake cutlets
20g butter
2 tablespoons olive oil, plus a little extra to serve
150g smoked bacon, cut into lardons
1 shallot, finely chopped
1 garlic clove, finely chopped
1 lemon
4 tablespoons chopped parsley
100g spinach, tough stalks removed
sea salt and black pepper

This is an unusually hearty fish dish. The strong flavour of hake cooked on the bone matches the meaty richness of bacon and lentils. Be sure to roast the hake in a hot oven, so that it cooks quickly and the skin crisps up.

Heat the oven to 220°C/Gas Mark 7. Rinse the lentils, put them in a pan with the bay leaf and water and simmer for about 20 minutes until tender. Drain through a sieve and set aside.

Place the hake cutlets in a lightly buttered small baking tin, season with salt and pepper and place half the butter on top of each one. Put in the top of the oven and roast for 10–15 minutes, until just cooked, basting with the juices halfway through.

Meanwhile, heat a heavy-based pan, add the olive oil and fry the bacon in it. When the lardons start to become crisp, lower the heat a little and add the shallot and garlic. Cook for a couple of minutes, until they start to colour. Then add the cooked lentils and a little splash of water to stop them sticking to the pan. Squeeze in the juice of half the lemon, stir in the chopped parsley and season to taste.

Cook the spinach briefly in a steamer until wilted, using a pair of tongs to wring out the excess moisture.

To serve, spoon the lentils on to 2 plates, put the spinach in the centre and lay the fish on top. Squeeze a little lemon juice over the fish and pour a little more olive oil on to the lentils.

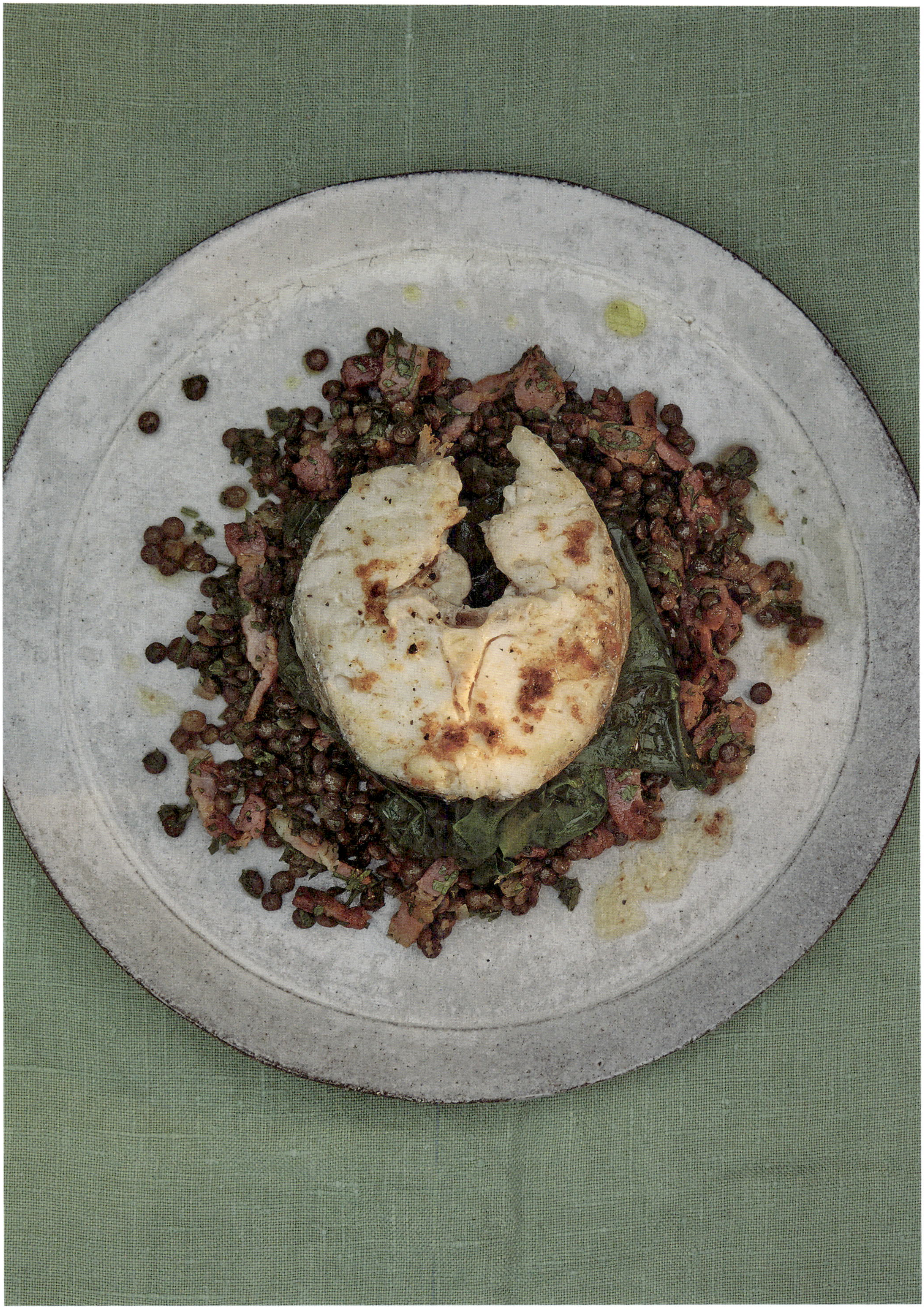

Braised chicory and bacon

SERVES 4

2 tablespoons olive oil

275g smoked streaky bacon, sliced into thin strips

1 large onion, chopped

500g chicory

150ml white wine

500ml chicken or vegetable stock

2 tablespoons crème fraîche or double cream

juice of ½ lemon

2 tablespoons chopped parsley

sea salt and black pepper

Chicory, often eaten raw in salads, tastes particularly good cooked. The chicons soften and sweeten, but retain their characteristic bitterness. This recipe makes a good supper dish served with plain boiled rice. If you omit the bacon, however, you could also serve it as a side dish; it goes especially well with chicken.

Heat the olive oil in a heavy-based frying pan, add the bacon and fry over a medium heat until it just begins to brown. Stir in the onion. If the bacon is very lean and has not produced much fat, you may need to add a little more olive oil to cook the onion. Allow the onion to soften for a couple of minutes.

Meanwhile, prepare the heads of chicory by cutting them lengthways into halves or quarters, depending on their size. If you have to trim the base, be very careful not to cut through the core, as you want the chicory pieces to stay intact. Place the chicory uncut-side down in the pan, which makes it much easier to turn over. Season with black pepper, but do not add any salt until you taste the sauce later, as the bacon will have introduced some. Allow the chicory to cook until the underside has some colour. Turn it over carefully and brown it as before. Turn up the heat, add the wine, and simmer until the alcohol has evaporated. Add the stock, bring to the boil, then reduce the heat and simmer gently for about half an hour, until the liquid has reduced to a gravy-like consistency and the chicory is very tender. Stir in the cream and lemon juice, then check the seasoning, adding salt if you like. Stir in the chopped parsley and serve straightaway.

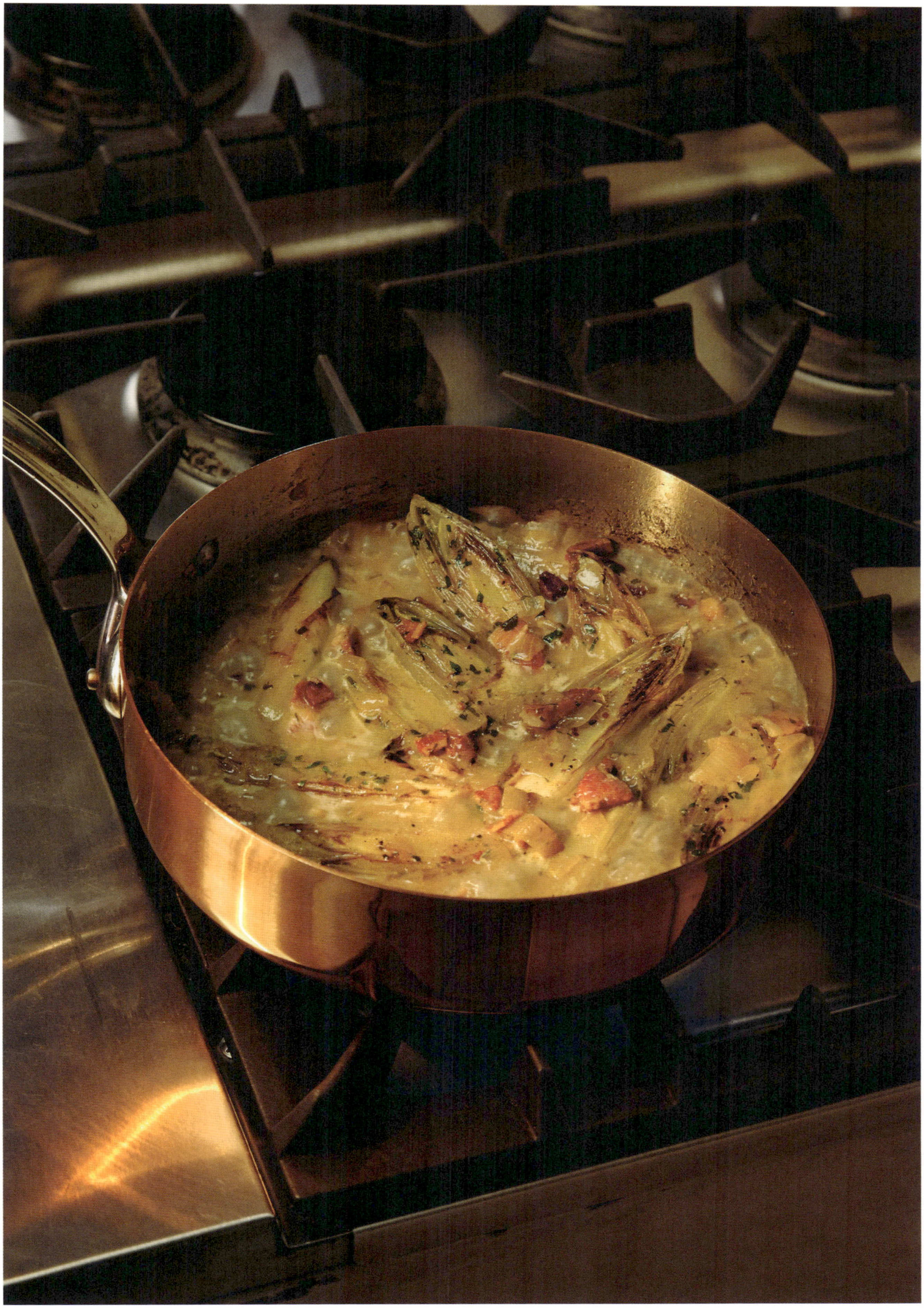

Working with the soil

WHEN WE CAME to Fern Verrow we were advised that our first crop should be potatoes. These tubers, with their robust root systems that could work deep into the soil, were a suitable crop to clean up an area of ground and move it towards productivity. We started by ploughing up half an acre of land, and with that first incision we opened up a conversation with the soil.

It has taken millennia to create the soil. The rocks and mineral deposits of the earth are the transformed remains of former life. All the products of disintegration – originating from plant and animal matter – gradually accumulate over time, layer upon layer, like pages in an ancient book. Year after year the cyclical processes of weathering – the rain, wind, frost and warmth – have also contributed to the gradual breaking down of substances. The soil is teeming with life, with billions of micro-organisms, earthworms and bacteria whose activity and decay contribute to the soil's fertility.

We develop our understanding of our soil by interacting with it. In early spring we use the plough to turn in the composted manure from our animals, which will provide fertility for the coming year's growth. Once the plough has done its work we walk over the field, kicking clumps of soil, scooping a handful, rubbing it between our fingers, squeezing it together, looking at its structure. When the time is right, we work the soil down to a fine tilth, alternately lifting and rolling until we get the right balance of moisture and crumb. Then we fill the beds with the young seedlings that we have been raising in the propagating greenhouse.

Throughout the summer months we tend to the growing plants by hoeing and removing weeds – giving the soil a little tickle – which helps the air, light and warmth to work into it, and the all-important water to penetrate to the plant roots. These regular cultivations greatly stimulate the development of our crops. The task in autumn is to renew and preserve fertility by applying compost to the permanent crops. The soil is our most valuable resource, and autumn's rich pickings remind us of the honest exchange we have with the land. Through our labour, skill and care, our efforts are rewarded with things of real substance and beauty.

Over the years that we've worked on this land, we've listened to the soil carefully and helped it become increasingly fertile and productive. Now it is more resilient, adapting to variations and extremes of moisture and temperature. The soil has become more forgiving, reminding us of the simple truth that we feed the soil and the soil feeds us.

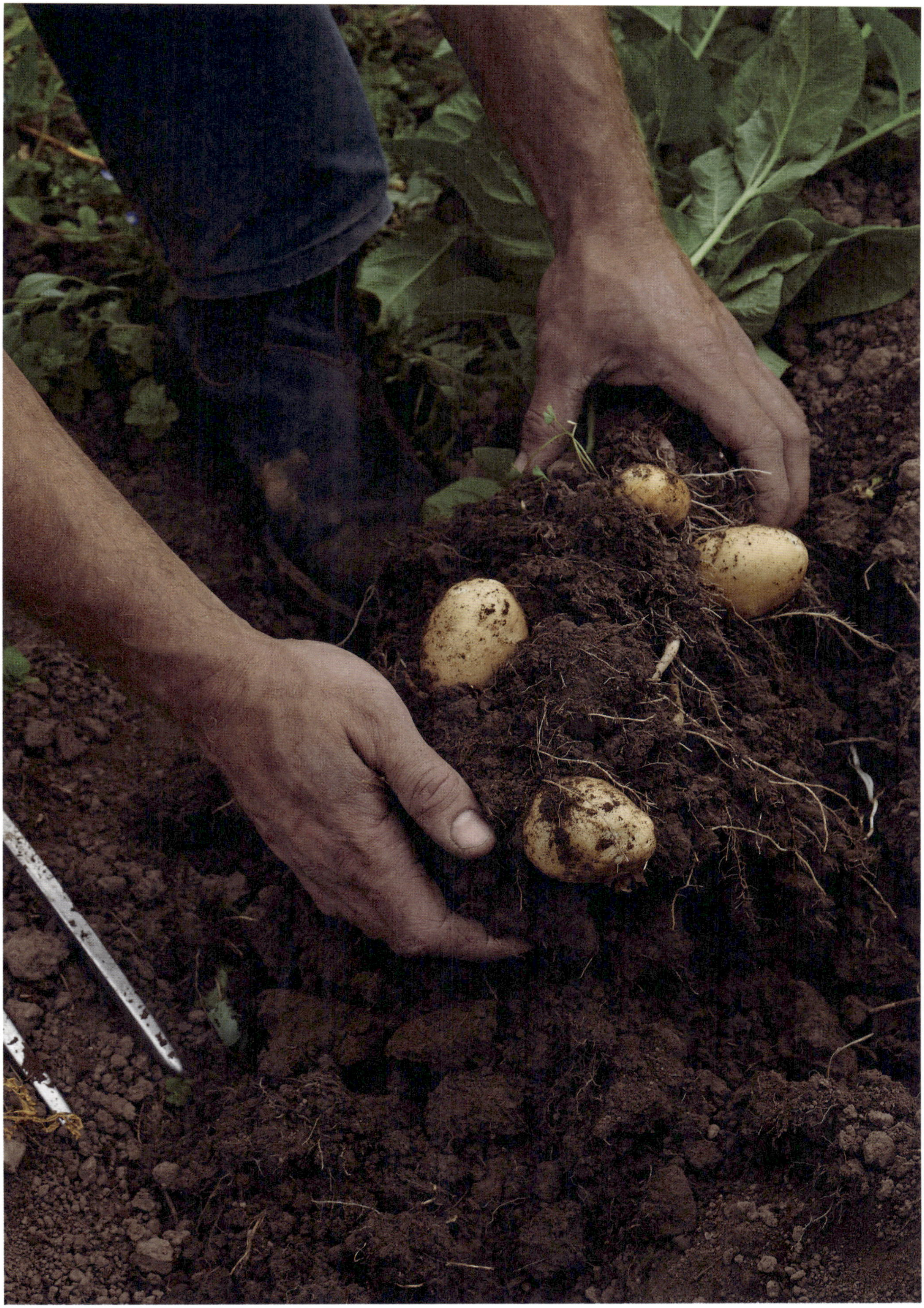

Pork chops with apple gravy

SERVES 4

8 small pork chops
2 onions, sliced
500ml dry cider
350g cooking apples, peeled, cored and quartered
8 juniper berries (optional)
sea salt and black pepper

This makes a good midweek supper dish. Use cooking apples for the gravy – Bramleys are ideal. They break down more easily than dessert apples, thickening the sauce, and their tartness blends beautifully with the salty fat of the pork. Serve with mashed potato and some lightly cooked kale or cabbage, if you wish.

Trim the rind and some of the fat from the pork chops. The amount of fat you remove is up to you; we trim ours to about 1cm. Place a large, heavy-based frying pan over a moderate heat and leave for a couple of minutes to heat up, then stand the chops, trimmed-edge down, in the pan, leaning them against each other so that they don't fall over. Cook until the fat runs, still on a moderate heat, but being careful not to let the fat burn. Once the trimmed edge is crisp and coloured and there is a good amount of fat in the pan, lay the chops down and cook for 15–20 minutes, turning occasionally until golden brown on both sides.

Remove the chops from the pan and set aside. Put the onions into the lovely pork fat and fry until soft, stirring well and scraping the pan to lift the sticky meat juices from the base. Season, then raise the heat a little and continue to cook until the onions are a dark caramel colour. Pour in the cider and bring quickly to the boil, then add the apples. Turn down the heat to a simmer. If you are using the juniper berries, add them to the pan at this point. Return the chops to the pan, nestling them into the sauce. Cover and cook for about 30 minutes, until the apples have disintegrated and the sauce has become the consistency of a thick gravy. Check the seasoning and adjust if necessary.

Spicy stuffed Savoy cabbage leaves

SERVES 4

1 Savoy cabbage
4 tablespoons sesame oil
2 shallots, finely chopped
4 garlic cloves, finely chopped
a piece of fresh ginger, two thumbs in size, finely chopped
500g minced pork
½ teaspoon crushed dried chilli
2 teaspoons Chinese five-spice powder
1 tablespoon sugar
1 tablespoon rice wine vinegar
2 tablespoons dark soy sauce
juice of 1 lime

In winter we often turn to spicy, strongly flavoured food. The body seems to crave what it needs. Ginger is a storecupboard staple in our house during the winter months. Food is never dull when it includes a knuckle or two of ginger.

Put a large pan of salted water on to boil. Carefully peel off 12 outer leaves from the cabbage, snapping them at the stem. Once the water is boiling rapidly, blanch the leaves in it for 2–3 minutes, then drain through a colander and refresh under cold running water to stop them cooking further.

Next make the filling. Put a large, heavy-based frying pan or a wok over a high heat. When it is hot but not smoking, pour in the sesame oil and fry the shallots, garlic and ginger in it for about a minute. Add the minced pork and cook, stirring with a wooden spoon, until it begins to colour. Sprinkle in the dried chilli and five-spice powder and continue to fry until everything starts to crisp. Turn the heat right down, add the sugar and vinegar, giving everything a good stir, then turn off the heat. Stir in the soy sauce and lime juice.

Shake off any excess water from the blanched cabbage leaves and place a heaped tablespoonful of the filling on each one. Fold in the sides, roll the leaf up, then secure with a cocktail stick. If they are difficult to roll, shave a thin slice off the back of the stalk on each leaf to make it more flexible.

Place the cabbage rolls in a steamer and cook for 8–10 minutes, until thoroughly heated through. Serve hot and steaming, being sure to keep the lid on the pan to keep the second helpings warm, if necessary.

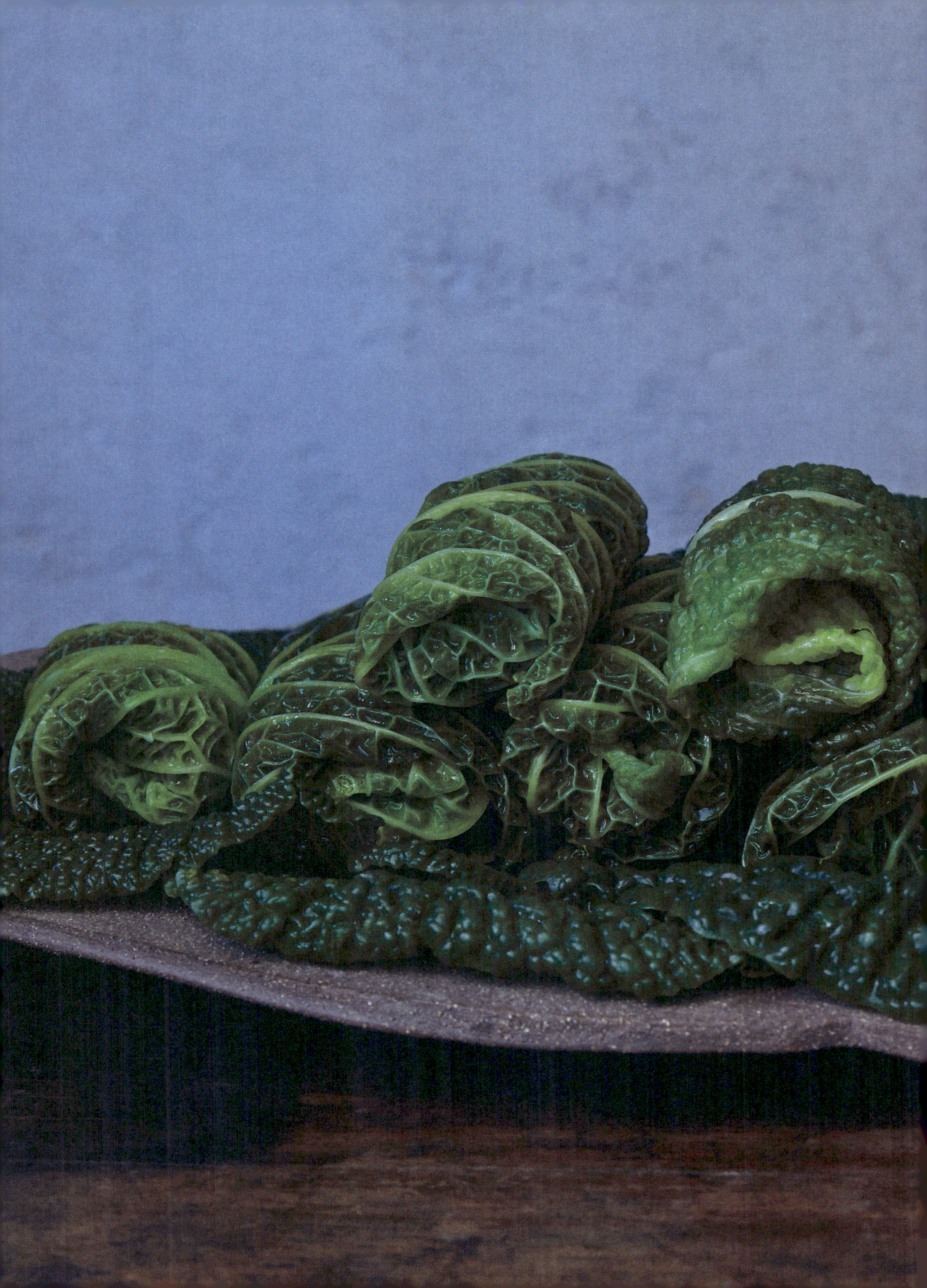

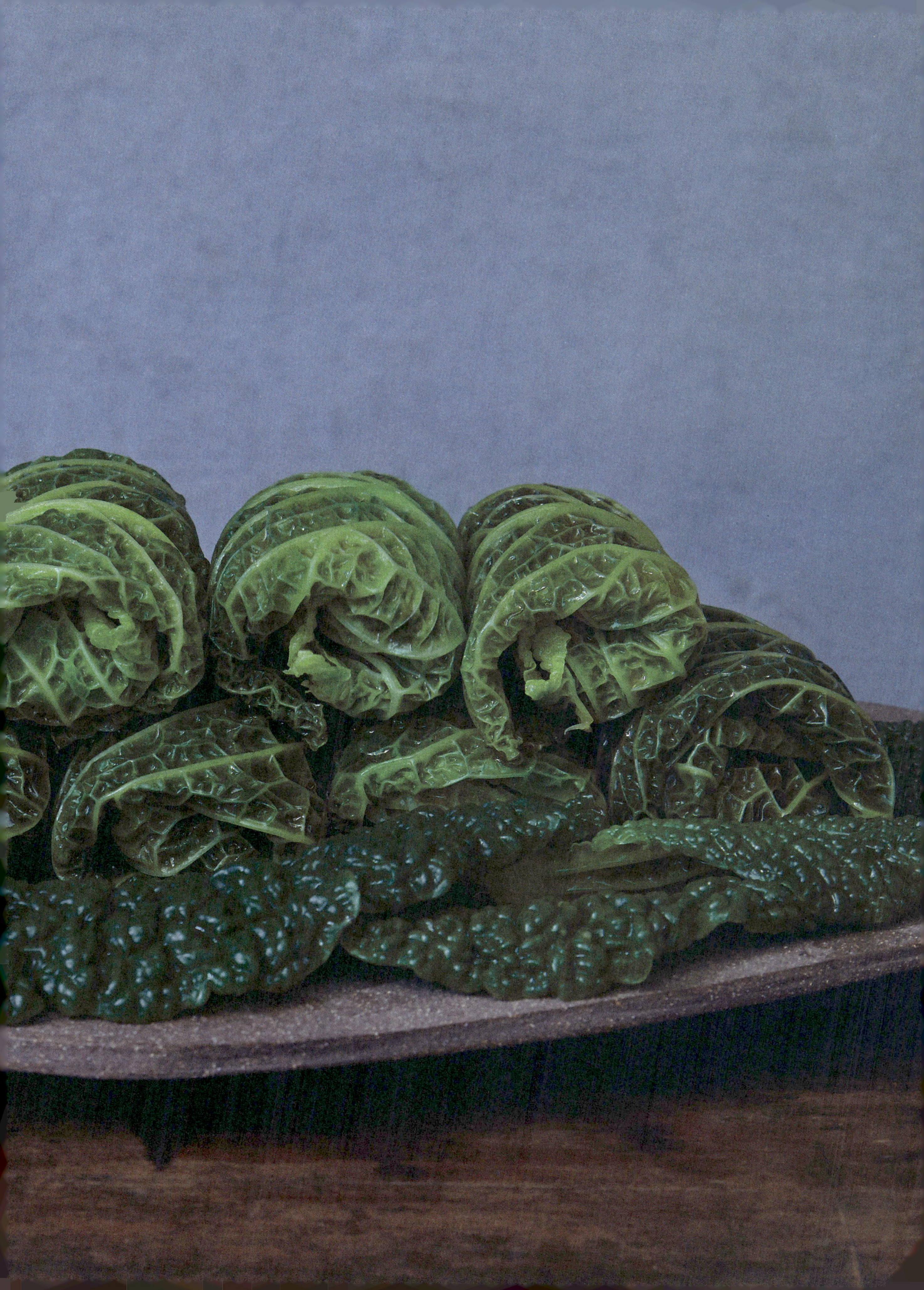

Beef stew with parsley dumplings

SERVES 4

1 tablespoon cooking oil or, if you have some, 25g beef dripping

800g stewing or braising steak, cut into cubes

25g butter

250g onions, sliced

1 garlic clove, crushed

1 tablespoon plain flour

1 wine glass of red wine or beer

1 dessertspoon tomato purée

1 dessertspoon Blackberry and Elderberry Condiment (see page 256; or use redcurrant jelly and 2 pinches of ground cinnamon)

250g celeriac, cut into 4–5cm batons

250g swede, cut into 4–5cm batons

450g carrots, cut into 4–5cm batons

800ml water

1–2 sprigs of thyme and rosemary plus 2 bay leaves, tied together

sea salt and black pepper

For the parsley dumplings

150g self-raising flour

¾ teaspoon baking powder

¼ teaspoon sea salt

75g shredded suet

4 tablespoons finely chopped parsley

It is usually best to eat a stew the day after it is made, allowing the flavours to combine and bring out the best in each other. It is important, however, that you reheat the stew thoroughly in the oven before adding the dumplings, otherwise they won't rise as well and they'll taste a little stodgy. If you get them right, the dumplings are the best part of this stew.

This is a meal in itself, but if you are extra hungry, a few thick slices of buttered bread are perfect for mopping up the juices.

Heat the oven to 150°C/Gas Mark 2. Place a large flameproof casserole over a medium heat, add the oil or dripping and allow it to heat up. Add the beef, in batches if necessary, and brown it all over as quickly as possible, then transfer to a plate. Lower the heat just a little, add the butter, followed by the onions and garlic, and fry until they are tender and golden. Sprinkle the flour over the onions. Stir and keep things moving for a minute. This will help to toast the flour and add flavour, but be careful not to let it burn. Place the meat back in the casserole. Pour in the wine or beer, add the tomato purée and simmer over a medium heat until the liquid has reduced by half. Season generously, spoon in the condiment and stir until dissolved. Then add all the vegetables to the pan and mix to coat them with the juices. Add the water and herbs and turn up the heat. Just as the liquid starts to bubble, place the lid on the casserole and transfer to the oven. Cook for at least 2½ hours, until the meat is very tender. Ideally, the casserole will be only about half full, so there is room for the dumplings to rise.

To make the dumplings, mix all the ingredients together in a bowl and add enough water to make a slightly sticky dough – about 100ml. On a floured surface, roll the dough into walnut-sized balls. Dot these over the surface of the stew and baste with some of the liquid. Cover and return to the oven for 40 minutes, until the dumplings are risen and fluffy. Baste the dumplings once more halfway through cooking.

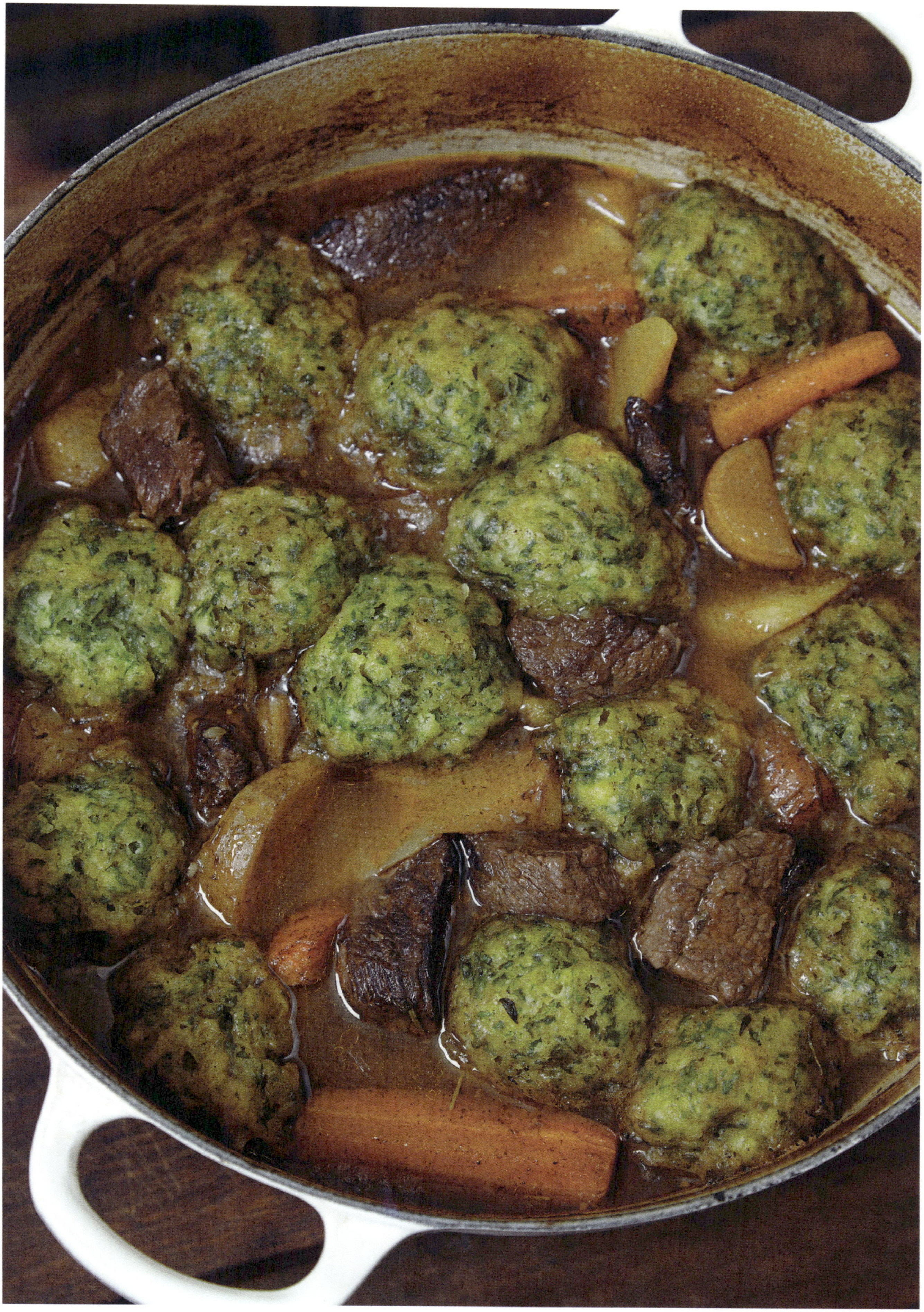

Paprika pork tenderloin with fennel seeds and buttered onion rice

SERVES 4

60g plain flour
3 teaspoons smoked paprika
750g pork tenderloin, cut into medallions 1cm thick
4 tablespoons sunflower oil
2 tablespoons olive oil
30g butter
4 garlic cloves, finely chopped
4 teaspoons fennel seeds
juice and grated zest of 1 lemon
sea salt

For the buttered onion rice
45g butter
1 onion, diced
½ teaspoon turmeric
250g basmati rice
500ml water

Pork tenderloin is effectively the fillet steak of the pig, as it is tender and needs only brief cooking. The buttery rice works really well with it here, complementing the toasted coating of the meat. Serve with a green endive salad or a chicory and blood orange salad.

For the rice, melt the butter in a medium pan over a low heat, then add the onion and turmeric. Cover and sweat until the onion has softened but not coloured. Add the rice and stir to coat it with the butter. Pour in the water, put the lid on the pan and bring to the boil as quickly as possible. Once you can see a stream of steam escaping, turn down the heat very low. Leave the rice to steam for approximately 15 minutes, until tender. Do not remove the lid during this time.

Mix the flour, paprika and a large pinch of salt together in a bowl. Using your hands, toss the pork medallions through the flour mix, ensuring that they are well coated. Heat the sunflower oil in a large frying pan over a medium heat. Add the pork in a single layer – cook it in batches if necessary. Cook for about 3 minutes, until browned underneath, then turn over and brown the other side. Keep the cooked meat warm on a plate while you fry the remaining pieces. When all the pork is cooked, wipe out the pan with paper towel to remove any burnt pieces of flour. Heat the olive oil and butter in the pan, add the garlic and fennel seeds and fry for a couple of minutes. Add the lemon zest, then reintroduce the meat to the pan, along with the lemon juice. Turn everything over to coat the meat with the fennel seeds, garlic and lemon and heat through gently.

Fluff up the rice with a fork and serve with the pork medallions.

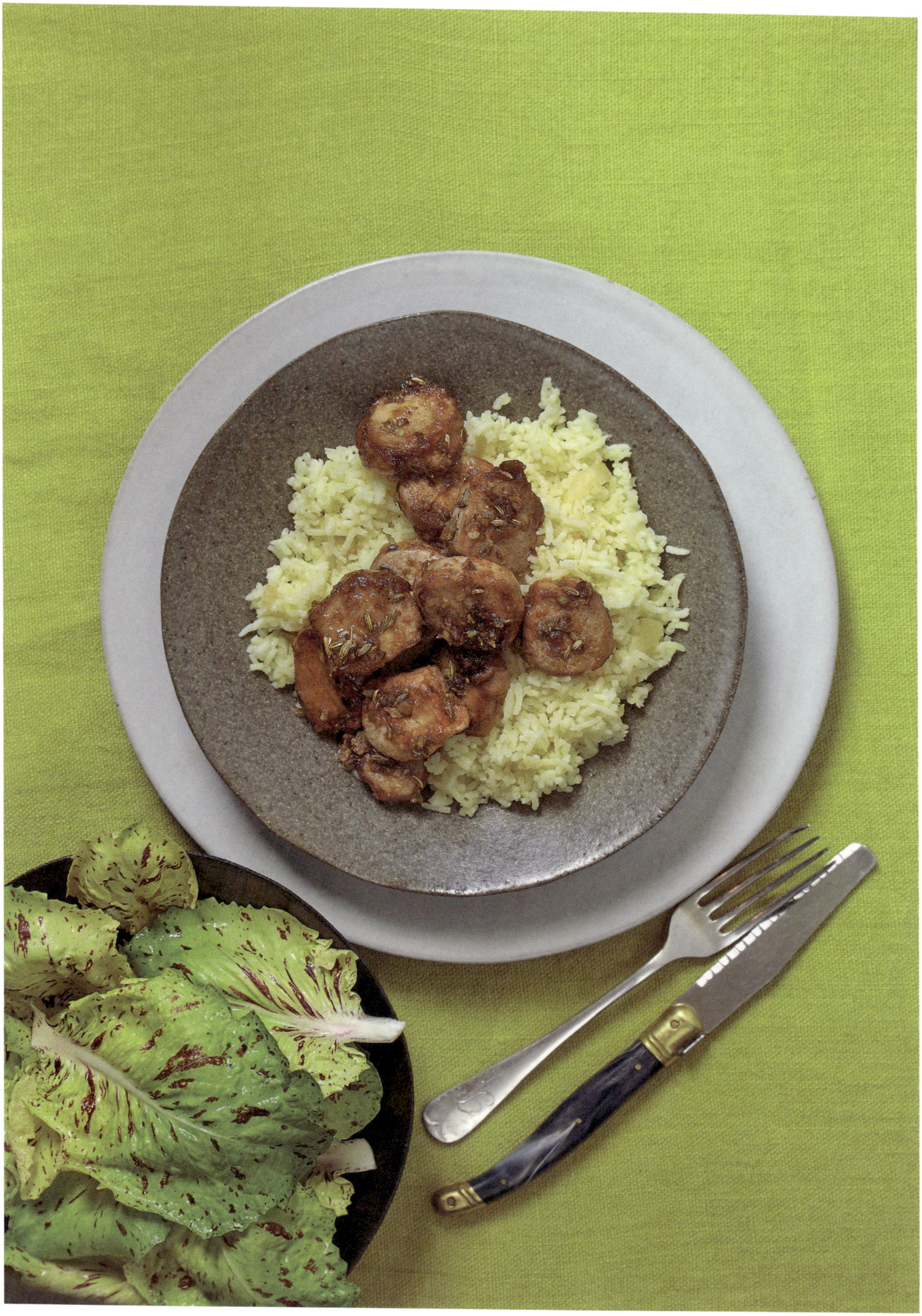

Roasted root vegetables with a fruit vinegar glaze

SERVES 4

1.5kg mixed carrot, beetroot, turnip, parsnip and celeriac (in whatever proportions you like)

2 sprigs of thyme

75ml olive oil

25g butter

2 red onions, peeled and cut into 6 wedges

1 bulb of garlic, broken into individual cloves, skins left on

3 tablespoons Fruit Vinegar (see page 196)

sea salt and black pepper

During winter, you can get a little tired of eating the same old vegetables, particularly in the later months as the autumn-harvested roots lose their just-picked flavours. The addition of fruit vinegar to a pan of roasted root vegetables gives them a little extra something. The bright colour and sweet-and-sour tang are a feast for the eyes and taste buds alike. It is important to leave the skin on the garlic, so it will melt down to a sticky, savoury pulp rather than drying out.

Use this recipe as a template if you wish, and mix and match with other vegetables, such as fennel or sweet potato. This dish is lovely on its own, or with a roast or some chops.

Heat the oven to 200°C/Gas Mark 6. Peel the root vegetables and cut them into largish chunks. Put them into a roasting dish with the thyme, pour over the olive oil and mix well to coat the vegetables evenly. Add the butter in small pieces over the top and season with salt and pepper. Roast for half an hour, then add the onions and garlic cloves. Turn the vegetables and baste them, ensuring that everything is well coated and browning evenly. Roast for another half hour, then splash in the fruit vinegar, mixing well. Cook for 10 minutes, until the vegetables are soft in the centre and coated with a shiny, almost caramelised glaze.

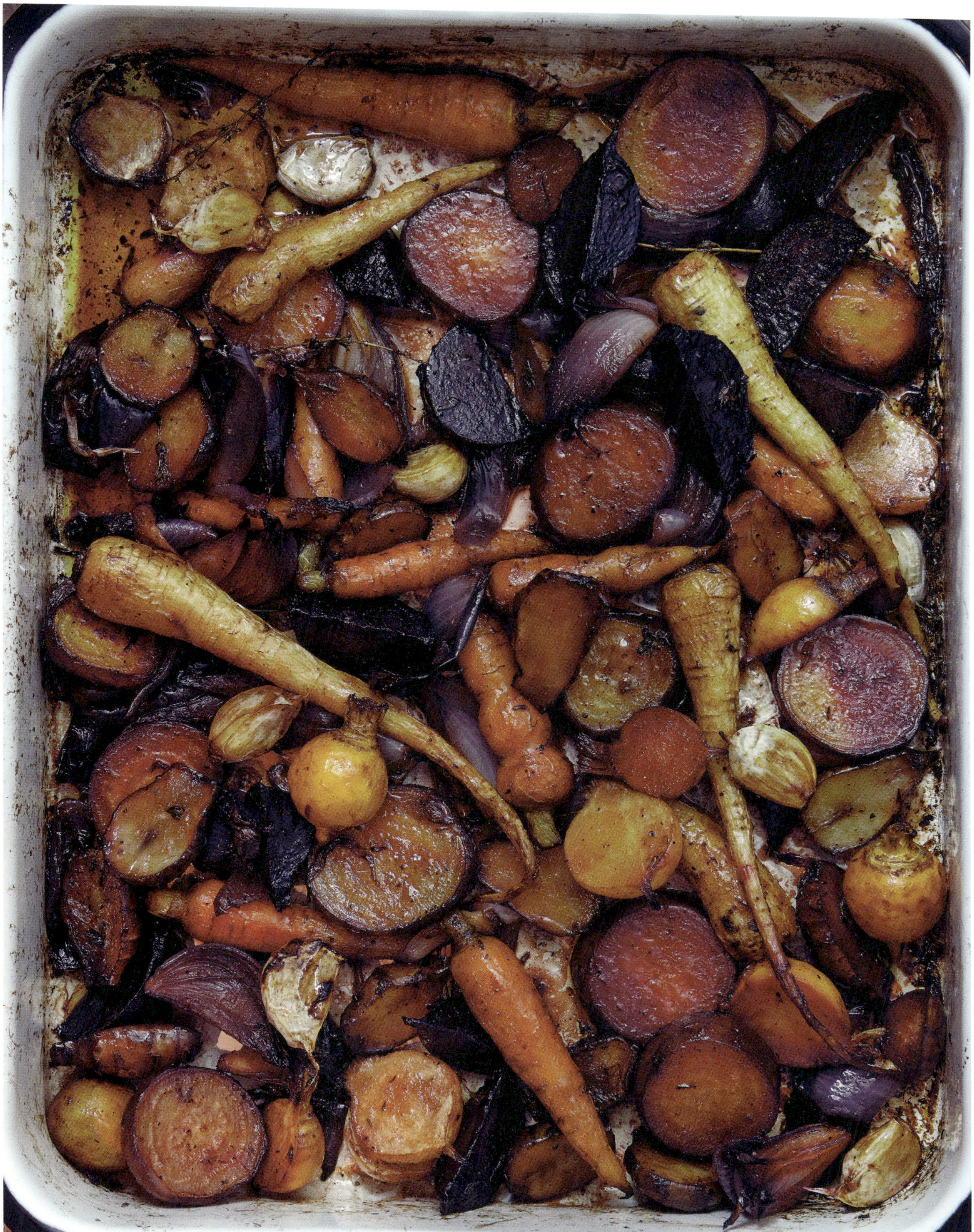

Seared wood pigeon with crispy kale, swede and hazelnuts

SERVES 2

4 wood pigeon breasts
1 tablespoon olive oil
4 tablespoons groundnut oil
150g kale, finely shredded
30g butter
1 shallot, finely chopped
1 garlic clove, finely chopped
2 teaspoons chopped thyme
100ml Madeira
50g hazelnuts, toasted and roughly chopped
sea salt and black pepper

For the swede
1 large swede (approximately 750g), peeled and cut into chunks
30g butter
3 tablespoons double cream
2 tablespoons freshly grated Parmesan cheese

After the wood pigeons have gorged themselves on acorns in the autumn, food for our feathered friends tends to become scarce. Not at Fern Verrow, however, where our fields turn into the local pigeon canteen and they demolish crops, particularly the purple sprouting plants, just as the purple buds are forming. We don't mind losing a few plants, but a little pigeon culling is necessary on occasion. Jane's son, Bill, is a keen hunter and keeps the numbers down, in the process bringing us one of the most delicious wild meats to eat.

It may not appear so, but this is a fairly quick meal to prepare.

Cook the swede in boiling salted water until soft, then drain well. Place in a food processor with the butter, cream and Parmesan and blitz until very smooth; it should resemble cooked polenta. Season to taste, then return to the pan, cover and set aside.

Have 2 frying pans ready, one for cooking the pigeon, the other for the kale. Put the pan for the pigeon breasts over a high heat; it needs to get very hot. Slice each pigeon breast in half horizontally. Season both breasts and lightly oil with the olive oil. When the pan is almost smoking, sear the meat for 10–15 seconds on each side, until well coloured on the outside but still pink inside. Remove from the pan and leave to rest. Meanwhile put the groundnut oil into the second pan and place over a high heat. When it is very hot but not smoking, throw in the kale (beware, it will spit) and push it around in the oil until it is very crisp; this will take only a minute or two. Remove the kale from the oil with a slotted spoon and leave on kitchen paper to drain. Season with salt.

Finish by quickly making the sauce. Melt the butter in the pan in which the pigeon was cooked, add the shallot, garlic and thyme and fry over a medium heat until softened. Pour in the Madeira and simmer until reduced by about a quarter, then place the pigeon breasts back in the pan to warm through. Finally add the hazelnuts.

To serve, gently reheat the swede purée, then divide it between 2 serving plates. Add a handful of kale to each one, put the pigeon on top and pour the sauce over.

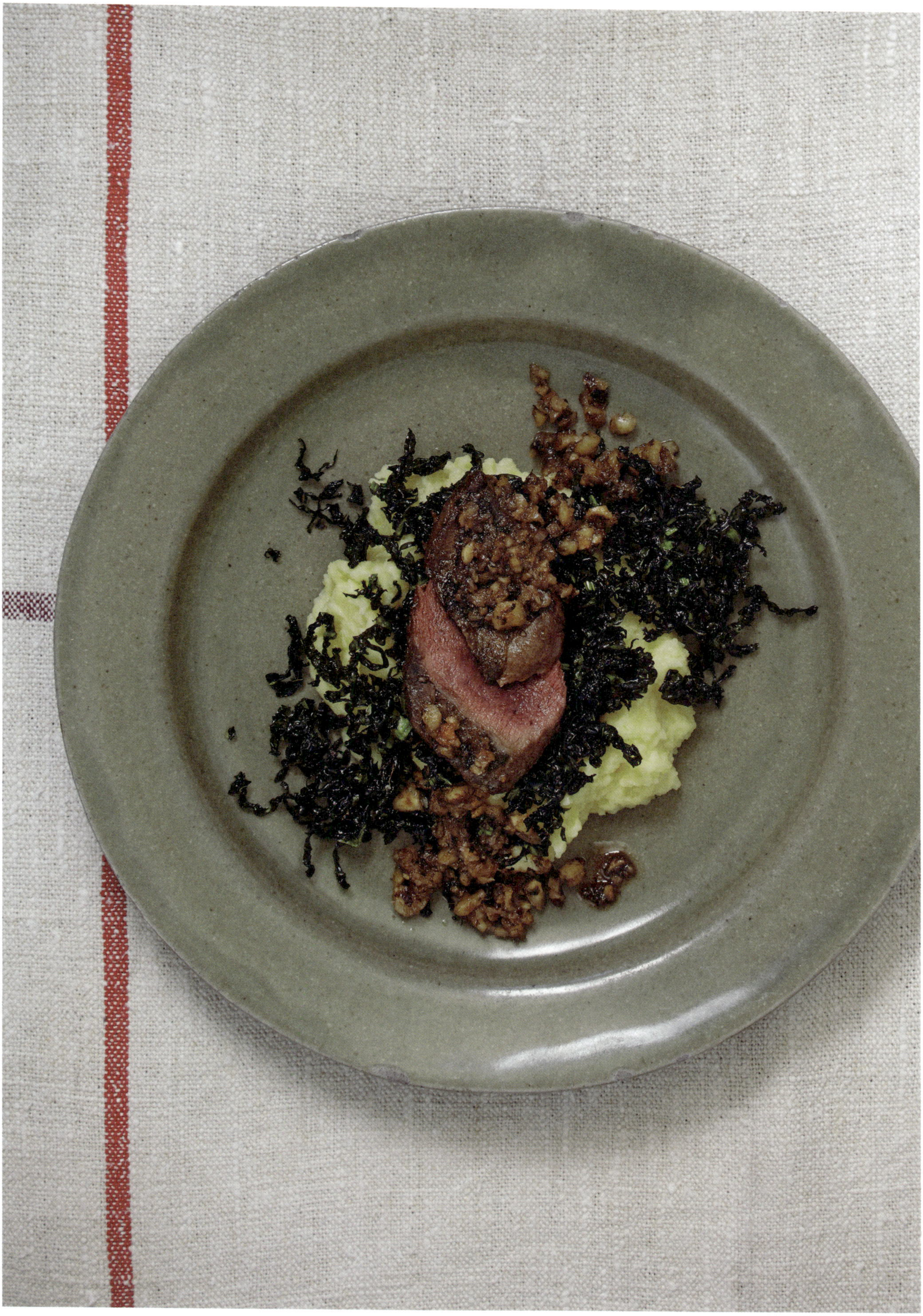

Cottage pie

SERVES 6

3 tablespoons olive oil
750g minced beef
2 onions, roughly chopped
1 garlic clove, chopped
250ml beef, chicken or vegetable stock
2 bay leaves
1 large carrot, coarsely grated
½ swede, coarsely grated
½ celeriac, coarsely grated
sea salt and black pepper

For the mash

1.5kg floury potatoes, peeled and cut into chunks
150ml milk
75g butter
75g Cheddar, Cheshire or Lancashire cheese, grated (optional)

The addition of coarsely grated root vegetables to cottage pie works really well and is a sneaky way of getting your children to eat more vegetables. It is important to add the raw vegetables to cool cooked mince, so that they are not overcooked and retain a nice, crunchy texture. Serve with any green vegetable. A splash of Worcestershire sauce on the plate is good, too.

First prepare the mash. Put the potatoes into a large pan of cold salted water and bring to the boil. Simmer until tender, then drain through a colander and leave to dry off for a few minutes. Meanwhile, put the milk and butter into the pan in which the potatoes were cooked and heat gently until the butter has melted. Return the potatoes to the pan and mash until fluffy and smooth. Season to taste and set aside.

Put a large, heavy-based frying pan over a high heat. When it is hot but not quite smoking, pour in the olive oil and then add the minced beef. Keep the mince moving with a wooden spoon, scraping the surface of the pan and breaking up any clumps of meat. Keep the heat high, so the moisture is driven out and the mince fries rather than stews. After about 10 minutes, add the onions and garlic and continue scraping the pan and breaking up the meat. Season with salt and pepper. Once the mince and onions begin to colour, add the stock and bay leaves and simmer for a few minutes until the stock has reduced by half. Remove from the heat and leave to cool.

Heat the oven to 200°C/Gas Mark 6. Add the grated carrot, swede and celeriac to the mince and mix well. Transfer to a casserole dish, pile the mashed potato on top and smooth it out evenly, then run the tines of a fork through the surface, creating furrows and ridges. Bake for about 45 minutes, until the filling is thoroughly heated through and the potatoes are lightly browned. If you are using the grated cheese, sprinkle it on top of the pie after 30 minutes in the oven.

Preserved bergamot lemons

MAKES 4 X 500G JARS

2.5kg bergamot lemons (or unwaxed organic lemons)
8 fresh bay leaves
4 teaspoons pink peppercorns
4 teaspoons coriander seeds
4 teaspoons fennel seeds
about 200g fine sea salt

Lemons are available to buy all year round, of course, but in Europe they are in season in late winter, so they tend to be better and cheaper then. Preserved lemons have become a must-have larder ingredient in our house. With their salty tang and lovely oily texture, they are so useful to brighten rice- and pulse-based dishes. Our Christmas couscous stuffing (see page 62) would not be the same without the addition of this wonderfully scented preserve.

If you can get your hands on some bergamot lemons, use these; they have a particularly high level of essential oil in their skin, which produces an exceptional preserve. Good-quality unwaxed organic lemons from Italy are superb, too.

If you like eating preserved lemons on their own, which we do, chop some up and serve as a nibble with a drink.

Set about 500g of the lemons aside. Wash and dry the remaining lemons, quarter them lengthways and pack very tightly into sterilised Kilner jars (see page 254), squeezing each quarter gently into the jar to release some of the juice. When the jars are half full, tuck the bay leaves in on each side of the jars, shiny side facing outwards. Put one teaspoon of each of the spices on top of the lemons and a heaped tablespoon of the salt. Pack in more lemons to fill the jar, leaving room for an additional tablespoon of salt.

Squeeze the juice from the lemons you have set aside and use it to fill the jars to the brim. The lemons must be fully covered with juice. Seal the jars and give them a good shake to distribute the salt and spices. Give them a daily shake, if necessary, until the salt dissolves. The lemons will be ready to use in 6 weeks.

Stir-fried leeks with lime juice and lime leaves

SERVES 4

4 good-sized leeks

3 tablespoons sesame oil

a walnut-sized piece of fresh ginger (or more, if you want a good ginger hit), finely chopped

1 garlic clove, finely chopped

2 fresh kaffir lime leaves, finely chopped

2 limes

sea salt

What would we do without our friend the leek? It's a wonderfully versatile, reliable and flavoursome contributor to winter cooking. When it's February, you haven't seen sunlight for weeks and are in need of a little lift, this dish is one of those just-right-for-the-moment meals. Bright, clean and zingy, it should be served with basmati rice, a good squeeze of lime juice and, if you like, a little sweet chilli sauce on the side.

Slit the leeks open lengthways to about 1cm of the root end, then rinse them thoroughly in a sink filled with plenty of cold water, gently spreading the leaves as you would a hand of cards. Drain well and slice on the diagonal into chunks about 2.5cm thick, using as much of the green part as looks tender and fresh.

Heat the sesame oil in a large, non-stick frying pan until very hot but not smoking. Add the leeks, ginger, garlic, lime leaves and a pinch of salt and stir-fry for 5–7 minutes, keeping everything well lubricated and on the move and being careful not to let the garlic burn. The leeks should be nice and crunchy. Serve on a bed of rice, squeezing lots of lime juice on top.

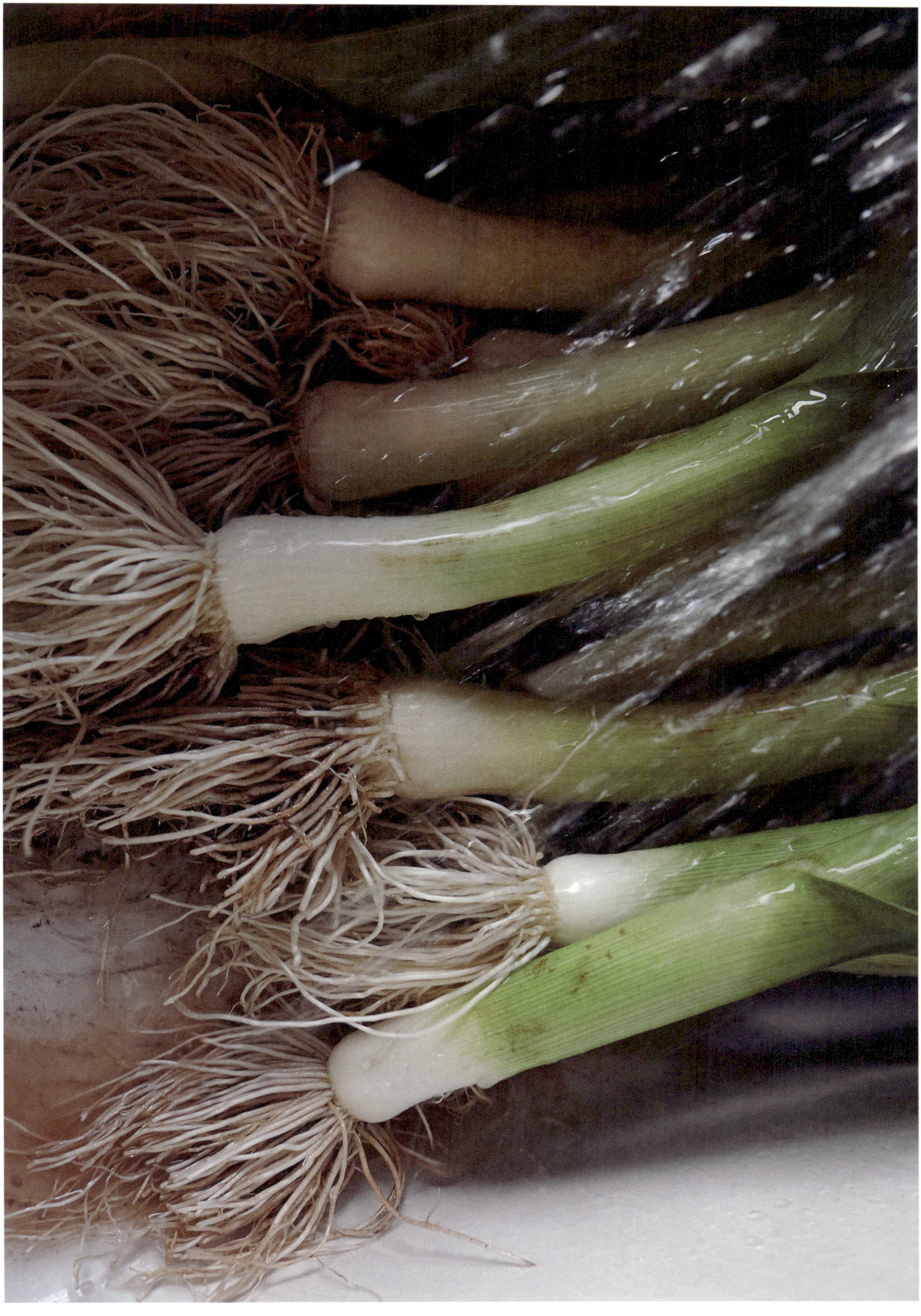

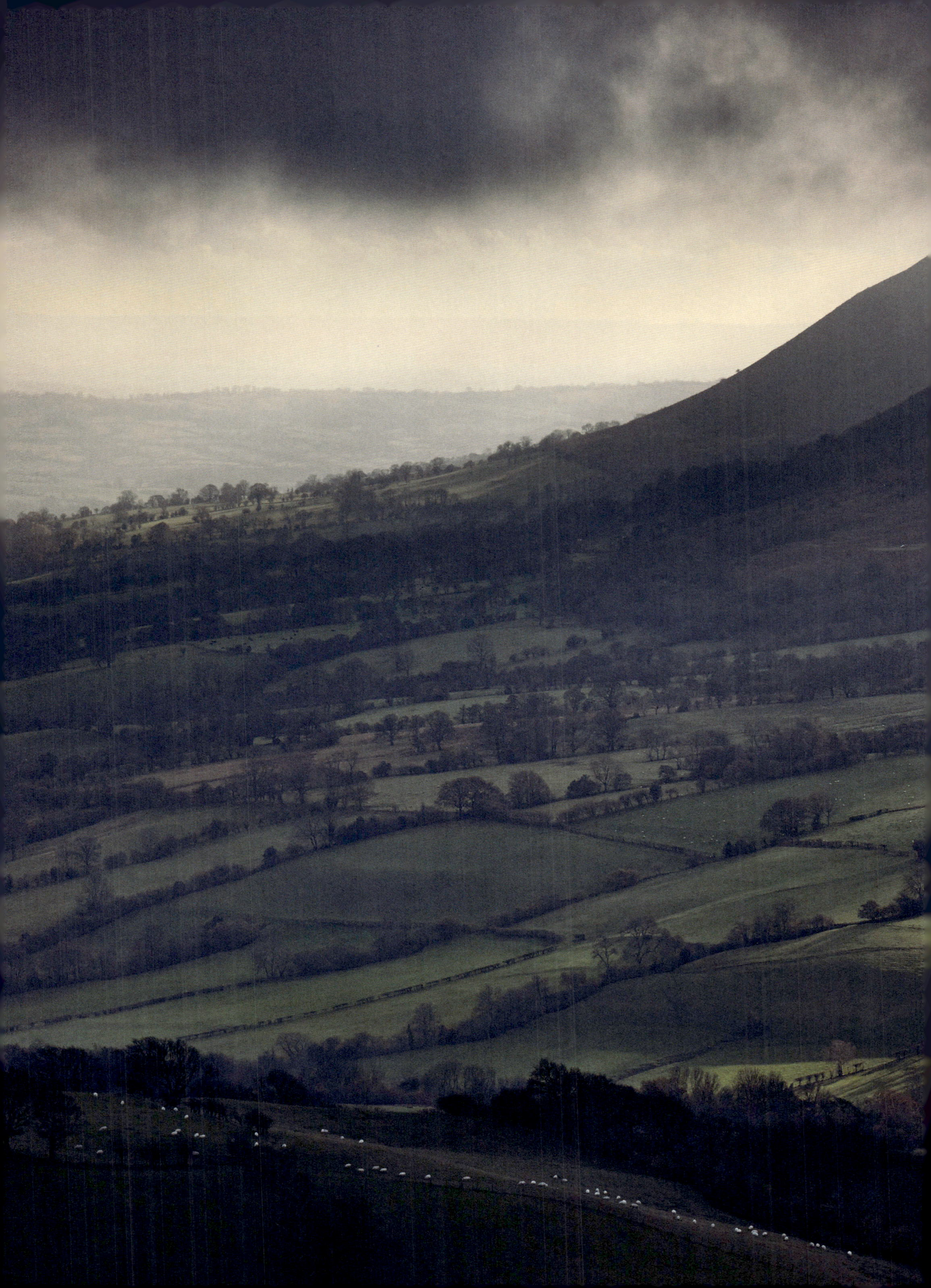

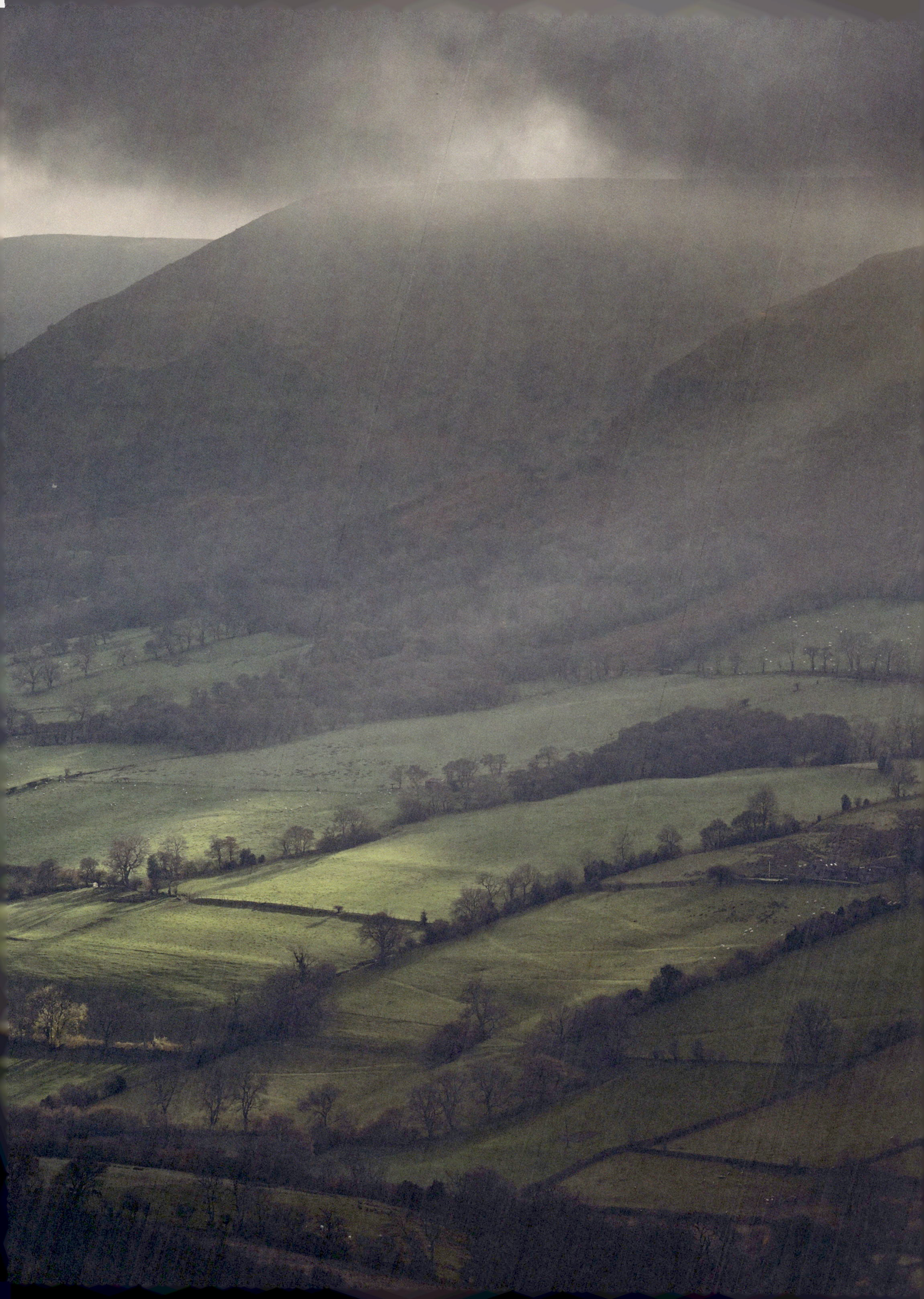

Blood orange jelly with stem ginger custard

SERVES 4

5–6 blood oranges

1 lemon

3 gelatine leaves

1 tablespoon granulated sugar, or to taste

25ml triple sec liqueur

For the stem ginger custard

1 vanilla pod

300ml double cream

3 egg yolks

1 teaspoon cornflour

30g caster sugar

30g stem ginger, finely chopped, plus 3 dessertspoons syrup from the ginger jar

This is jelly and custard for grown-ups. You can, of course, omit the triple sec liqueur from the jelly for younger diners – and the ginger from the custard, if necessary. A fun thing to do with this pudding is to create a striped jelly by making half of it with ordinary oranges and then setting it in alternate layers with the blood orange jelly. Allow extra time for this, as each layer of jelly needs to set before you add the next.

Squeeze the juice from the oranges and lemon and strain it into a measuring jug. You will need 450ml juice. Soak the gelatine in cold water for 5 minutes. Meanwhile, put the juice and sugar in a pan and heat gently until the sugar has dissolved. Add the triple sec, then taste and add more sugar if desired. Lift the gelatine sheets from the water, gently squeeze out the excess liquid and add the gelatine to the warm juice. Stir until it has dissolved. Leave the juice to cool for an hour, then strain it into a jug again. Divide it between 4 wine glasses and place in the fridge for about 2 hours to set. The jelly should be firm but have a nice wobble to it.

While the jelly is setting, make the custard. Slit open the vanilla pod and scrape out the seeds. Pour the cream into a saucepan, add the vanilla pod and seeds and place over a low heat. Bring to just under a simmer, then remove from the heat. Whisk the egg yolks, cornflour and caster sugar together in a bowl with a balloon whisk. Pour the hot cream on to the egg mixture, whisking vigorously, then return the mixture to the pan and place over a low heat. Whisk gently for about 5 minutes, until the custard has thickened. Leave to cool a little, then stir in the ginger pieces and syrup. Let the flavours infuse for an hour, then taste and add more ginger and syrup if desired.

Once the jelly is set, dollop the custard on top of it, filling the glasses. Cover with cling film and chill for at least another 30 minutes before serving.

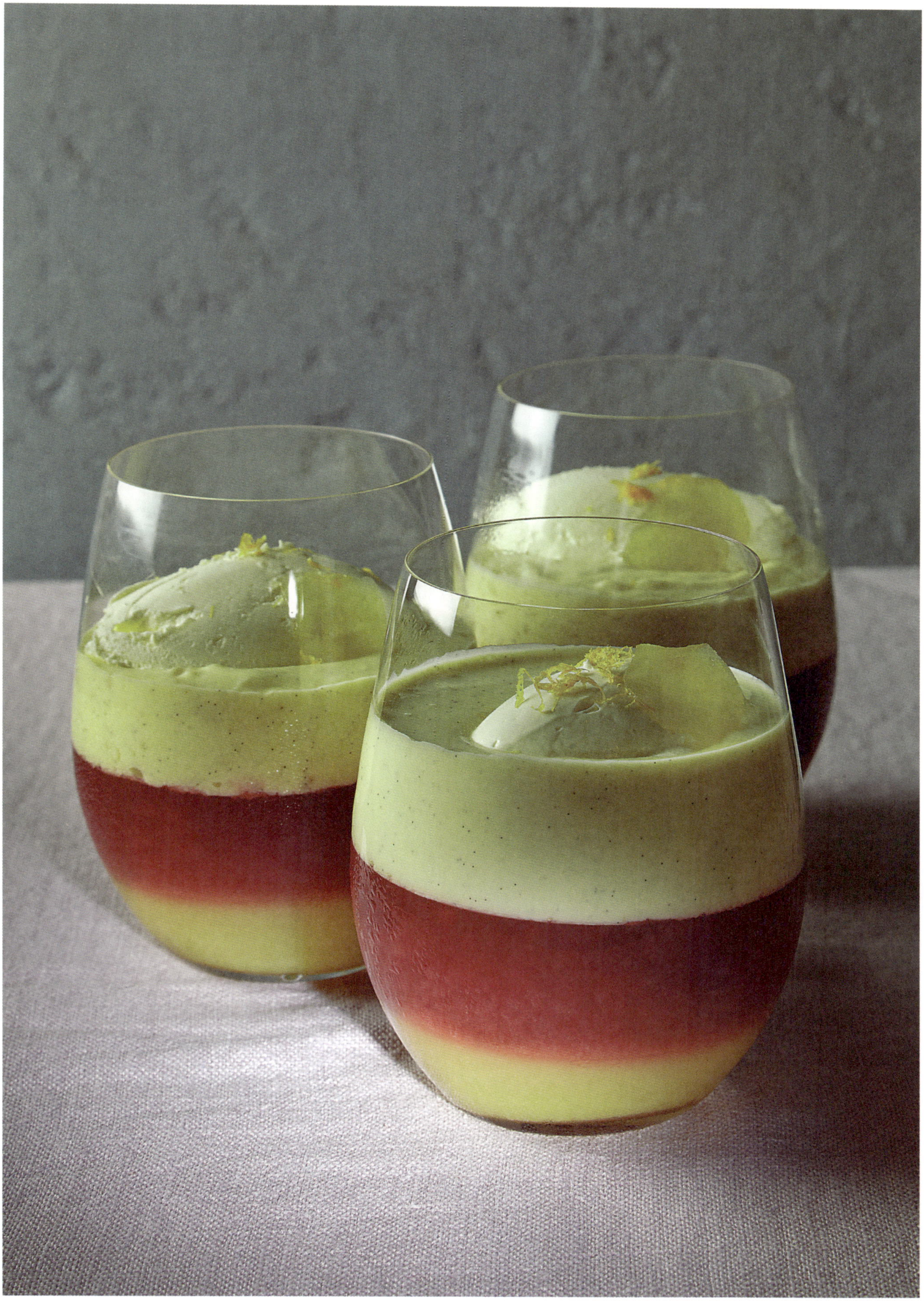

Apple and lemon crumble with a nutty topping

SERVES 4

500g Bramley apples, peeled, cored and thinly sliced

1 tablespoon golden granulated sugar (or to taste)

grated zest of 2 large lemons

juice of 1 large lemon

For the crumble topping

50g whole hazelnuts

75g plain flour

100g ground almonds

90g unsalted butter, cut into cubes

65g golden granulated sugar

The classic British crumble is a national treasure of a pudding. In this recipe Bramley apples, with their fabulous snowy texture, are combined with lots of lemon zest to make a wonderfully tangy pudding. If you use a different variety of apple, perhaps a less sharp one such as James Grieve or Egremont Russet, you may prefer to omit the tablespoon of sugar. Serve with cream, custard or ice cream – or all three, if you wish!

Heat the oven to 180°C/Gas Mark 4. Spread the hazelnuts out on a baking tray and toast in the oven for about 15 minutes, checking them occasionally and giving them a shake to ensure they toast evenly. The skins will split and the nuts inside will be golden. Grind them in a food processor, leaving them slightly chunky. Alternatively, allow the nuts to cool a little, then place in a plastic bag, seal and give them a good bash with a rolling pin.

Put the flour and ground almonds in a mixing bowl, add the butter and rub it in with your fingertips until the mixture resembles breadcrumbs. Stir in the sugar and hazelnuts.

Put the apples in a shallow 20cm ovenproof dish and scatter the sugar over them. Add the lemon zest and juice. Spoon the crumble over the apples and bake at 200°C/Gas Mark 6 for 15 minutes. Reduce the heat to 180°C/Gas Mark 4 and cook for a further 30 minutes, until the topping looks toasted and the apples are bubbling and juicy underneath.

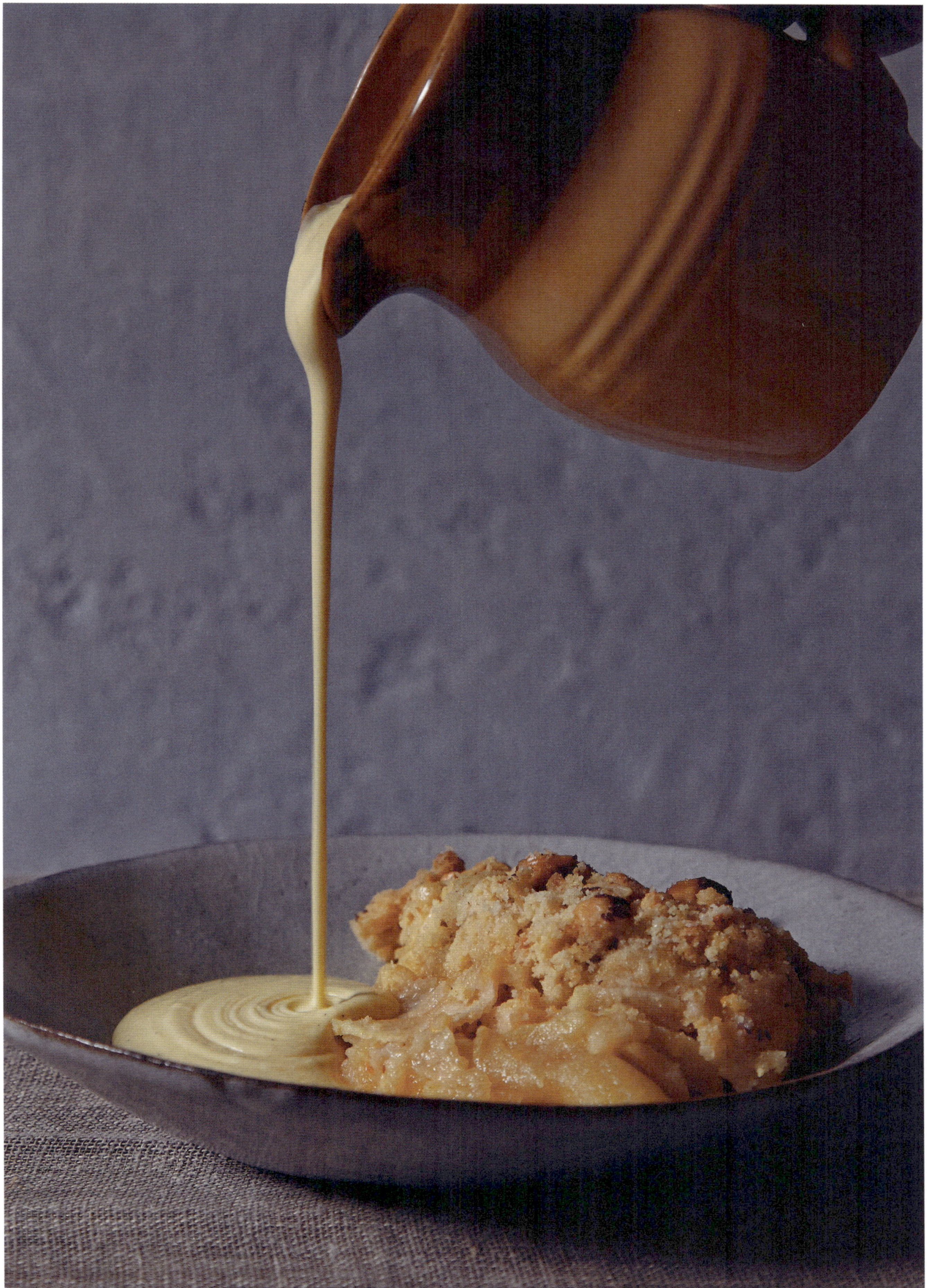

Parsnip and hazelnut oat biscuits

MAKES ABOUT 18

150g plain flour

½ teaspoon bicarbonate of soda

a pinch of salt

1 teaspoon ground nutmeg

1 teaspoon ground ginger

100g porridge oats

100g butter

50g light soft brown sugar

grated zest of ½ lemon

3 heaped dessertspoons set honey

150g cooked and puréed parsnip

1 egg, lightly beaten

1 teaspoon vanilla extract

50g hazelnuts, roughly chopped

These wholesome biscuits make a hearty addition to a lunchbox. The parsnips give them sweetness and an almost cake-like texture. Pumpkin would also work well, and you could substitute other nuts for the hazelnuts.

Heat the oven to 180°C/Gas Mark 4. Line a baking tray with baking parchment. In a bowl, mix together the flour, bicarbonate of soda, salt and spices, then stir in the porridge oats and set aside.

Using an electric beater, cream the butter with the sugar and lemon zest until soft and fluffy. Beat in the honey, followed by the parsnip purée, egg and vanilla. Add the flour and oat mixture, along with the chopped hazelnuts, and stir until well combined.

Using a teaspoon, drop golf-ball-sized pieces of the mixture on to the baking tray, spacing them 3cm apart and gently squashing them down with the spoon. Bake for 20 minutes, until golden brown, then remove from the oven and transfer to a wire rack to cool.

Carrot and almond cake

170g unblanched almonds
4 large eggs, separated
200g caster sugar
grated zest of 1 orange
3 drops of vanilla extract
250g carrots, finely grated
1 heaped tablespoon self-raising flour
60g ground almonds
icing sugar, for dusting

We are all familiar with carrot cake made with dark molasses sugar and oil and finished, if we're lucky, with a sweet cream cheese topping. This recipe is based on an Italian one and uses no fat and only a little flour. Quite different from its cousin, it is very sweet and light. Rather nice with a good cup of black coffee – *bellissima*, **in fact!**

Heat the oven to 180°C/Gas Mark 4. Line the base and sides of a deep 20cm cake tin with baking parchment.

Grind the unblanched almonds in a food processor, but leave them fairly chunky, as this will give a nice texture to the cake. Put the egg yolks, caster sugar, orange zest and vanilla extract in a bowl and beat with an electric whisk for about 5 minutes, until very pale, thick and creamy. Gently stir in the carrots, flour and both lots of almonds. In a separate bowl, whisk the egg whites until stiff. Gently fold them into the cake mixture with a large metal spoon. Turn the mixture into the prepared tin and bake for 40–45 minutes, until the cake is well risen and a skewer inserted in the centre comes out clean. Leave to cool in the tin, then turn out and dust with icing sugar.

Caramel Seville orange marmalade

MAKES 7 X 500G JARS

1.35kg Seville oranges
2 lemons
3 litres water
2.7kg granulated sugar

This marmalade is best made over two days. The long, slow cooking means that the sugar develops a beautiful caramel colour and flavour. Combined with the bitter citrus taste of the Seville oranges, it makes this the most delicious marmalade we have ever eaten.

Day one

Wash the fruit and remove any stalks. Place the whole fruit in a preserving pan, add the water and bring to a gentle simmer. Cover the pan with a tight-fitting lid if you have one; if not, cover with a well-secured piece of foil. This is important to prevent the steam escaping. Poach the fruit at a gentle simmer for 3 hours. Leave, still covered, until cool enough to handle, then remove the fruit from the poaching liquid with a slotted spoon, keeping the liquid in the pan.

Cut the oranges and lemons in half and scoop out all the flesh and pips into a saucepan. Keep all the empty orange halves, but discard the lemons. Add 500ml of the poaching liquid to the pulp in the saucepan and simmer over a medium heat for 15 minutes, stirring occasionally to prevent sticking. Pour the pulp into a muslin-lined sieve placed over a bowl and allow it to drip through.

Meanwhile, cut the empty orange halves in half again and then slice into strips. The thickness is up to you; we slice ours as thinly as possible to produce glassy slivers. Add these to the poaching liquid in the preserving pan. Once all the pulp has dripped through the muslin, gather the corners of the muslin and twist it into a ball, then squeeze as hard as you can to extract the remaining sticky juice. This juice contains the all-important pectin that will help the marmalade to set. Add the juice to the sliced peel, cover and leave overnight.

Day two

Place the preserving pan on the heat and allow the contents to get warm – they should be a little more than hand hot. Add the sugar approximately a kilo at a time, stirring well with a wooden spoon to dissolve. Once the sugar has fully dissolved, turn up the heat and bring slowly to the boil, stirring frequently. Reduce the heat and allow the marmalade to bubble gently for 3 hours, stirring once in a while. The marmalade will gradually thicken and darken to a caramel brown. Your kitchen will smell gorgeous! If you don't have a sugar thermometer, put a small plate in the fridge ready for testing the set. If you do have a thermometer, after 3 hours use it to take a reading from the middle of the pan, being careful not to touch the bottom, as this will give a false reading. If it reads 104.5°C, setting point has been reached.

Alternatively the good-old wrinkle test will do just as well: spoon a teaspoon of marmalade on to your chilled plate and leave in the fridge for a couple of minutes, then run your finger gently through; if the marmalade wrinkles, then setting point has been reached. You may need to do several tests but once you get that wrinkle, turn off the heat.

Leave the marmalade to stand for 10 minutes or so; this will help ensure the peel is evenly distributed in the jars. Pot it in sterilised jars (see page 251), using a jam funnel if possible, or you can use a sterilised mug. Seal the jars tightly and leave undisturbed for 12 hours. Label and use within a year.

Kippers with marmalade

You know when someone tells you about a food combination that sounds odd? Well, this is one of those. Kippers and marmalade is truly a marriage made in heaven. The smoky, meaty kippers combined with the bittersweet caramel of the marmalade on a piece of buttery toast is a winner. It is probably our favourite 'day-off' breakfast.

We tend to poach our kippers rather than grill them. Put the kippers in a large frying pan or saucepan, cover them with cold water and bring to a simmer. Poach for 3–4 minutes. Lift the kippers out of the water and serve straightaway, with lots of toast and marmalade.

Christmas lunch at Fern Verrow

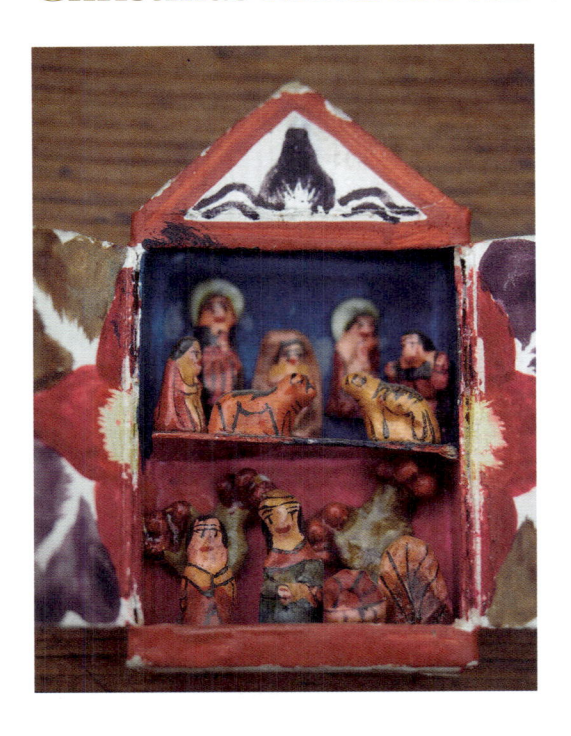

OUR CHRISTMAS HOLIDAY time begins when we return from the last market of the year, having sold all the Christmas birds and the cratefuls of sprouts and parsnips. It is a time when we close the doors, stay in the warm and enjoy our home. We take a couple of days to get ready for the big day, starting by decorating the house. With secateurs in hand we venture outside snipping and gathering holly, ivy and mistletoe from the farm. Back in the house we arrange the greenery with candles and lights around the doorways and window frames.

With Christmas music playing, our spirits are high and we look forward to our family and friends arriving. We cook all day on Christmas Eve and relish the fact that most of what we prepare has been grown or raised on the farm. We always think of our customers tucking into our produce and hope they enjoy it as much as we do. It is the goose that is the real treat at this time.

From the end of March when they are born, the geese we rear graze and fatten on our pastures. The green grass and herbage gives the meat its unique character. An organic, free-range goose should have a thick layer of golden fat under the skin, helping to keep the lean, dark meat beautifully moist, sticky and delicious. Goose is our most popular Christmas bird with customers who reorder every year. Of course, our own Christmas lunch wouldn't be complete without the golden goose.

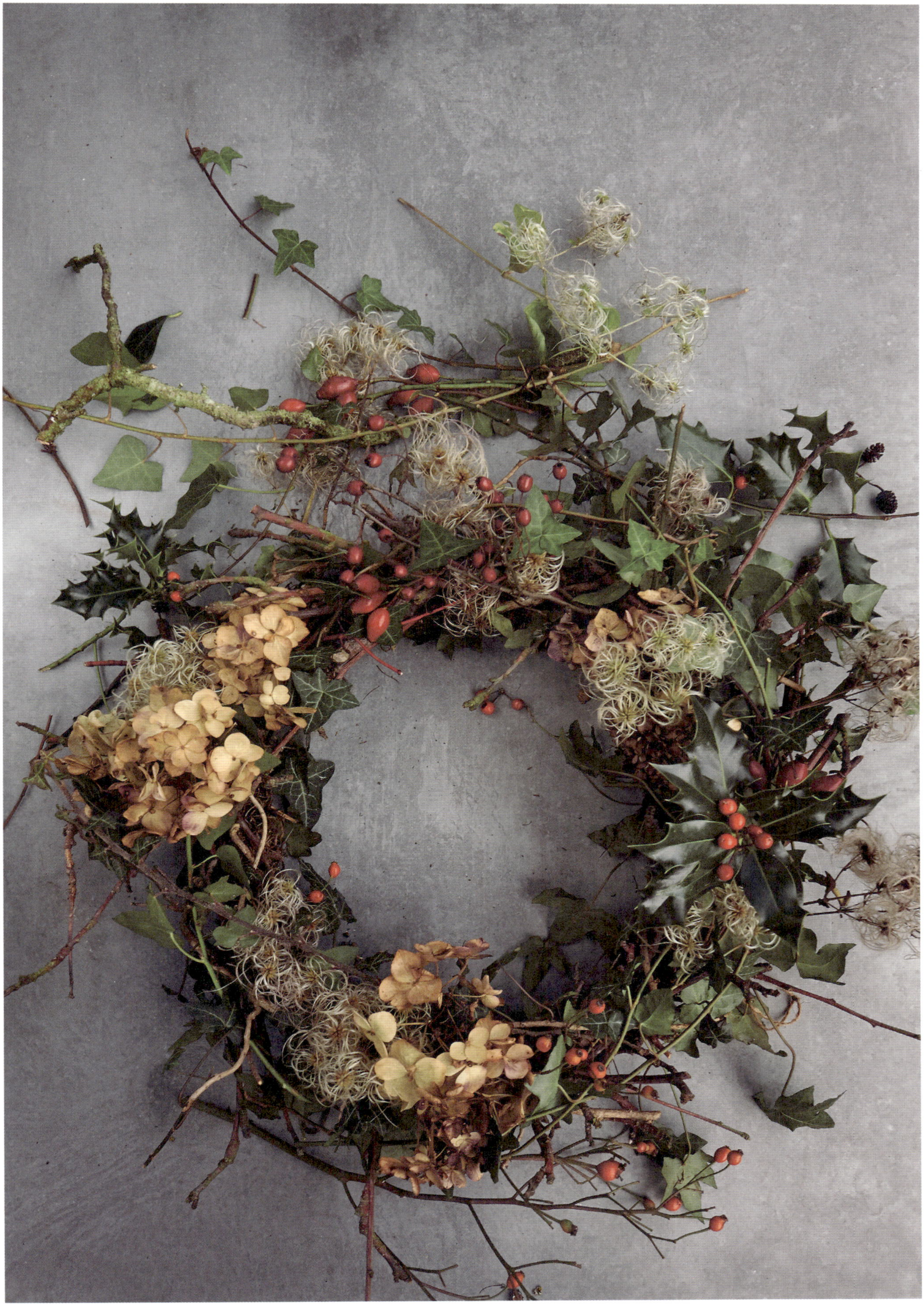

Roast goose

SERVES 6–8

a 4–5kg goose

Preserved Lemon, Prune, Quince and Couscous Stuffing (see page 62)

Herb and Chestnut Stuffing (see page 62)

quince or redcurrant jelly, for brushing (optional)

sea salt and black pepper

For the gravy

1 onion, roughly chopped

1 bay leaf

½ wine glass of white wine

750ml chicken stock

For the accompaniments

Gooseberry Sauce (see page 62)

Roast Potatoes (see page 63)

Bread Sauce (see page 63)

Braised Red Cabbage with Apple (see page 64)

Swede and Nutmeg Purée (see page 64)

Braised Brussels Sprouts with Chestnuts (see page 64)

Cook the goose in a roasting tin, preferably on a poultry rack if you have one; if not, make sure you spoon off the excess fat regularly or the bird will broil in the fat. Keep this precious liquid gold for roasting potatoes. Goose fat reaches a higher temperature than other oils, and produces wonderfully crisp roast potatoes.

The stuffings for your Christmas bird can be made the day before.

Heat the oven to 190°C/Gas Mark 5. Put the goose on a rack in a roasting tin and trim some of the fat from the cavity. Put the giblets in the base of the tin. Stuff the bird with the two stuffings – we find it easiest to hold the goose upright with the legs facing us and push the stuffing in with our hands. We put them both in via the cavity, as the neck opening is very narrow, making it difficult to stuff. Make sure the flap of skin at the neck end is tucked under the goose to stop the stuffing escaping. Don't pack it in too tightly, as it will swell during cooking. It is a good idea to stitch the cavity opening closed with a trussing needle and string to stop the stuffing oozing out during cooking. Any leftover stuffing can be baked in a small buttered ovenproof dish for about 30 minutes.

Wrap the fat you took from the cavity over the legs. Prick the skin all over with a fork and season with salt and pepper. Cover the bird loosely with foil and place in the oven. A 4kg bird (stuffed weight) needs to roast for about 3 hours; a 5kg bird for 3½ hours and a 5.5kg bird for 4 hours – the bigger the bird, the less time it will take to cook per kilo. Baste with the cooking juices every 30 minutes and remember to skim off the excess fat. Remove the giblets from the tin after an hour and feed them to the dog, if you have one; they will have left flavoursome juices behind that will enrich the gravy.

Half an hour before the end of the roasting time, remove the foil so the skin can brown. Brushing over some quince or redcurrant jelly will add a glaze that really complements the flavour of the goose.

To test that the bird is done, insert a sharp knife into the thickest part of the thigh; the juices should run clear. Remove from the oven, transfer to a warmed serving dish and leave to rest for half an hour.

While the goose is resting, make the gravy. Pour off most of the cooking juices and fat from the roasting tin, leaving behind a layer about 5mm deep, then set the tin over a medium heat on the stove. Add the onion and bay leaf, stir well and let the onion brown for about 5 minutes. Pour in the wine, stirring and scraping the 'Marmite' from the base of the tin. When the wine has reduced a little, pour in the chicken stock and bring to the boil, stirring constantly. Simmer until the gravy has reduced to the consistency and flavour you like. Season to taste, then strain into a jug.

Carve the goose and serve with all the accompaniments.

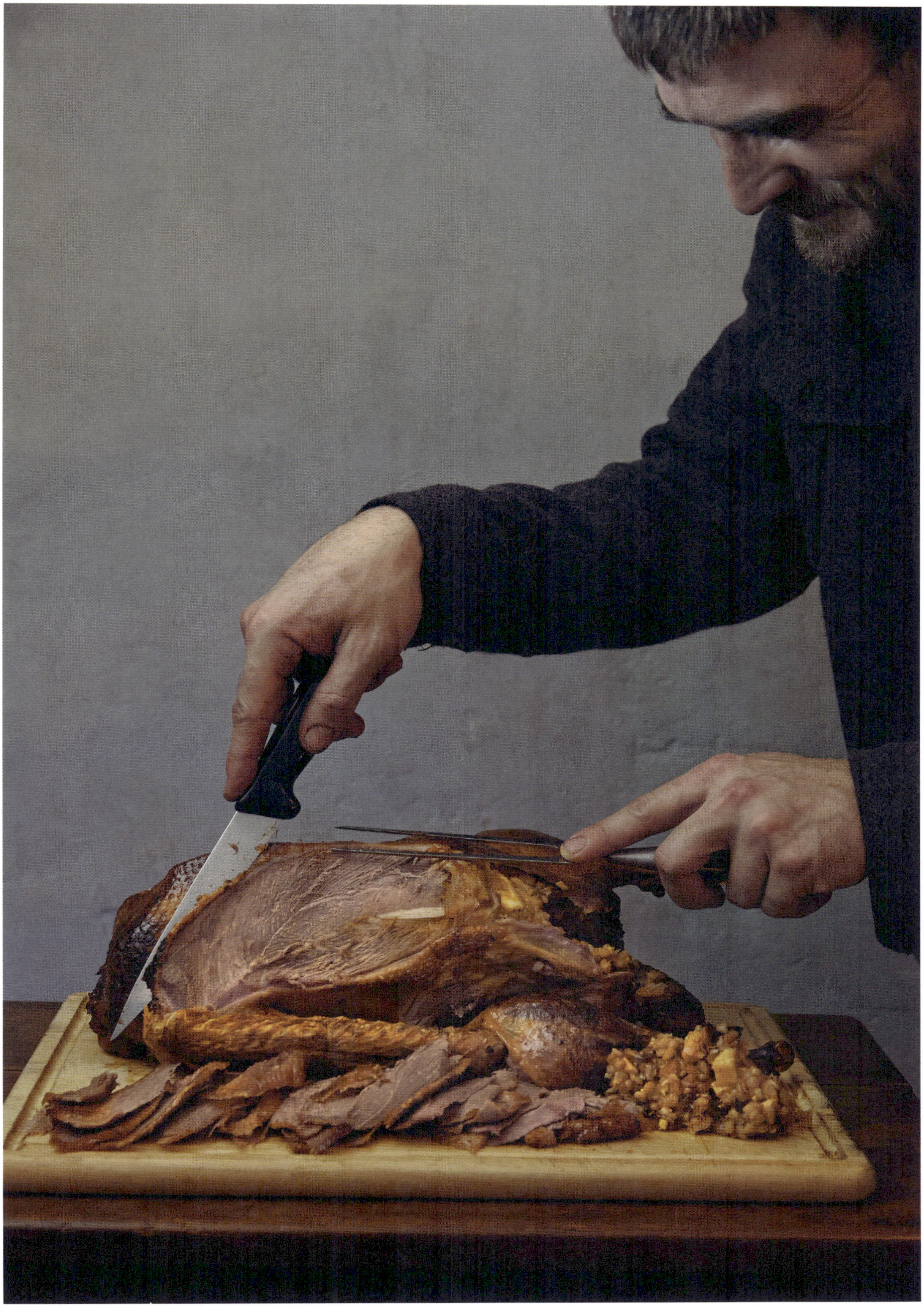

Preserved lemon, prune, quince and couscous stuffing

SERVES 6–8

100g wholewheat couscous
300ml boiling water
25g fresh ginger, finely chopped
1 red onion, diced
100g dates, stoned and chopped
100g prunes, stoned and chopped
1 quince, peeled, cored and chopped
175–200g preserved lemons, chopped
1 dessertspoon juices from the preserved lemons
black pepper

It's much more convenient to make the stuffings for your Christmas bird the day before. This one is fruity, salty and citrussy, which works perfectly with the gamey meat of the goose. Using couscous here in place of the usual breadcrumbs works very well indeed.

Put the couscous in a bowl, pour over the boiling water, then cover and leave to soak for 10 minutes. Fork through the couscous and leave to cool. Add all the remaining ingredients, seasoning with pepper, and mix well.

Herb and chestnut stuffing

SERVES 6–8

225g fresh chestnuts (or 150g vacuum-packed chestnuts)
25g butter
1 onion, diced
3 celery sticks, sliced
a small bunch of sage, chopped
a bunch of thyme, chopped
a bunch of parsley, chopped
150g fresh breadcrumbs
1 egg, lightly beaten
sea salt and black pepper

This traditional stuffing is much loved, with good reason.

If using fresh chestnuts, score a deep cross on the base of each one with a sharp knife. Add to a pan of boiling water and cook for 30 minutes, then drain. As soon as they are cool enough to handle, peel off the skin and the thin inner skin to reveal the wrinkled chestnut. Chop them roughly.

Melt the butter in a small pan, add the onion and celery and sweat for a few minutes, until softened but not coloured. Stir in the herbs, chestnuts and breadcrumbs and season with salt and pepper. Mix in the beaten egg. The mixture should hold together if squeezed in your hand.

Gooseberry sauce

SERVES 6–8

300g gooseberries
1 level teaspoon sugar, or to taste

There is no way of making this sauce unless you have a few gooseberries in the freezer. So when you see them in June, bountiful and cheap, buy an extra 300g and freeze them. It couldn't be simpler to make and is a pleasant change from cranberry sauce, although we must admit we often have both!

Put the frozen gooseberries into a small pan with the sugar and a dash of water, then cover and place over a very low heat. Once the gooseberries are simmering, remove the lid and continue to cook, stirring frequently, until they have a pulpy consistency. Taste and add more sugar, if necessary – though it is best with the goose if you leave it on the sharp side. Serve cold.

Roast potatoes

SERVES 6–8

2.5kg even-sized potatoes, peeled
6 tablespoons goose fat
sea salt

We love roast potatoes and grow a specific variety for roasting. This is Arran Victory, a purple-skinned spud that, if care is taken with the par-boiling, produces the perfect roast potato, with a crisp outer shell and a very fluffy interior – ideal for absorbing all the delicious gravy. Desiree, Cara and King Edward do a fine job, too.

Put the potatoes in a large pan of cold water with a good pinch of salt. Bring to the boil and simmer for about 4 minutes, until the outer layer of the potato is just beginning to break down. Keep a careful eye on them, as overcooking may mean that they fall apart. Drain and allow all the steam to evaporate.

While the potatoes are letting off steam, put the goose fat in a large roasting tin and place it in a hot oven (it can go in the same oven as the goose). Once the fat is hot, add the potatoes to the tin, turning them to coat and baste them with the golden fat. Sprinkle some salt over the potatoes and return to the oven. Cook for about an hour, basting them every 20 minutes and turning them each time so they are golden and crisp all over.

Bread sauce

SERVES 6–8

280g white bread, crusts removed
1 onion, peeled and cut in half
12 cloves
500ml full-fat milk
1 large bay leaf
grated nutmeg, to taste
1 knob of butter (about 15g)
sea salt and black pepper

Bread sauce is one of those things that everyone has their own way of making; this is ours. It works best with slightly stale bread, but fresh bread will do if necessary. Do not use sourdough as it can curdle the milk and the sauce will taste sour. Actually, the best bread sauce we have ever had was made with ordinary white sliced bread.

Cut the bread into dice-sized cubes. Stud the onion halves with the cloves and put them into a saucepan with the milk and bay leaf. Season with nutmeg, salt and pepper. Bring to the boil, then turn off the heat and leave to infuse for at least 30 minutes.

Add the cubed bread to the milk and slowly bring it back to the boil, stirring frequently to make sure that it doesn't catch and burn. Continue to stir over a low heat until it is thick and gloopy and the aroma delightful. Stir in the butter, adjust the seasoning and serve warm.

Braised red cabbage with apple

SERVES 6–8

50g butter
1 onion, sliced
1 large red cabbage (about 1kg), shredded
1 large cooking apple, peeled, cored and sliced
200ml red wine
300ml cider vinegar
freshly grated nutmeg, to taste
1 dessertspoon sugar
sea salt and black pepper

Although we eat this tangy, sweet-and-sour dish hot with our Christmas lunch, we are always happy to have leftovers to be enjoyed cold with cheese or meats.

Melt the butter in a large, heavy-based pan. As it begins to bubble, add the onion and cook gently for a few minutes, until softened but not coloured. Add the shredded cabbage, mixing it through the butter until it begins to wilt and settle in the pan. Stir in the slices of apple, then pour in the wine and vinegar. Grate in the nutmeg, season with salt, pepper and the sugar and stir to mix in all the seasonings. Cover and braise over a low heat for 30 minutes, allowing the cabbage to simmer gently in the vinegar and wine. Taste and adjust the seasonings as necessary. Continue to cook for an hour, stirring occasionally and keeping everything moist.

Swede and nutmeg purée

SERVES 6–8

1 large swede (approximately 750g), peeled and cut into cubes
50g butter
freshly grated nutmeg, to taste
sea salt and black pepper

Swede is a great vehicle for soaking up gravy. When you're not making this for Christmas lunch, try adding 100g grated Comté or Gruyère cheese – too rich for Christmas with all the other treats on the plate, but perfect for a bangers and mash sort of day instead.

Boil the swede in plenty of salted water until very soft, then drain. Return it to the pan and work in the butter with a potato masher until the swede is very smooth. Grate in some nutmeg and plenty of salt and black pepper. Serve piping hot.

Braised Brussels sprouts with chestnuts

SERVES 6–8

300g fresh chestnuts (or 200g vacuum-packed chestnuts)
500g Brussels sprouts
50g butter
sea salt and black pepper

There is a fine line between sprouts tasting amazing and their resembling a nasty school-dinner green. Keeping a little crunch in the centre of the sprouts and not overcooking them is the secret of success with this wonderful vegetable.

If using fresh chestnuts, score a deep cross on the base of each one with a sharp knife. Add to a pan of boiling water and cook for 30 minutes, then drain. As soon as they are cool enough to handle, peel off the outer skin and the thin inner skin to reveal the wrinkled chestnut.

Use a small knife to trim the base of the sprouts, removing any unsightly outer leaves. Melt the butter in a heavy-based pan, add the sprouts, then cover and cook over a low heat for 10–12 minutes, giving the pan an occasional shake. The sprouts will soften in the steam. Remove the lid, add the chestnuts and continue to cook and stir gently for a few minutes until the sprouts and chestnuts are browning in the butter and the sprouts are tender on the outside but still quite firm in the centre. Season to taste.

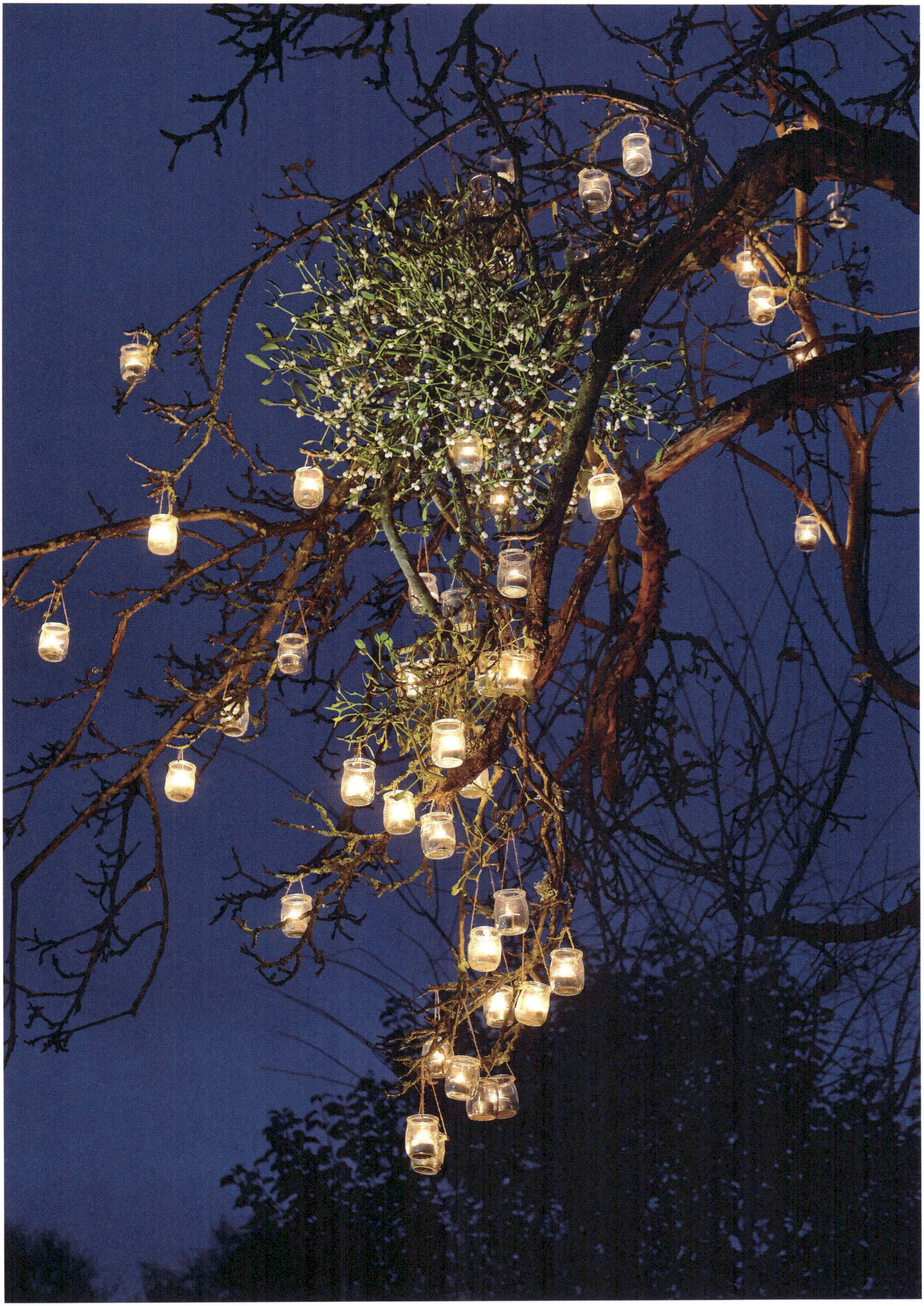

Sour cherry Christmas pudding

SERVES 6–8

90g unblanched almonds
60g self-raising flour
¼ teaspoon salt
¼ nutmeg, finely grated
½ teaspoon ground mixed spice
½ teaspoon ground ginger
85g suet
85g muscovado sugar
85g mixed candied peel, finely chopped
110g dried figs, chopped
60g dried apricots, chopped
170g dried sour cherries
60g large raisins
85g fresh breadcrumbs
juice and grated zest of ½ orange
½ quince, peeled and grated
2 small eggs
80ml ale or stout
2 tablespoons brandy, to flame the pudding (optional)

Christmas would not be the same without the licking sapphire flames on the Christmas pudding. The sour cherries lighten the flavour of this one. It can be made any time from the beginning of December.

Pour some boiling water on to the almonds and leave to soak for about 5 minutes. Drain, then slip off the skins. Slice the almonds into slivers.

Sift the flour, salt and spices into a large bowl. Add the suet, sugar, candied peel, dried fruit, breadcrumbs, almonds, orange zest and grated quince and mix well. Lightly beat the eggs together, then mix in the beer and orange juice. Add the liquid to the fruit mixture and stir thoroughly.

Butter a 1-litre pudding basin and turn the mixture into it. Cover the surface with a buttered circle of baking parchment. Then take a piece of foil, fold a 3cm pleat in the middle and use to cover the pudding basin; there should be a roughly 4cm overlap. Tie a piece of string round the lip of the basin to secure the foil, making an extra loop of string to use as a handle.

Place the basin in a large saucepan and add boiling water to just below the string. Cover the pan and simmer for 4 hours, replenishing with boiling water as necessary. Remove the pudding from the pan, replace the baking parchment and foil with fresh pieces (not buttered this time) and secure with string once more. Store the pudding in a cool, dry place.

On the big day, boil the pudding for 2 hours, then remove the foil and baking parchment, run a knife around the edge of the pudding and turn it out on to a serving plate. If you want to flame it, pour 2 tablespoons of brandy into a small saucepan and heat it slowly, until it is just too hot to touch. Pour it over the pudding and, standing well back, immediately ignite it with a match. Have someone ready on the light switch as you present your pudding in all its flaming glory.

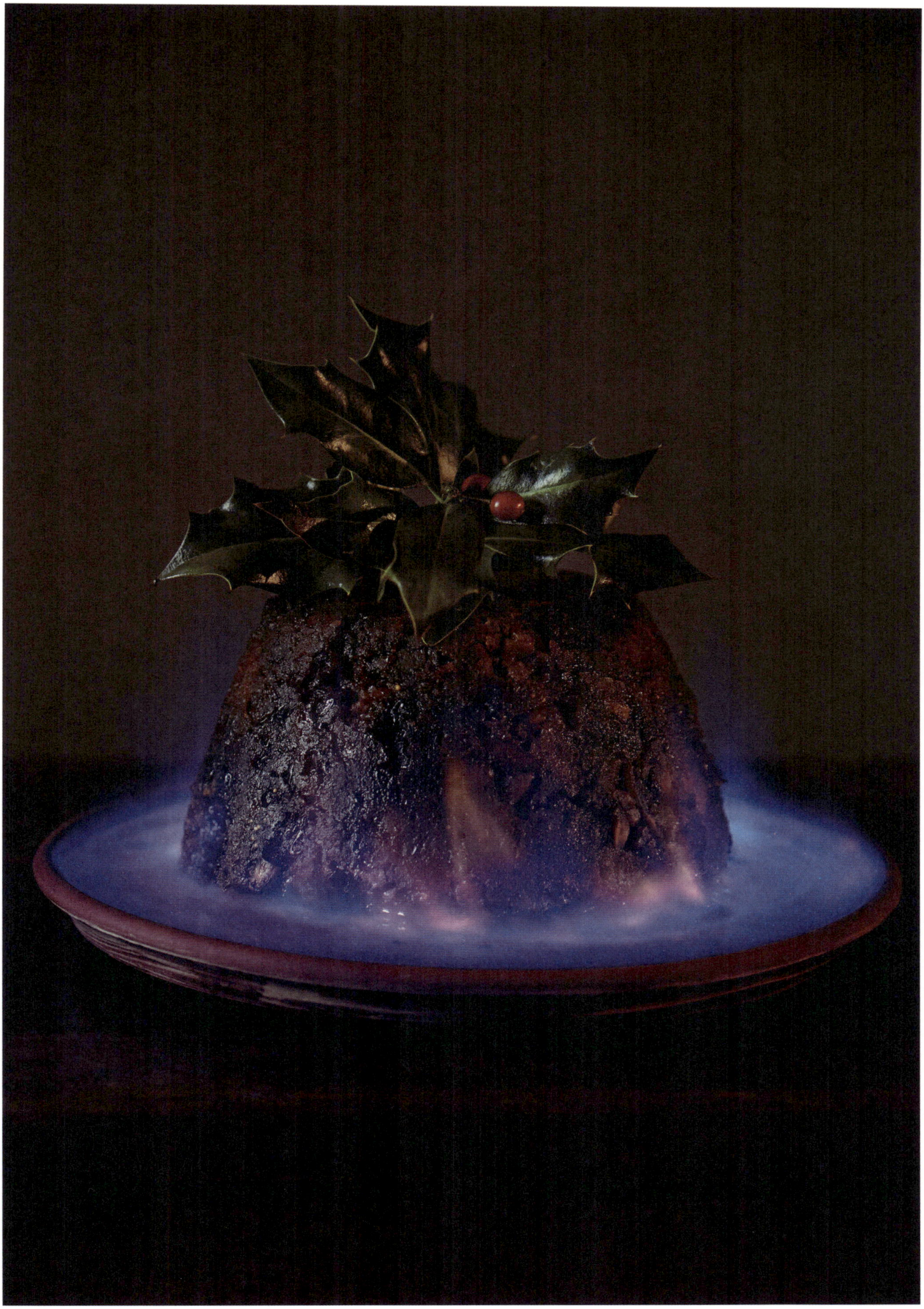

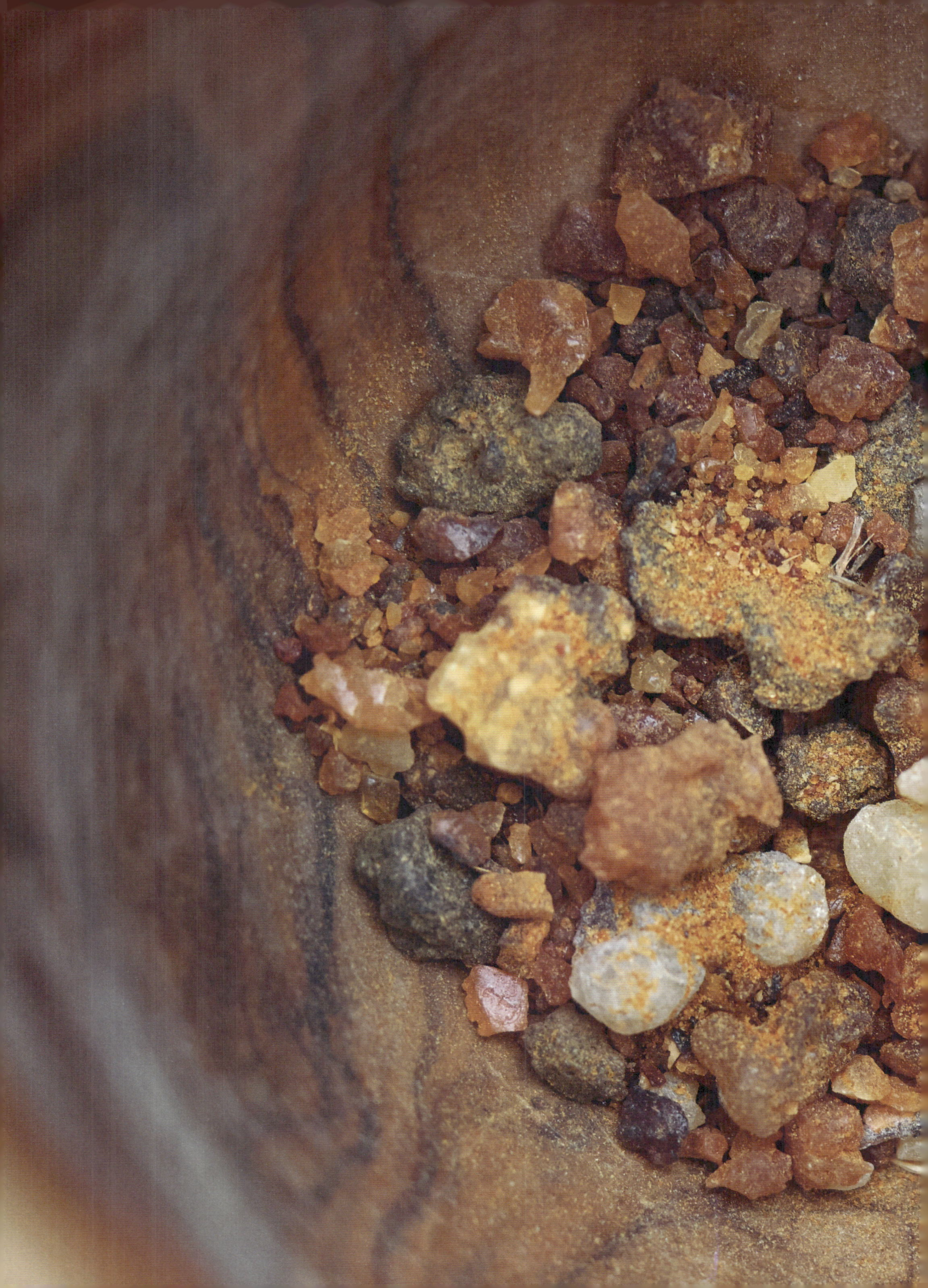

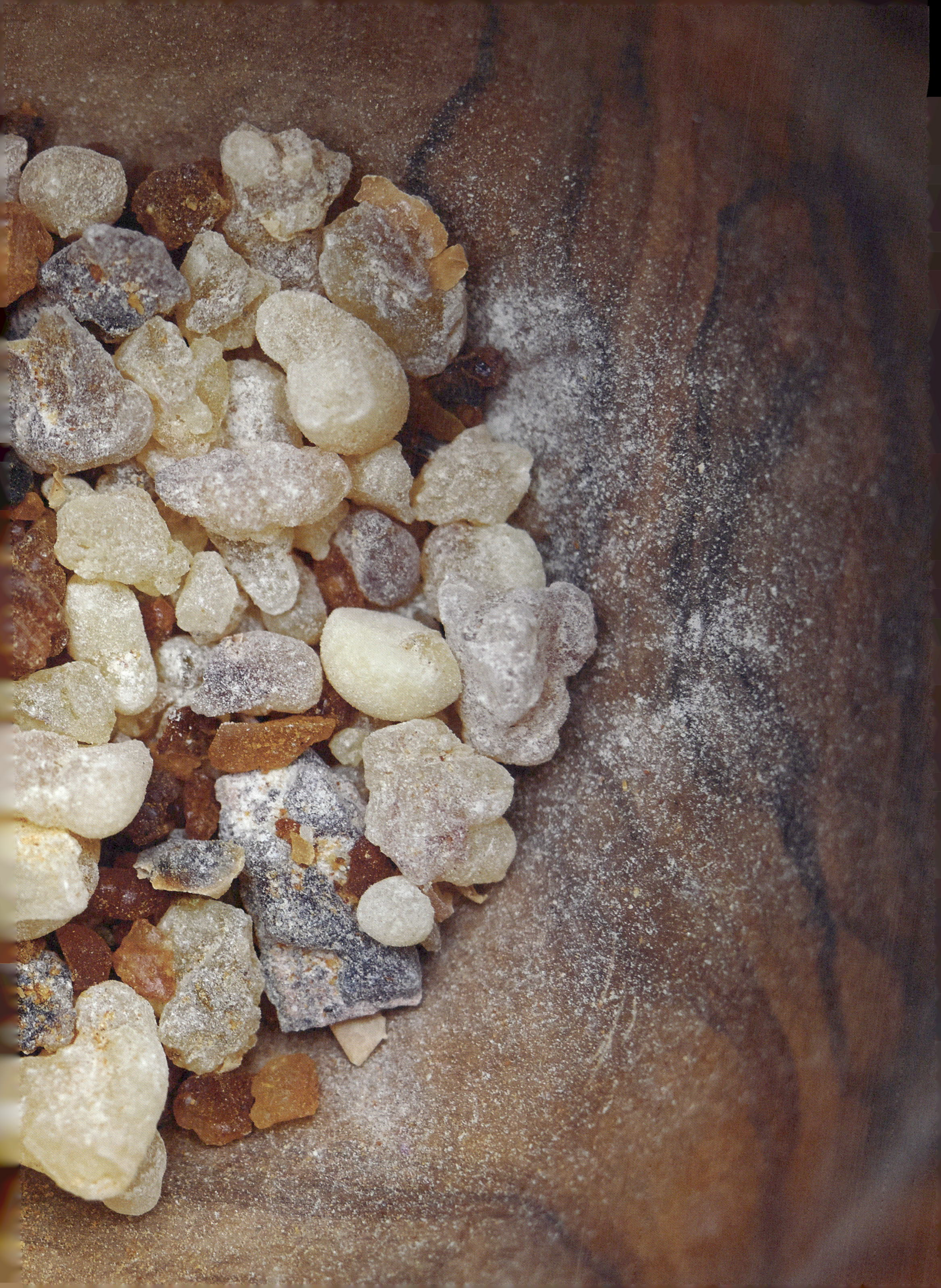

Three Kings Day

THREE KINGS DAY, which falls on January 6, is a celebration that encapsulates our approach to our work on the farm. From Christmas Eve to Epiphany, a time that used to be widely known as the 13 Holy Nights, we have a rest from the practical work outside, just feeding and tending to the animals. January 6 marks the start of our endeavours for the new working year, a whole new growing cycle.

On this day we make the Three Kings Preparation. Developed by a biodynamic farmer and researcher, Hugo Erbe (1895–1965), the Three Kings Preparation is an offering to the elemental world and a blessing for the earth. In the morning we begin in the kitchen by grinding gold, frankincense and myrrh to a fine powder using a pestle and mortar. These three sacred substances have been used through the ages as symbols to acknowledge the spiritual activity that weaves within the physical world. Gold symbolises the wisdom of the past; frankincense the transience of the present; and myrrh the victory of life over death. We take turns to mill the resins as we talk about the year ahead with excited anticipation.

In the afternoon we go out to stir the finely ground mixture in a barrel of water (see page 105). It's our first real physical exertion after the excesses of good food, drink and company over the festive time. We sit well wrapped up, sensitive to the cold and wind. As we stir we notice that the water seems to become lighter, warmer and thinner over the course of an hour, and the highly diluted scent of the frankincense and myrrh is pleasing, combining the regal with the spices of Christmas.

Over the year we don't usually have much time to walk the boundaries of the farm, but on this day we set off together around this less familiar route, along the hedgerows and over fences, criss-crossing the streams, ducking under branches in the woodland. We notice it all: every forgotten corner reminding us of its need for our attention and care. We each carry a bucket and a hand-brush and sprinkle the preparation as we go. All the while we are wishing good things to manifest on the farm this coming year and feeling gratitude towards the elemental world. By identifying the physical boundaries of the land in our care, we're marking out the stage on which the coming year will be played. This ceremonial mapping reaffirms our constantly evolving partnership with the farm.

PREVIOUS PAGE: *The Three Kings Preparation – gold, frankincense and myrrh*

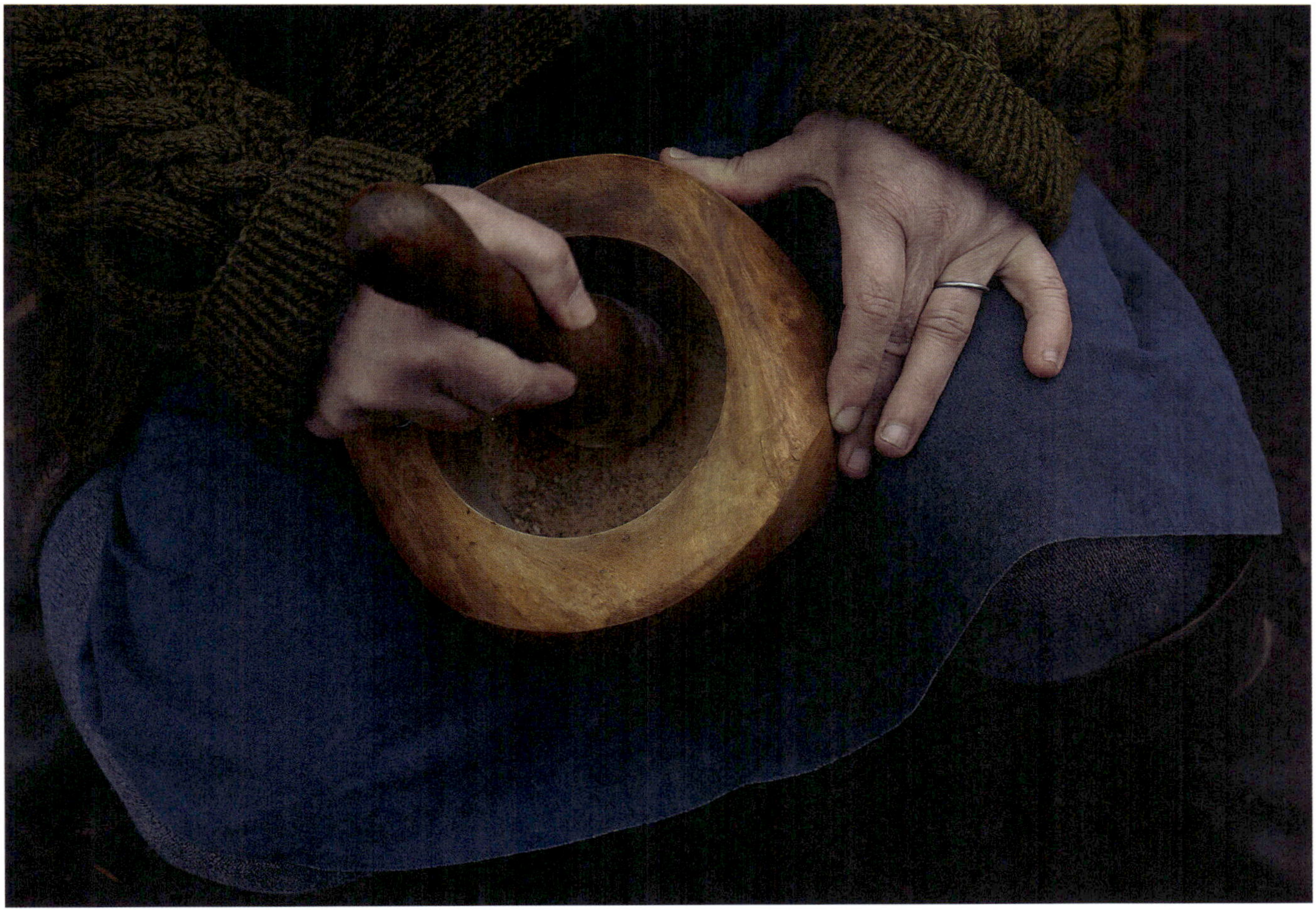

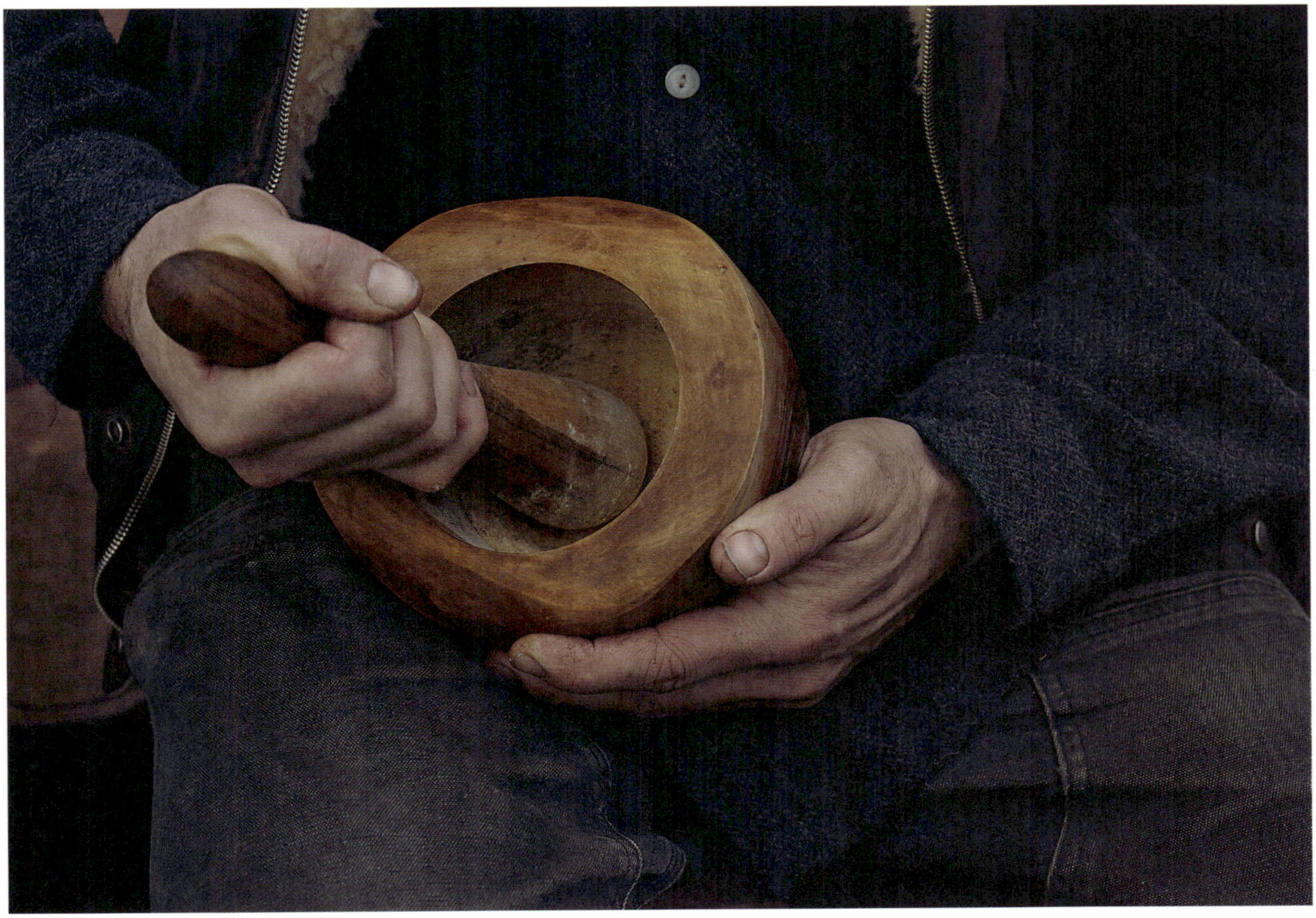

▽

WATER
Spring

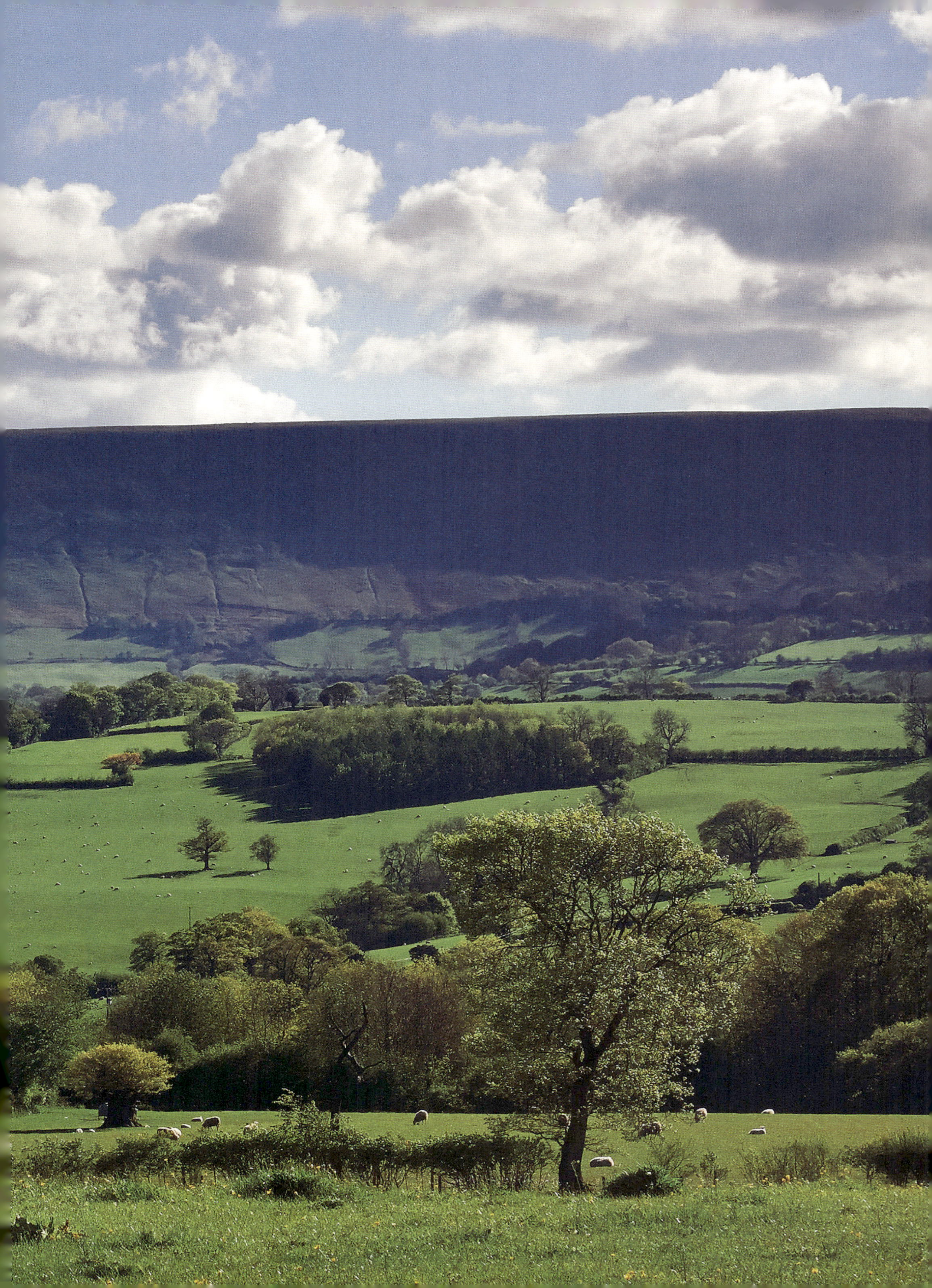

THE FIRST SHOW of snowdrops in February tells us that spring is on its way – still a number of weeks away, but it is a little nudge, signalling us to start making preparations for growing again. Here on the farm that moment of the year, out in the field, when for the first time we feel the warmth of the sun on our faces, is always a joyful occasion. The endurance of winter is coming to a close, and we bask in the sun's light with gladness, feeling it reach the deepest depths and spark an overwhelming will to participate. We are roused from the hibernation of winter, carrying with us feelings of optimism and the excitement of new beginnings. Spring is the honeymoon season of the year, with everything in its infancy, when all is fresh and new.

In the morning the birds in the trees announce the air is warming and light and colour returning, as the impulse of the sun starts to show itself in all living things. Each comes out of itself. 'The Earth exhales her soul,' and so begins 'the interweaving of all things'.*

In this westerly part of Herefordshire, renowned for its higher than average rainfall, we are blessed with generous displays of spring. The landscape quickly transforms into a spectacular palette of greens and myriad colours of wild flowers. Every day brings more treasures to behold. Bulbs sprout out of the ground, whites give way to yellows and everywhere there is green spreading upwards and outwards. New shoots rise from the soil, leaves grow from branches, and buds open to announce nature's rebirth. Flowers and fruit blossoms unfurl, and the heavenly pollinators are busy at work. At this time of year, it feels that anything is possible, and we relish the challenge ahead of us.

We eagerly open new seed packets and sow their contents into compost-filled modules in the propagating greenhouse; as germination and growth begin we tend to the young seedlings lovingly and skilfully. As growers, we always hope for an early start to the season, with favourable weather conditions to work with; however, our temperate climate often tests our patience. Nothing can be rushed: we must wait, with open hearts and minds, ready in the wings, and make our entrance in a timely and appropriate manner. But once there is some consistency of light and heat in the days, and the soil begins to warm, we are carried with the flow.

The beginning of spring is also punctuated by the needs and habits of our animals. We time the birth of our lambs to coincide with the new growth of grass and herbage that will get mothers and their offspring off to the best start. You can spot the imminent arrival of a lamb, as the ewe detaches herself from the rest of the flock and, if there is wind and rain, finds a sheltered spot in which to give birth. If all goes well, within an hour the lamb is born; the bond between mother and her young is forged by the ewe licking the lamb clean and softly bleating, while the warmth and contact from the mother

*From *The Four Seasons and the Archangels: Experience of the Course of the Year in Four Cosmic Imaginations* by Rudolf Steiner (Rudolf Steiner Press, 2002).

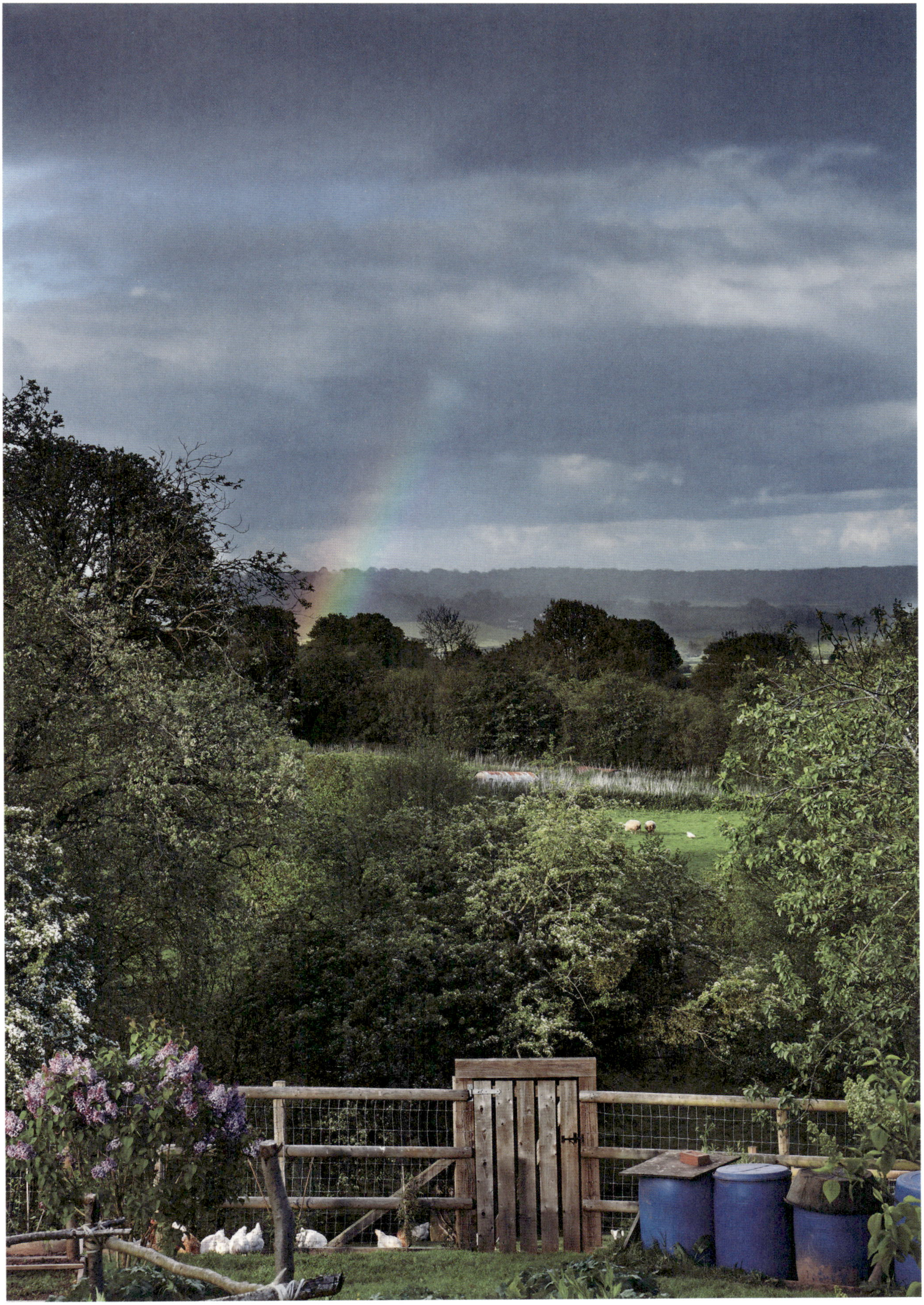

stimulate the lamb's instinct to stand and feed. There are rarely problems, except that on occasion the first-time mums need a little guidance and encouragement from us. The care and love with which sheep tend to their young never fails to astonish us. We always look forward to lambing time, and being close to our flock.

Usually in March, providing the ground is not too wet, we take the cows from the barn, where they have spent the winter months eating the summer-made hay, out on to the pastures. This is always an amusing occasion. It's a short trailer-ride up to the Tump (see the map on pages 6–7). We open the gates and the ladies surge forwards, grabbing hurried chunks of grass here and there. We wait with anticipation, and are never disappointed as, suddenly realising that they are out in the open, the animals take off at full gallop in every direction, kicking their back legs with a yee-ha! Within a month our Herefords will have shed their thick winter coats, which are replaced with sleek copper ones. We are all full of the joys of spring.

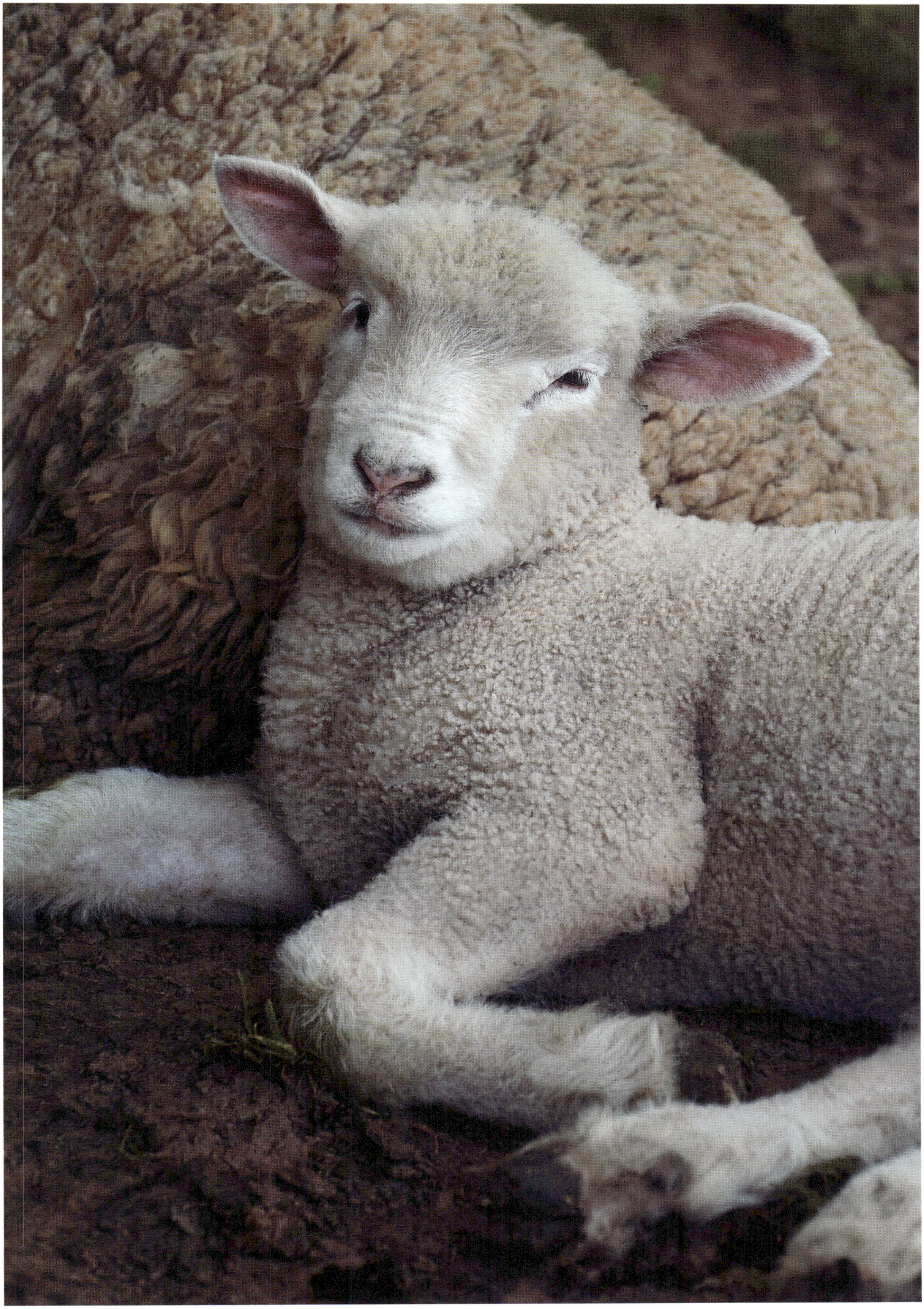

Nettle soup

SERVES 4

1 colander full of nettle tops (about 300g)

3 tablespoons sunflower oil, olive oil or butter

2 leeks, including the green tops, sliced

1 colander of perpetual spinach or chard (about 300g), chopped

1 litre vegetable stock

crème fraîche, single cream or yoghurt, to serve

sea salt and black pepper

We always leave nettles to grow in the hen run purely for making this soup – there are usually enough by March. The soup is a real tonic – you can feel it doing you good and clearing away the winter cobwebs. Wearing rubber gloves, we take just the fresh growth (about 12cm long) at the top of each shoot. Nettles continue to produce nettle tops after they've been picked so we make this soup right up to midsummer. We change it slightly according to what's available (see the variations below), but the basic recipe is much the same each time.

Wash the nettle tops in cold water and leave to drain in a colander. Gently heat the oil or butter in a large saucepan, add the leeks and sweat for 5 minutes, stirring occasionally, until softened but not coloured. Add the nettles, cover the pan and allow them to wilt. Add the spinach or chard and let that wilt, too. Pour in the stock and bring to the boil. Reduce the heat and simmer for 20 minutes.

Liquidise the soup in a blender or food processor and then return it to the saucepan. Reheat and season to taste. Serve with a spoonful of crème fraîche, single cream or yoghurt added carefully on top of each portion, plus a twist of freshly ground pepper.

Variations

For a heartier soup, add 200g diced potatoes with the leeks.

Substitute onions, spring onions or shallots for the leeks.

A little later in the year, you can use spinach instead of perpetual spinach or chard.

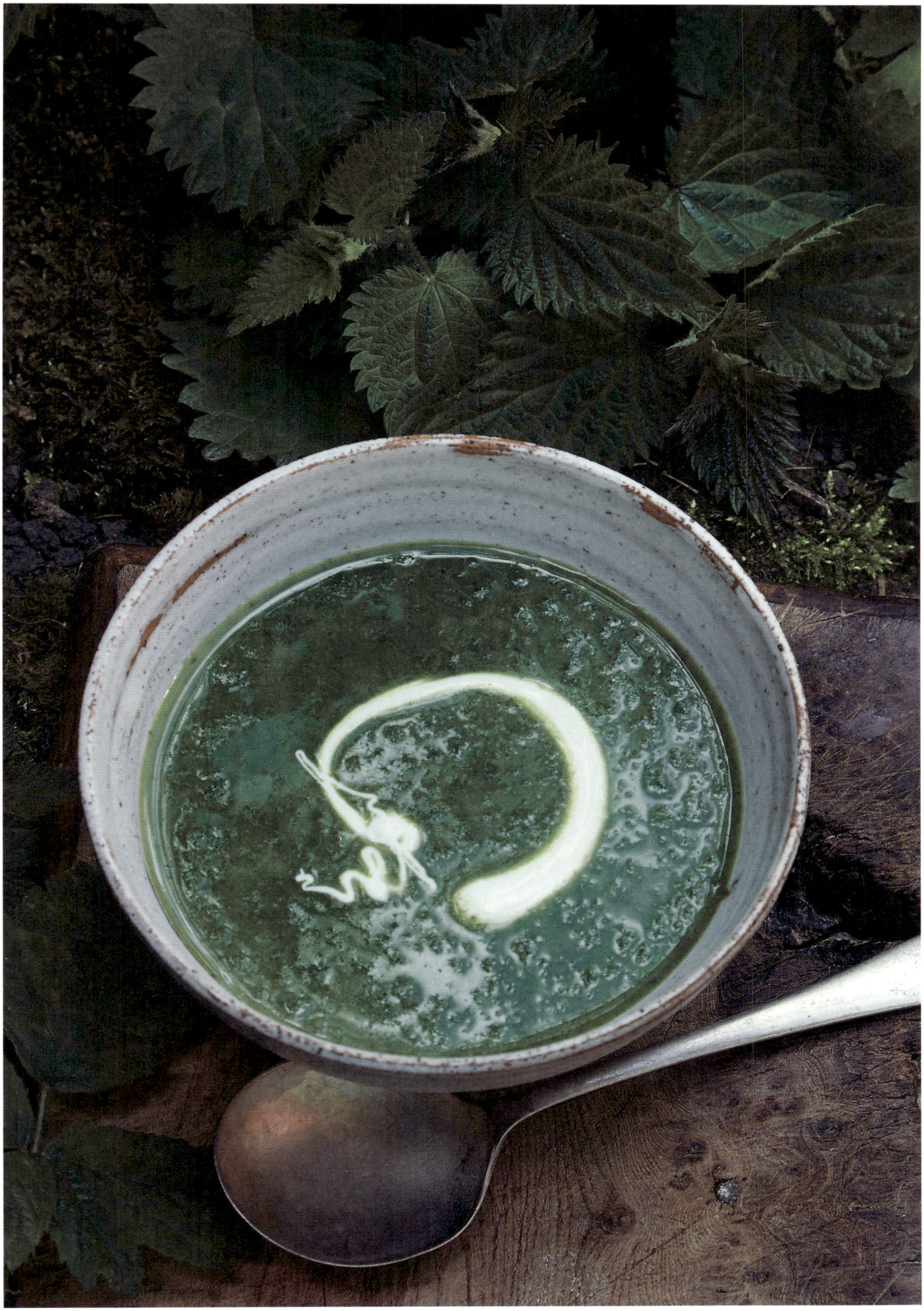

Lovage and potato soup

SERVES 4

50g butter
1 large onion, chopped
500g potatoes, peeled and diced
500ml vegetable or chicken stock
500ml milk
4–5 sprigs of lovage (about 25g)
a little double cream, to serve
sea salt and black pepper

Lovage is a delicious herb, but hugely underrated these days. Native to the Mediterranean, it used to feature widely in English gardens owing to easy cultivation and a generous perennial growth habit. It has a pungent aroma and taste, similar to celery. Try adding it to a tomato sauce – just one leaf will give a strong, aromatic flavour.

Melt the butter in a pan, add the onion and cook gently until softened. Add the diced potatoes and continue cooking for a few minutes, stirring now and then and adding a generous seasoning of salt and pepper. Pour in the stock and the milk and cook at a very low simmer for at least 20 minutes, until the potatoes are soft.

Chop the lovage leaves and stalks, add to the pan and cook for 5 minutes, then remove from the heat. Blitz the soup with a stick blender or in a food processor and check the seasoning. Serve in warm bowls with a swirl of double cream and, if you like, some croûtons.

Braised lettuce with peas, spring onion and mint

SERVES 4

1 large butterhead lettuce

75g butter

6 large spring onions, cut on the diagonal into 3cm chunks

1.5kg peas in their pods, shelled

1 small bunch of mint, finely chopped

sea salt and black pepper

In May the first peas begin to appear. It is one of the highlights of our growing season. Once the flowers blossom, we make sure to water the plants regularly, helping the fruits to set, and just a few weeks later the pods begin to swell with their emerald-green jewels inside.

Shelling peas may be a little time consuming, but there is something very comforting and homely about the task. A family affair, sitting on the back doorstep in the warm spring sunshine, the job is a pleasurable one. There is nothing like the taste of a sweet, fresh pea. Freshness is very important, as the natural sugars turn to starch within hours of picking.

This dish is very good served on its own for lunch or to accompany a roast chicken. A thrifty tip here is to use the discarded pods to make a flavoursome vegetable stock.

Remove the outer leaves of the lettuce right down to the paler soft heart. Depending on the size of the lettuce, cut the heart into 4 or 6. Rinse and pick it over carefully, removing any wildlife, then leave to drain on a tea towel.

Melt the butter in a wide pan over a low heat. When it begins to bubble gently, add the spring onions, cover and sweat for about 5 minutes, until softened. Add the lettuce pieces to the pan, spooning a little butter over them, then add the podded peas, some salt and pepper and about 3 tablespoons of water. Cover the pan and let the vegetables braise for 7–8 minutes, until the sauce has a very creamy consistency, the peas are tender and the lettuce wilted. Garnish with the mint and serve.

Barbecued asparagus with sheep's cheese and lemon

SERVES 4

800g asparagus
6 tablespoons olive oil
a few pinches of paprika
juice of 1 lemon
100g Manchego, Berkswell or other hard sheep's milk cheese, grated
sea salt and black pepper

In May, when the asparagus begins to spear out of the ground, we are reminded that all good things come to those who wait. The asparagus season is defined by the temperatures and rainfall of early spring. The spears do not start protruding through the soil until the earth has warmed, which usually means we are finally into proper spring weather. The outdoor-grown asparagus season is a short one, usually about a month, but when it does burst on to the scene it is a time of celebration. This recipe is an opportunity to stoke up the barbecue and enjoy the warmer evenings, basking in the promise of sunny days ahead.

The quantities given here are for a main meal of asparagus, at a time when the spears are at their best and most bountiful. If you cannot get hold of a hard sheep's milk cheese, a sweet, nutty Parmesan will do just as well. Cooking this dish is a casual affair. Have everything you need at the barbecue; it is important to keep the spears moving and brushed with oil.

Trim the bases of the asparagus spears, then put them in a roasting tin and dress with the olive oil, paprika, half the lemon juice and some salt and pepper. The spears need to be fully coated and glistening with oil.

Once the yellow flames of the barbecue have subsided and the embers are hot, arrange the asparagus spears in such a way that they won't fall into the fire, as they shrink during cooking. Cook for 10–15 minutes, until tender. Keep turning and rolling the spears so that they cook evenly and don't char, brushing them occasionally with a little of the oil left in the roasting tin to keep them moist. When they are almost cooked, sprinkle with a generous amount of the cheese. Allow the cheese to melt and stick to the asparagus spears, then roll them over and repeat. Keep turning until they are cooked and have begun to blacken a little. Squeeze the remaining lemon juice over the asparagus and serve immediately.

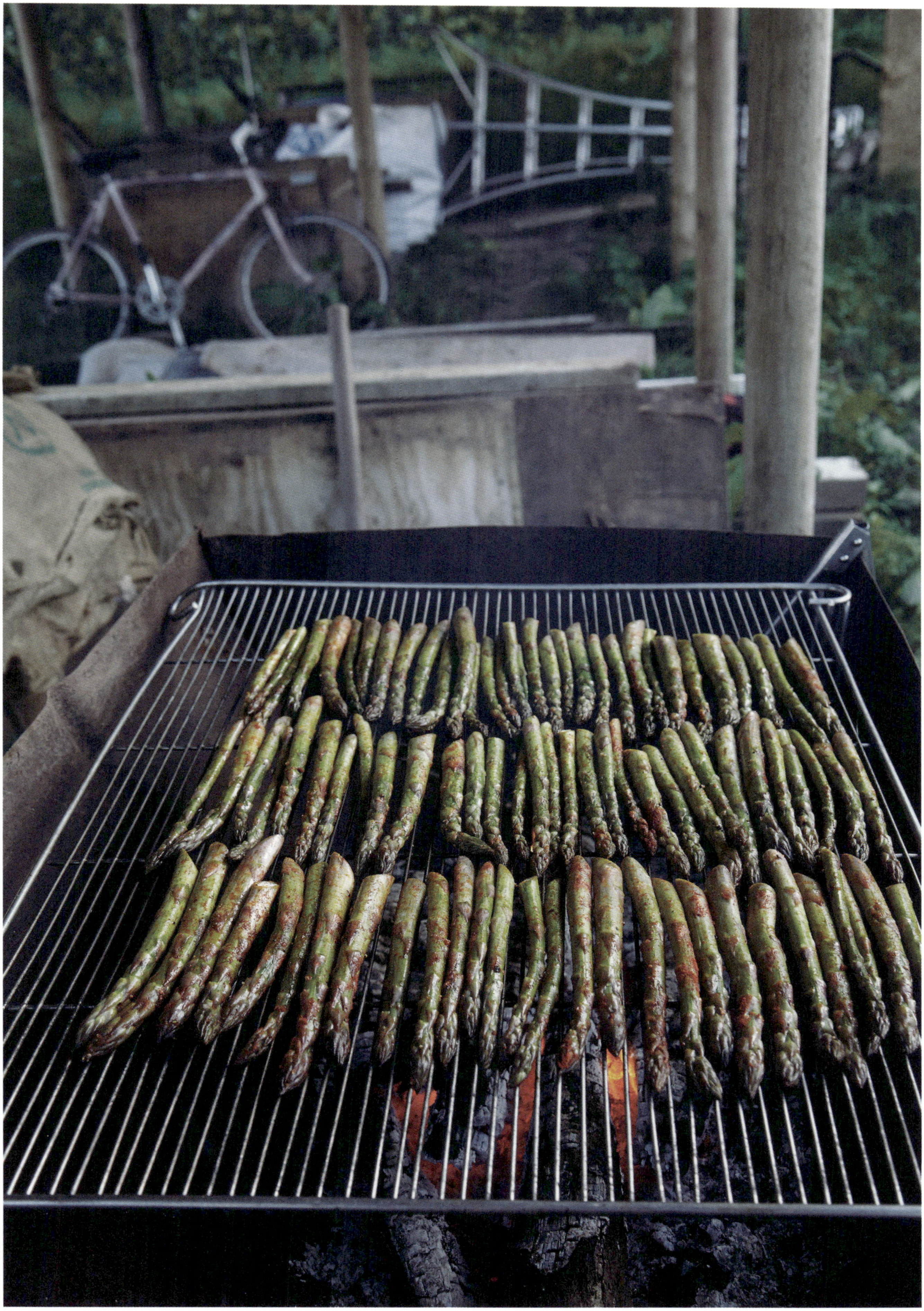

Gathering from the wild

THE ARRIVAL OF spring brings a craving to eat fresh green shoots, an atavistic yearning for what does us good. We see the effects of the sun in the green of the leaves; it is as if we crave the chlorophyll – the blood of the plant – as a tonic for the circulation, a cleanser for the metabolism, a stimulant to take our minds and bodies into the warmer months with renewed strength. It is the benevolent kingdom of nature that makes these restorative properties available to us.

This is the time of year we growers call the 'hungry gap'. The overwintering cabbages and kales have gone to seed and are past their best, and frankly we've had our fill of the brassica family. So at this time we forage for our fresh greens from the hedgerows and woodland around the farm. The first

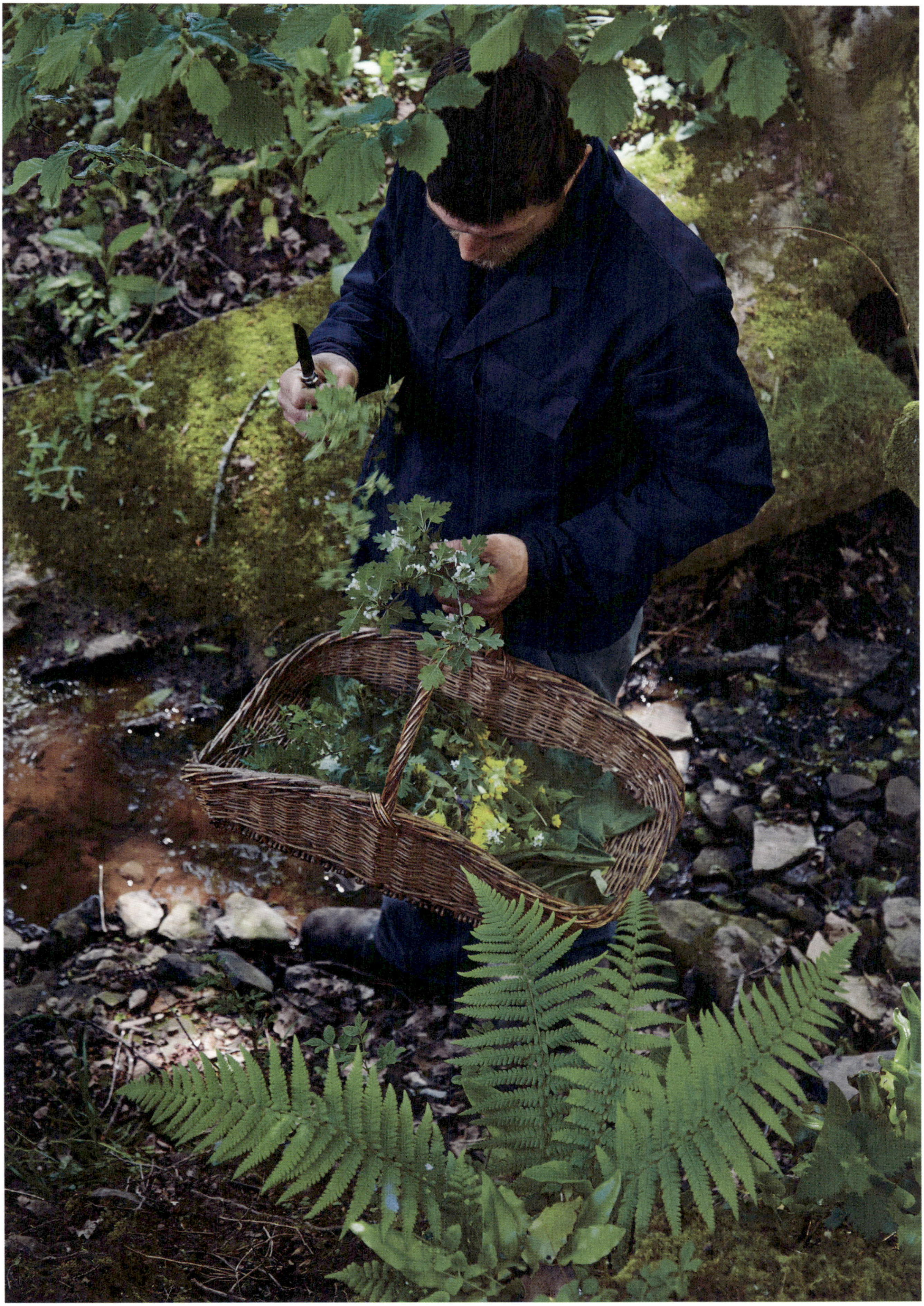

shoots of spring are the most tasty, young and tender without the toughness of the more developed foliage.

Gathering wild herbs, leaves and flowers is rewarding and satisfying; it is always good fun to wander around the farm collecting our lunch or supper. It reminds us of our partnership with the land and what it provides for us. In our work as biodynamic growers, we are always aware of nature's generosity. With these thoughts we gather the foraged crops with respect and modesty. We never take too much, choosing from abundant patches so as not to inhibit future growth or seed production, and in turn the multiplication and survival of these so-called weeds.

Foraged leaves and flowers can make a lovely salad. We collected those in the photograph, opposite, in the second week of May. Among the mix are leaves and flowers of wild garlic, dandelion, the hot, peppery jack-by-the-hedge; hawthorn leaves and buttercup also feature.

To gather your own leaves and flowers take a basket or tray and wander in your garden, or along a hedgerow or in a patch of woodland. A good, simple plant identification book is *Wild Food* by Roger Phillips. Try to avoid areas that are close to busy roads, or where dogs are walked frequently. Pick the leaves and flowers just before serving if you can, so that they are as fresh as can be and have not begun to wilt, which can happen very quickly.

Try to avoid washing your gathered greens: just pick them over for mud and bugs and toss them in a bowl with your hands. Generally the flavour of these spring shoots is either bitter (in a good way) or hot and mustardy, so a simple dressing will do. Crumble a good pinch of sea salt over the leaves and evenly trickle over two teaspoons of vinegar – a sweet fruit vinegar (see page 196) or balsamic is perfect – and then do the same with two tablespoons of olive oil. Toss the salad and eat it straightaway.

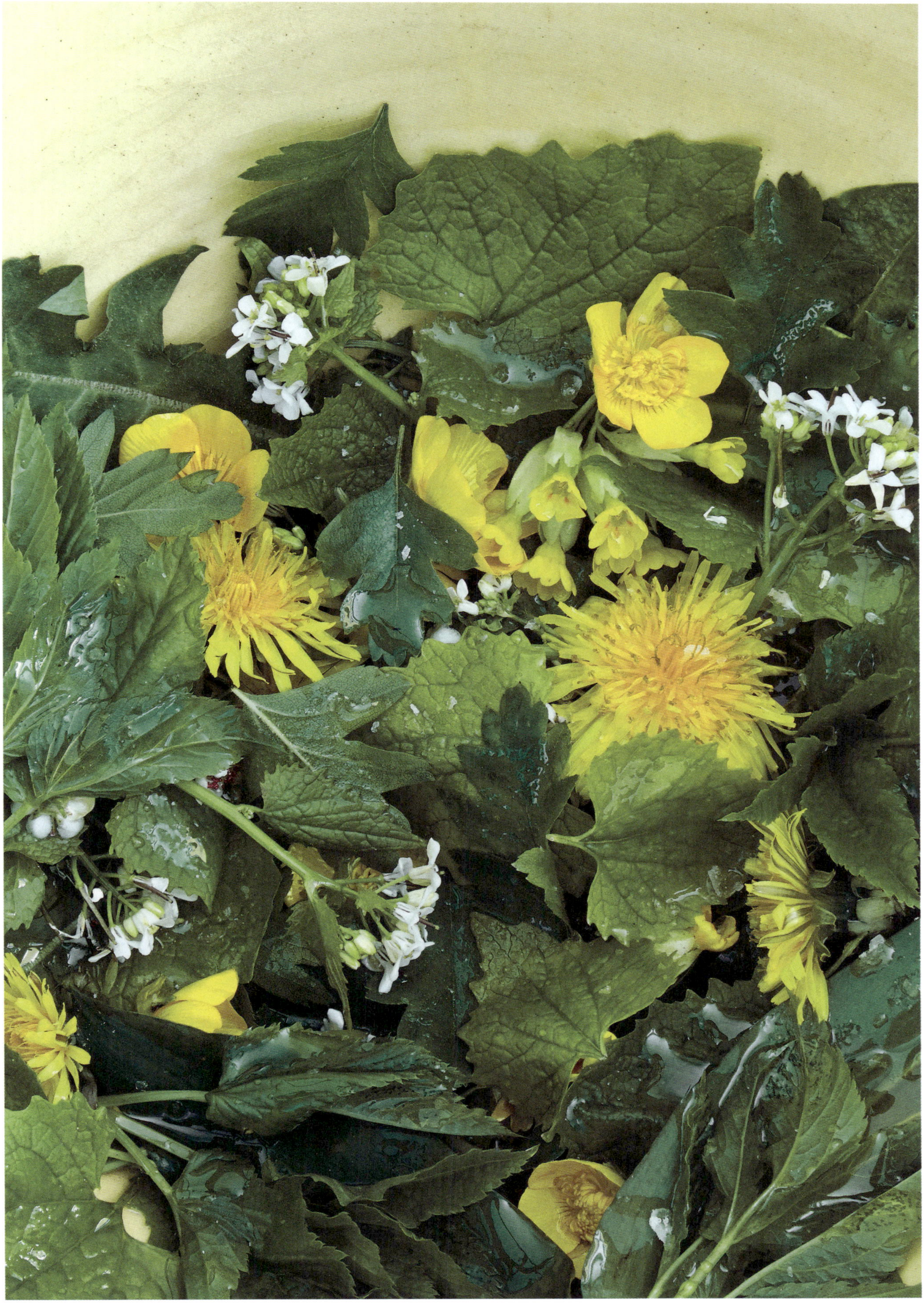

Spring fritters with wild garlic mayonnaise

SERVES 4

150g plain flour
a good pinch of salt
330ml lager
2 egg whites
a selection of fresh herbs, leaves and flowers
groundnut or sunflower oil, for frying

For the wild garlic mayonnaise
2 egg yolks
1 teaspoon Dijon mustard
juice of 1 lemon
150ml olive oil
150ml groundnut oil
a handful of wild garlic (about 30g)
2–3 tablespoons water
sea salt and black pepper

This basic recipe for savoury fritters is a good opportunity to use your imagination and creativity, as what you put into the batter is up to you. Any tender new green leaves work well: try lovage, dandelion, nettle, sage, borage, sorrel, ground elder, comfrey or wild garlic. Spring onions and asparagus are delicious, too. Later in the year try slivers of courgette, slices of cauliflower, celery leaves or finely sliced fennel.

First make the mayonnaise. Put the egg yolks, mustard and lemon juice in a food processor and blend briefly. With the machine running, gradually add the oils, pouring them in very slowly at first while the emulsion begins to form. Add the wild garlic and some salt and pepper and continue to blend. Mix in enough water to thin the mayonnaise to a good dipping consistency. Transfer to a bowl and leave in the fridge.

For the batter put the flour and salt into a mixing bowl and add the beer in a slow, steady stream, whisking constantly and being sure to knock out any lumps, until you have a smooth, thin paste. Leave this to sit for at least half an hour. Just before you begin cooking the fritters, whisk the egg whites until stiff and gently fold them into the beer batter.

Heat some groundnut or sunflower oil in a large, heavy-based frying pan over a moderate heat – a centimetre deep is plenty. Drop a little of the batter in to gauge whether the oil is hot enough to begin frying; the batter should sizzle when it meets the oil and turn golden within about a minute. Then gently dip a few leaves or flowers at a time into the batter, lift out and allow any excess batter to drip off before placing them in the hot oil. Be generous with available space in the pan; a fork is useful for flipping over the fritters. Cook for 3–4 minutes, until both sides are golden, then lift out on to some kitchen paper and season with salt immediately. You can gather the fritters together and flash them in a hot oven for a minute before serving, or eat them as you go along. Serve with the mayonnaise for dipping.

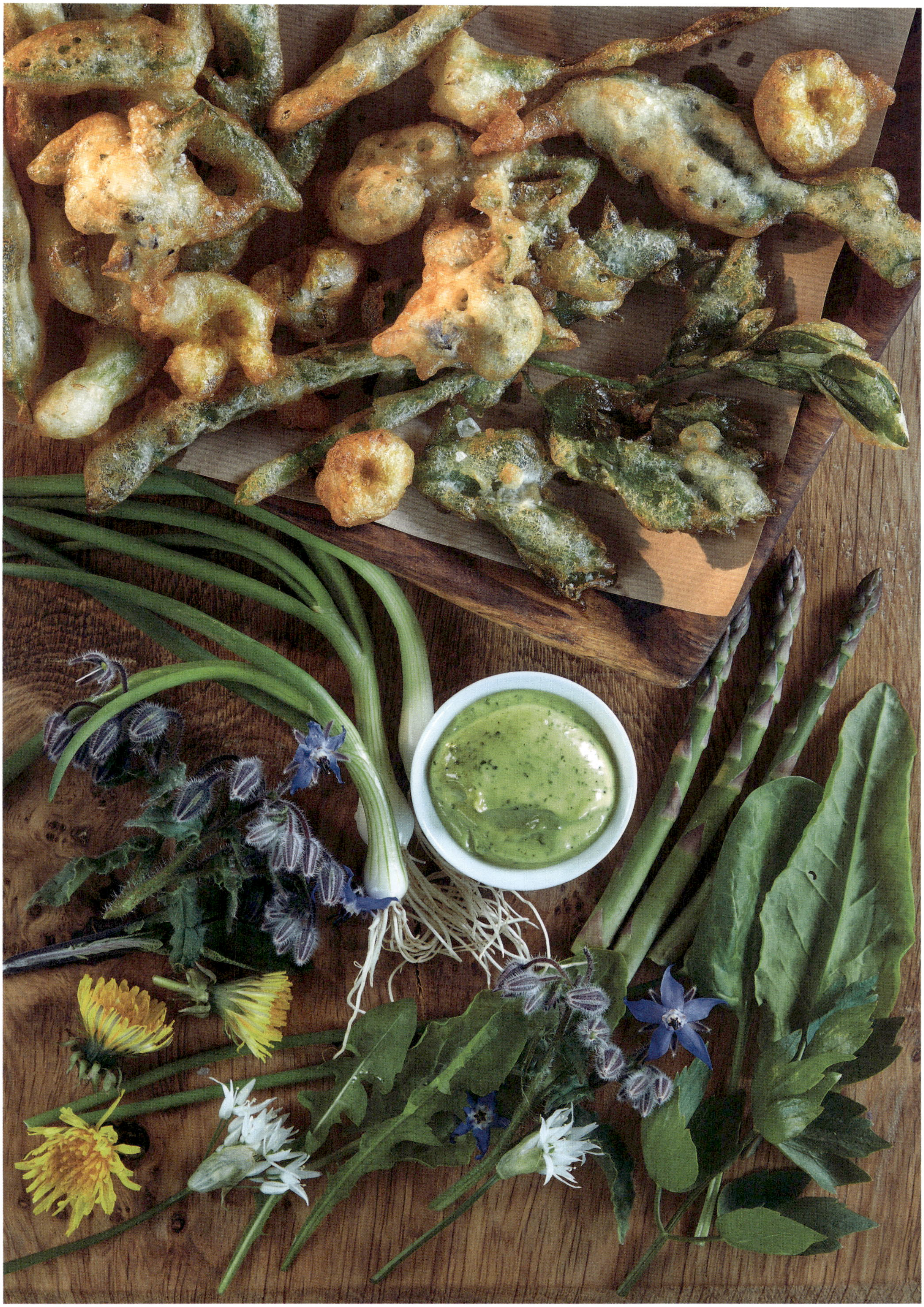

Herbs and teas

MOST EVENINGS AFTER supper before going to bed we drink a herbal tea, or tisane – a soothing digestif that punctuates the end of our day, aiding a good night's sleep. The benefits of herbal teas have been recognised for thousands of years, and documents discussing their enjoyment and properties have been found dating back to ancient Egypt and ancient China. Many herbal teas are believed to help strengthen the immune system and detoxify.

In general we tend not to mix our herbs, enjoying the pure, individual characters. However, there are exceptions to the rule, such as the addition of ginger to chamomile, or blending the different aniseed flavour variations in so many herbs. We keep a teapot solely for these infusions, so that the tannin of regular tea never taints the delicate herbal flavours.

If possible, pick the herbs as you need them – in general, two to three leaves or six to eight flowers per person is enough. Scrunch the herbs into the teapot and pour freshly boiled water directly on to them, then leave to brew for at least five minutes. You can, of course, also make the infusions in a cup or mug if you prefer. We pour ours into heatproof glasses. They seem to taste better when you can see the stunning green shades in the glass.

The best way to store freshly picked herbs, or any other green leaves for that matter, is in the fridge, loosely sealed in a plastic bag with enough air so that it resembles a puffed pillow. This method provides a perfect, moist and cool microclimate, keeping the herbs perky and hydrated for several days.

While fresh is best, if you have lots of fresh herbs available, it can be a good idea to dry some while they are plentiful in the spring and summer months and store them for use in the winter. Always select good-quality leaves and flowers, picking them in the morning on a dry day. (Moisture-rich herbs such as mint and sweet cicely do not dry well and are best used fresh.)

One drying method is to remove the individual flowers or leaves from their stalks and lay them out evenly, with plenty of space between, on a piece of clean paper or cardboard. Put them in a dark and warm place such as an airing cupboard, turning them over carefully once a day for three or four days. If you don't have an airing cupboard, you can hang them to dry tied into loose bunches inside a paper bag, again in a warm, dry space. A kitchen ceiling works well, providing the kitchen is airy.

The idea is to dry the herbs slowly, out of direct sunlight, to ensure that the leaves don't 'cook' and therefore lose their flavour and oils. Once dried, the leaves should be a little crisp, and the flowers shrivelled but still colourful. Discard any stalks, throw away any leaves or flowers that have yellowed or blackened, then store in sealed jars or tins in a dark place. It is always a good idea to label the jars, as once the herbs are dry they can be difficult to identify.

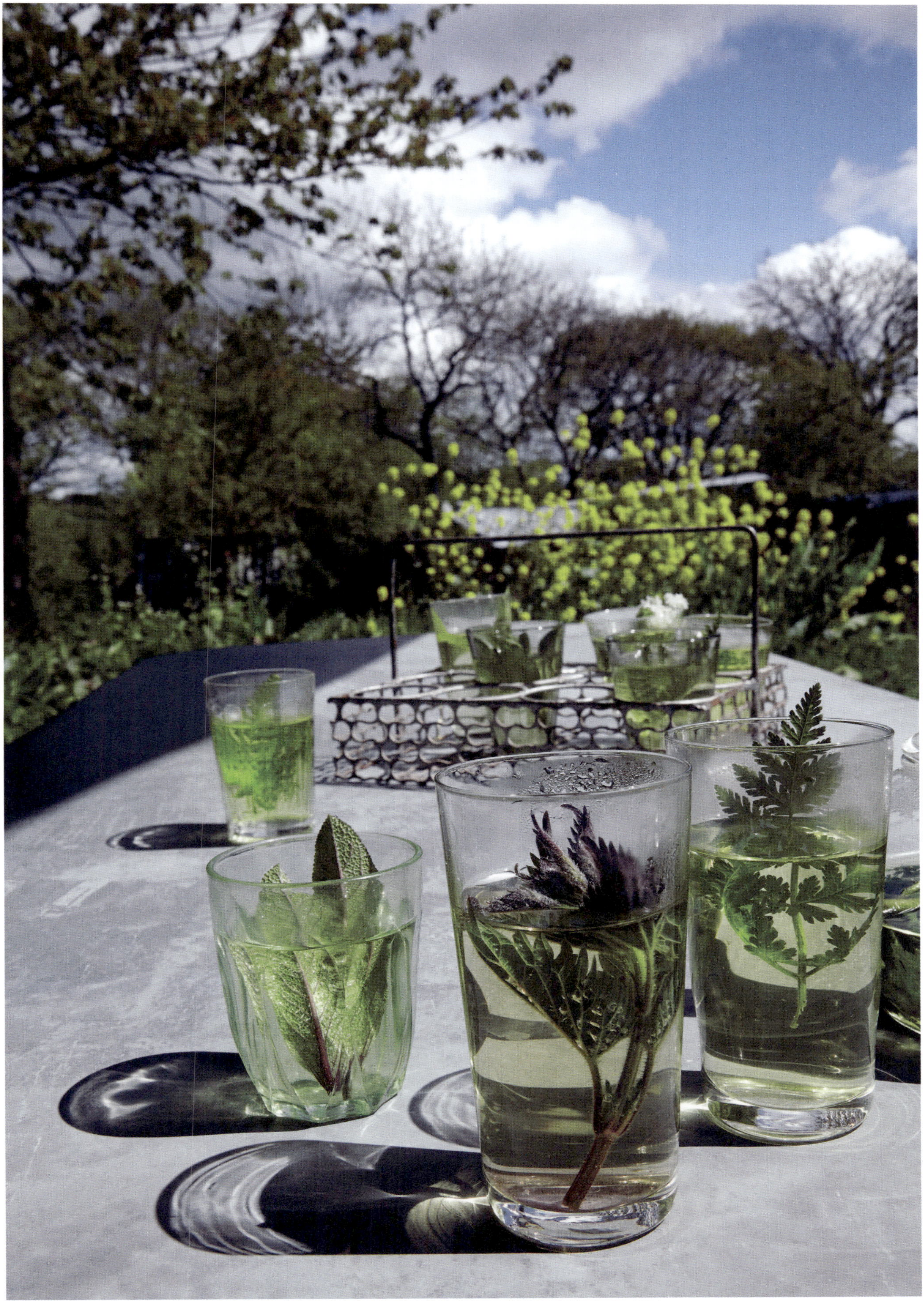

Making that first pot of fresh tea from the new growth in the spring is always a thrill. But equally there is immense pleasure and satisfaction to be had when opening a tin of dried herbs and flowers and bringing them back to life. The scents and warmth rise with the steam, as you drink, taking you back to those sunny days.

Here are the herb teas that we make most often:

Sweet cicely

Probably our family favourite, this grass-green herb has fernlike, downy leaves and dainty tufts of white flowers. It has a sweet, mildly aniseed flavour. Sweet cicely was in the past used as a natural sweetener – not unlike angelica, which is from the same family of *Apiaceae*. As well as using the leaves for an infusion, try adding a few to a fruit compote during cooking for a hint of sweetness.

Fennel

This is another sweet-tasting herb, but with a stronger aniseed flavour than sweet cicely. The two together is a more savoury combination. Fennel is easy to grow, a hardy, generous perennial. In spring and early summer, the leaves can be used not only for teas, but also for cooking. In autumn, try harvesting and drying the seeds for use in cooking throughout the year.

Lemon balm

Nicholas Culpeper, the renowned seventeenth-century English herbalist, said that lemon balm helps lift the spirits. It makes a pleasant tea to drink at breakfast time, with its zingy flavour. Lemon balm has a strong taste that can be overpowering – use only a few leaves. The addition of a teaspoon of honey makes the tea taste delicious.

Mint

The almost black Moroccan mint is particularly good for a thirst-quenching and refreshing tea. However, it is not as easy to find as regular spearmint, which will do just as well. Try putting a leaf or two of lemon balm in with your mint infusion. We drink this tea throughout the day in the summer. With a little sugar or honey, it helps as a bit of a pick-me-up, especially on a scorching hot day while we're weeding out in the fields.

Lemon thyme

Of the many varieties of thyme, lemon thyme is ideal for infusing. Just smelling the wonderful lemony aroma as the hot water releases the essential oil is a delight to the senses.

Lime or linden flowers

The flowers of the lime or linden do not appear until late June, but when they do this tea is a favourite of ours. It has an intoxicating floral taste. The flower clusters grow on slender stalks on the underside of the heart-shaped leaves. Beekeepers believe that the sticky honeydew found on lime trees produces some of the finest-tasting honey. We planted two lime trees on the farm especially with our bees and their honey in mind.

Chamomile

Chamomile comes a little later in the year than many other herbs, usually from July onwards, when you can gather the dainty, daisy-like flower heads for a calming, honey-scented tea. Select flowers in bloom, with plenty of petals and a firm yellow centre. Adding a knuckle of fresh ginger to the chamomile infusion works very well. We like this tea at any time of the day;

however, with its reputation as an aid to sleep, it makes a soothing bedtime drink, and is especially beneficial if you are feeling a little under the weather.

Elderflower

In common with other spring-flowering trees with white blossom, the elder had strong associations with Faery- and Goddess-centred mythology. It was thought of as a protective tree, and it was an auspicious sign if an elder grew near your dwelling. Elders are very common here in Herefordshire. The flowers are so beautiful and the scent heavenly. We tend to make cordial from the flowers, but a blossom or two added to a lemon balm or mint tea is delicious, adding a hint of wonderful muscat aroma.

Sage

The flavour of sage is fresh and restorative. The essential oil is pungent, so just a couple of young leaves will make a full-flavoured, almost medicinal-tasting (in a good way) infusion. The sixteenth-century botanist John Gerard said: 'Sage is singularly good for the head and brain, it quickeneth the senses and memory, strengtheneth the sinews, restoreth health to those that have the palsy, and taketh away shakey trembling of the members.'

Valerian

We grow valerian primarily for use in our biodynamic compost preparations. However, we often take some of the ripe flowers to make a herb tea. The scent is pleasantly heady and strong. We are drawn to drinking a valerian infusion when we feel a little stressed. We find it relaxing and calming, properties described by Hippocrates, the father of Western medicine. Galen, the highly influential Greek physician, later prescribed valerian as a cure for insomnia.

Nettle

Nettles are a good source of iron. Leaves from the first flush of spring growth are the nicest for an infusion. Later in the season, the flavour can be overpowering. It is best to remove the leaves from the pot after five minutes of brewing, as they can become a little sulphurous after a while.

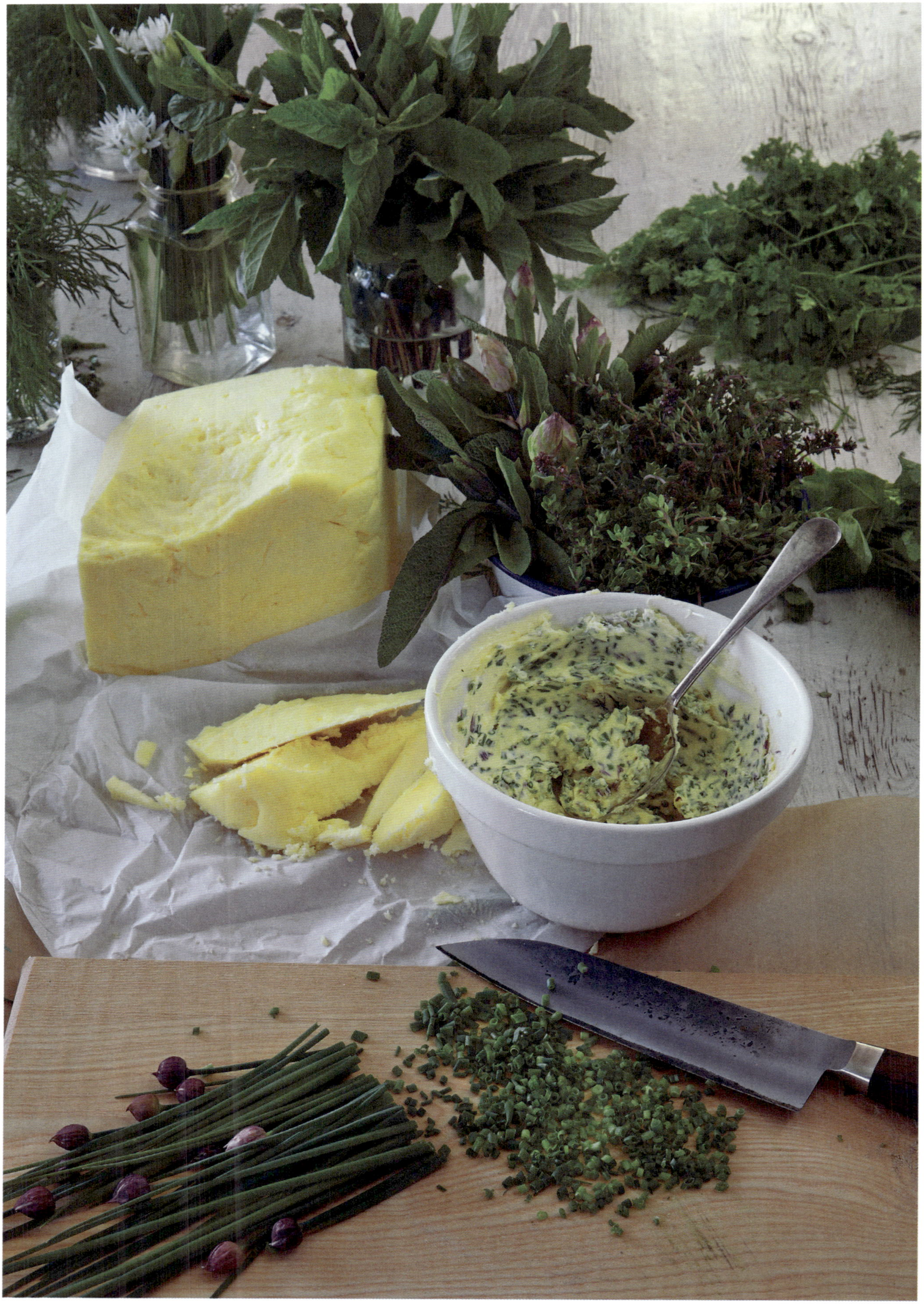

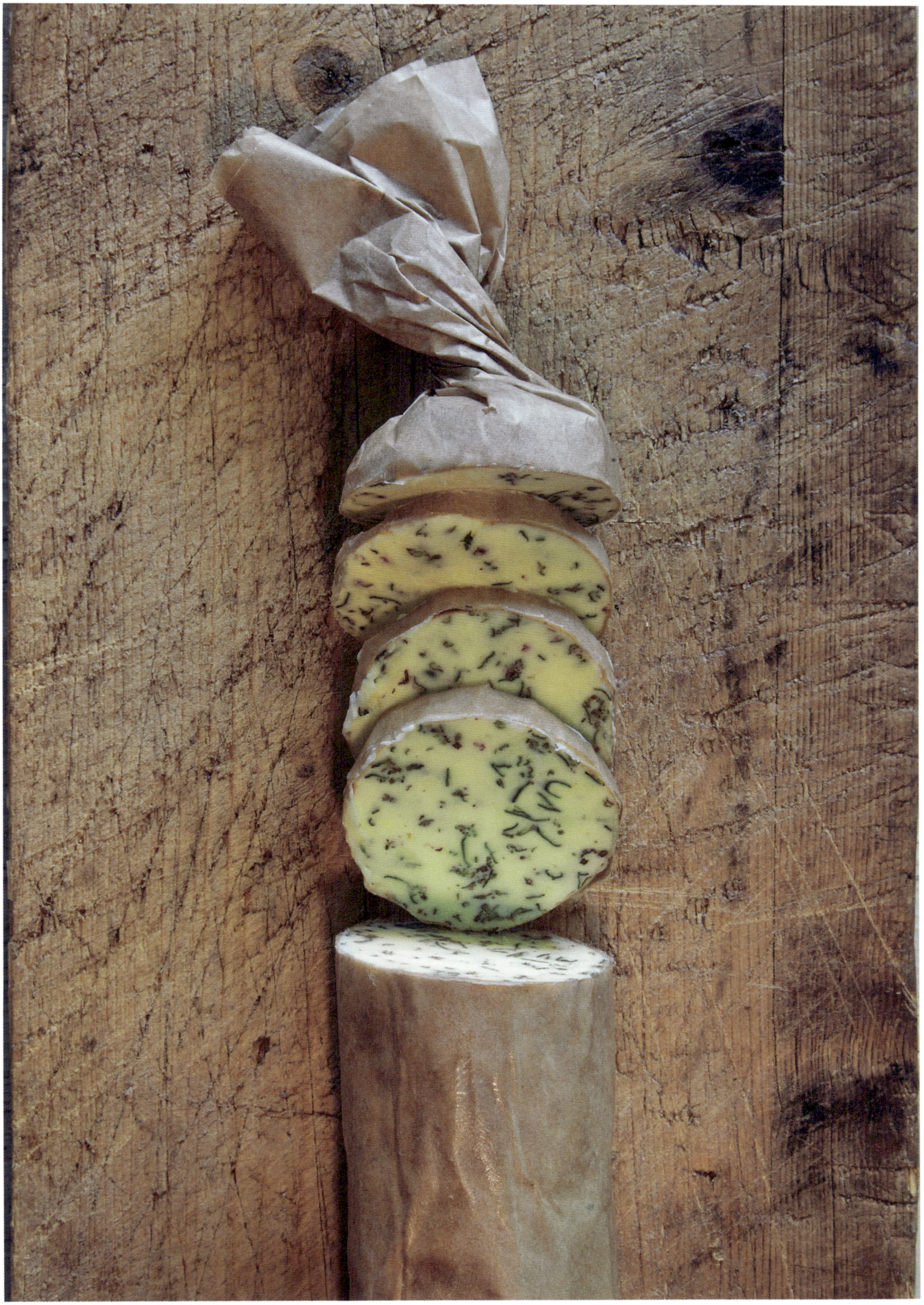

Herb butters

250g butter, softened at room temperature

5 tablespoons finely chopped herbs (see suggestions below)

lemon juice (optional)

If you have a herb patch in your garden, you're likely to have more herbs than you can use at this time of year. Regular harvesting is necessary to keep most herb plants in tiptop form, encouraging regular supplies of new shoots and leaves for a good, long spell from early spring to autumn. Making a batch of herb butters in the spring and freezing them keeps the kitchen larder bountiful all year round. A herb butter can lift a plain meal into a sophisticated one: try a couple of discs of parsley and chive butter in a baked potato, or a plate of greens dressed with mint butter and a squeeze of lemon, for example.

With a fork or in a food processor, cream the butter until it is very soft and easy to work. Mash the chopped herbs into the butter until they are well distributed, adding a squeeze of lemon juice if liked. Divide the butter into 4 and transfer each portion to a piece of baking parchment or cling film. Lift the end nearest to you over the butter and, with the palms of your hands, roll the butter into an even-sized oblong. Roll the butter up in the paper and twist the ends firmly. Chill for a couple of hours before serving, to allow the herbs to release their flavours. Alternatively, freeze and use within 9 months.

A few suggestions

Finely chopped coriander, chilli, lime zest and mint – a clean-tasting butter that will add a bit of zing to a lamb chop or steak.

Chive flowers – not only do these look very attractive but they taste strongly of chives. This butter makes a great baked potato filler.

Parsley, chervil, tarragon and chives – either place a disc of two on top of a fish for grilling, or melt the butter with a little lemon juice for a delightful sauce to accompany fish or steamed vegetables.

Tarragon – a disc or two of tarragon butter slipped under the skin of a chicken before roasting makes it very special indeed. French tarragon has the best flavour and is a major player in our herb garden.

Sweet cicely and orange zest – a sweet butter to serve with hot cross buns etc.

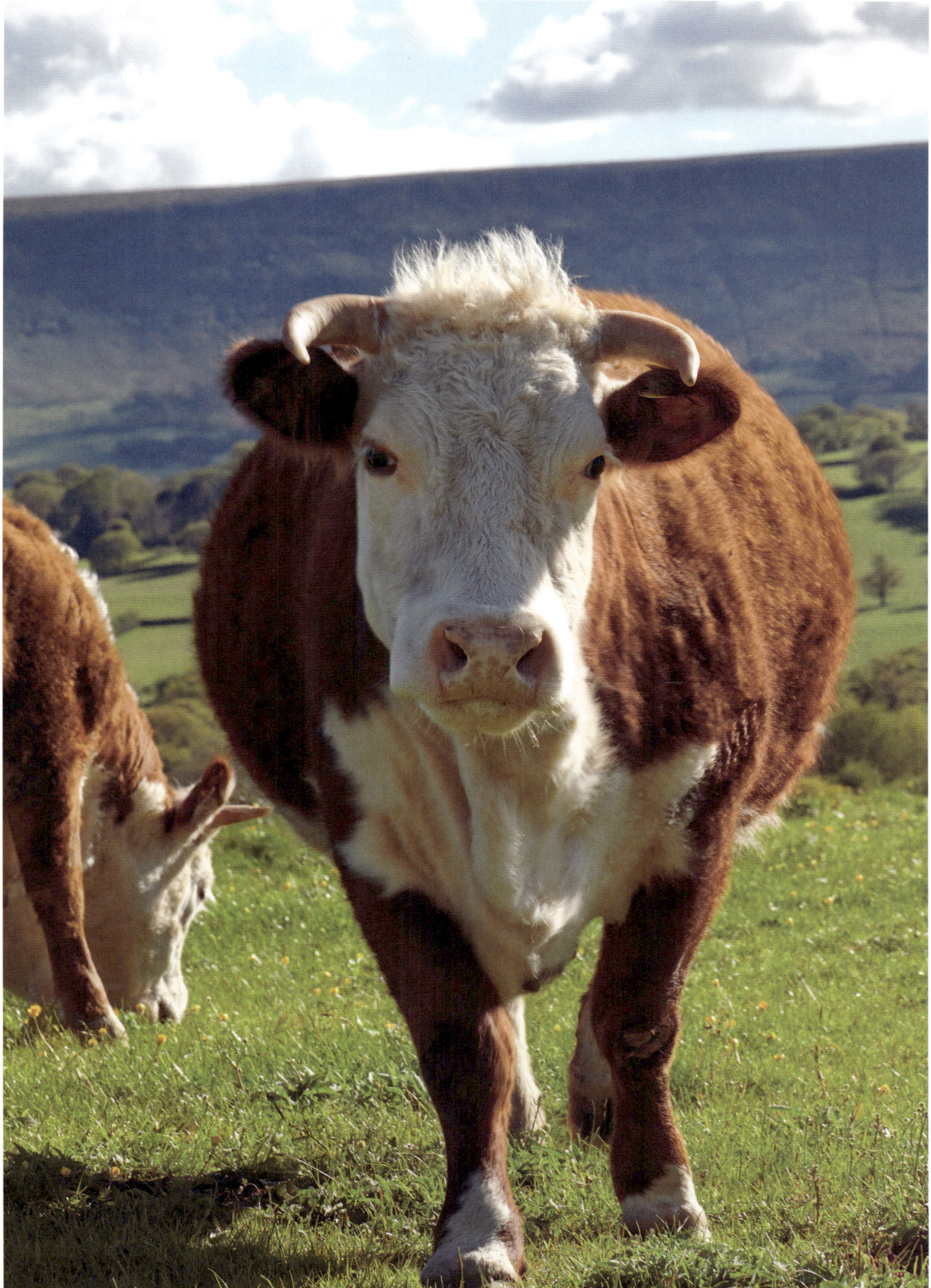

Spring garden sandwiches

Sandwich making is an art form. The type of bread you use for different fillings is so important, as is how thick or thin you make your slices. But above all, it is the layering of textures and flavours that turns an adequate sandwich into a great one. We are lucky to have a greenhouse where we can grow salad leaves in a protective atmosphere, so that their texture is soft and lush. The spring garden sandwiches that we make tend to come from first-of-the-season shoots.

A few suggestions

Slice a radish into thin lengths and sandwich between thickly cut seeded, grainy bread. The addition of one or two leaves from the radish makes the sandwich tasty and provides some heat. You could also include cress varieties such as Persian cress. Thin slivers of cold butter placed on the bread with a sprinkling of salt work very well with the hot radish flavour.

The fourth or fifth leaf of growth from young chard or beet plants is a good-sized and flavoursome addition to a sandwich. The iron flavour of beet leaves is particularly good with goat's cheese. A good-quality white loaf, sliced thinly, suits this sandwich very well.

Butterhead lettuce is one of the best types for a sandwich – crisp but tender, with a delicious, gentle, creamy flavour. Try it with a crusty white loaf, adding a sprinkling of olive oil to the bread and lettuce – no butter. The inclusion of some salami is nice, too.

For a new take on an egg and cress sandwich, chop a hardboiled egg, mix with 2 tablespoons of mayonnaise and spread on to a medium-thick piece of sourdough rye bread. Add a layer of Persian cress or even some foraged jack-by-the-hedge for heat and contrast. Very thin slivers of spring onion laid on top of the cress adds extra bite.

Chives and their flowers are very pretty in a sandwich. Break up one or two of the purple flower heads and sprinkle the petals over the buttered bread. Cut the chives to fit the sandwich and place on top of the petals, together with a piece of your favourite cheese – we like a farmhouse Caerphilly.

Parsley leaves are one of our favourite fillings for a spring garden sandwich. We always use flat parsley, and only the leaves. Their strong flavour with slivers of cold butter and some salt on white or brown bread is delicious and needs nothing else.

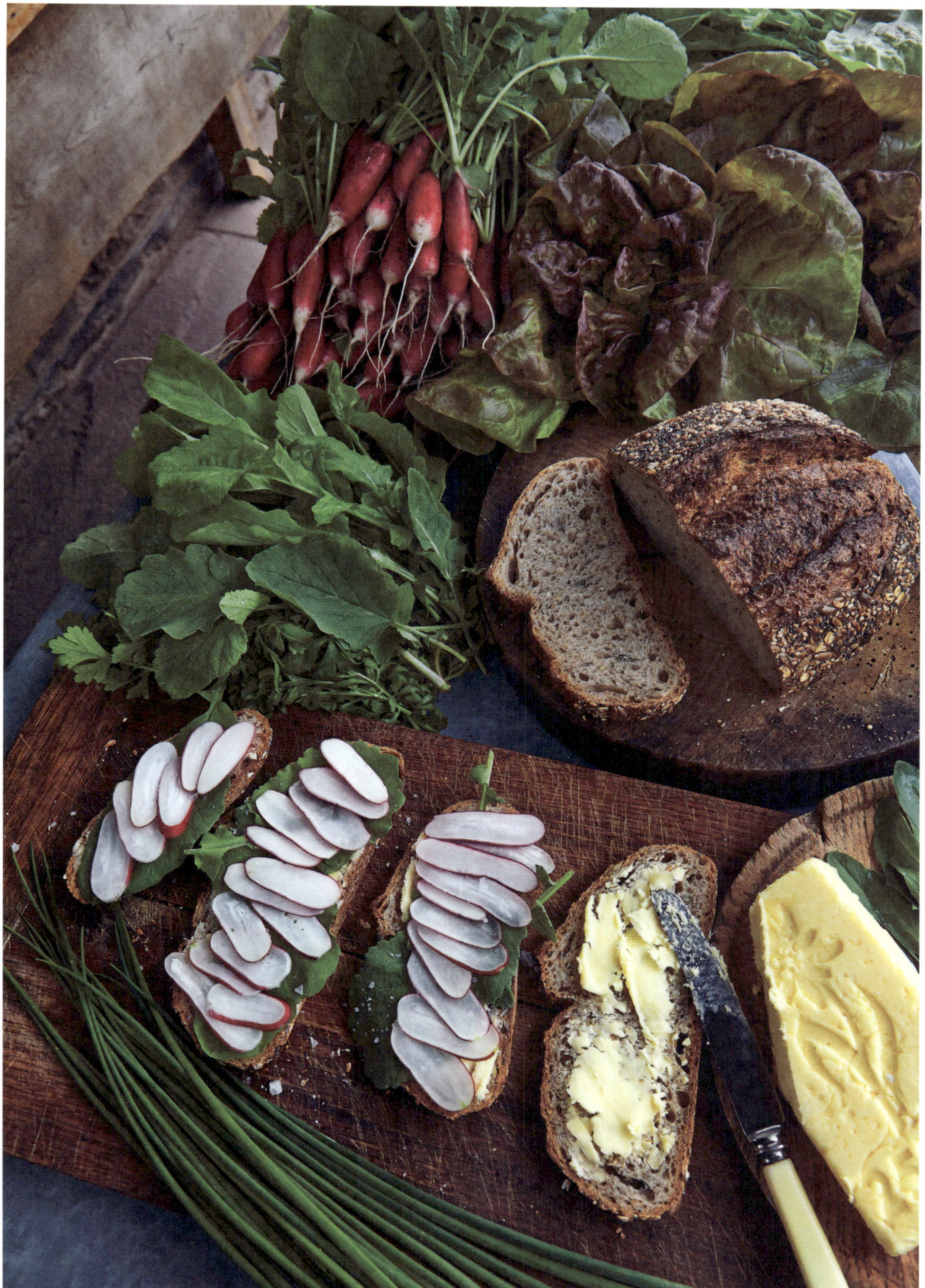

Pasta with green sauce

SERVES 4

200g mixed herbs

½ teaspoon sea salt

200g goat's curd or ordinary curd cheese

100ml olive oil

400g spaghetti (or ribbon pasta, such as tagliatelle)

freshly grated Parmesan cheese, to serve (optional)

We are fortunate at Fern Verrow to have an abundant and varied supply of fresh herbs with which to make this very fresh and grassy green sauce. If you don't grow your own herbs, buy a good quantity and variety from a farmers' market, where you can pretty much guarantee the freshness and quality that are essential to the success of this dish. The different herbs and their relative proportions are left to the whim and taste of the cook. However, we think the following makes a good combination.

Mint – use lots, stems and all.

Lovage – a very strong, sometimes overpowering herb; just a leaf or two is enough, but do use it as it is delicious and adds that celery flavour that is so good with pasta.

Parsley – it may be a little early for new-season parsley; however, if you planted your parsley in the late autumn, the new shoots in early spring will be bright, tender and full of vitamins.

Thyme – this takes its time to start new growth, but trimming and taking those first new shoots only helps to encourage the plant to swell and achieve good growth throughout the summer.

Chives – usually the first crop of herbs to show in the spring, chives are a water-loving plant with a delicate onion flavour; cut the whole plant at the base and new shoots will come again very quickly.

Rosemary and sage – these are both powerful flavours, so use sparingly; again, just pinch out a few of the new, soft shoots.

Wild garlic and jack-by-the-hedge – these wild herbs have a strong garlic flavour.

A food processor makes the preparation of the sauce very quick. Simply put all the herbs in it and process until they become a bright green paste. Add the salt, curd and oil and blend again until thoroughly combined. The sauce needs to be a nice spoonable consistency.

Cook the spaghetti in lots of boiling salted water (as salty as the Mediterranean, as the Italians say) until it is *al dente*; the brightness of the sauce will simply not be the same if the pasta is overcooked and starchy. Drain the pasta in a colander and quickly warm the sauce through in the pasta pan. Return the pasta to the pan and toss gently, making sure it is well coated. Serve straightaway, with a grating of Parmesan, if you like.

Creamed sorrel and spinach sauce

SERVES 4–6

500g sorrel
200g spinach
25g butter
1 shallot, finely chopped
200ml double cream
1 egg yolk
sea salt and black pepper

With its lemony tang, sorrel complements perfectly a simply grilled or fried piece of white fish. If the weather is warm, this sauce is also very good served cold with poached salmon. The addition of spinach helps to make it a little more pleasing to the eye because the sorrel browns a little on cooking. If you increase the amount of spinach in the recipe, you can serve the sauce as an accompanying vegetable dish.

Remove any thick stems from the sorrel and spinach. Steam the leaves (or blanch them briefly in a large pan of boiling water) until they are just wilted. To remove the excess water, put the leaves into a colander or sieve, place a small plate on top and press down firmly, squeezing out as much liquid as you can. Chop the leaves finely, either by hand or in a food processor.

Heat the butter in a saucepan, add the shallot and cook gently until soft and translucent. Stir in the sorrel and spinach. Beat the cream and egg yolk together, add to the pan and allow the sauce to thicken slightly over a gentle heat. Blend to a smooth purée with a stick blender, season to taste and serve immediately – or, if serving cold, leave to cool, then cover and chill for at least 2 hours.

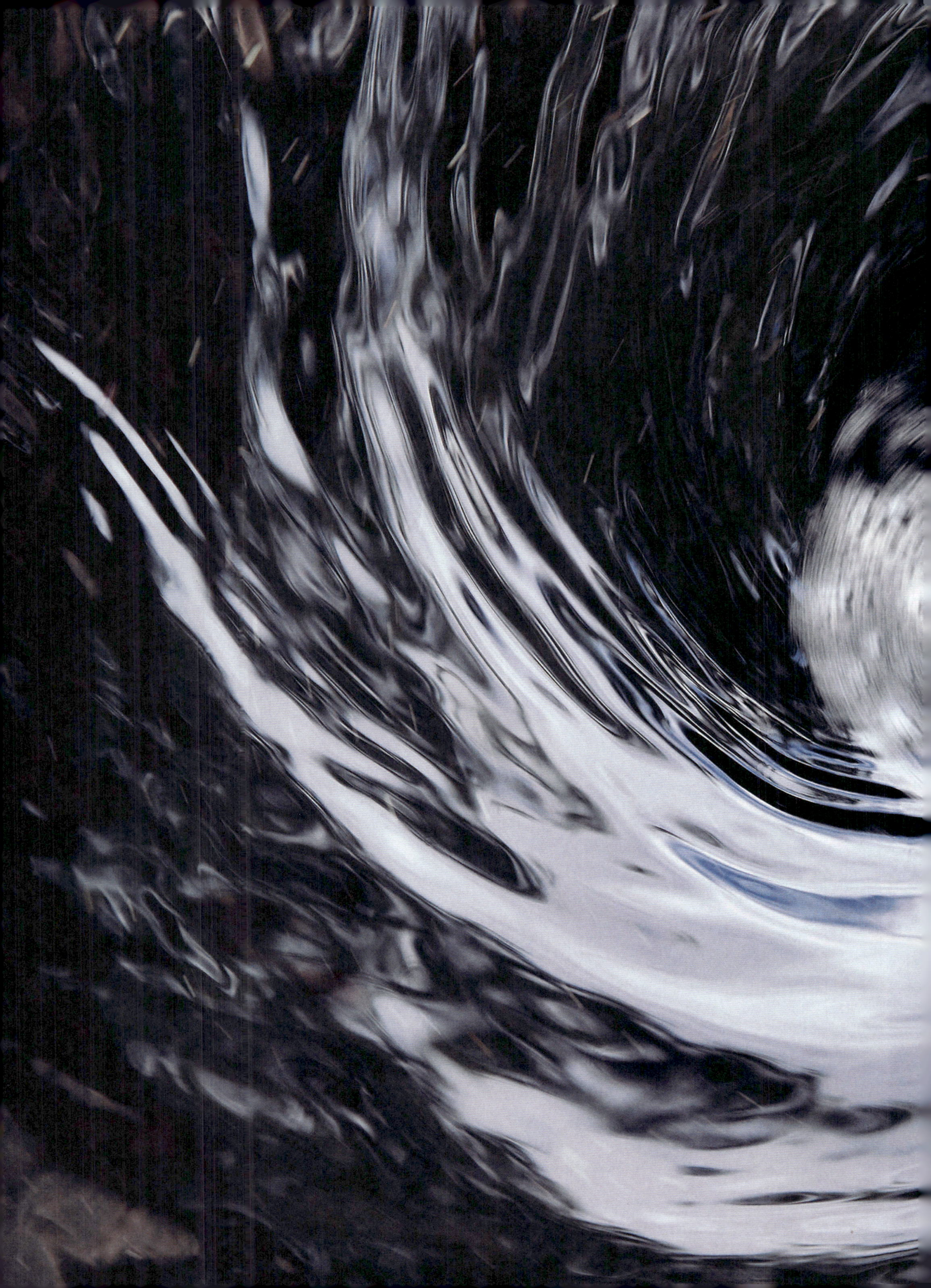

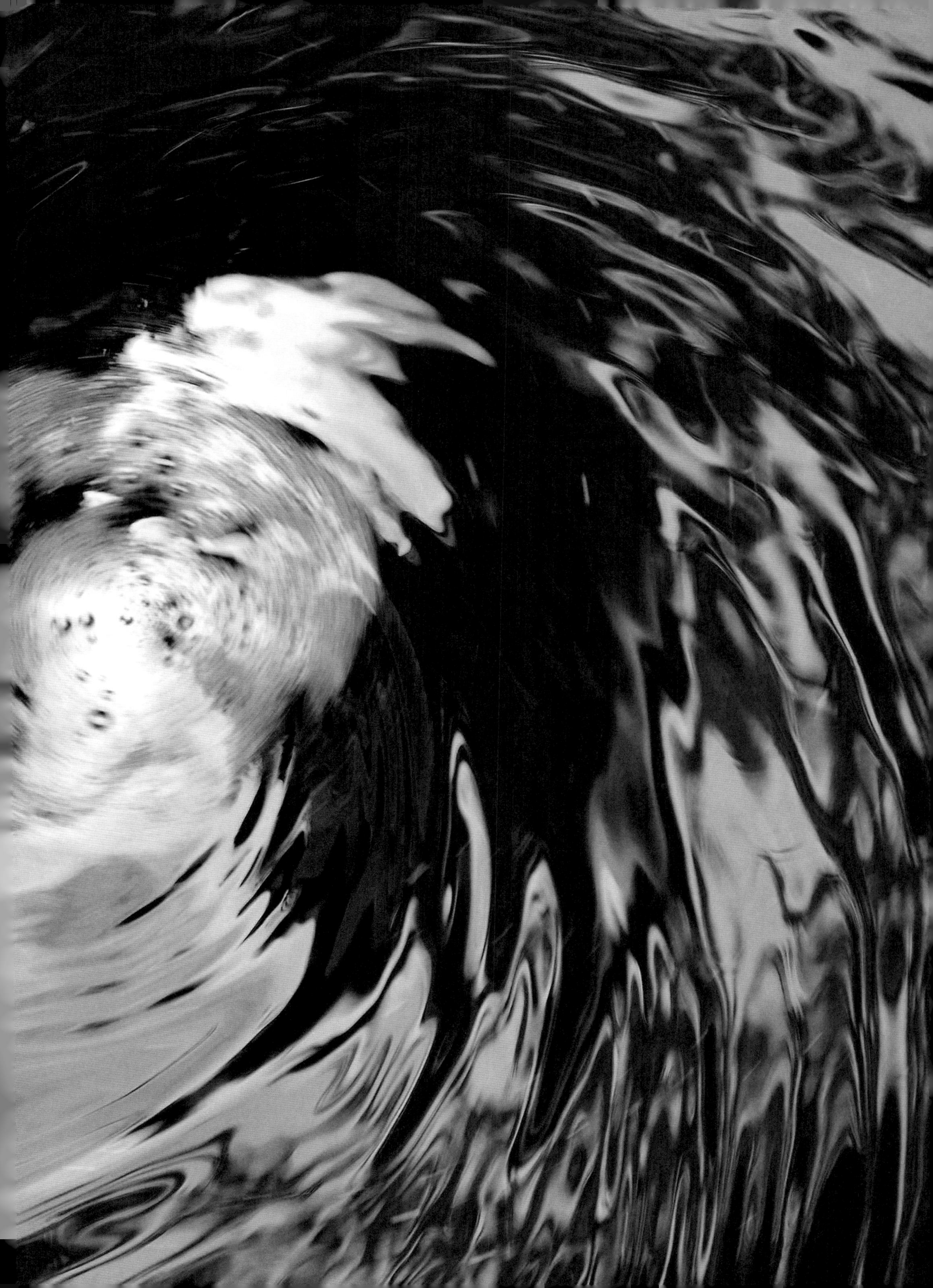

Living water

WATER IS A constant presence at Fern Verrow. This part of England, on the border with Wales, has a high annual rainfall, which gives rise to its rich, verdant landscape. The word Verrow itself has its roots in an old French term that describes a split in the land around which water flows. Many place names throughout the Welsh Marches derive from old Norman words, illustrating the region's history following the invasion of 1066. Its many parish churches and castle ruins stand testament to the Normans' knowledge of masonry as well as their influence on the expansion of Christianity in these parts.

Our small farmhouse was built in 1734, nestled into the hillside, sheltered by rising slopes to the north and west. Beside the stone building is a spring from which pure water seeps out of the ground. It is the source of a small stream that winds its way through the garden and onwards, past the propagating greenhouse and then steeply down into the dingle, through the woodland and beyond.

Above the spring stand twelve mighty oak trees, over 20 metres tall, which help to draw water up out of the ground to the spring's outlet and also provide further shelter from the strong winds that whip down off the Black Mountains. Within a stone's throw of the farmhouse carve three more small watercourses, carrying water down from the hillsides.

When there is heavy rain, the flow rises and gains strength and intensity, and the four arteries of water that weave their different ways within the farm converge so that torrents sweep through its heart. Ferns, meadowsweet, ragged robin and lady's smock grow around these waterways and among the woodland and stream banks.

All the water that we use on the farm comes from the spring. A pipe at its outflow carries some of the spring water down the gentle slope of the garden and fills a 200-litre holding tank that stands beside an old pear tree, next to the stream. From here, the collected water flows through a metal pipe with a steep five-metre drop and pushes into a hydraulic ram. The Hydram, an ingenious device, first manufactured in Accrington by John Blake in 1867, uses a simple principle of physics to transport water by its own power. The pressure of water flowing down the pipe compresses the air and water within the cast-iron pump and the trapped water is pushed out through another pipe that runs all the way back up to the highest point of the farm. One hundred metres from the pump, the water is stored in a much larger tank at the top of Maya's field, at a vantage point looking out on to the whole farm spread out below.

The pump runs 24 hours a day, seven days a week and delivers three litres of water per minute to the storage tank. From here we have dug a whole series of pipes underground that, with the aid of gravity, carry water to every area of

PREVIOUS PAGE: *The creation of a vortex in a barrel of water.*

the farm, allowing us to use the fresh, clean water wherever the animals, the plants or we ourselves need it. This living water is the blood of the farm.

In a favourite spot, perched on a raised stone patio, overlooking the herb and flower garden with views to the Malvern Hills on the distant horizon, we have built a small shed for storing our biodynamic preparations. These are recipes we make using ingredients from the mineral, plant and animal kingdoms, which serve to enhance the effects of our traditional fertilising practices of manuring and composting. When it rains, water runs off the tin roof of the preparation shed, along the gutter, and falls into a large wooden barrel that sits on the stone paving. To this collected water we add small amounts of either composted cow manure or finely ground quartz (see pages 166–167), and enliven the liquid before applying it to the land and plants. We stir the water in the barrel by hand, energetically building up a vortex with circular movements around the edge of the barrel.

We roll our sleeves right up, and use as much of our arm as possible to create a strong spiral in the centre of the water. When everything is rotating rapidly, we change direction. The water abruptly and noisily turns into chaos. Then we start to build another vortex in the opposite direction, working the centripetal motion up to a perfect and powerful rhythm. We continue this pattern of activity for a whole hour. This newly energised water, brimming with life-potential, we then carry out and spray all over the farm. Our intention is to enhance the receptivity of the soil and plants, to draw towards them what they need in order to grow and thrive.

Buckwheat galettes filled with spinach béchamel

SERVES 4

125g buckwheat flour
50g plain flour
a pinch of sea salt
1 egg
175ml milk
175ml water
25g butter, melted

For the spinach béchamel
500g spinach, tough stalks removed
500ml milk
1 small onion, finely chopped
1 bay leaf
a little grated nutmeg
40g butter
40g plain flour
150ml double cream
100g Comté or Gruyère cheese, grated
sea salt and black pepper

The nutty taste of buckwheat flour is key for these traditional French savoury pancakes. There are many different fillings, but we particularly like this one.

Put the buckwheat flour, plain flour and salt into a mixing bowl and make a well in the centre. Break the egg into the well and whisk while you slowly add the milk and water. Keep whisking out any lumps as you gradually draw all the flour into the liquid. When the batter is smooth, stir in the melted butter. If you can, allow the batter to sit in the fridge for half an hour before you cook the galettes.

Meanwhile, prepare the spinach béchamel. Bring some salted water to the boil in the largest pan you have. When it is boiling rapidly, immerse the spinach in it for 30 seconds, using a pair of tongs to dunk the leaves so that they all soften. Drain the spinach through a colander and run some cold water over it until it is cool enough to handle. Squeeze out as much of the moisture as you can, then chop it up and set aside.

Put the milk, onion, bay leaf and nutmeg into a small saucepan and bring to a simmer. Remove from the heat and leave to infuse for 20 minutes or so. Then, in another saucepan, melt the butter and stir in the flour to make a roux. Cook the roux over a gentle heat for a minute or two, stirring with a wooden spoon, until it starts to brown and smell nutty, then gradually strain the infused milk into it, whisking until the sauce thickens. Simmer for a few minutes, then add the cream and simmer for a minute or two longer. Remove from the heat and stir in half the grated cheese plus the chopped spinach. Season to taste and set aside.

Next cook the galettes. Heat a 20cm frying pan or pancake pan over a medium heat and use a wad of paper towel to rub a little butter around it. Ladle in about 2 tablespoons of the batter, quickly lifting and tilting the pan to spread the batter evenly. Once the underside of the galette is brown, flip it over and cook for a minute or so longer, then transfer to a plate. Repeat the process, adjusting the heat and the cooking time until you find a good rhythm. You can pile the galettes on top of each other as they're done; they will not stick. You should have 8–10 galettes altogether.

Heat the oven to 190°C/Gas Mark 5 and lightly butter a baking tray. Place a heaped tablespoon of the spinach béchamel in the centre of each galette and spread it out a little. Fold the galette in half and then in half again, so you end up with a triangle. Arrange the parcels snugly on the baking tray, add any remaining filling and sprinkle the remaining grated cheese on top. Bake for 10–15 minutes, until thoroughly heated through. Serve with a green salad.

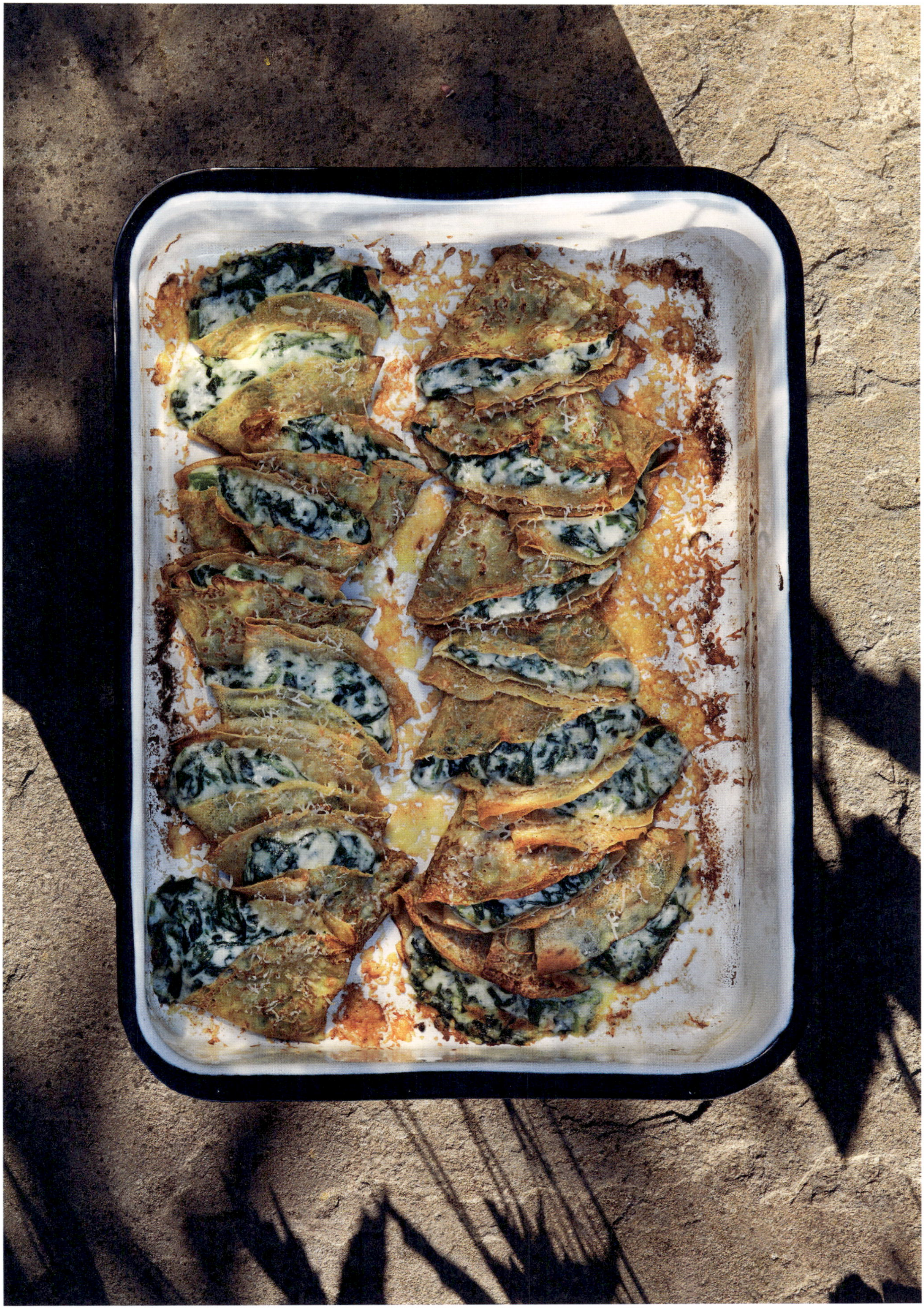

Butterhead lettuce with crème fraîche and parsley dressing

SERVES 4

2 large pinches coarse sea salt

1 teaspoon Dijon mustard

1 tablespoon lemon juice

3 tablespoons good-quality olive oil

3 tablespoons crème fraîche

2 tablespoons finely chopped parsley

1 large or 2 small butterhead lettuces

We are often asked which vegetable we like growing the most. We enjoy them all; they are all different and require varied skills. We do, however, have a soft spot for lettuces. Over many years of growing, we have trialled and eaten lots of varieties. A lettuce is truly a gardener's friend. Easy and quick to grow and beautiful to look at, lettuces come in so many types, shapes and sizes. One family favourite, and one of the most popular, with good reason, is the butterhead. It has floppy, tender, sweet leaves with contours just asking to be dressed. The butterhead lettuce prefers the cooler growing temperatures of spring and autumn.

There is nothing like harvesting the first outdoor-grown lettuces of the year, with their milky sap and pert, squeaky leaves. Gently peel off each leaf, checking for any bugs or slugs, and tear up the bigger outer leaves, working your way to the tight head of blanched leaves.

Mix together the salt, mustard and lemon juice in a small bowl, then whisk in the olive oil a tablespoonful at a time. When the dressing is nice and thick, whisk in the crème fraîche and parsley. Just before serving, pour the dressing over the lettuce leaves and toss well.

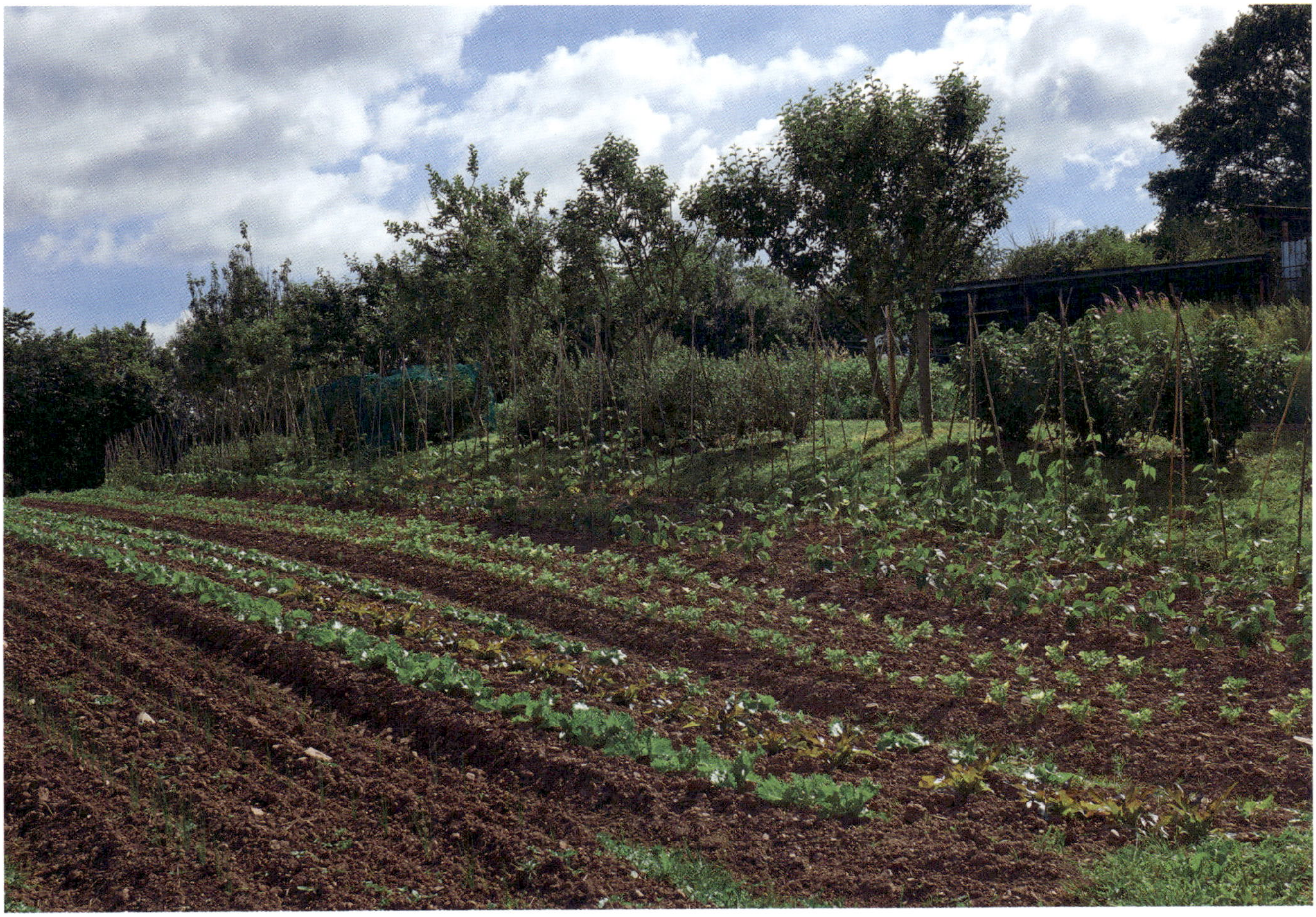

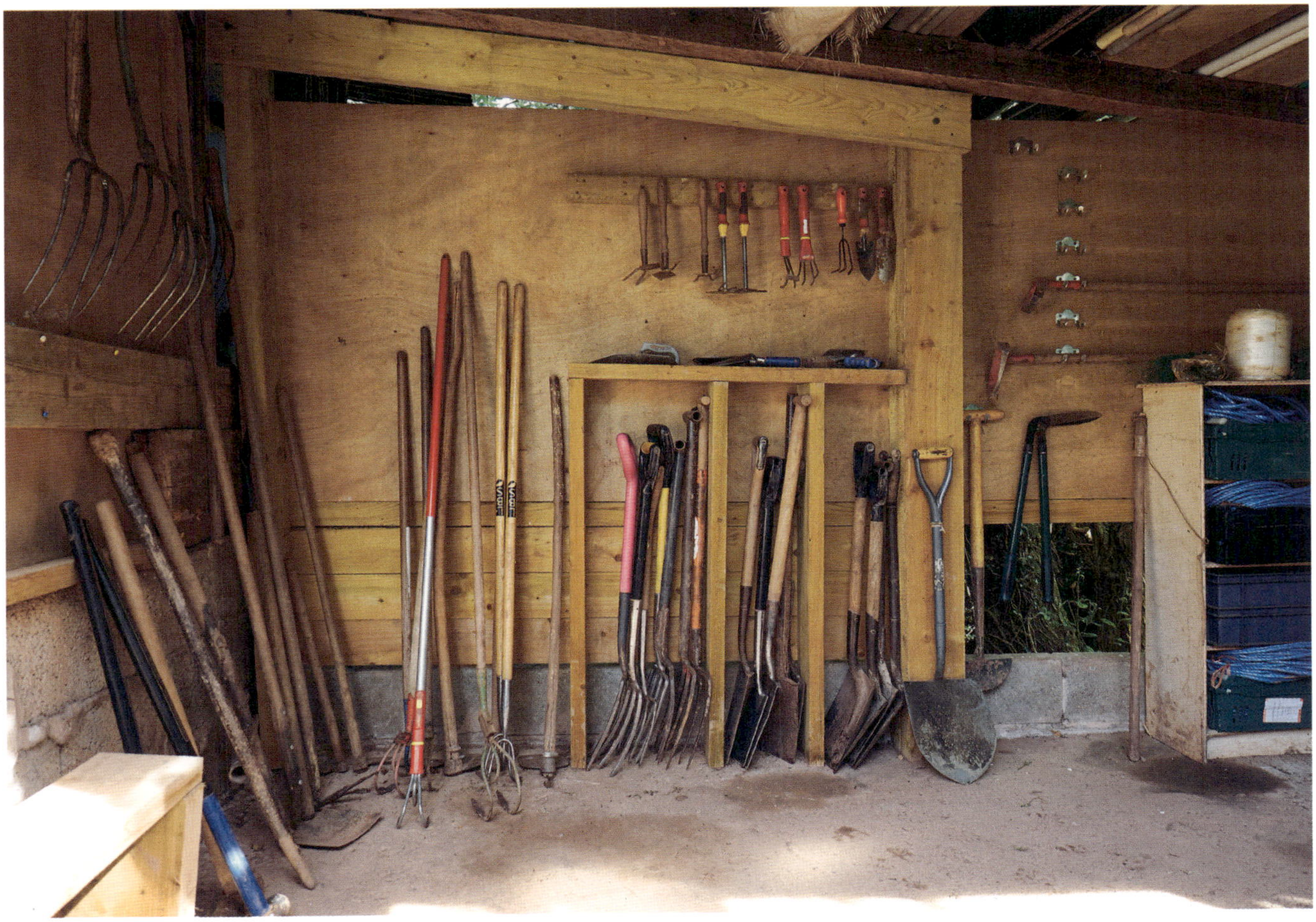

Pak choi and spring onion stir-fry

SERVES 4

500g pak choi

3 tablespoons sesame oil

a knuckle of fresh ginger, peeled and finely chopped

2 garlic cloves, finely chopped

1 scant teaspoon dried chilli flakes

8 spring onions, cut on the diagonal into 4cm lengths

a pinch of five-spice powder

5 drops of fish sauce, or to taste

4 fresh lime leaves, finely shredded

Pak choi is a fast-growing, cool-season vegetable from the brassica family. The flavour is fresh and mustardy with just the right amount of heat. This dish is packed full of flavour and makes an excellent light lunch. Serve it with a bowl of boiled jasmine rice.

Cut the pak choi in halves or quarters, according to size. Heat the sesame oil in a wide pan over a medium heat, add the ginger, garlic and chilli and fry gently for a couple of minutes to release the flavours. Add the spring onions and cook until wilted, then sprinkle in the five-spice powder.

Arrange the pak choi in the pan, turning it over to make sure it is coated with the spices. Turn up the heat a little and add a splash of water; there should be about 1cm of liquid to make a broth. Put the lid on the pan and leave the vegetables to steam for about 10 minutes, until tender. Stir in the fish sauce, then taste and add more if you like, a drop or two at a time. Stir in the lime leaves and let them warm through. Serve in bowls, with jasmine rice.

Cauliflower salad with Dijon mustard and parsley dressing

SERVES 4

1 cauliflower, broken into florets
2 teaspoons Dijon mustard
2 tablespoons cider vinegar
4 tablespoons olive oil
2 tablespoons finely chopped parsley

The secret of this very simple salad is to get your hands on a freshly harvested spring-headed cauliflower. This variety is planted in autumn, then 'over-wintered', with the growth held dormant until spring. These are the best-tasting cauliflowers. The curds should be tight and a bright, creamy-white colour, while the leaves should still have body and be a soft green, without any yellowing. A farmers' market or village shop is a better place to look for good fresh cauliflowers than in supermarkets, where the vegetables have usually been harvested many days earlier and stripped of their leaves.

If you cannot get a very fresh cauliflower for this salad, it is best to blanch the florets for 2 minutes, as stored cauliflowers can have a rather mouth-burning flavour when raw. The salad may be served as a starter, but it also goes very well with cold meats, pâté and charcuterie.

Cut the cauliflower florets into slices 2mm thick. A mandolin will do this perfectly, but if you don't have one, use a large, sharp knife and cut as thinly as possible. Place the mushroom-shaped florets in a large salad bowl. Mix the mustard with the vinegar, then whisk in the olive oil a tablespoon at a time until emulsified. Stir in the chopped parsley. Pour the dressing over the cauliflower and turn it until it is coated.

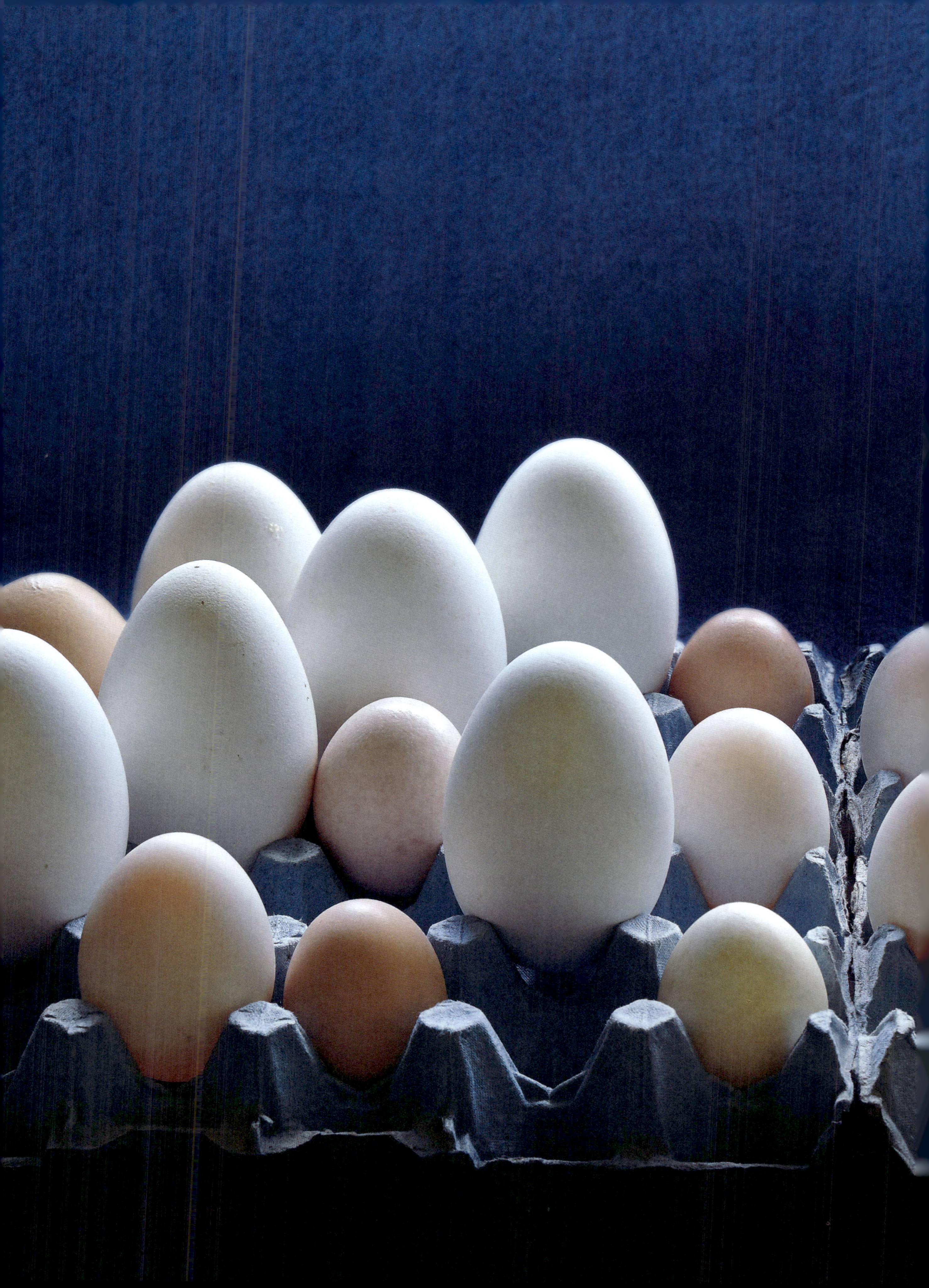

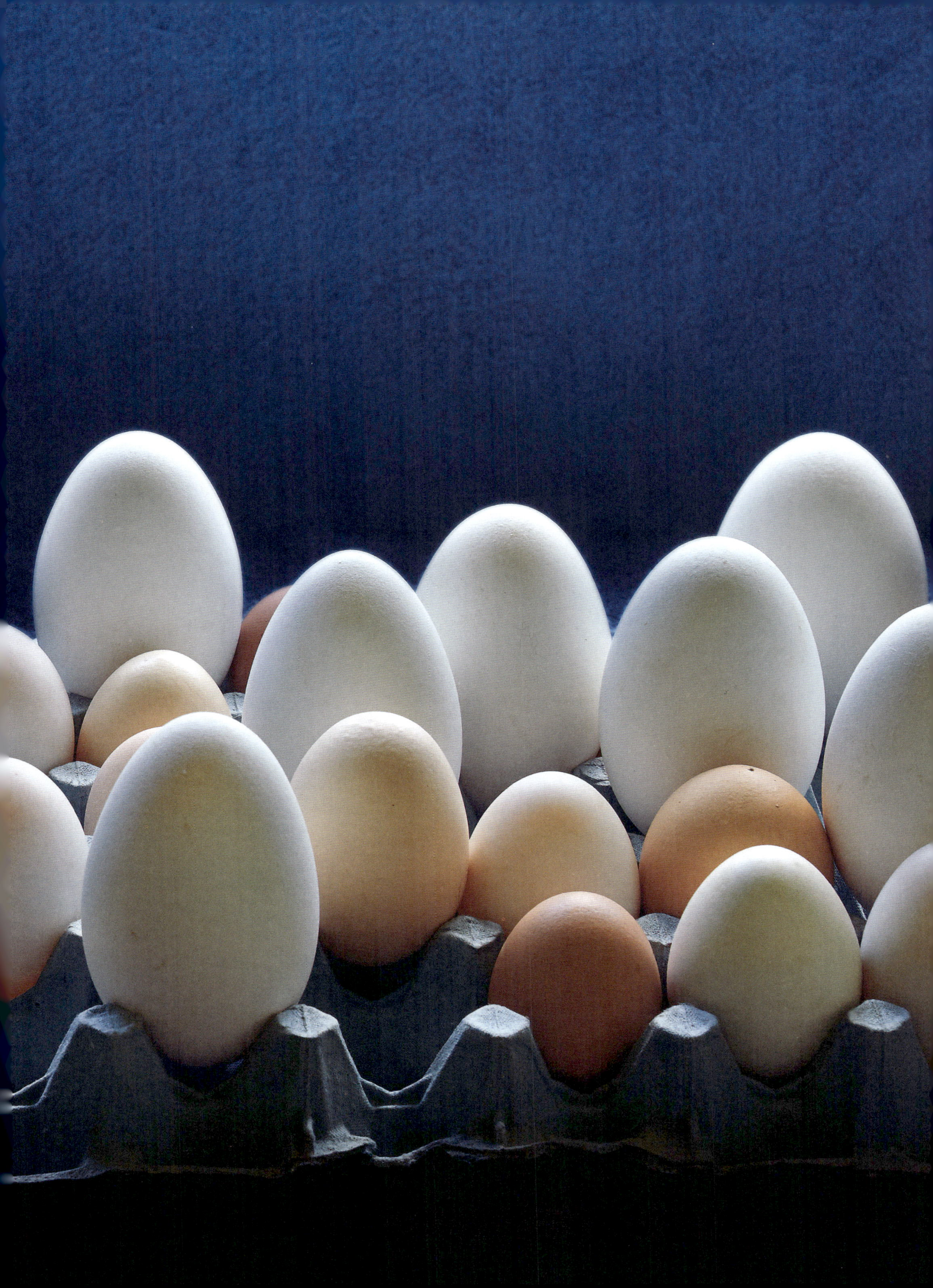

The magic in an egg

WHAT A PIECE of work is an egg! We all take for granted the ubiquitous chicken egg, its elegant form too often overlooked, but there is beauty in cupping an egg in your palm and feeling the fine, silky, almost ceramic texture. This enclosed form holds the potential for new life, and within each eggshell lie remarkable properties of transformation.

Once a female bird has laid a suitable number of fertilised eggs she sits patiently on them, providing warmth and humidity to develop the embryo. The length of incubation differs a little between species: with the poultry we raise on the farm, it is 21 days for the chickens and turkeys, and 28 days for the ducks and geese. The dedicated mother carefully covers the eggs, rising only briefly to feed herself, drink a little and stretch her legs, and to turn each egg a few times a day.

It is during this incubation period that magic takes place. Protected by its calcium shell, the embryo evolves within the yolk, surrounded by the watery element of egg white, slowly growing and becoming more solid. Three days from the end of incubation, the chick begins to 'pip', little by little pecking its way out from inside the shell. Once the shell cracks open, the young chick wriggles out, exhausted. The wonder then is how the new arrival emerges into the world ready to feed independently, quite unlike humans and other mammals, which must first feed on their mothers' milk.

The egg has long symbolised new beginnings. We can still see this at Easter, with the egg as metaphor for rebirth. At this time of the year we celebrate the victory of life over death and the immortality of the human soul. The date of Easter changes each year, despite some moves to fix it to a specific day. It always falls on the first Sunday after the first full moon following the spring equinox: a reminder that in the past, people were far more aware than we are today of the influence of the sun and the moon and their relationship with the earth.

Perhaps the most obvious place we can directly appreciate the potential in an egg is in the kitchen. How limited cookery would be without this most versatile of performers. You can cook an egg in its entirety, but as soon as you separate yolk and white – the metaphorical sun and moon – you open up a multitude of possibilities for transformation.

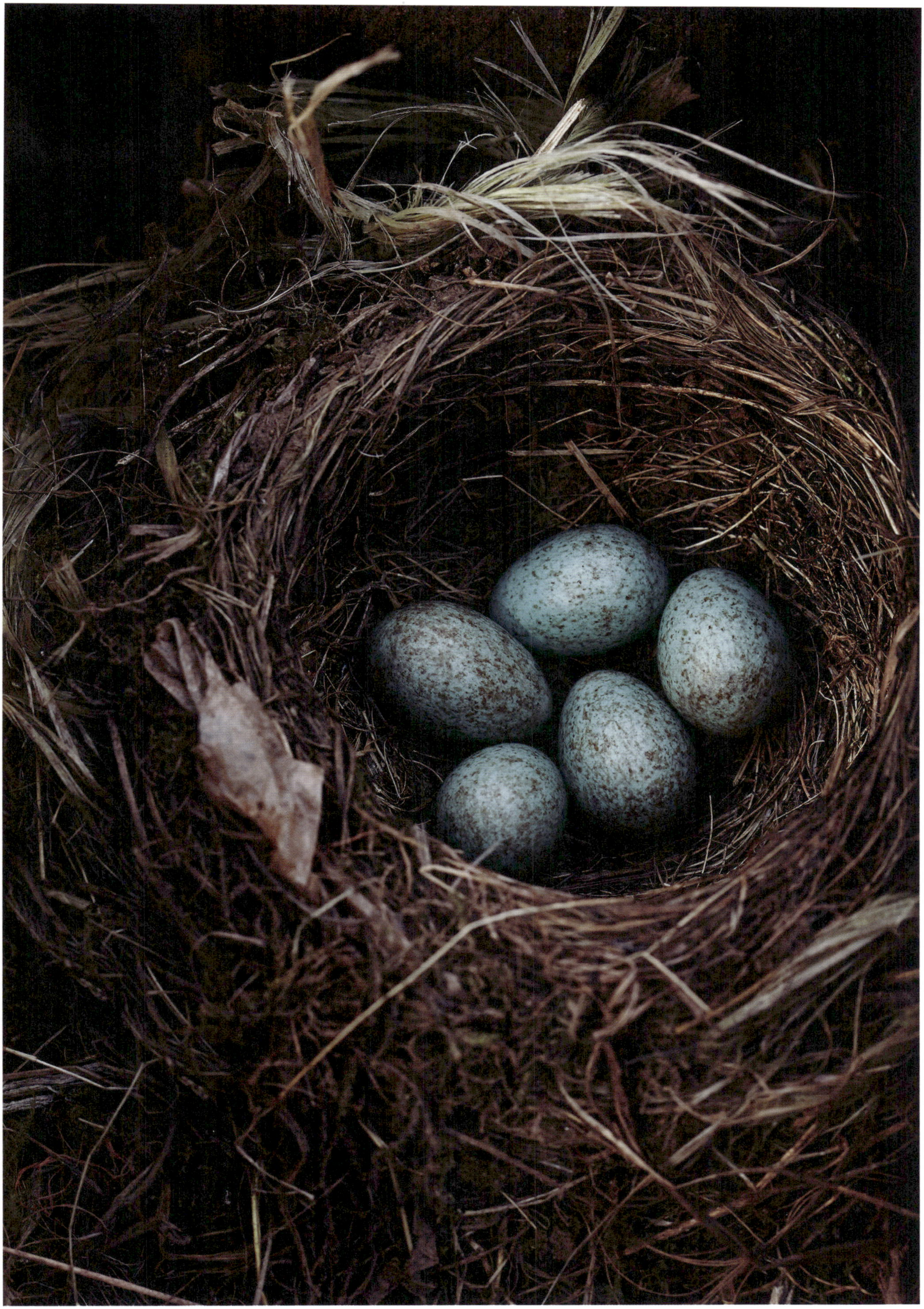

Fried duck egg with asparagus, sage and Parmesan

SERVES 2

2 bunches of asparagus
25g Parmesan cheese
10 sage leaves
60g butter
2 duck eggs
juice of ½ lemon
sea salt and black pepper

Unlike chickens, which lay eggs most of the year, ducks tend to lay seasonally, in the spring. The eggs are very beautiful, coming in a range of pale, semi-translucent shades of white and sometimes blue. The texture of the shell is like alabaster – quite different from a chicken's egg. Inside the shell the egg is different, too: a large yolk equivalent to two chicken yolks and a relatively small white. The flavour is stronger and richer. Duck eggs are also marvellous for baking, with the large yolks adding extra richness and a wonderful yellow colour to a sponge cake.

Put a large pan of salted water on to boil. Meanwhile, snap off the dry, woody base from each asparagus spear. Using a potato peeler, shave the Parmesan into thin slivers and crumble them up a little with your fingers. Slice the sage leaves as thinly as you can.

Once the water is boiling rapidly, add the asparagus and cook for about 2 minutes, until just tender. Drain through a colander and set aside.

Melt half the butter in a frying pan, break in the duck eggs and fry, seasoning with a little salt and pepper as they cook. Quickly heat the remaining butter in a separate frying pan, large enough to hold the asparagus. When it begins to brown, throw in the sage and squeeze in the lemon juice. Add the cooked asparagus, season with a little salt and pepper and toss gently so that the asparagus is well coated in the butter and lemon.

Share the asparagus out between 2 warm plates, put the eggs on top and sprinkle with the Parmesan. Serve with bread and butter.

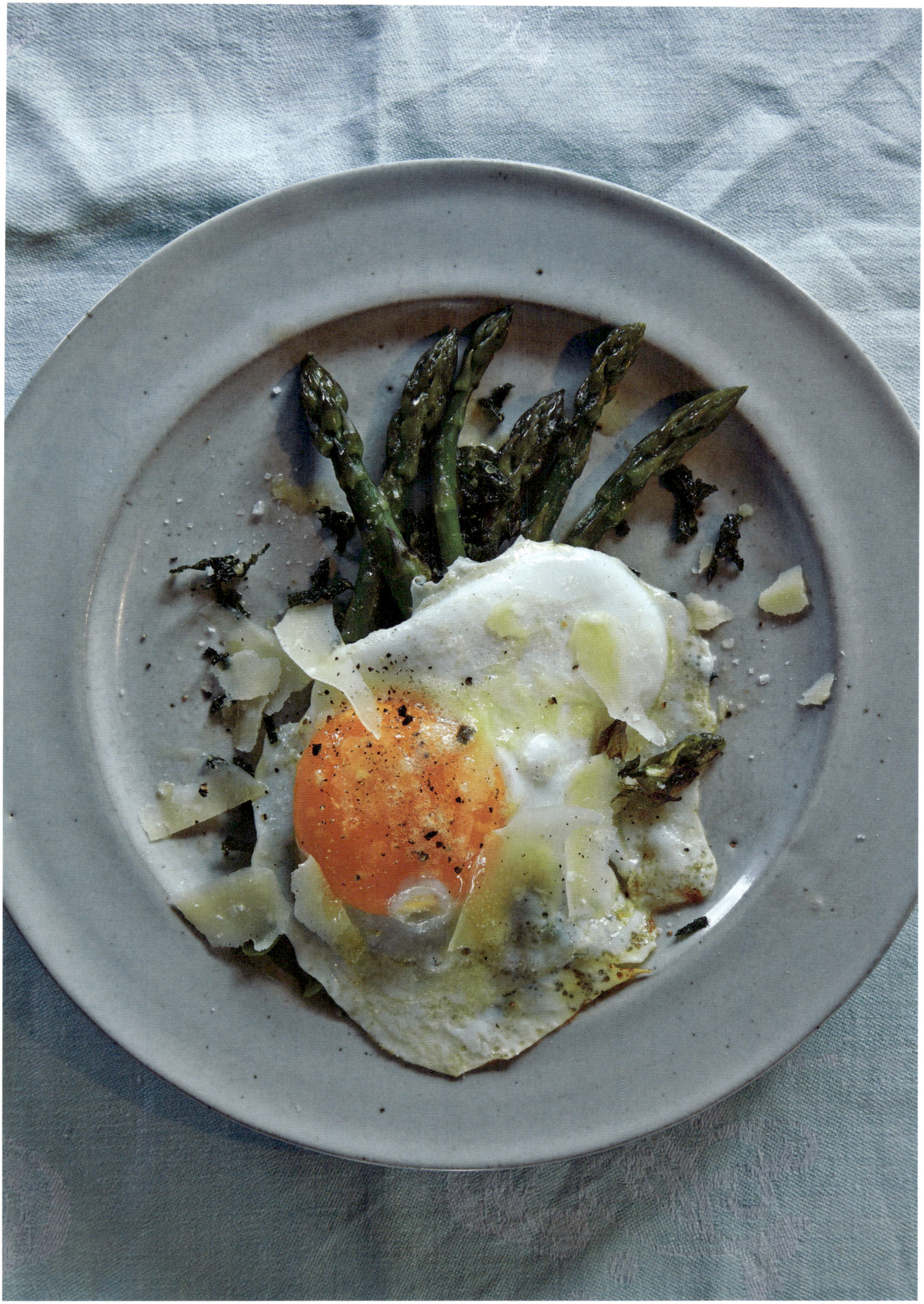

Chive, sorrel and ramson frittata

SERVES 2–4

8 eggs
a bunch of chives
a handful of sorrel (about 25g)
a handful of wild garlic (about 25g)
30g butter
sea salt and black pepper

This is a refreshing mixture of greens and eggs and very quick to make. The sorrel will turn brown on cooking, but it gives a sharp tang that lifts the mellow flavours of the chives and wild garlic, or ramsons.

Crack the eggs into a mixing bowl, season with salt and pepper and whisk with a fork. Slice the chives with a sharp knife or snip them with scissors. Tear the sorrel from its stems and shred. Roughly chop the wild garlic. Add the greens to the bowl and give the mixture a gentle stir.

Melt half the butter in a large frying pan over a medium heat. Tilt the pan to coat the sides, then pour in the egg mixture. Cook for 3–4 minutes, until set around the edges but still slightly runny in the centre, then use a palette knife to tease the frittata away from the edge of the pan. Remove from the heat, put a plate over the pan and, with a tea towel in each hand, turn the frittata out on to the plate by flipping the pan. Then return the pan to the heat with the remaining butter, again tilting it to coat the sides. Slip the frittata back in and cook the underside for a minute or two, until set. Slide it out on to a chopping board and allow to cool a little before slicing and serving. This frittata is also very nice eaten cold.

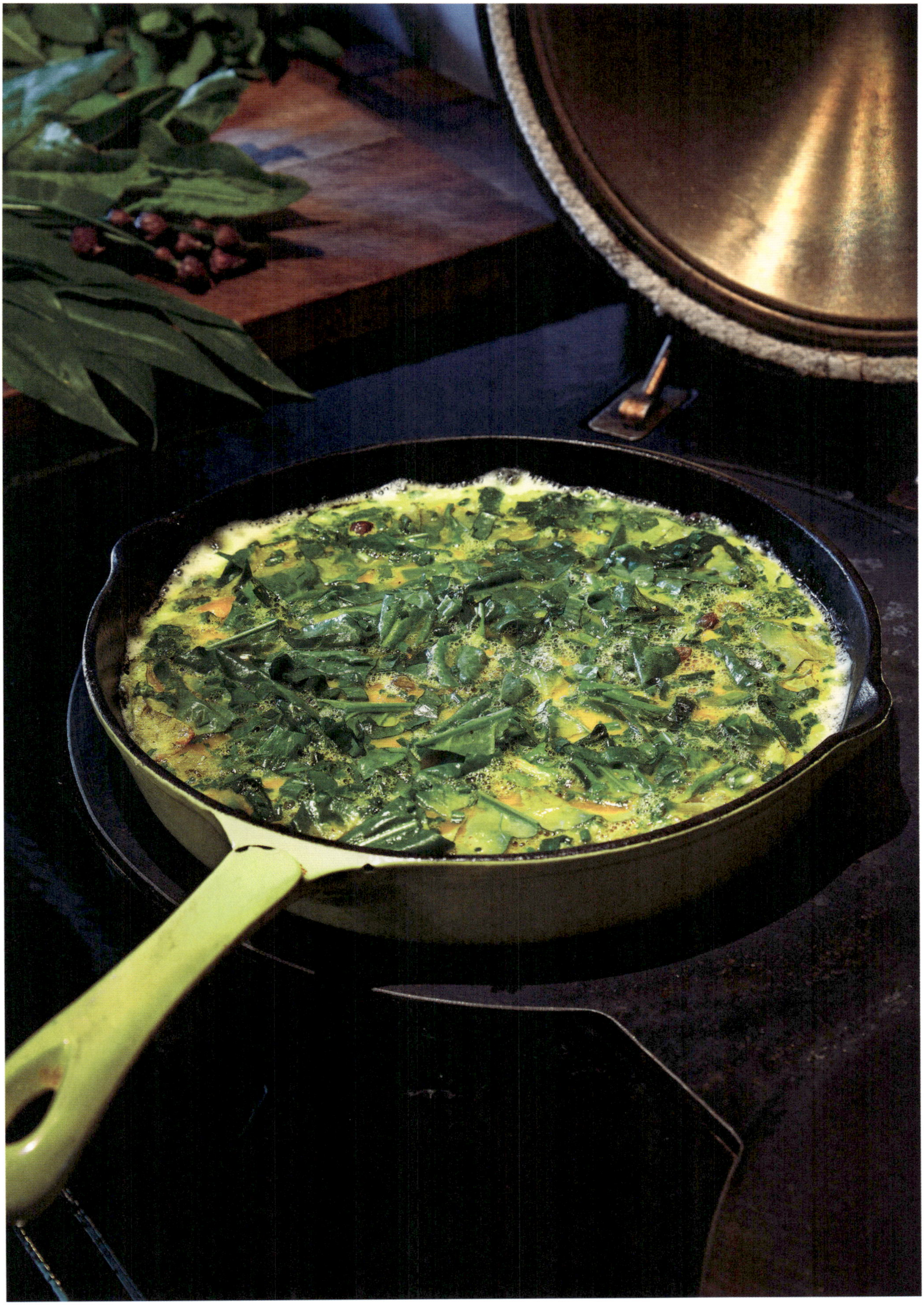

Baked trout in a new-season herb crust with beurre blanc

SERVES 2

50g butter, melted
50g fresh breadcrumbs
grated zest of 1 lemon
1 tablespoon chopped dill
2 tablespoons finely chopped chives
2 tablespoons chopped parsley
1 egg
a little plain flour, for dusting
1 large trout, filleted
sea salt and black pepper

For the beurre blanc
2 small shallots, finely chopped
50ml white wine vinegar
50ml water
200g chilled butter, cut into small chunks
juice of ½ lemon

The key to making this simple but extremely delicious dish is to ensure that there is plenty of the breadcrumb mix on top of the fish. Push the fillets firmly into the crumbs to ensure a good, thick layer. Baking the fish sealed within its coating in a hot oven produces a crunchy crust and moist, perfectly cooked flesh. Serve with boiled new potatoes and purple sprouting broccoli.

Heat the oven to 230°C/Gas Mark 8. Brush a baking tray with a little of the melted butter to prevent the fish sticking. Put the breadcrumbs in a shallow bowl, add the lemon zest and herbs and mix with a fork. Break the egg into a separate shallow bowl and beat lightly with a fork. Put some flour on a plate.

Season the trout fillets with salt and pepper. Dip them, flesh-side only, in the flour, then the egg and finally the breadcrumb mixture. Lay them skin-side down on the baking tray. Put any remaining breadcrumb mixture on top, filling any gaps, and spoon the rest of the melted butter over.

Cook the fish at the top of the oven for 10–15 minutes, depending on size. The crust should be golden brown, but be careful not to overcook the fish.

While the trout is baking, make the beurre blanc. Put the shallots, vinegar and water in a small saucepan and boil rapidly until almost all the liquid has evaporated and only about a tablespoon remains. Immediately turn down the heat as low as it will go and whisk in the butter a piece at a time. Incorporating the butter should take only a minute or two. It is important that the pan remains warm as you make the emulsion, but if it gets too warm the sauce will split. If it looks as if this is about to happen, lift the pan off the heat briefly. Once the butter has transformed into a rich yellow sauce, squeeze in the lemon juice and season with salt and pepper. Serve immediately, with the trout.

Goose egg lemon curd

MAKES 4 X 225G JARS

finely grated zest and juice of 8 large unwaxed lemons

400g granulated sugar

200g unsalted butter, cut into small cubes

2 goose eggs, lightly beaten

In our first year at Fern Verrow, an elderly neighbour recited, 'A good woman's goose should lay by Valentine's Day.' That year, our first egg was laid on that very day – it has never happened since. In general, weather conditions allowing, the geese lay from about the middle of February until mid-May. What a joy it is to find that first egg, pure white in colour, just like goose feathers. It's a sign that spring is only a month away. It takes 28 days for a goose egg to hatch, so when the goose has finished her period of confinement, the new-season shoots of grass and herbage have arrived in time to feed the young goslings.

One goose egg is equivalent to three chicken eggs, but the proportion of yolk to white is higher, adding richness when used in baking. Geese are grazing animals, and can survive and thrive eating only grass during the summer months. Many a time we have seen our geese in a police sweep-search line, heads down, working their way through the pastures. This factor certainly adds to the quality of flavour in their eggs.

Lemon curd made with goose eggs is in a class of its own. The neon-yellow shines through the jar. Try to find the freshest possible eggs – your local farmers' market is probably the best bet, as it is likely that the person selling them is also the one who gathered them.

Put the lemon zest and juice, sugar and butter into a heatproof bowl and place it over a pan of simmering water, ensuring that the base of the bowl does not come into contact with the water. Stir occasionally until the sugar has dissolved and the butter has melted. The mixture should be nice and warm, but not hot or the eggs will curdle. Strain the beaten eggs through a sieve into the bowl. Using a balloon whisk, whisk the curd gently for about 15 minutes, until it thickens to a custard-like consistency and feels heavy on the whisk.

Remove the bowl from the heat and leave to cool, stirring occasionally. Pour the curd into sterilised jars (see page 251) and seal. Store in the fridge and use within 28 days.

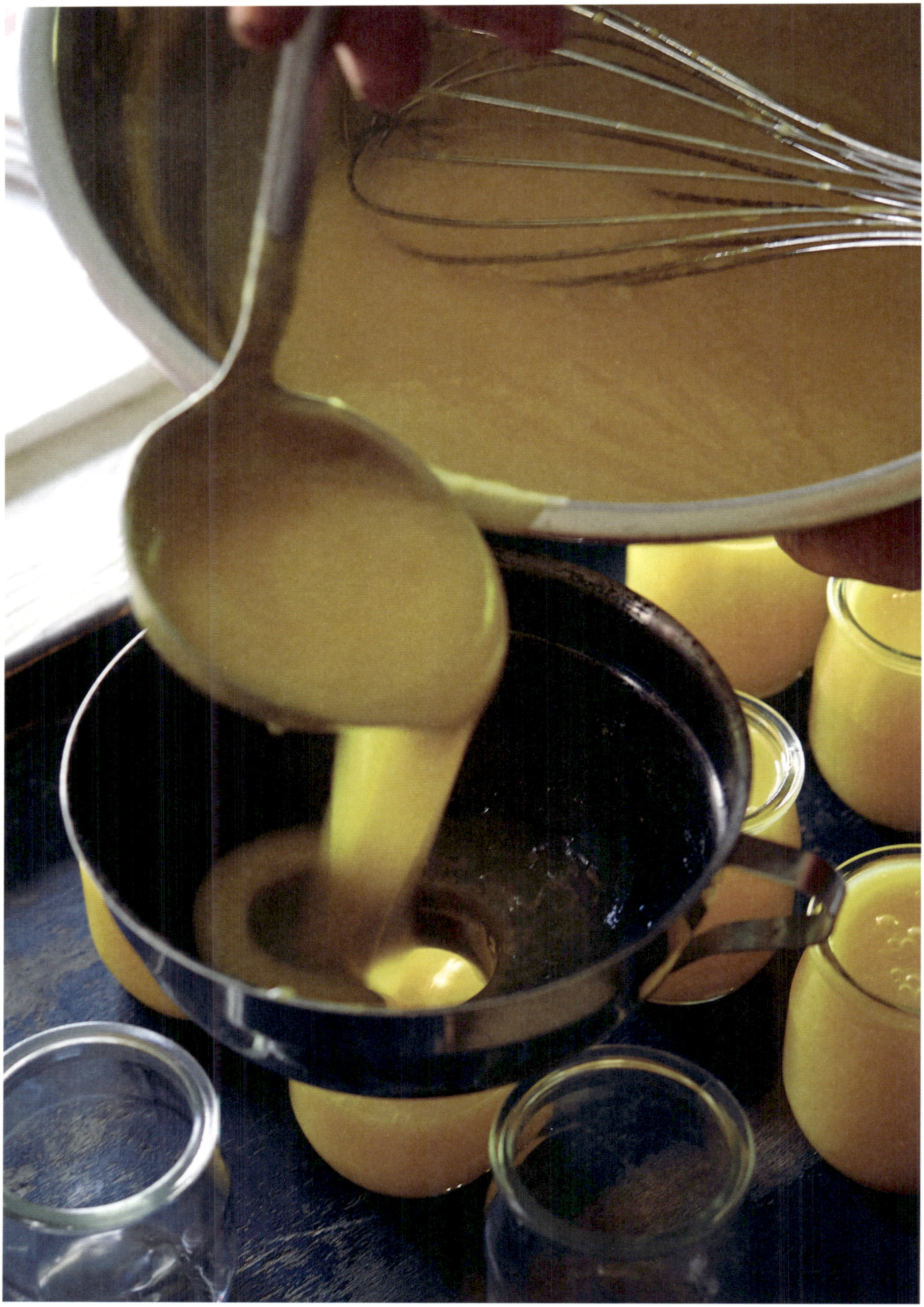

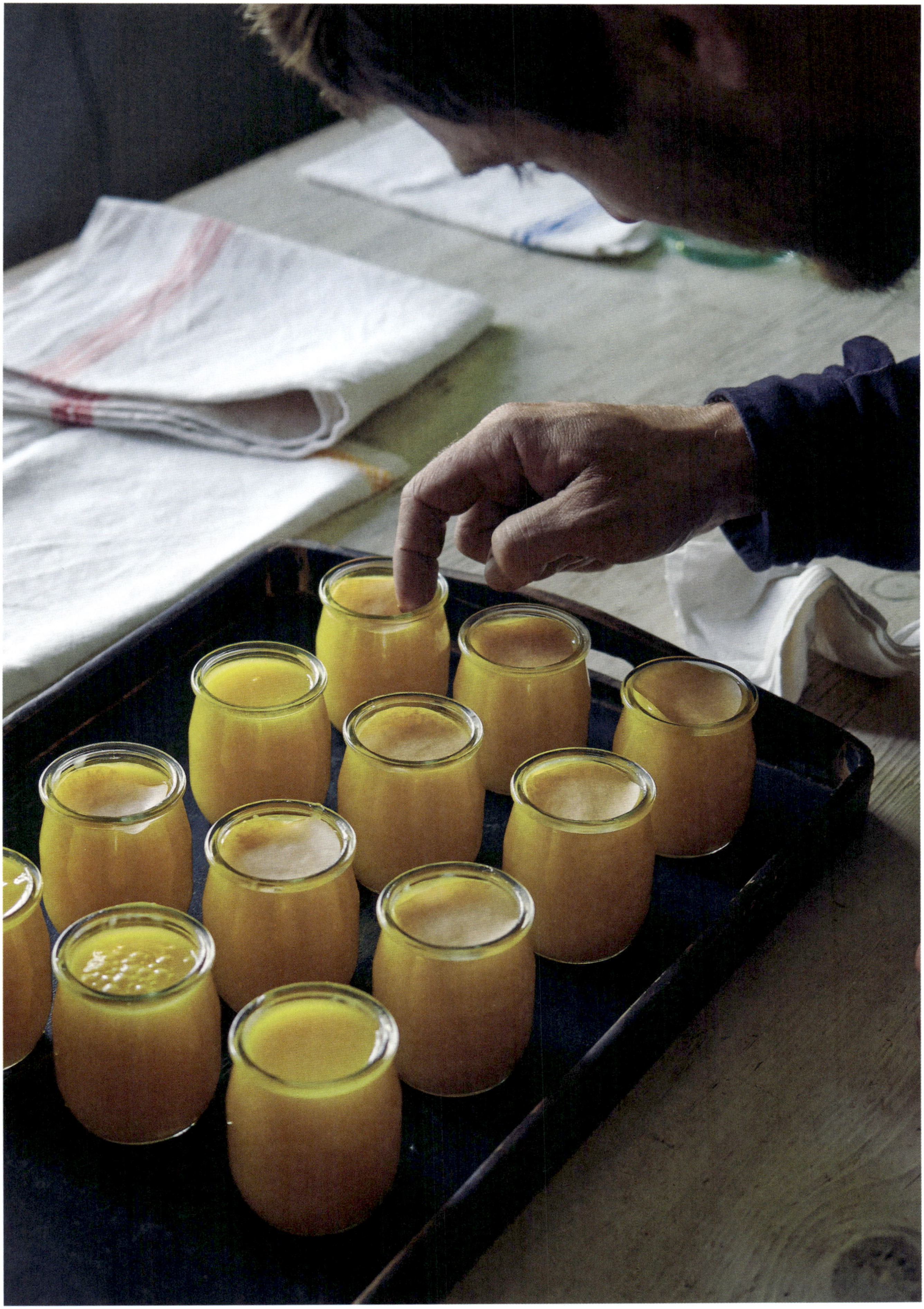

Rhubarb and custard fool

SERVES 6

For the rhubarb compote
500g rhubarb, cut into 3cm lengths
100g granulated sugar
50ml water

For the custard
250ml full-fat milk
2 egg yolks
15g caster sugar
1 level teaspoon cornflour
300ml double cream

A good friend once told us that when he was a child his mother used to give him a homemade dip-dab of sugar and a stick of rhubarb. This would be nicest with an early season stalk from one of the finer varieties – champagne rhubarb, for example. To keep your rhubarb tender and not tough and stringy, as it can be in late spring, pick it often, by tugging, not cutting, at the base to remove the petioles (stalks to you and me, but petiole is a lovely name). Keep the plant well watered and you can be picking rhubarb for months.

To make the compote, place the rhubarb, sugar and water in a 22cm diameter saucepan (not an aluminium one), cover and bring slowly to the boil. Immediately reduce the heat as low as possible and leave the rhubarb to steam, without stirring, for about 15 minutes, shaking the pan gently a couple of times to help disperse and melt the sugar. When the rhubarb is done, it should be tender but still holding its shape. Turn off the heat and leave to cool with the lid on the pan. Check for sweetness.

To make the custard, bring the milk slowly to simmering point in a saucepan. Meanwhile, whisk together the egg yolks, sugar and cornflour in a large bowl. Gradually pour the hot milk on to the egg mixture, whisking vigorously with a balloon whisk. Return the mixture to the pan and whisk gently over a very low heat until the custard thickens to a whipped cream consistency. This can take 15 minutes or so. Leave to cool, stirring occasionally to prevent a skin forming.

Whip the cream until thick, then fold it into the cold custard. With a slotted spoon, remove the rhubarb from its juice, leaving a few pieces to use later for decoration. Add 6 tablespoons of juice to the custard and then fold in the rhubarb carefully. Chill, then serve in individual glasses or bowls, decorating with the reserved pieces of rhubarb and trickling more of the pink juice over the top.

Variation

The addition of a knuckle of peeled fresh ginger or 2 or 3 strips of orange zest to the rhubarb as it cooks can make the compote even more delicious.

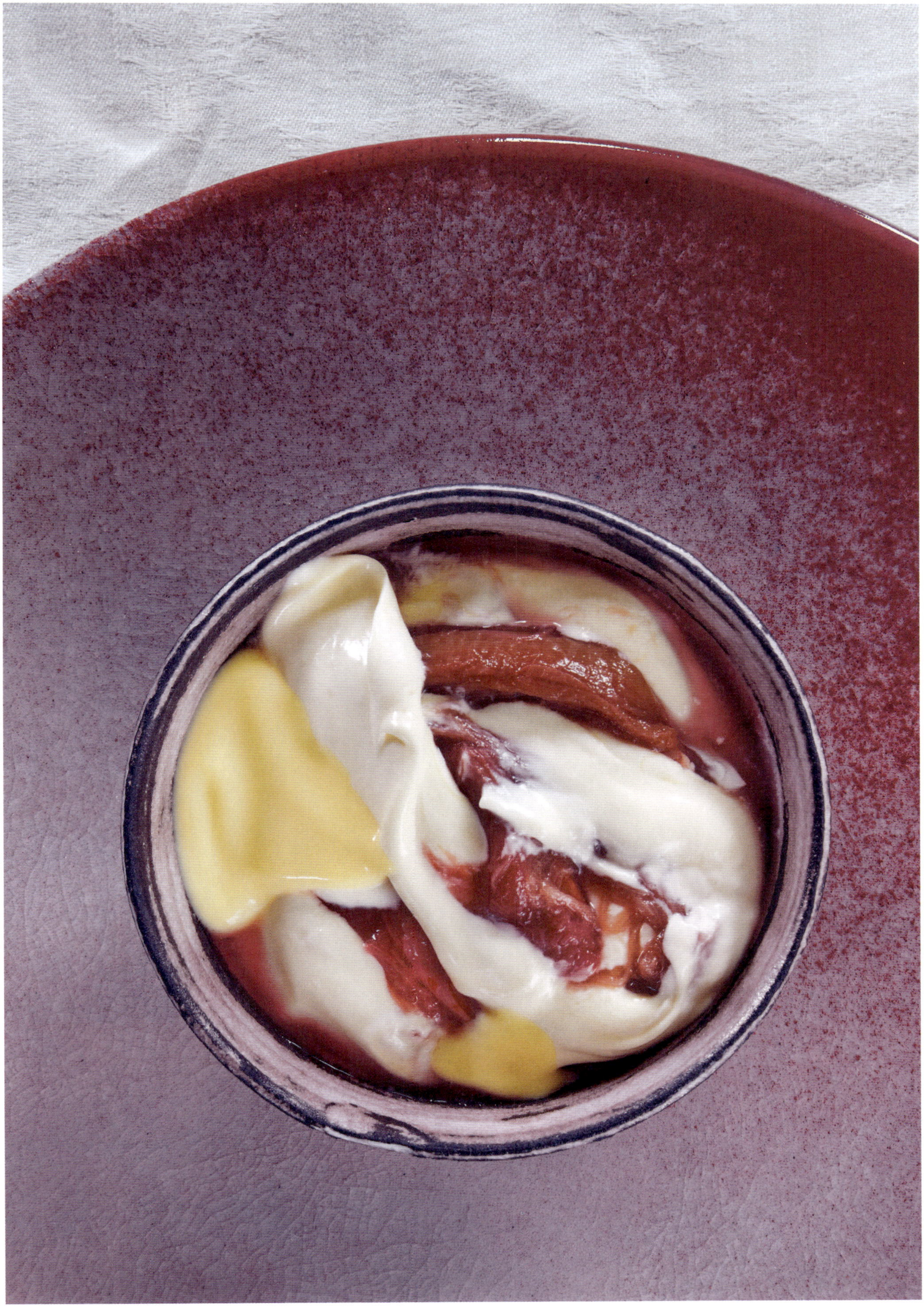

Baked cheesecake with rhubarb compote

SERVES 6–8

175g ginger nut biscuits
50g butter, melted
550g full-fat cream cheese
180g caster sugar
¼ teaspoon salt
1 teaspoon grated lemon zest
2 teaspoons vanilla extract
4 eggs, separated
200ml double cream, lightly whipped
50g cornflour
icing sugar, for dusting
rhubarb compote, to serve (see page 124)

We like to make this cheesecake well in advance as it tastes better chilled. The sharpness of the rhubarb compote cuts through the richness of the cheesecake, and the pale pink is very pretty against the gold and cream. In summer, you could replace the rhubarb compote with another fruit compote such as gooseberry or blackcurrant.

Heat the oven to 160°C/Gas Mark 3. Lightly grease the base and sides of a 22cm springform cake tin. Put the ginger biscuits in a food processor and whiz to make crumbs. Combine them with the melted butter, then spoon into the tin and press evenly on to the base.

Mix the cream cheese with half the sugar, plus the salt, lemon zest and vanilla. Beat in the egg yolks and then fold in the whipped cream. In a large bowl, whisk the egg whites until they hold soft peaks. Add the remaining sugar a tablespoon at a time, whisking constantly, until the whites are very stiff. Sift the cornflour over the surface, then add the cream cheese mixture and fold it in gently. Pour the mixture into the prepared tin.

Place in the oven and bake for about 1 hour 20 minutes. Don't open the door for the first hour or the cheesecake may sink. Once it is golden brown and the surface has begun to crack, revealing the creamy curd inside, turn off the oven. Leave the cheesecake in the switched-off oven for a couple of hours to cool. Cover the tin with cling film and chill for at least 2 hours.

Remove the cheesecake from the tin and dust with icing sugar. Serve with the rhubarb compote.

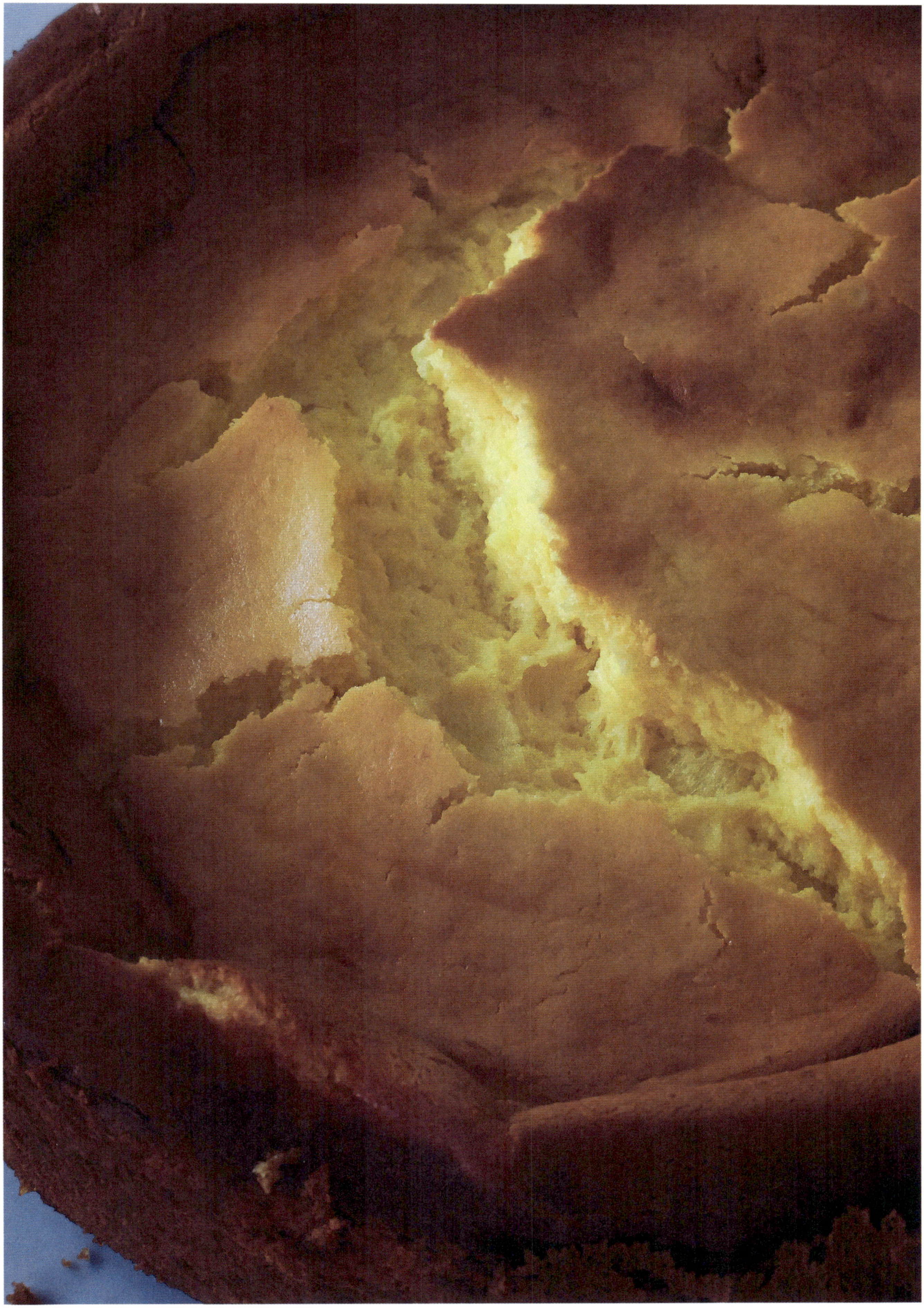

Working with the sun

THE RHYTHM OF daily life on the farm and the pattern of work that plays out over the course of the year are set by the sun and its activity. The changing character of the sun, the quantity and quality of the light and warmth that it gives, influences everything. And we are always following it, making the most of every opportunity that it offers. Working in the light, resting in the dark.

Within the fixed perimeters of the farm, inside the familiar frame of hedges and trees, the picture is always changing slightly. We walk to the poultry houses every single morning to let the birds out and feed them, always looking up to the sky to clock the position of the rising sun. And we take the same route at dusk, closing the birds safely in their houses and looking to see where the sun has just set, using the trees like markings on a compass. Sunrise and sunset gradually move around the horizon, the two points never meeting, but lengthening the day for half the year, and for the other half lengthening the night.

The daily routine of walking the familiar track through the flower garden to the poultry houses each morning, noon (to collect eggs) and night, is always an opportunity for observing the changes that occur through the seasons. In the summer, first thing in the morning, the dew is still on the closed flower heads, then at noon the fully opened blooms revel in the sunshine, while the chickens further down the hill scratch the ground in the shade of the trees. The long evening shadows seem to change the dimensions of the flowerbeds. In the winter there is very little colour around, but the different forms of the many deciduous trees are always there to admire.

We often find ourselves thinking in opposites – of the extremes of darkness and light. On the shortest working day, just before Christmas, when the sun makes its lowest and narrowest arc over the southern tree line, we have barely seven hours of daylight: both we and the animals spend far more time inside than out. At midsummer, the sun fills the sky above our heads for seventeen hours, with each day rolling into the next, drawing everyone up and out. And within these two poles, every possible variation, laid down by the beat of the sun.

The pace of work also shifts over the course of the year: increasing into spring, up to the high pitch of summer, then the gradual slowing down through autumn, into the long walk through winter. The growth of plants and animals are synchronised with the sun at every turn. And we are always trying to keep up, staying in the company of the sun. Catching it in the leaves and flowers, holding it in the ripening fruit and storing it in the swelling roots. Finding a beginning in every end.

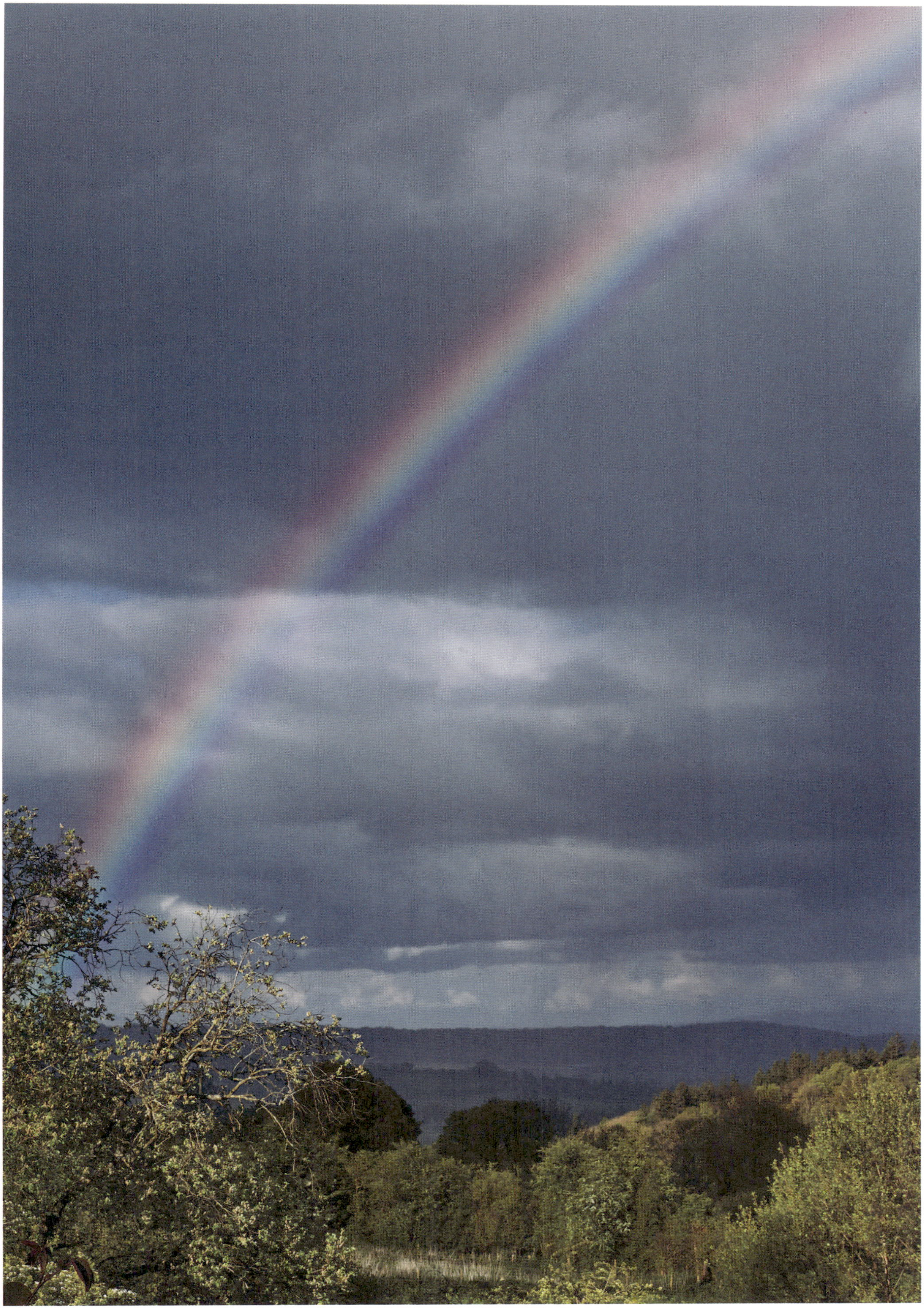

Rhubarb cordial

MAKES ABOUT 2 LITRES

4kg rhubarb, cut into 5cm lengths
400ml water
about 1.2kg granulated sugar
juice of 4 lemons, strained

Although it is treated as a fruit, rhubarb is technically a vegetable. It has also been used as a medicinal plant for centuries – the Chinese, for example, add rhubarb roots to many of their herbal medicine preparations. Some people believe that rhubarb helps to promote blood circulation – something we all need at the end of a long winter. This cordial is indeed a tonic. Not only does it taste delicious but it also does you good. The sherbet-pink concentrate is a great cocktail mixer for alcoholic drinks or for the ultimate pink lemonade (see below).

Place the chopped rhubarb in a pan (not an aluminium one), add the water and bring slowly to the boil. Turn the heat down to a low simmer, cover and leave to stew for 30 minutes, until the rhubarb is soft and the juice is very pink. Turn off the heat and allow to cool a little.

Line a large sieve with a sterilised piece of muslin and set it over a large bowl. Tip the rhubarb carefully into the muslin so the juices drip through into the bowl. Tie the corners of the muslin together, suspend it over the bowl and leave for at least 6 hours, overnight if possible. Do not be tempted to squeeze the bag as this will cloud the cordial.

Measure the juice and pour it into a clean pan. For each litre of juice, add 600g sugar. Add the lemon juice, then heat, stirring, until the sugar is fully dissolved, then bring to the boil. Pour into sterilised bottles (see page 251) and seal immediately. The cordial should keep for a year, or for a week in the fridge once opened.

A few suggestions

Rhubarb gin fizz – shake or stir 60ml gin, 30ml lemon juice and 60ml rhubarb cordial vigorously with lots of ice. Pour into a glass and top up with soda water, then stir gently.

Pink lemonade – put 60ml rhubarb cordial and the juice of 1 lemon into a tall glass with some ice. Top up with water and stir, adding more cordial or lemon to taste. Decorate with a borage flower or two, if available; if not, a twist of lemon looks pretty.

Rhubarb bellini – purée a tablespoon of stewed rhubarb until smooth and add 2 teaspoons of rhubarb cordial. Place in a chilled wine or champagne glass and top up with champagne or prosecco.

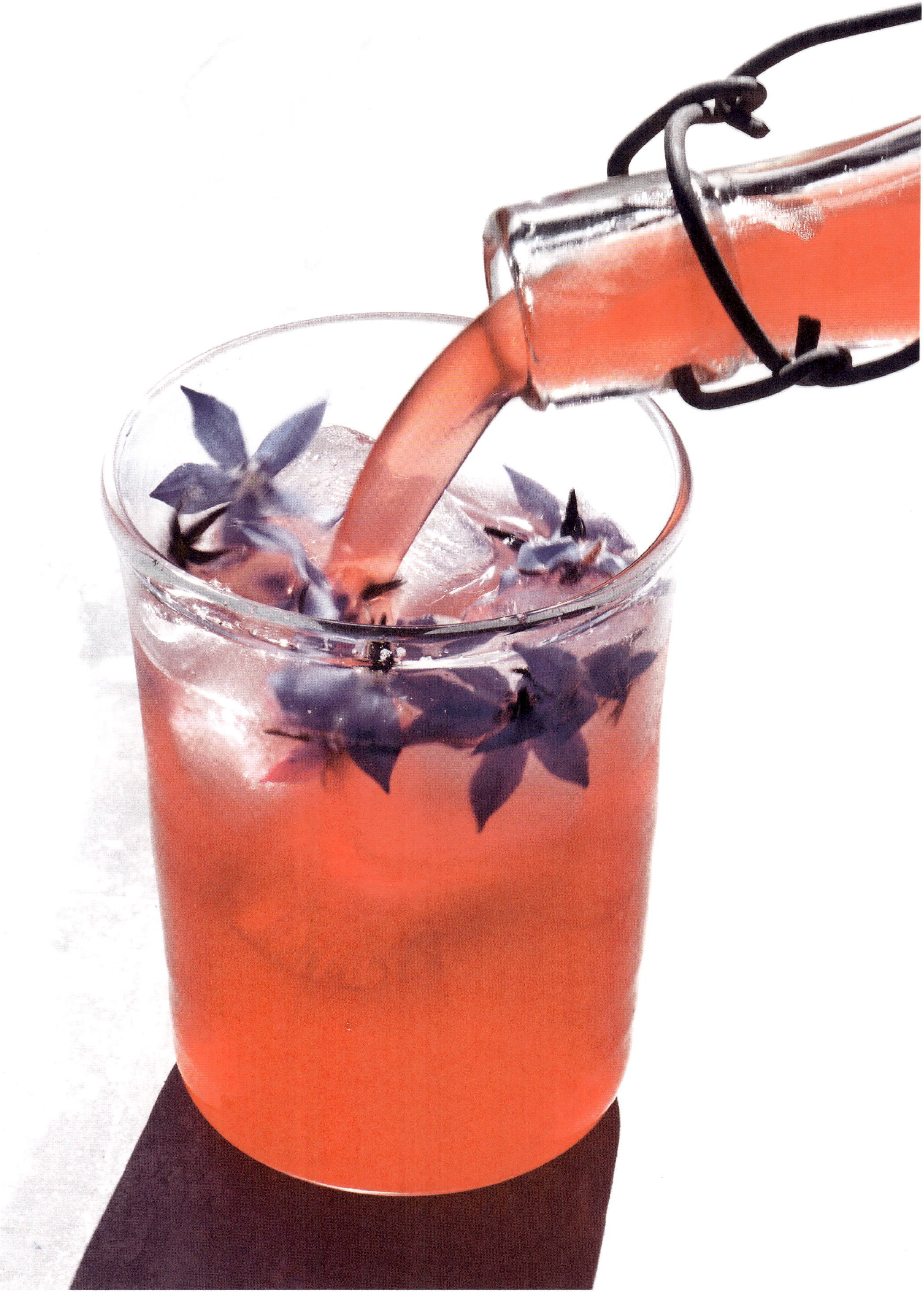

Elderflower cordial

MAKES 2 LITRES

50 freshly picked elderflower heads
4 lemons
2 litres boiling water
about 1.5kg granulated sugar

Collecting flowers to make elderflower cordial has to be one of the top good-to-be-alive moments. May is when we see the first of the elderflowers coming into bloom. They are the prettiest of flowers – tiny, lacy blossoms, hundreds of them on each stem, in nature's most exquisite shade of cream.

Pick the flowers first thing in the morning before they are fully open, on a dry day. Choose a tree that is full of flowers, as this will mean that the majority of flower heads are in their prime; the heady Muscat scent should be almost overwhelming. Choose the whitest heads and snip them at the base of the flowers, keeping the heads whole. Shake them gently to remove any insects, but do not wash.

To dilute the cordial, we suggest four parts fizzy or still water to one part cordial. The addition of the juice of half a lemon makes this a fragrant and very refreshing lemonade.

Place the elderflower heads in a large bowl. Slice 2 of the lemons, add them to the bowl and pour over the boiling water. Cover the bowl with a tea towel and leave overnight to infuse.

The next day, strain the infusion through a muslin cloth into a saucepan. Juice the 2 remaining lemons, then strain the juice into the pan. Add the sugar and heat gently, stirring frequently, until the sugar has completely dissolved. Simmer for a few minutes, until the mixture reaches 90°C on a sugar thermometer. Pour the hot syrup into sterilised bottles (see page 251) and seal. The cordial should keep for a year.

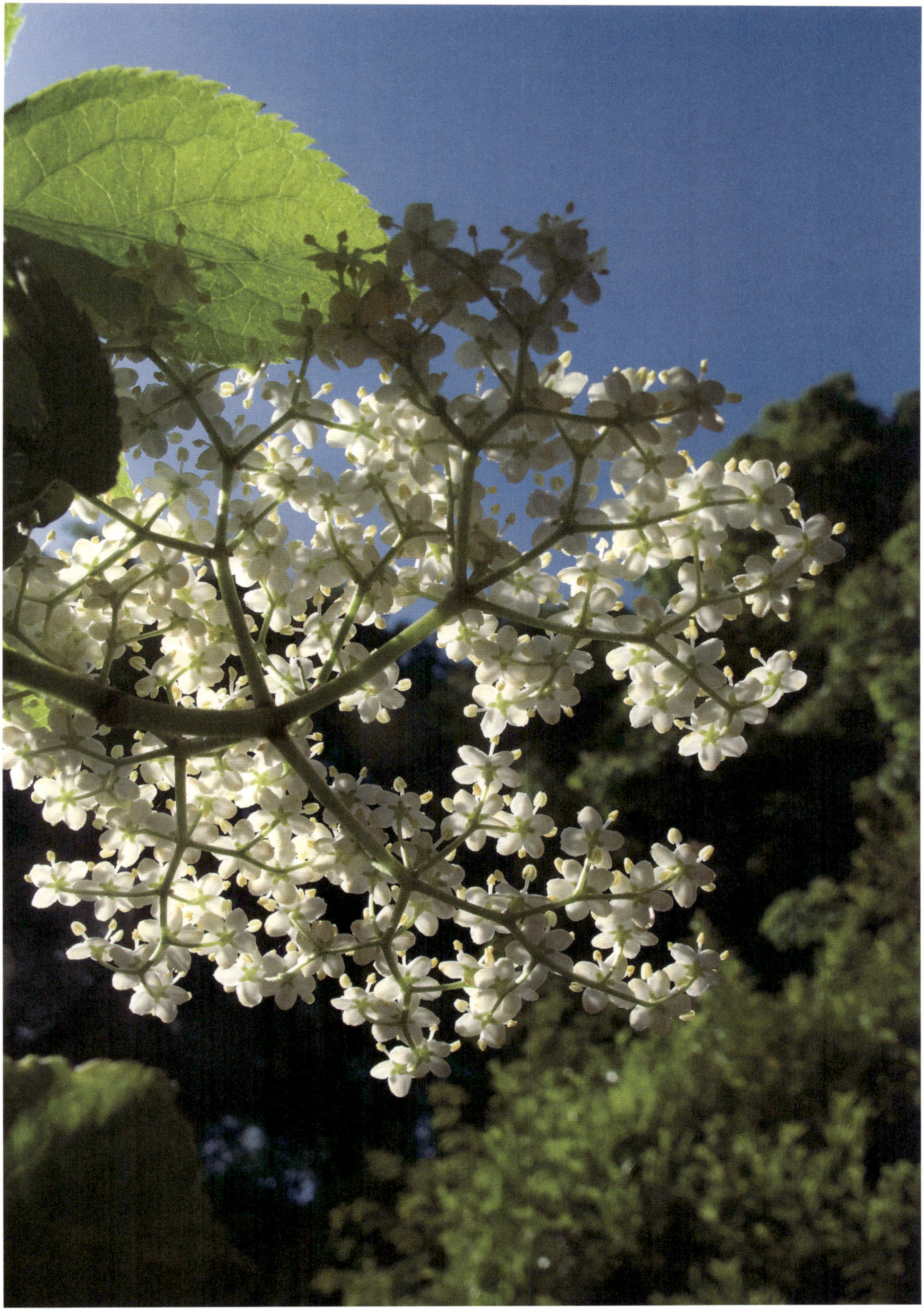

Elderflower cake

6 eggs
170g caster sugar
1 teaspoon vanilla extract
170g plain flour, sifted twice
75g unsalted butter, melted
4 large heads of fresh elderflower, flowers removed from the stalks, plus a few flowers to decorate

For the buttercream
60g granulated sugar
4 tablespoons water
2 egg yolks
170g unsalted butter, softened
3 tablespoons Elderflower Cordial (see page 132)

For the icing
200g icing sugar
2 tablespoons Elderflower Cordial
about 1 tablespoon lemon juice

This is a basic génoise sponge, or French butter sponge cake, scented with fragrant elderflower. The cake is light and delicate. It is not difficult to make, providing you follow the instructions carefully. For the best results, use an electric whisk, which will introduce the air and volume the cake needs to help it rise without the aid of baking powder. You can also use the sponge mixture to make a fantastic Swiss roll.

Heat the oven to 180°C/Gas Mark 4. Grease 2 deep 20cm cake tins and line the bases with a circle of baking parchment.

Break the eggs into a large mixing bowl and add the sugar. Whisk with an electric hand mixer (or a balloon whisk and plenty of elbow grease) until the mixture is pale and mousselike; it should be thick enough to leave a ribbon trail on the surface when the whisk is lifted. Add the vanilla extract. Carefully fold in about half of the sifted flour with a large metal spoon. Pour the cool melted butter over the surface and fold it in, immediately followed by the remaining flour. Finally fold in the elderflowers. It's important to do all this as quickly and lightly as possible, so you don't lose too much air.

Divide the mixture between the prepared cake tins and bake for 25–30 minutes, until the cakes are golden and beginning to shrink from the sides of the tins. Leave in the tins for 5 minutes, then turn out on to wire racks to cool.

Meanwhile, make the buttercream. Put the sugar and water in a heavy-based pan and heat gently until the sugar has dissolved. Turn up the heat and bring to the boil. Continue to boil until the syrup reaches the thread stage (115°C on a sugar thermometer). Gradually trickle the warm sugar syrup on to the egg yolks in a bowl, whisking with an electric hand whisk until thick and mousselike. Cream the butter until very soft and fluffy. Then gradually beat it into the egg mixture a little at a time. Finally beat in the elderflower cordial. Sandwich the cakes together with the buttercream.

To make the icing, sift the icing sugar into a small bowl and stir in the elderflower cordial and enough lemon juice to make a fairly thick but spreadable icing. Spread it over the top of the cake, letting it run down the sides a little. Decorate with a few elderflower petals.

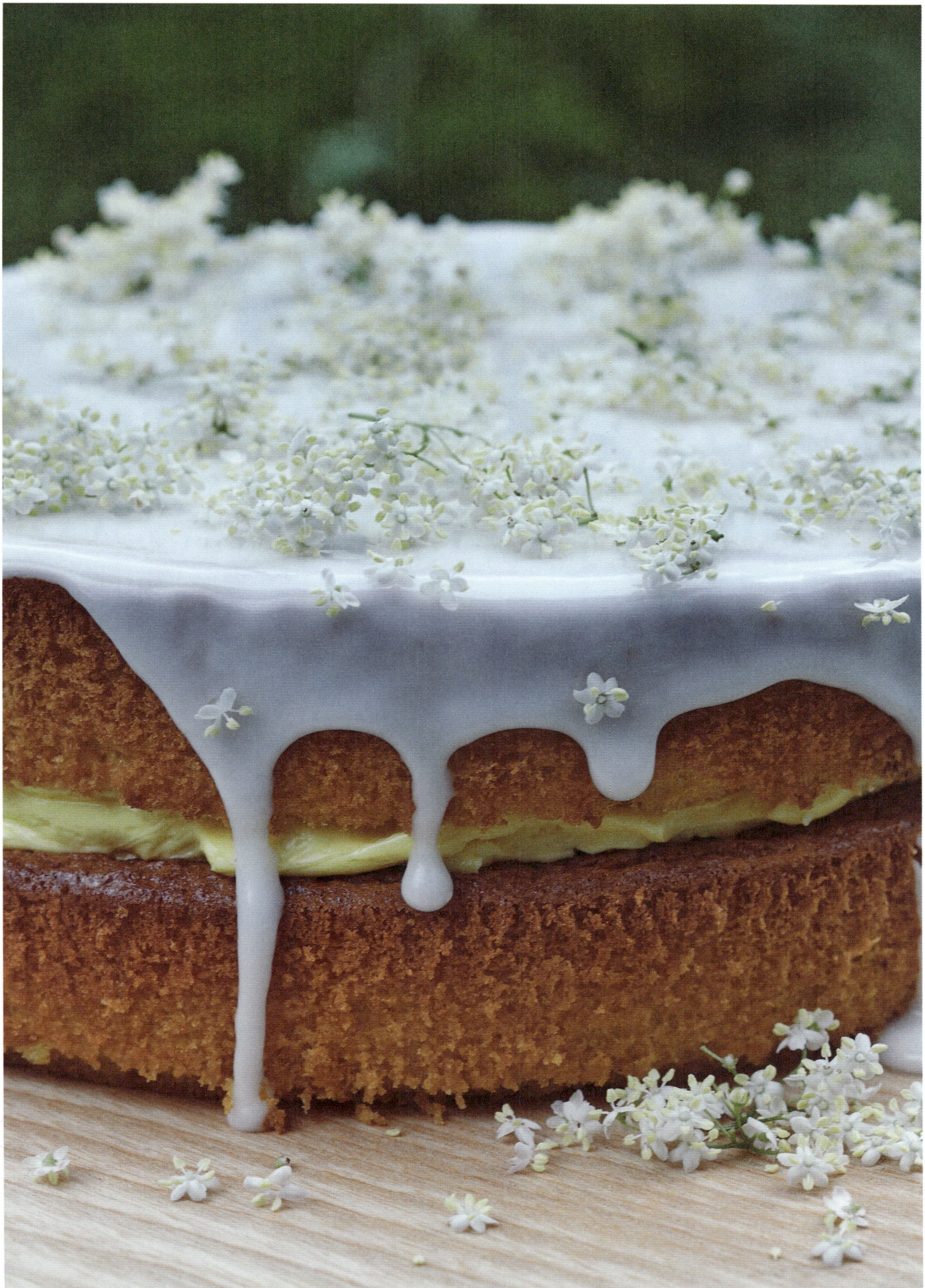

AIR
Summer

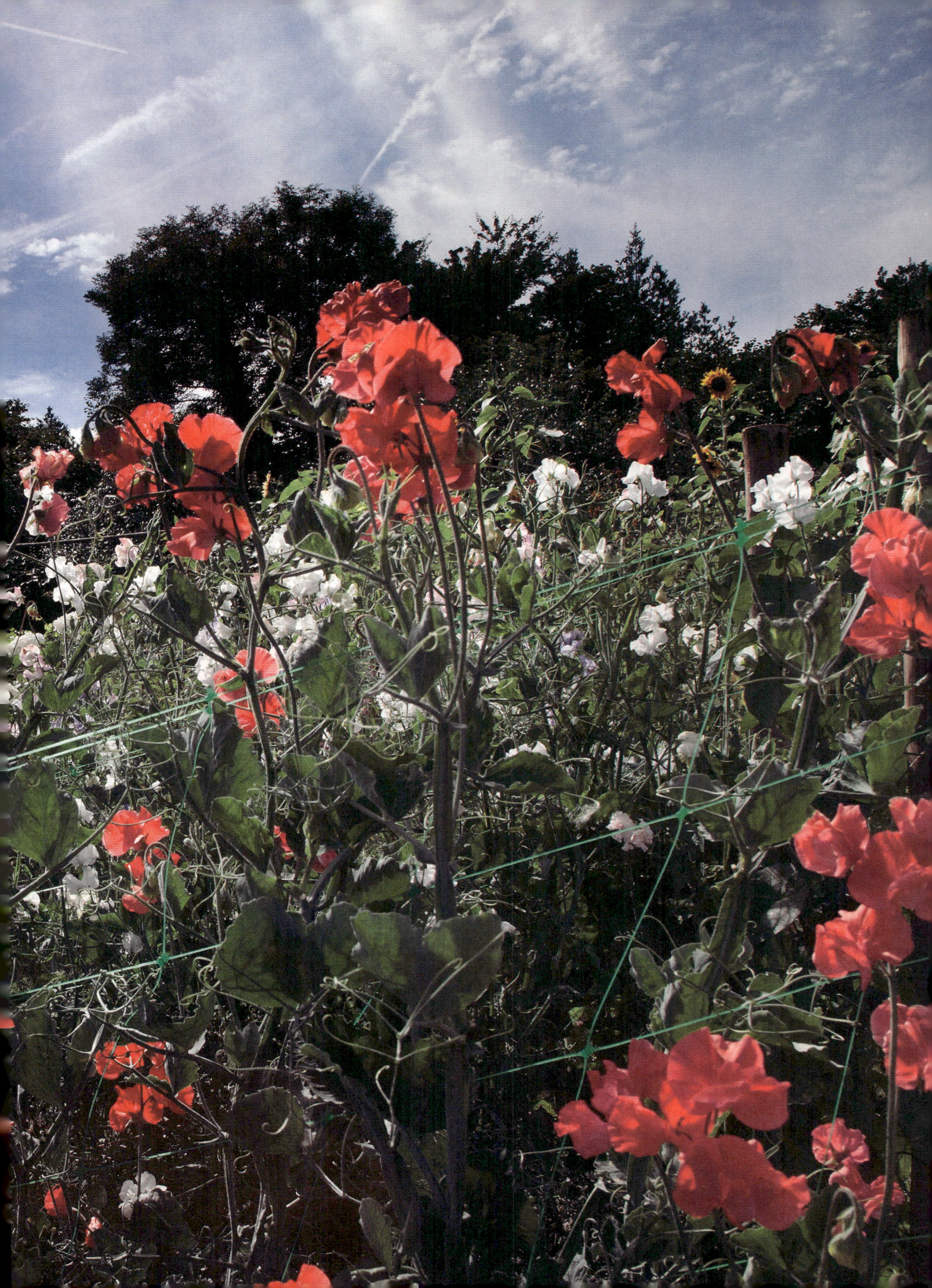

EACH MORNING AT this time of year we wake to the sound of the cockerels competing with each other for the greatest crow. The noise in the confined space of the chicken house must be deafening. The wild birds are all up bright and early, welcoming the day with song, then off to find breakfast for their young. It's lovely to lie in bed and listen as the light arrives, gathering thoughts for the day's work ahead.

In the summer months things are really getting in the swing. The quantity and variety of crops to care for and harvest multiply from the end of May, with the early spring sowings now ready to sell and eat. The newness is met with great enthusiasm from our customers. Everyone wants to eat salads and greens, to feel light and summery. The propagating greenhouse fills and empties with an ever-increasing array of young vegetable and flower seedlings, successively taking their places out in the generous, fertile soil.

In June the first of the soft fruits are ready – bushes laden with green gooseberries, a reminder to be vigilant and net the redcurrants and any other reddening, sparkling jewels against the keen-eyed birds. We find ourselves checking the strawberry beds daily for the first ripe fruits: a sweet assurance that summer has truly arrived. Soon, more and more treasures colour up in the sunshine, and the picking and jam-making begin in earnest. White currants hang in chandelier clusters. Blackcurrants are bursting with juice, packed full of flavour for jellies and pies. In mid-July we reach the soft-fruit climax with the arrival of raspberries, tayberries, loganberries and jostaberries. On the drive to London, the heady fragrance of the just-picked punnets of fruit makes for heavenly company.

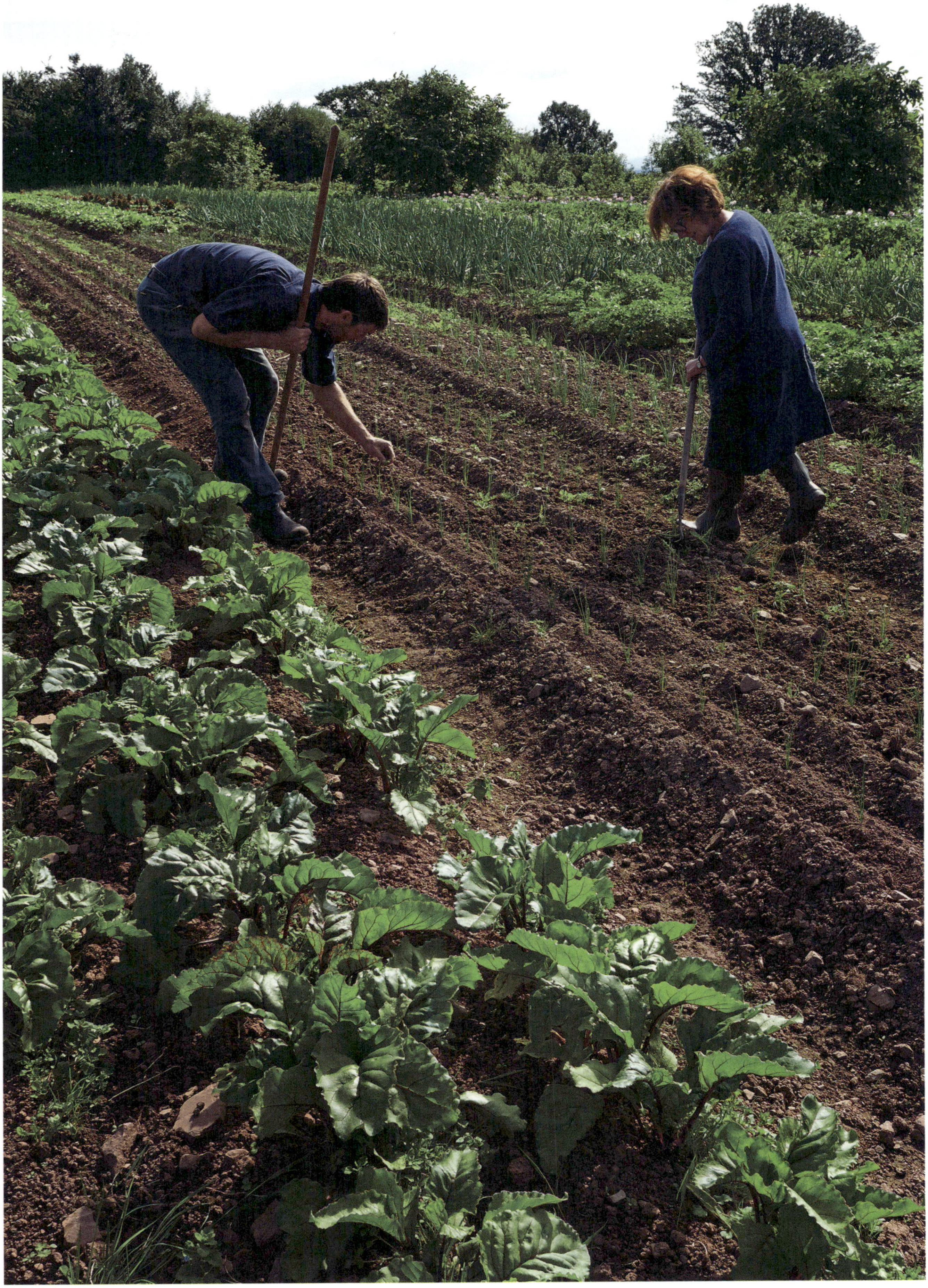

There is a deepening concentration of colour in both berries and flowers – and this is accompanied by a progression of more complex and elaborate arrangements in form. The flowers chime louder and ever bolder in their joyous performance.

We dash about like clucky hens, trying to keep up with all the jobs that need to be done. Sowing, planting, irrigating, cultivating. Encouraging what is wanted, removing what is not. The number of crops to look after and their rate of growth are always on the increase, and we have to move with the times. Everything expands under the summer sun, in the constant interplay of the elements. The bees are ceaseless in their activity, back and forth, gathering nectar and pollen from the furthest reaches of the farm and returning to the hive, filling their majestic comb with liquid sunshine.

The sheep are hardly recognisable once relieved of their thick woollen coats. They seem to relish their top-to-toe makeover and take to the rich pastures and meadows with renewed vigour. The lambs are growing up strong, fed on a diet of grass and mother's milk. The calm, wise cows, with their dreamy inward gaze, harmoniously chew the cud. The geese are growing in size and confidence, becoming more raucous each day, bossing around the ducks and bullying the chickens, especially so at meal times.

We watch the skies and check the forecast many times each day to see what's coming our way. The weather becomes obsessive viewing. Its co-operation can make all the difference to a successful season. High pressure up in the atmosphere means high pressure for us down on the farm: we have to water plants early in the morning or late at night, to ensure as little moisture as possible is wasted through evaporation in the parched days. At hay-making time in July and August, a heat wave is welcome. When there is the promise of a dry week we cut, turn, bale and bring in the sweet ripe grasses that will nourish the cattle and sheep through the winter.

The extremes of weather can test and stretch our patience and skills. There have been years with unseasonal amounts of summer rainfall. This hinders our progress and stops us from cultivating and tending to the plants at the time when it is most important. But wait we must, and of course in time the weather does change and everything continues and generally works out just fine.

The summer days are long. The farm is looking at her best, groaning with abundance and richness of colour. Our weekly farm walk on a Sunday helps us to organise the forthcoming week; it is always a delight to slow down, lift our heads and observe what is around us, admiring the plants in their tidy rows, pert and healthy. The thrill of it all!

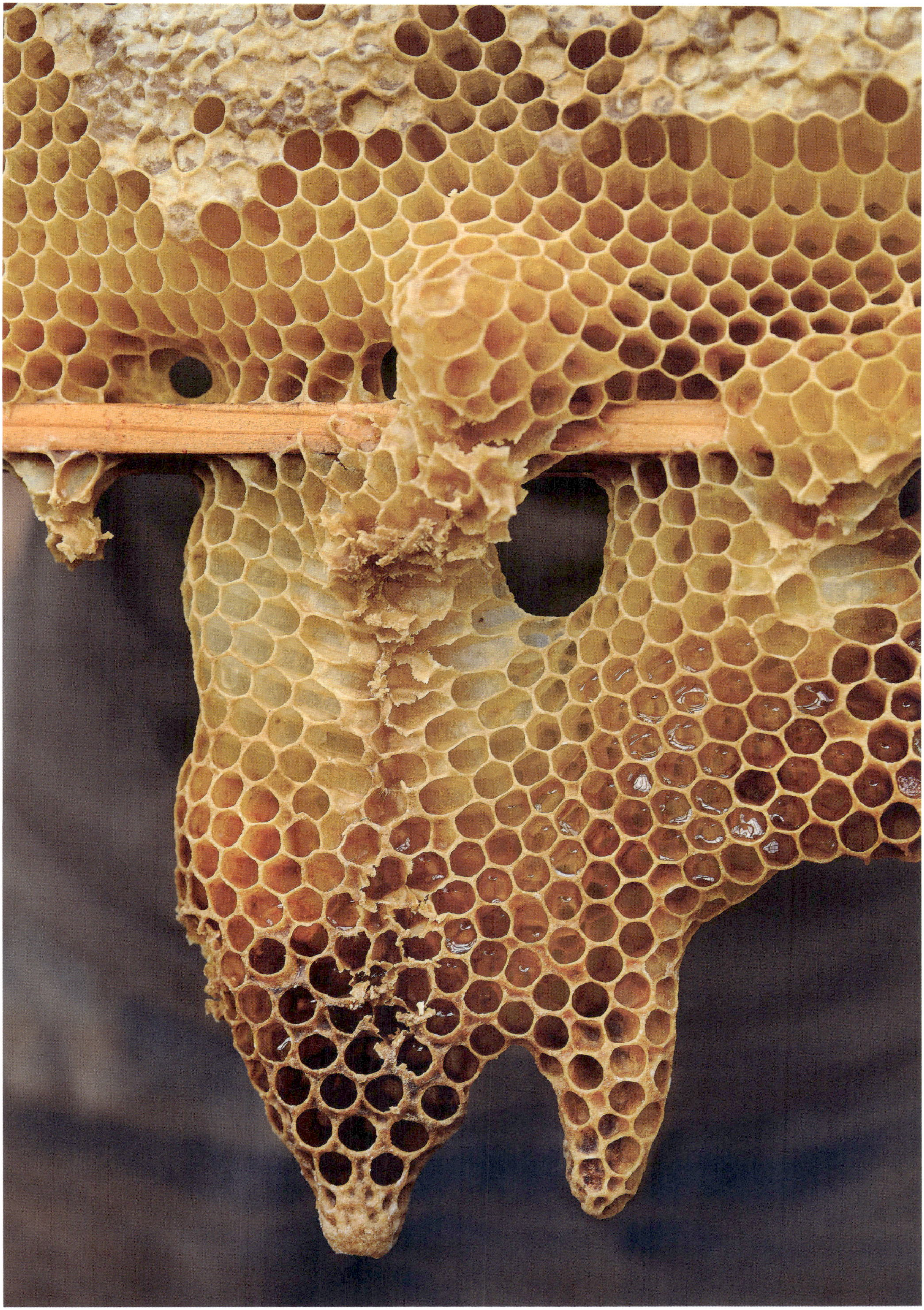

Broad bean hummus

SERVES 3–4

about 1.5kg broad beans in their pods (you will need 400g shelled beans)

4 garlic cloves, peeled

a sprig or two of summer savory

½ teaspoon paprika, plus extra to serve

juice and grated zest of 1 large lemon

olive oil

sea salt

This is a very simple dish to prepare. You can use the first tiny, sweeter-than-sweet, no-need-to-peel broad beans if you have them, but it is more economical to use the large, mealy, later-season ones. They will give the hummus a texture more like traditional chickpea hummus. Use in sandwiches, with flatbreads, as a dip for crisps and crudités or as a topping for burgers.

Summer savory is a strong, aromatic herb that tastes very good with beans of all kinds. It can be hard to find in shops so, if you don't grow it, use another pungent herb such as oregano or marjoram instead.

Shell the broad beans, collecting the smaller, less developed ones in a separate bowl. Have a large pot of salted boiling water ready. Plunge the smaller beans into the water and cook for about a minute, until tender; you will need to taste one to check. As soon as the beans are cooked, scoop them out of the pan with a slotted spoon and immediately refresh them under cold running water. Peel off the skins to reveal the bright green beans inside. This may seem a bit of a faff, but if you are using late-season beans it is essential. Cook the remaining, larger beans until they are very tender. Refresh them in cold water, drain and remove the skins.

Put all the beans into a food processor with the garlic, summer savory, paprika, a pinch of salt, about half the lemon juice and 3 tablespoons of olive oil. Blend, adding more olive oil and lemon juice to give the consistency and taste you prefer.

Transfer to a bowl and add a generous topping of olive oil, so there is a nice moat of oil on the plate when you serve it, plus a sprinkling of paprika and the lemon zest.

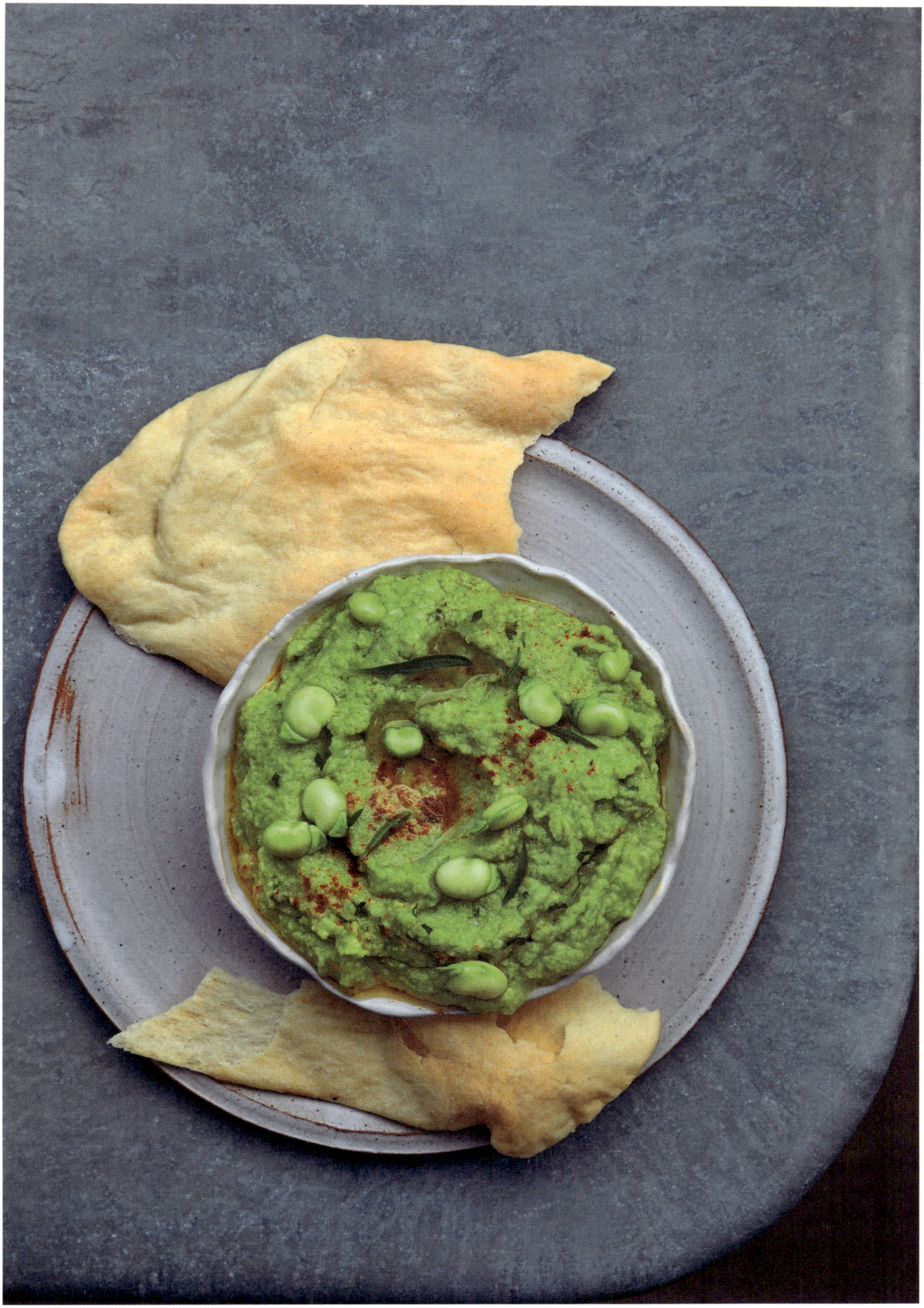

Tomatoes on toast with herbed goat's cheese – a summer brunch

SERVES 2

4 dessertspoons good olive oil

4–6 medium tomatoes, or 2 large ones if using a variety such as Marmande, roughly chopped

6 sprigs of lemon thyme (regular thyme will do if you have no lemon thyme)

200g soft, fresh goat's cheese or goat's curd

2–3 tablespoons chopped mixed herbs – we use plenty of parsley, plus basil, thyme, chives and their flowers, a small leaf of lovage and 2 tarragon leaves

a little lemon zest

2 medium-thick slices of bread (sourdough is particularly good)

sea salt and black pepper

This is a favourite of ours on a summer Sunday after our work is done for the morning and we have taken our work-planning walk around the farm. A few slices of good Parma ham or salami add greatly to the meal. Usually we buy goat's curd ready strained, but occasionally we make it ourselves and hang it in muslin to separate the curds from the whey.

The type of tomato is important here. You need a so-called heirloom variety – the kind we grow or you might find for sale by the roadside in France or Italy. Farmers' markets are a good source here in the UK. Our favourite for this dish is Olirose, a beautiful thin-skinned, plum-shaped, pinkish-red variety that is full of juice and flavour. Marmande, a beefsteak type, is also very good. The most important thing is to select a tomato that is not too red. Choose a tomato that is not over-ripe as the slight acidity goes well with the creaminess of the cheese. Don't be tempted to add any onions, as this makes the dish taste like a pasta sauce … not what you want at 11 o'clock on a summer's morning.

Warm the oil in a heavy-based frying pan over a low heat. Add the tomatoes and the lemon thyme, then raise the heat slightly. As the tomatoes start to cook, stir well, coating them with the olive oil and squashing them with the back of the spoon to release the juices. Turn down the heat, allow the tomatoes to bubble for a few minutes, then season with salt and pepper. Meanwhile, put the goat's cheese or curd in a bowl, add the herbs and lemon zest and mix well.

Toast the bread, then spread the cheese over it generously and spoon over the tomatoes.

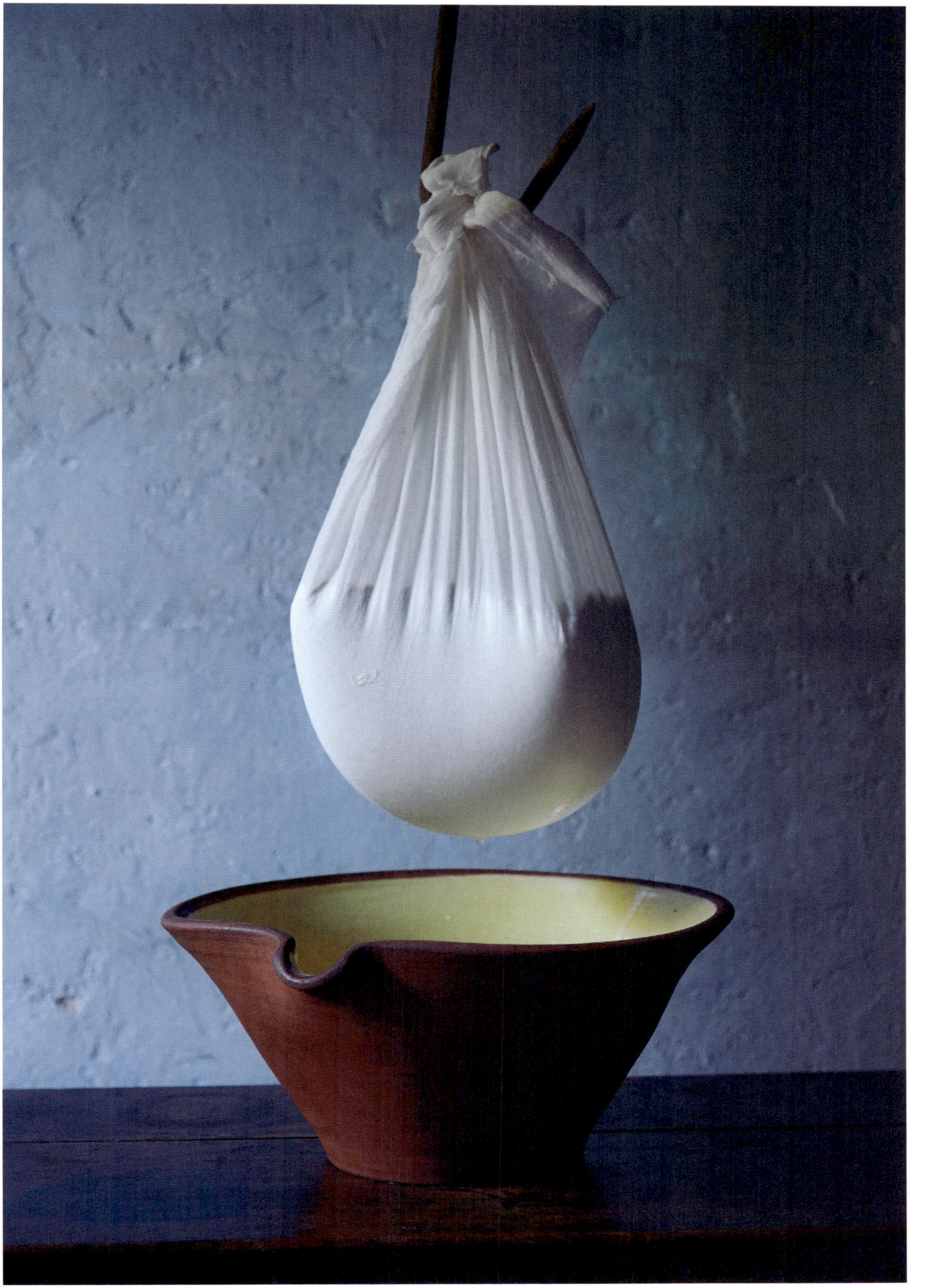

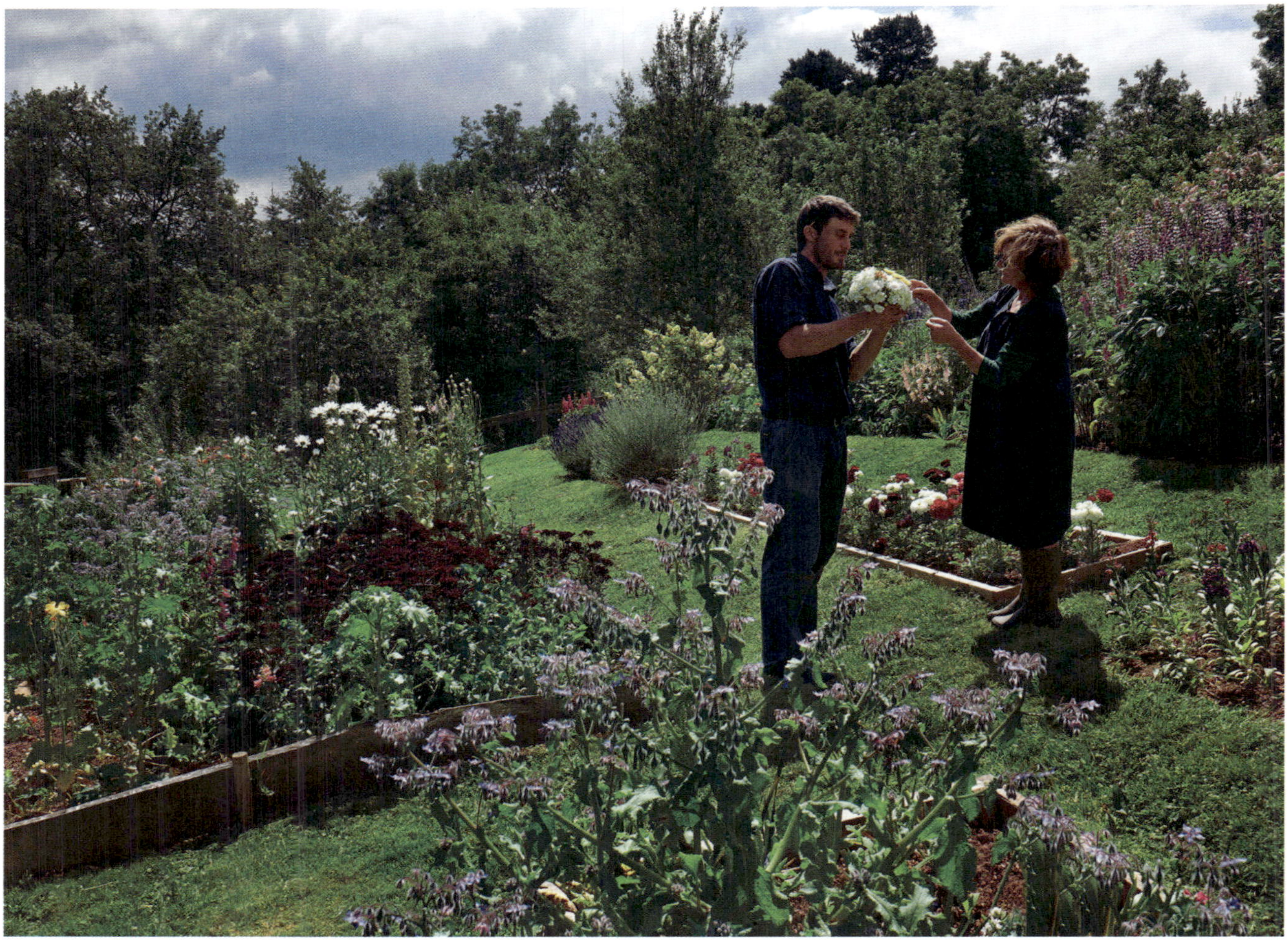

Fresh pea and mint soup

SERVES 4–6

about 2kg peas in their pods (you will need 500g shelled peas)

175g butter

150g spring onions (or white onion), chopped

1 garlic clove, chopped

1 small butterhead lettuce heart

1.25 litres water

a little single cream, to garnish

chopped chives or mint, to garnish

sea salt and black pepper

Very fresh peas need no cooking at all and are delicious eaten raw in salads. Grow your own if you can, or buy them from a farmers' market where you know that they will be as fresh as can be. Always keep some of the pods, which have a fabulously strong, sweet-pea flavour and make the very best of vegetable stocks. If you don't have time to make stock, you can always freeze the pods to use another day.

This soup is a genuine treat, perhaps to be eaten in celebration of summer having truly arrived. Don't be alarmed by the amount of butter it contains. It's essential for a creamy flavour and texture.

Shell the peas, reserving 8 large, bright green pods. Heat the butter in a large pan, add the spring onions and garlic, then cover and sweat very gently for about 15 minutes, until soft. Tear up the lettuce leaves and add them to the pan with the reserved pea pods. Stir until the lettuce has wilted and is coated in the butter. Season with salt and pepper, then add the peas and water and bring to the boil. Simmer for about 5 minutes, until the peas are tender; be careful not to overcook them or the colour will not be as bright.

Pass the soup through a mouli-légumes or blitz in a food processor, then pass through a sieve to remove any stringy threads from the pods. Reheat gently, until hot but not boiling, and adjust the seasoning if necessary. Serve with a swirl of single cream and a generous garnish of chopped chives or mint.

Broad beans in parsley sauce on fried bread

SERVES 2

1kg broad beans in their pods, shelled
4 slices of thickly cut bread
4 dessertspoons olive oil
coarse sea salt
25g butter
25g plain flour
300ml milk
2 tablespoons chopped parsley
lemon juice
sea salt and black pepper

There is nothing quite like the first freshly picked broad bean of the year. An old friend returning for a short visit, it should be enjoyed during its stay as much as possible. Here, broad beans make a simple lunch or supper dish. You may leave on the skins if you wish, but skinning them does turn this 'beans on toast' into a more elegant affair. Without the toast, this dish makes a very good accompaniment to roast lamb.

Heat the oven to 200°C/Gas Mark 6. Cook the beans in a large pan of boiling salted water for 2 minutes, then drain and remove the skins.

Place the bread on a baking sheet, trickle the olive oil evenly over the slices and sprinkle some coarse sea salt on top. Bake for 10–15 minutes, until the bread is golden and has absorbed all the oil.

Meanwhile, melt the butter in a small pan over a low heat, add the flour and cook, stirring, for a minute or two. Gradually stir in the milk, then raise the heat and bring to a simmer to make a thick, smooth sauce. Continue to cook over a low heat for 3–4 minutes. Stir in the chopped parsley. Mix the broad beans into the sauce and add a squeeze of lemon juice to taste, plus some salt and pepper.

Spoon the broad bean sauce on to the crisp bread slices. Return to the oven for 5 minutes or so, then serve piping hot.

Lemon and courgette flower risotto

SERVES 4

1 litre chicken or vegetable stock

50g butter, plus a knob of butter to finish

1 onion, finely chopped

1 celery stick, finely chopped

2 garlic cloves, crushed

2 teaspoons chopped lemon thyme (or ordinary thyme)

300g arborio rice

250ml white wine

juice and grated zest of ½ lemon

8 courgette flowers, finely shredded

100g Parmesan cheese, freshly grated

sea salt and black pepper

At its best, risotto is a simple, versatile and delicious dish. Never hurry a risotto – the rice needs constant gentle stirring. Often we try to multi-task when cooking supper, but it's better to think of risotto as a meditation. Relax and give it 20 minutes or so of your undivided attention, then you will be rewarded with a perfect plump, creamy, glossy dish.

Courgette flowers are tricky to find in shops, as they wilt very quickly after picking. Ideally they should come straight out of the garden. The flavour of the flowers is not dissimilar to saffron, but with a little heat. This dish is a good way to use up the male flowers – the ones on stalks that don't bear the fruit.

Heat the stock in a saucepan and keep it at a gentle simmer. Melt the butter in a wide, heavy-based pan, add the onion, celery, garlic and thyme, then cover and sweat for about 5 minutes, until the onion is soft and translucent. Add the rice and stir until it is luxuriously coated with the butter. Turn up the heat a little, pour in the wine and stir until the rice has absorbed all the liquid. Season generously with salt and pepper. Add the hot stock a ladleful at a time, stirring the rice constantly with a wooden spoon and waiting until the stock has been fully absorbed before adding more. When you have added all the stock, the risotto should be rich and creamy and not at all watery in appearance. Taste the rice; the grains should be soft on the outside and have a gentle, not hard, bite in the centre.

Stir in the lemon juice and zest. If the risotto is a little too thick and stodgy, add a few tablespoons of freshly boiled water. Gently stir in the shredded courgette flowers and half of the grated Parmesan, along with a knob of butter. Serve immediately and sprinkle the rest of the Parmesan on top.

Courgettes in saffron and basil butter

SERVES 2

4 courgettes (preferably with flowers attached)
50g butter
1 tablespoon olive oil
a pinch of saffron strands
2 tablespoons water
a handful of basil leaves
juice of ½ lemon
sea salt and black pepper

Try to choose very fresh courgettes to avoid the metallic flavour that can develop when they are stored. If you can find them, courgettes with their flowers still attached are great for this recipe. Finely shred the flowers and add them at the same time as the basil, allowing them to wilt just a little. Serve with rice.

Slice the courgettes lengthways into manageable strips about 8mm thick. Heat the butter and olive oil in a large, heavy-based frying pan. Once the butter begins to bubble and foam, lay the courgette strips in the pan and cook over a medium heat for a few minutes until they start to brown. Turn them over, season and continue to cook for a minute. Add the saffron and water and cook for a couple of minutes longer, until the butter has taken on the golden colour of the saffron. Tear in the basil leaves, pour the lemon juice over the top and serve immediately.

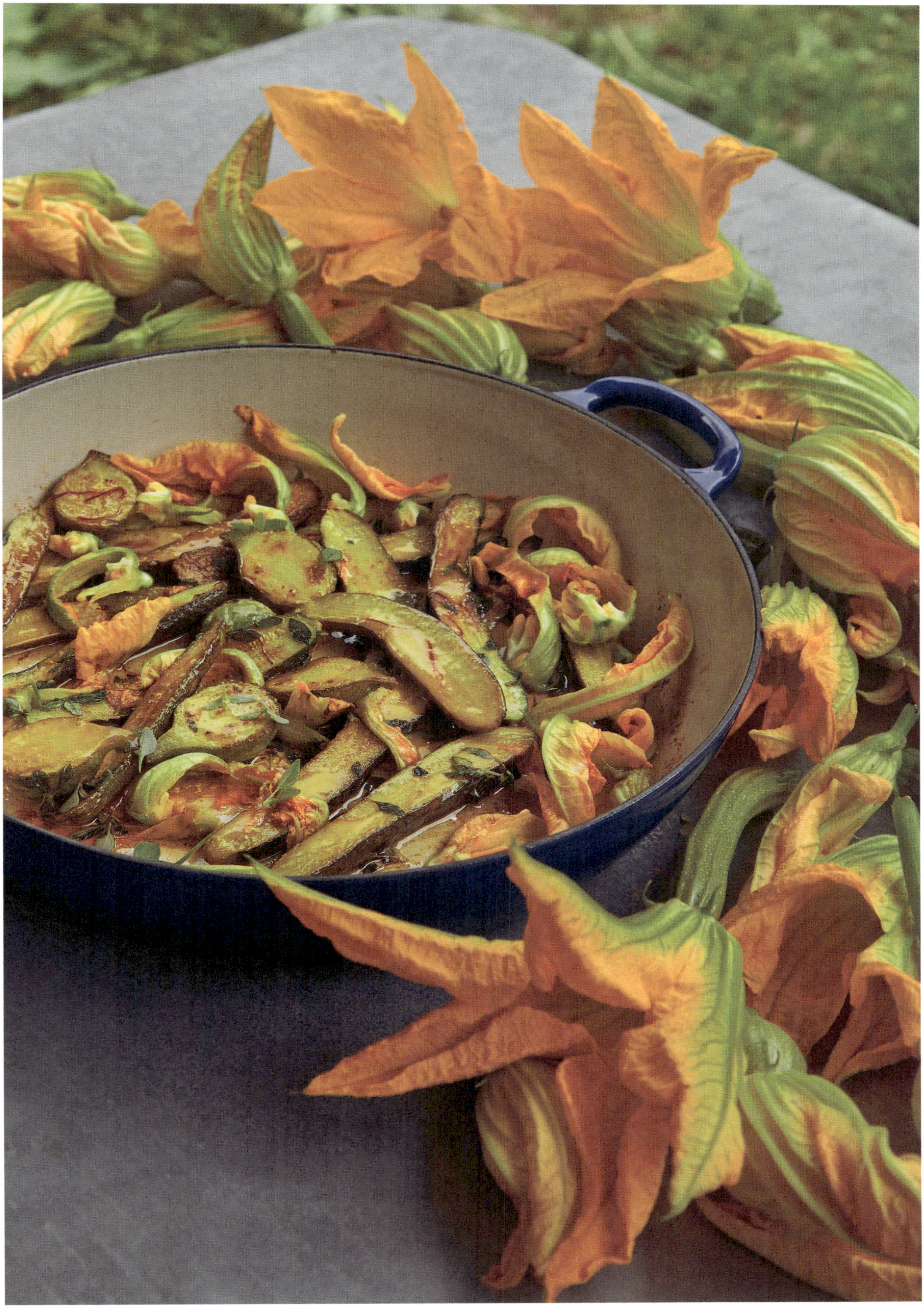

Edible flowers

THERE IS SOMETHING luxurious and intimate about eating a flower, tuning into a plant's life cycle at its most seductive moment. We grow and eat flowers all year round. It started for us one year in the late winter, during an unseasonably warm spell in early March. Our over-wintering cabbages and kales had begun to run to seed with the warm weather, the tall yellow flowers pushing their way through the tops of the cabbages. They looked beautiful and alien, and we were drawn to them. Having tasted their buds full of sweet nectar with tender, soft stems, we decided they were every bit as delicious as the parent plant. So we started selling the flowering tops, with much success, and have done so ever since.

The use of flowers in recipes dates back thousands of years. Dandelions are believed to be one of the bitter herbs mentioned in the Old Testament, and the Romans added mallow, rose and borage to many of their dishes. The Victorians used flowers to decorate their salads and make fragrant flower waters; they also candied violets and roses to adorn cakes and puddings, and gave them as gifts to impress friends and lovers.

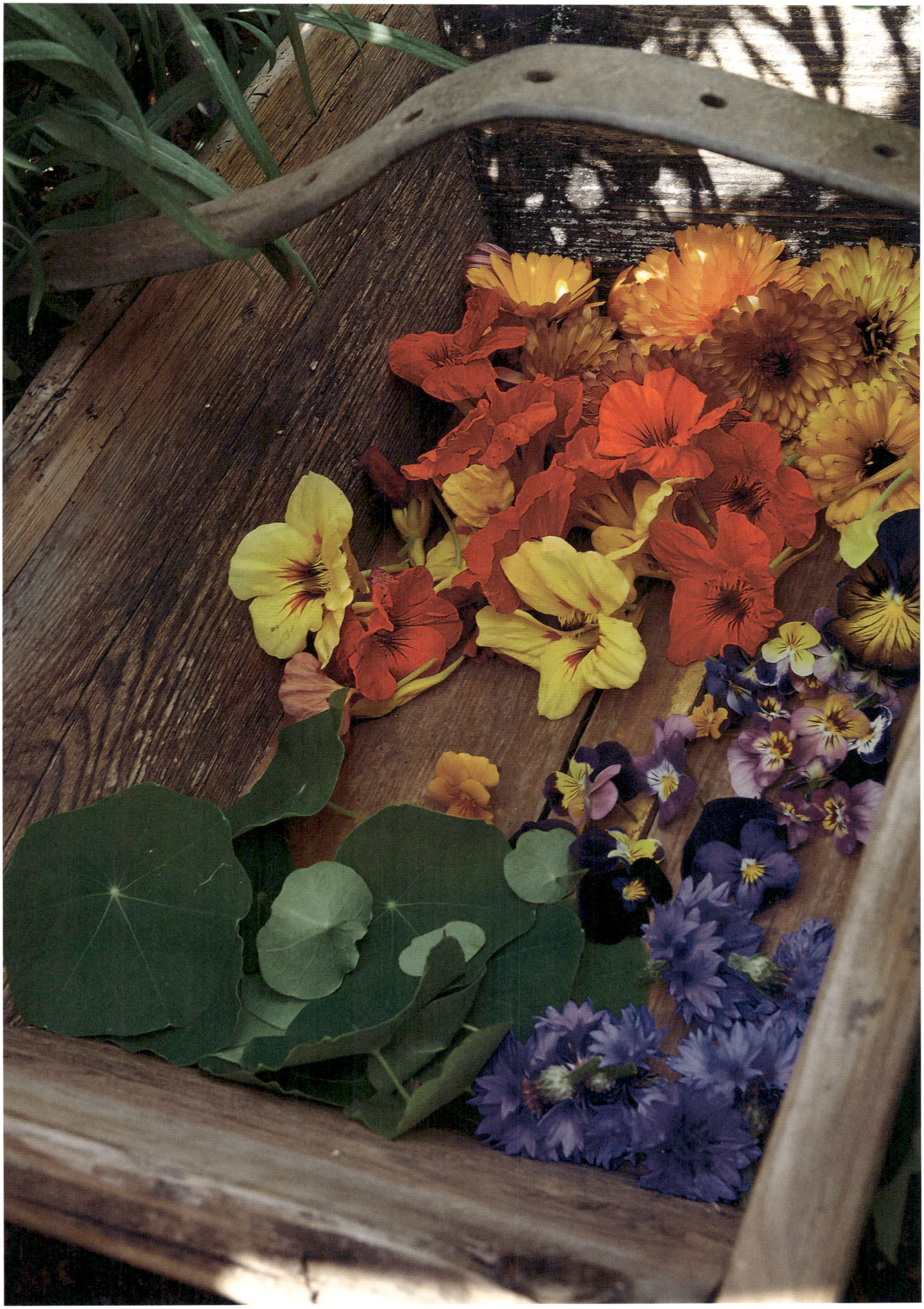

You could look deeply into the use of flowers for health and medicinal purposes, but for us they are first and foremost a bit of fun and make us feel happy. Mostly we grow edible flowers to enhance our salad mixes – they certainly add great eye appeal, and people find them hard to resist.

Pick your flowers on a dry day if possible, once the petals have opened. Flowers are very delicate and need careful handling. Pinch out the blooms with your thumb and forefinger, holding them at the base and trying not to touch the flower face. Place them carefully in a single layer on a tray. Once back in the kitchen you can use a pair of scissors to snip off any of the green that you don't want.

While all edible flowers will look pretty, we try to make sure that they taste good, too. Here are a few examples of the flowers that we cultivate throughout the seasons. All are really easy to grow and look amazing both in your garden and on your plate. Many prefer shade and not too rich a soil, so are ideal for the urban grower. Even if you only have a window box, you can get the best of both worlds: the beauty and form of the plants to enjoy and fresh-picked flowers to adorn your meal.

Nasturtium

Probably the tastiest of all: a delicious, spicy-hot flower that is a welcome addition of colour and interest to a green salad. The wonderful, evocative floral trumpets come in many shades of sunshine, red, peachy pink, and yellow with orange freckles – just gorgeous. You can pickle the fat green seedpods that appear in late summer and use them as an alternative to capers, while the lily-pad leaves can be served as a salad on their own, or with the flowers, or as part of a mixed salad.

Sow nasturtium seeds in spring. These annual plants tend to sprawl, so three or four sown in April will supply lots of flowers from late June or early July right through to the first frosts of autumn. They can also maintain themselves for several years through self-seeding. Nasturtiums prefer full sun and a light, well-drained soil. They grow well in containers, on a trellis against a wall if space is tight, or even in a hanging basket. Keep well watered in hot weather. If caterpillars or black fly appear, remove the creatures and infested leaves as you see them; the plant should recover if you are attentive.

Pick the flowers throughout the summer for immediate use. The more you pick, the more your plants will produce. It is always best to add the flowers after you have dressed your salad, as the dressing can weigh down the delicate petals and damage them.

Lavender

This beautiful and highly scented flower can be used in many puddings, jellies, ice creams, biscuits and cakes. Adding it to flavour shortbread is particularly delightful. Lavender has a high essential oil content and the taste is strong, so be sparing. Leave a few heads of lavender to sit in a sealed container full of sugar, as you would a vanilla pod, and you will have a scented sugar for baking or sprinkling on fruit.

An evergreen perennial shrub, lavender grows best in an open, sunny position. The plants become woody and leggy with age, but you can prune them back immediately after flowering or in the spring to maintain vigour. It's best to pick the flowers when they first open, before the seeds form.

Sweet violet

The small, multicoloured flowers of sweet violet, or violas, are wonderful for decorating cakes and puddings as they are so intricate and dainty, with pretty, monkey-like faces. These flowers are among the only edible flowers available in winter and early spring. Their fresh flavour is good in salads, and they add a stunning, easy decoration to fruit salads and desserts. Sweet violets thrive in rich soil in a semi-shaded spot. They do well in containers, but need to be placed in a cool position throughout the summer.

Pansy

Pansy flowers come in a huge range of colours. Many varieties bloom throughout the winter, although the flowers may not be quite so prolific in the colder months. The darker shades of purple and red petals have a rich, velvety colour and texture (see the Summer Fruit Trifle on page 186). Use pansy flowers in the same way as sweet violets.

Pot marigold

The orange or yellow flowers of pot marigolds are strongly flavoured: use only the petals. Marigolds can make a good substitute for saffron, adding that wonderful glow to rice and eggs. The petals can also be dried and stored for use in winter.

Sow seeds in spring, after the last frost. The plants are not too fussy about soil quality, but do prefer a sunny spot. Marigolds are wonderful self-seeders, so if you leave a few to go to seed it is likely they will reappear the following year. Keep picking the flowers regularly to encourage a continuous supply.

Chives

The purple pompom flowers of this perennial herb have a distinct, oniony flavour but it is not overpowering. Scatter chive flowers on to a potato salad or mix into a herb butter, where they look beautiful with the green of other herbs (see page 96). We have also cooked with chive flowers, adding them to the filling in a cheese and onion tart. They change to a darker, almost red hue once cooked, adding a splash of colour to what can otherwise be a rather pale-looking dish.

You can propagate chives either from seeds or by splitting clumps in the autumn. Best grown in rich, well-drained soil in full sun, chives must be kept well watered. They also perform well in pots, so are another good plant for a small garden or window box. Harvest the flowers as they are just opening.

Borage

An annual herb with star-shaped flowers that are the most delectable shade of bright blue and have a mild flavour of cucumber. The flowers are excellent tossed in a salad, as a garnish for a summer soup, or floated on cordials and cocktails, such as Pimm's (also see the Rhubarb Cordial on page 130). If you have time and want to impress, try freezing the flower heads in ice cubes. A few borage flowers added to lemonade will turn pink with the acidity of the lemon juice – a trick for a child's party, perhaps. You can also crystallise them for cake decorations (for the method, see Rose Angel Cake with Crystallised Rose Petals, page 192).

Sow borage seeds in the spring. When you harvest the flowers, remove the prickly part at the base. Borage is another prolific self-seeder. Bees love these plants and they are beneficial for the pollination of other species.

Cornflower

The cornflower is a tall, slender plant. Its rich shades of blue, crimson and sometimes white are eye-catching and generous. The petals of blue cornflowers look beautiful with a green lettuce salad or sprinkled on top of broad beans or peas: a good trick to encourage young children to eat their greens!

This hardy annual likes a sunny spot, growing in most well-drained soil types. The plants will need some support or they can appear untidy, but can be grown up against a wall. Deadheading helps to prolong the flowering season, as does autumn sowing: an option that will produce larger and earlier-flowering plants the following summer.

Rose

The rose with its archetypal charm has inspired poets and artists for centuries as a symbol of love and beauty. A scented rose petal can taste as good as it smells: fragrant and perfumed. Probably our favourite flower for decorating cakes, you can use rose petals fresh, or else crystallise them (for the method, see Rose Angel Cake with Crystallised Rose Petals, page 192) and store in an air-tight jar for winter. Place some petals in a jar of sugar for a flavoured sweetener to sprinkle on fruit, or make whitecurrant jellies with rose petals set into them.

Rocket, kale and cabbage flowers

At the end of their growing season, most leafy vegetables will flower and run to seed. Rocket tends to bolt in warm summer weather and at this stage the leaves become tough and overly peppery. Pinch out about 6cm at the tip of the flowering stem and add to a salad or sandwich.

In late winter and early spring the over-wintered kale and cabbage tops and flowers are very tasty. Pinch out an 8cm tip and wilt in a little olive oil or butter to make a welcome vegetable dish at a time when fresh seasonal produce is scarce.

Courgette and squash flowers

Although regarded as vegetables, the courgette and its cousin the squash are in fact fruit. These plants produce generous supplies of large, bell-shaped, golden flowers. These can be stuffed with ricotta cheese and herbs, then shallow fried. Alternatively, shred a few flowers into a risotto for colour and to add a delicious, saffron-like flavour (see Lemon and Courgette Flower Risotto, page 149). The flowers must be garden fresh, as they quickly wilt.

Wild flowers

Some wild flower species, such as cowslips and primroses, are edible. They make a pretty decoration on an Easter cake or to eat in a spring salad. We recommend that you grow your own. Many species of wild plants are becoming scarcer from the constant strimming of hedges and verges, and the use of herbicides and pesticides. If you are gathering from the wild, choose a wooded, out-of-the-way spot, only take from an area with a proliferation of wild flowers, and don't take too many.

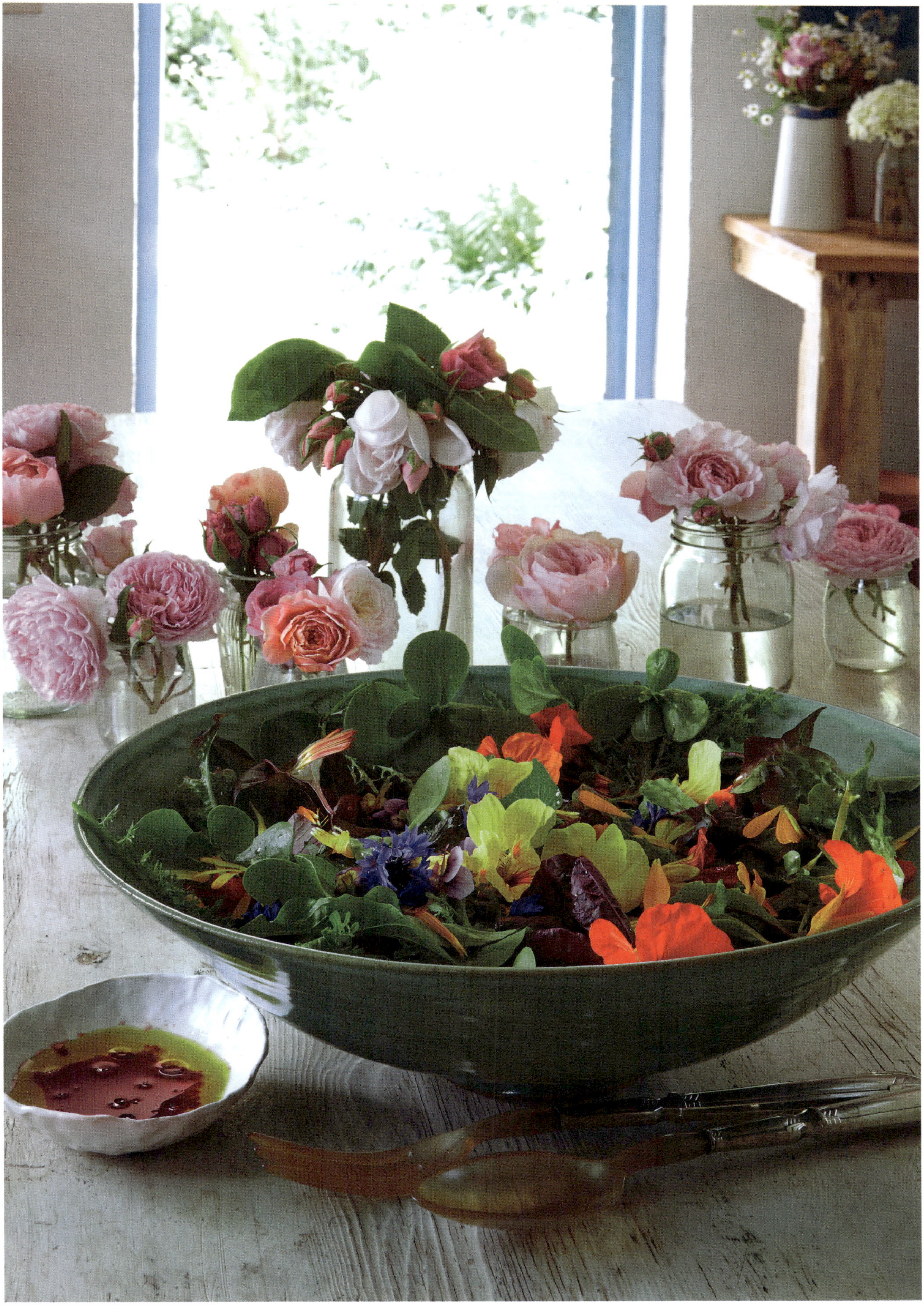

Pizza with summer vegetable toppings

MAKES 4

4 teaspoons dried yeast
6 tablespoons warm water
450g strong white flour
2 teaspoons sea salt
4 tablespoons olive oil
170ml cold water

For the tomato sauce
3 tablespoons olive oil
1 onion, finely chopped
3 garlic cloves, crushed
1 celery stick, roughly chopped
½ carrot, roughly chopped
750g tomatoes, roughly chopped
a bunch of thyme, chopped
sea salt and black pepper

For the blond sauce
2 balls of mozzarella cheese
4 dessertspoons cream

All good pizzas should have an authentic crisp crust. For this you need to roll out the dough thinly and cook the pizzas in a very hot oven – as hot as it will go. We nearly always use tomato as a base, though a blond sauce base makes a pleasant change and complements the more delicate, individual flavours of some of the vegetable toppings. We've given both options below. As far as the toppings go, pizza is a blank canvas and you are the artist. See the suggestions below to help inspire you.

The tomato sauce is best made with fresh cooking tomatoes – Italian plum varieties are ideal. Otherwise, use canned plum tomatoes. If you do find in-season plum tomatoes at a bargain price, it is worth making a big batch of the sauce and freezing it in bags, as it also comes in very handy as a pasta sauce.

Mix the yeast with the warm water until it has dissolved. Leave in a warm spot for 15 minutes.

Put the flour and salt into a mixing bowl and make a well in the centre. Pour in the oil and most of the cold water, then add the yeast liquid. Stir gently with a wooden spoon, drawing in the flour as you go, and adding enough of the remaining water to give a soft but not sticky dough. Turn out on to a lightly floured surface and knead for about 10 minutes, until smooth and elastic. Place the dough in a lightly oiled bowl, cover with cling film and leave in a warm, draught-free place for an hour or so, until doubled in size.

If you are making the tomato sauce, it is good to get it under way while the dough is rising. Heat the olive oil in a pan, add the onion, garlic, celery and carrot, then cover and sweat gently until soft but not coloured. Stir in the tomatoes and thyme and simmer for 45–60 minutes, until the sauce is thick. Season to taste and leave to cool. Purée in a food processor or blender to make a smooth, spreadable sauce.

Knock back down the dough with your knuckles and knead for 2–3 minutes. Divide it into 4, shape each piece into a ball and leave to rise, covered, on the floured work surface for a further hour. This is a good time to prepare the toppings and the blond pizza sauce, if you have chosen that. For the blond sauce, roughly chop the mozzarella and put it in a bowl with 4 dessertspoons of the liquid from the packet, the cream and some seasoning. Mix well.

Heat the oven to 240°C/Gas Mark 9. Roll each piece of dough into a circle 2–3mm thick and place on a lightly floured pizza stone or baking sheet (if you have only 2, prepare the pizzas in batches). Spread a thin layer of tomato sauce over each one or pour the blond sauce over. Add the toppings of your choice (see page 160), then trickle a little olive oil over the top and bake, 2 at a time, in the hot oven. Make sure the oven has reached the correct temperature, as you need it to be really hot. Cook for 8–10 minutes, until the base is lightly coloured and the cheese has melted. If your oven is anything like ours, you will have to swap the pizzas around for the last few minutes so the bottom one gets a stint on the top shelf.

continued overleaf

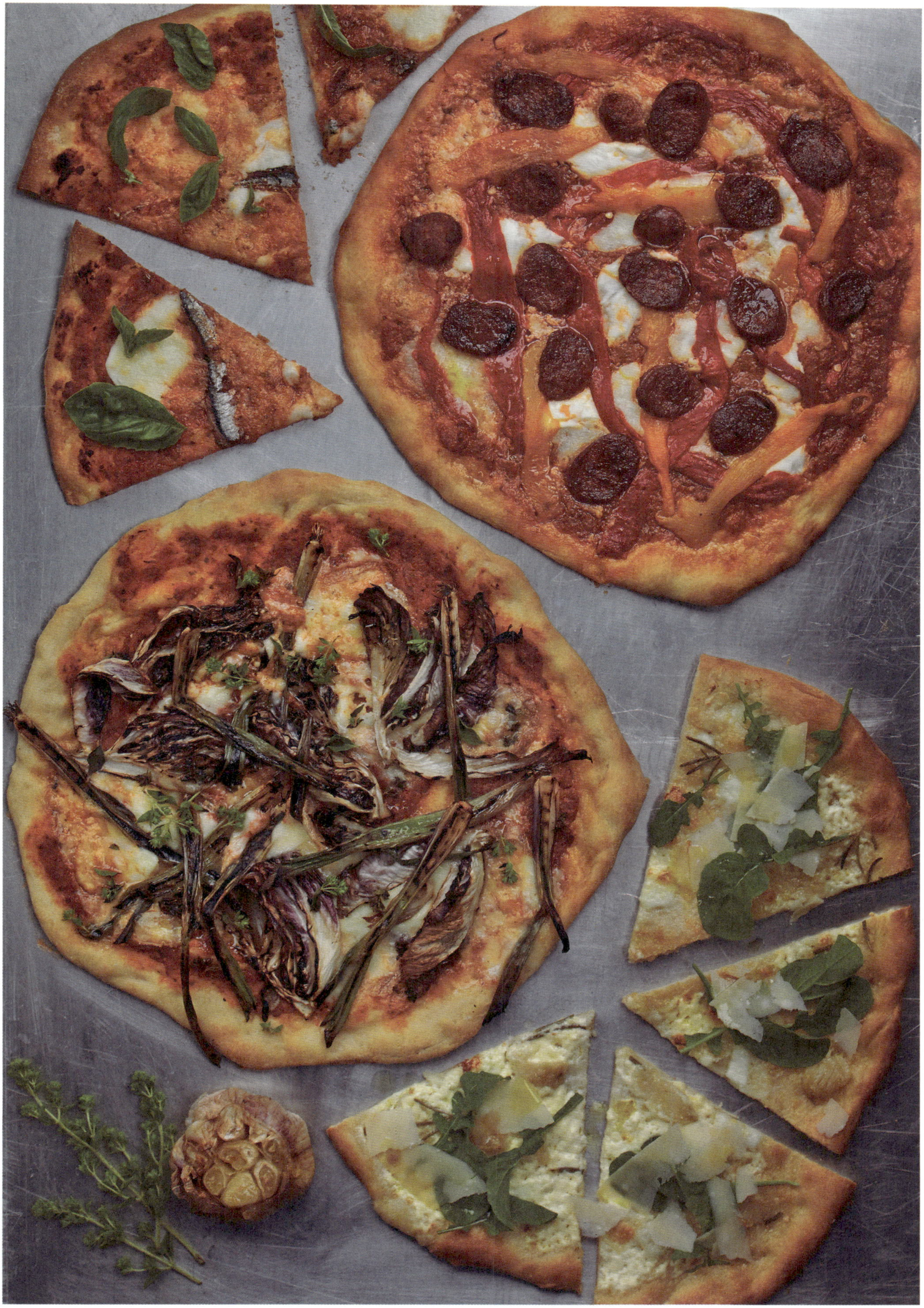

A few suggestions
(each makes enough for 2 pizzas)

Roasted garlic, rosemary, rocket and Parmesan – Trickle a teaspoon of olive oil over a bulb of garlic and roast in a moderately hot oven for about 20 minutes, until soft and withered. Trickle a little olive oil over the pizza bases, spread with the blond sauce, then squeeze a few of the garlic cloves out of their skins and scatter them over the dough, squishing them gently with a fork. Scatter over the leaves from a sprig of rosemary and bake the pizzas as above. As soon as they are cooked, sprinkle a handful of rocket and Parmesan shavings on top, trickle over some more olive oil, particularly on the rocket, and serve with freshly ground pepper.

Chargrilled courgette, aubergine, onion, chilli, mozzarella and basil – Cut 5 slices of aubergine about 7mm thick and steam them for 5 minutes (this helps prevent them becoming leathery). Slice 1 courgette 3–4mm thick. Grill the aubergine and courgette on a griddle pan (you could do it under a grill but the criss-cross marks created by the griddle pan look very smart on the pizza). Spread the pizza bases with tomato sauce and top with the courgette, aubergine, 1 finely sliced red onion, 1 deseeded and finely sliced red chilli, a ball of mozzarella, torn into small pieces, and a handful of basil leaves. Bake the pizzas as above and dress with a little olive oil before serving.

Tomato and mozzarella with anchovies and basil – Spread the pizza bases with tomato sauce, then scatter over 1 mozzarella cheese, torn into chunks, 6 anchovy fillets per pizza, and a handful of basil leaves. Bake as above.

Chorizo and roasted red pepper – Spread the pizza bases with tomato sauce, then scatter over 1 mozzarella cheese, torn into chunks, 12 slices of cooked chorizo and a roasted large red pepper, cut into 5mm slivers. Bake as above.

Grilled radicchio, spring onions and Taleggio – Cut a head of radicchio into 8 pieces, making sure they stay intact. Brush with a little olive oil and cook on a griddle pan, turning frequently, for 10–15 minutes, until wilted and a beautiful reddish-brown colour. Trim 12 spring onions to about 8cm long, leaving some of the green top on them. Cut in half lengthways, brush with olive oil, then cook on the griddle, turning frequently, until soft and coloured. Arrange over the pizza bases (tomato sauce and the blond base both work well here). Slice 100g Taleggio cheese, cut it into 3cm squares, then scatter it over the pizzas and bake as above.

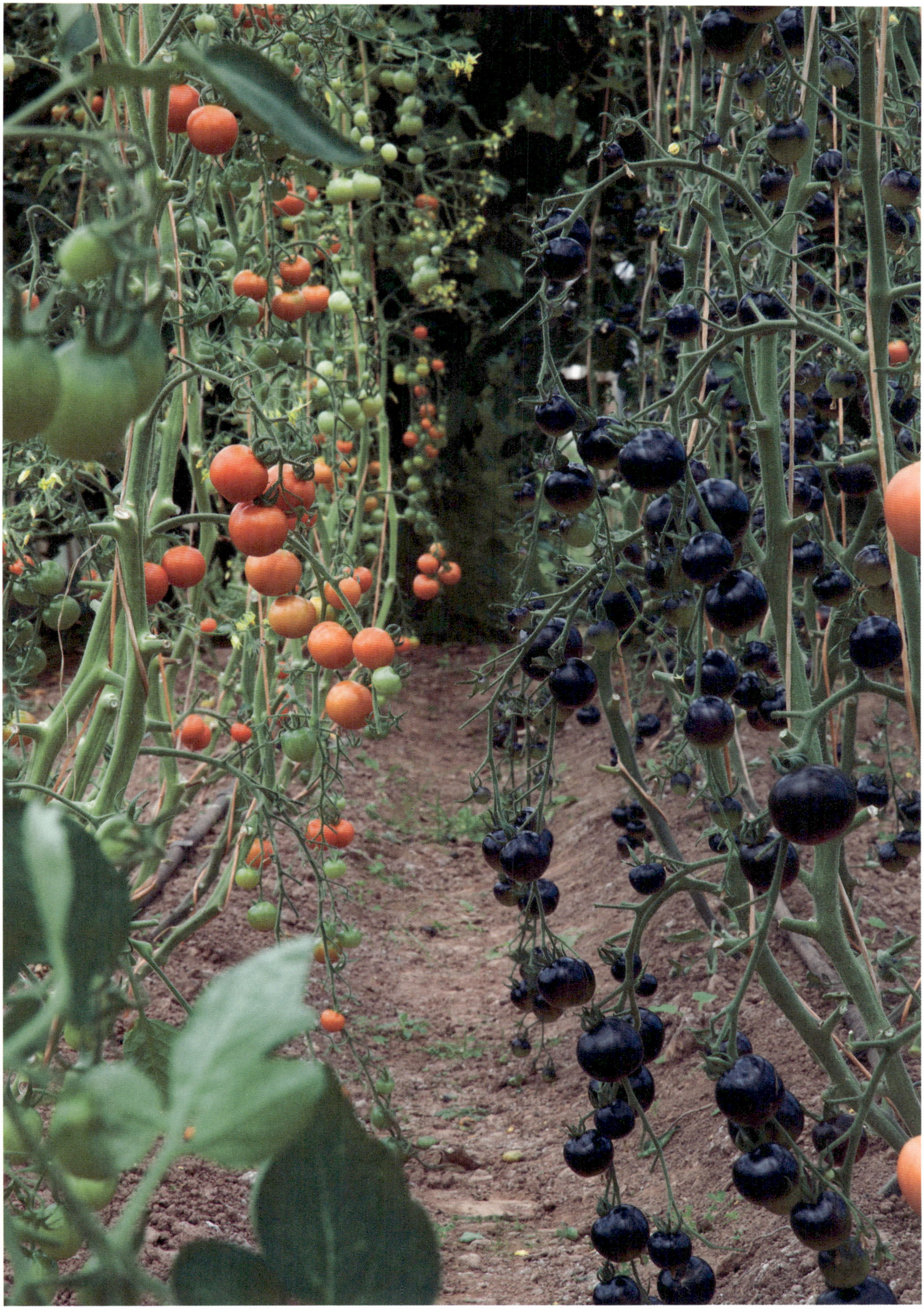

Summer vegetable lasagne

SERVES 8

2 aubergines (about 700g in total)

500g courgettes

2 teaspoons sea salt

4 red peppers

4 tablespoons olive oil

500g Swiss chard

400g dried or fresh lasagne sheets

2 balls of mozzarella cheese

125g basil

100g Parmesan cheese, grated

sea salt and black pepper

For the tomato sauce

5 tablespoons olive oil

1 large onion, finely diced

1 celery stick, finely diced

1 carrot, finely diced

3 garlic cloves, crushed

2 teaspoons finely chopped thyme

2 teaspoons finely chopped oregano

2 bay leaves

50ml red or white wine (optional)

2kg ripe plum tomatoes, cut into quarters, or 4 x 400g cans of tomatoes

1 dessertspoon tomato purée

For the béchamel sauce

1.5 litres milk

1 bay leaf

1 small onion, peeled and halved

90g butter

90g plain flour

1 teaspoon mustard

150g Comté cheese, or similar melting cheese such as Gruyère or Emmental, grated

This luxurious lasagne takes quite a long time to prepare and uses many in-season summer vegetables. The method for layering it ensures it stays really moist and luscious. To make a version using minced beef, simply reduce the amount of tomatoes by a quarter, fry 750g mince with a finely chopped large onion and then stir this into the prepared tomato sauce.

For the tomato sauce, heat the olive oil in a heavy-based pan over a moderate heat. Add the onion, celery, carrot and garlic and stir to coat in the oil. Reduce the heat, cover and sweat the vegetables for about 10 minutes, until soft. Stir in all the herbs, cook for 2 minutes, then turn up the heat and pour in the wine, if using. Stir until most of the wine has evaporated. Lower the heat and add the tomatoes. Season to taste. Cover and stew until the tomatoes begin to break down. Stir in the tomato purée and simmer, uncovered, until thick. Depending on how juicy the tomatoes are, this might take up to an hour.

While the sauce is cooking, prepare the vegetables. Heat the oven to 200°C/Gas Mark 6. Trim the aubergines and courgettes and slice them lengthways into strips about 5mm thick. Lay the aubergine slices out on a roasting tray and sprinkle the sea salt over them. Set aside for at least half an hour, to sweat out any bitter flavours. Meanwhile, put the peppers on a baking sheet and roast for about 30 minutes, until they are soft and lightly charred. Seal the hot peppers immediately in a plastic bag. When they are cool enough to handle, cut them in half, remove the seeds and the green stem, then peel off the skin. Cut the peeled peppers into long strips and set aside.

Rinse the aubergines and drain, then pat dry. Lay the slices on a clean baking sheet. Do the same with the courgette slices. Spoon over the oil and place in an oven preheated to 220°C/Gas Mark 7. Roast for 20–30 minutes, turning once, until lightly browned on both sides. Shred the chard and steam it very briefly so that it wilts but doesn't cook. Drain well.

Finally, make the béchamel sauce. Pour the milk into a pan, add the bay leaf and onion and bring slowly to boiling point. Remove from the heat and set aside for about half an hour to infuse. Melt the butter in a pan over a low heat, add the flour and cook, stirring, for a minute or two. Gradually strain in the milk, omitting the bay leaf and onion, then raise the heat and bring to a simmer to make a thick, smooth sauce. Continue to cook over a low heat for 3–4 minutes. Add the mustard and grated cheese and season to taste.

Layer the lasagne as you wish – or try our method, which works well, and cooks the pasta so that it remains nice and moist. There are 3 layers of tomato sauce and pasta and 2 of béchamel sauce. Spoon a layer of tomato sauce into a 25cm x 35cm lasagne dish or a deep roasting tin. Add a layer of pasta sheets, followed by another layer of tomato sauce, then a layer of aubergine and courgette. Tear the mozzarella into small pieces and dot them over the aubergine and courgettes. Add another layer of pasta and arrange the peppers on top. Next arrange the chard leaves evenly in the dish and pour half the béchamel over it. Now add another layer of pasta and the final layer of tomato sauce. Spread the basil leaves over the top and then pour the remaining béchamel evenly over, making sure it spreads into the corners. Scatter the grated Parmesan over the top and place in the middle shelf of an oven preheated to 200°C/Gas Mark 6. Bake for about 1 hour, until the sauces are bubbling and the top is lightly browned. Serve with a green salad.

Tondo courgettes stuffed with peas, marjoram and goat's curd

SERVES 4

4 cricket-ball-sized round courgettes
2 tablespoons olive oil
1 onion, diced
1 garlic clove, crushed
1 tablespoon chopped marjoram
grated zest of ½ lemon
250g shelled peas (or baby broad beans)
150g goat's curd or ordinary curd cheese
sea salt and black pepper

Tondo di Nizza is a round courgette with a light green, mottled, shiny skin. The flavour is every bit as delicious as that of regular-shaped courgettes. The round shape also makes them very good vessels for stuffing. Ideally, we pick them when they are about the size of a cricket ball.

Heat the oven to 180°C/Gas Mark 4. Choose courgettes that are of an even size. If necessary, cut a thin slice off the base so they sit flat, being careful not to make a hole. Cut a lid off each one and set aside. With a teaspoon, carefully scoop out the flesh from the courgettes, leaving a shell about 5mm thick; make sure you don't pierce the skin. Slice about a third of the flesh into thin strips; you won't need the rest.

Heat the olive oil in a small pan. Add the onion, garlic and sliced courgette flesh and fry until they soften and start to colour. Stir in the marjoram and lemon zest and cook for a minute longer. Remove from the heat and stir in the peas (or broad beans). Mix in the curd cheese and season to taste.

Fill the courgette shells with the stuffing and put the lids on top. Place the stuffed courgettes on a baking sheet and cover them loosely with foil. Bake for 30 minutes or until the courgettes are tender. Serve with a green salad and some crusty bread.

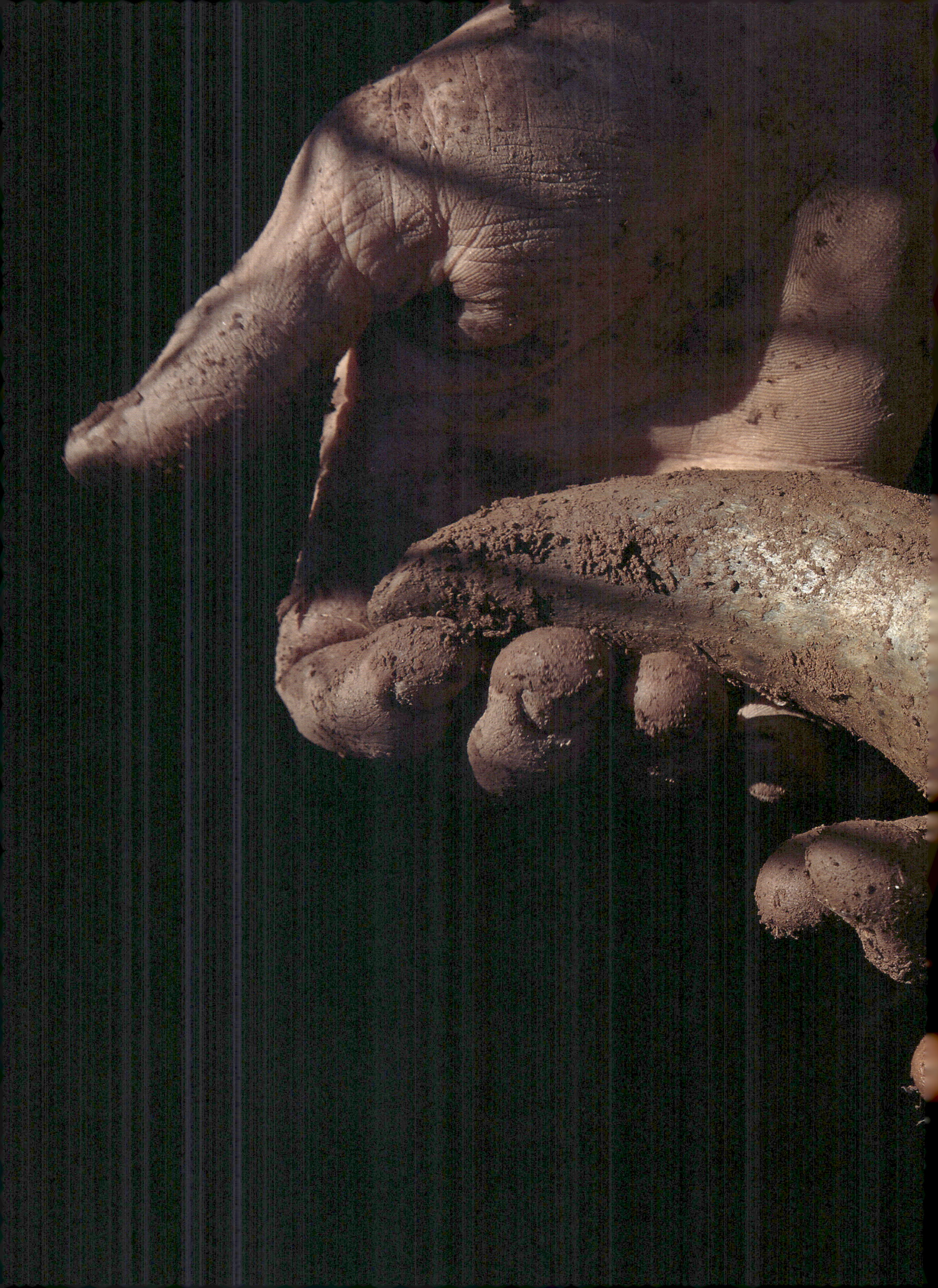

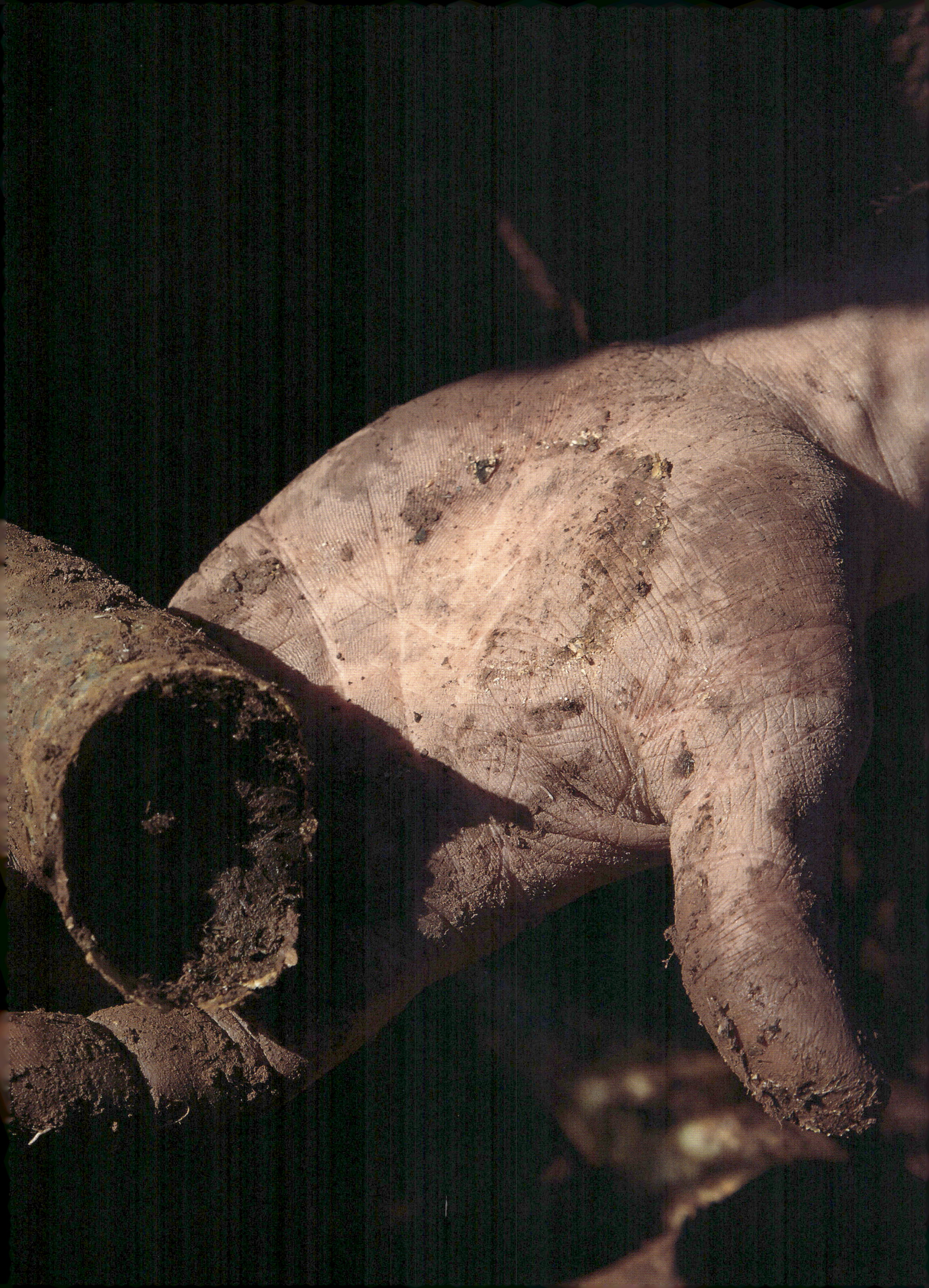

Helping our crops reach their potential

HUMANKIND HAS BEEN using cow manure for thousands of years because of the fertility it carries, and its highly beneficial properties in building and stabilising the humus – the decayed organic component of the soil. Whenever we harvest crops from our fields, we always take something from the earth. We fertilise our soil to return not only substance but also vitality.

In our work as biodynamic farmers, we take particular measures to try to enhance our manuring practice. As well as making compost preparations (see page 212), we make two field sprays: horn manure and horn silica (known respectively as preparations 500 and 501). We apply these with the aim of better uniting our crops with the life emanating from the earth, and with the influences coming from the starry skies above (see page 176).

We don't really know how to quantify the effects of these biodynamic field sprays, but there is no question in our minds that there is a visible difference in the vigour of the growing plants. Once we harvest the plants, the qualities we can discern in their depth of colour, taste and improved storage are very apparent. We regularly make the time to stir and apply the sprays throughout the growing season.

Horn manure (Preparation 500)

In late autumn we take cow horns and fill each one with fresh manure from our cows. We then bury the manure-filled horns in the ground, down in rich, fertile soil, where they remain throughout the winter. Rudolf Steiner explains the process like this: 'If the horn is buried for the entire winter – the season when the earth is most inwardly alive – all this life will be preserved in the manure, turning the contents of the horn into an extremely concentrated, enlivening and fertilising force'*.

We dig up this buried treasure in the spring, remove the now sweet-smelling, humus-like preparation and place a large handful in a barrel of rainwater. This we stir vigorously for an hour, to create the vortex described on page 105. For this horn-manure preparation we always do the stirring in the late afternoon and apply it by walking over the newly cultivated fields with a bucket in one hand and a hand brush in the other. We dip the brush in the bucket and flick the potent liquid left and right; the ground breathes in the falling droplets. We do this right at the beginning of the growing process, when ploughing, sowing or planting, with the purpose of impregnating the soil with formative growth forces. We see this as a nourishing encouragement, stimulating the life in the soil and giving the young plants strong foundations.

*From Spiritual Foundations for the Renewal of Agriculture by Rudolf Steiner (Biodynamic Farming and Gardening Association, 1993).

Horn silica (Preparation 501)

The aim of this second spray preparation is to help the growing plants to fully harness the light. The earth's crust is composed primarily of silicate minerals. In the springtime we take quartz, a hexagonal, transparent crystal, and crush it with a pestle and mortar and then grind it between two pieces of glass. We are left with a very fine powder, resembling flour, which we mix with a little water to make a paste. We fill a cow horn with the mixture and again bury it in fertile ground, exposing it to the summer life of the earth. Here it remains until the autumn, when we dig it up, place the contents of the horn in a jam jar, and store this on the windowsill in full light, ready for use the following spring and summer.

To apply this horn silica we take a few pinches and mix thoroughly in a barrel of rainwater – this time not in the afternoon, but early in the morning, in order to catch as much of the sun as possible. After an hour's vigorous stirring, we fill a backpack sprayer and walk out across the dew-covered fields to spray a fine mist over the growing plants. Our intention is to help our crops develop their flavour, form, and true character and beauty. It is striking that we can go out the day after we have sprayed and see what could be described as a glow or shine in the plants. Overnight they have come to stand proud – it's as if they are all reaching up and singing 'Hallelujah!'

Soused mackerel with cucumber and dill

SERVES 4

4 mackerel fillets
2 slices of lemon
1 tablespoon olive oil
250ml white wine vinegar
1 small onion, thinly sliced
1 teaspoon coriander seeds
½ teaspoon black peppercorns
a pinch of sea salt
1 bay leaf

For the cucumber and dill
1 cucumber
2 tablespoons olive oil
1 tablespoon chopped dill
a generous pinch of coarse sea salt
black pepper

Mackerel is particularly good in this unusual and very tasty lunch or supper dish. You could use any other fish, including white fish. The raw fish becomes pickled in the hot vinegar and you eat it cold. It's very good served with a dollop of soured cream and some new potatoes.

Place the mackerel fillets skin-side down in a large, shallow dish. Put the lemon slices on top and drizzle over the olive oil. Put the vinegar, onion, spices, salt and bay leaf in a saucepan and bring to the boil. Pour the hot vinegar over the fish fillets, making sure that they are completely covered. Leave to cool, then cover the dish with cling film and leave in the fridge for at least 6 hours or overnight. Remove from the fridge about an hour before serving to allow the fish to come to room temperature.

Peel the cucumber if you wish and cut it into long, thin strips. Add the remaining ingredients and mix together. Serve with the fish.

Baked fish with fennel and saffron

SERVES 4

2 fennel bulbs, very thinly sliced
a few threads of saffron
a few sprigs of lemon thyme
a sprig of leaf fennel
2–3 sprigs of parsley
3 slices of lemon
a 2–2.5kg fish, such as sea bass, gutted and cleaned
75g butter
50ml white wine
sea salt and black pepper

This is a very classy dish, despite being remarkably easy to prepare. Sea bass is ideal here, but you can use any non-oily fish. One weighing 2–2.5kg will feed four people very well.

Slice the fennel on a mandoline, if you have one. It is by far the best way to get beautifully glassy, thin slices that can make all the difference to the finesse of this dish. If you don't have a mandoline, use a sharp grater or the slicing attachment of a food processor.

Heat the oven to 180°C/Gas Mark 4. Cover a roasting dish with a piece of foil that is large enough to wrap the fish in. Scatter the thinly sliced fennel down the centre of the foil, then sprinkle the saffron on top. Put the herbs and lemon slices into the cavity of the fish, then lay the fish on top of the fennel. Dot the butter evenly over the fish and pour the wine over, then season with salt and pepper. Gather up the edges of the foil and squeeze them together to seal. Leave the parcel puffy so that the steam can circulate properly and cook the fish evenly.

Bake the fish for 25–30 minutes. To check it is done, open the foil and insert a knife near the backbone; the flesh should flake easily.

Serve the fish off the bone, giving each person a helping of fennel and a generous spoonful of the sauce. It goes well with buttered new potatoes and some steamed green leaves, such as chard or spinach.

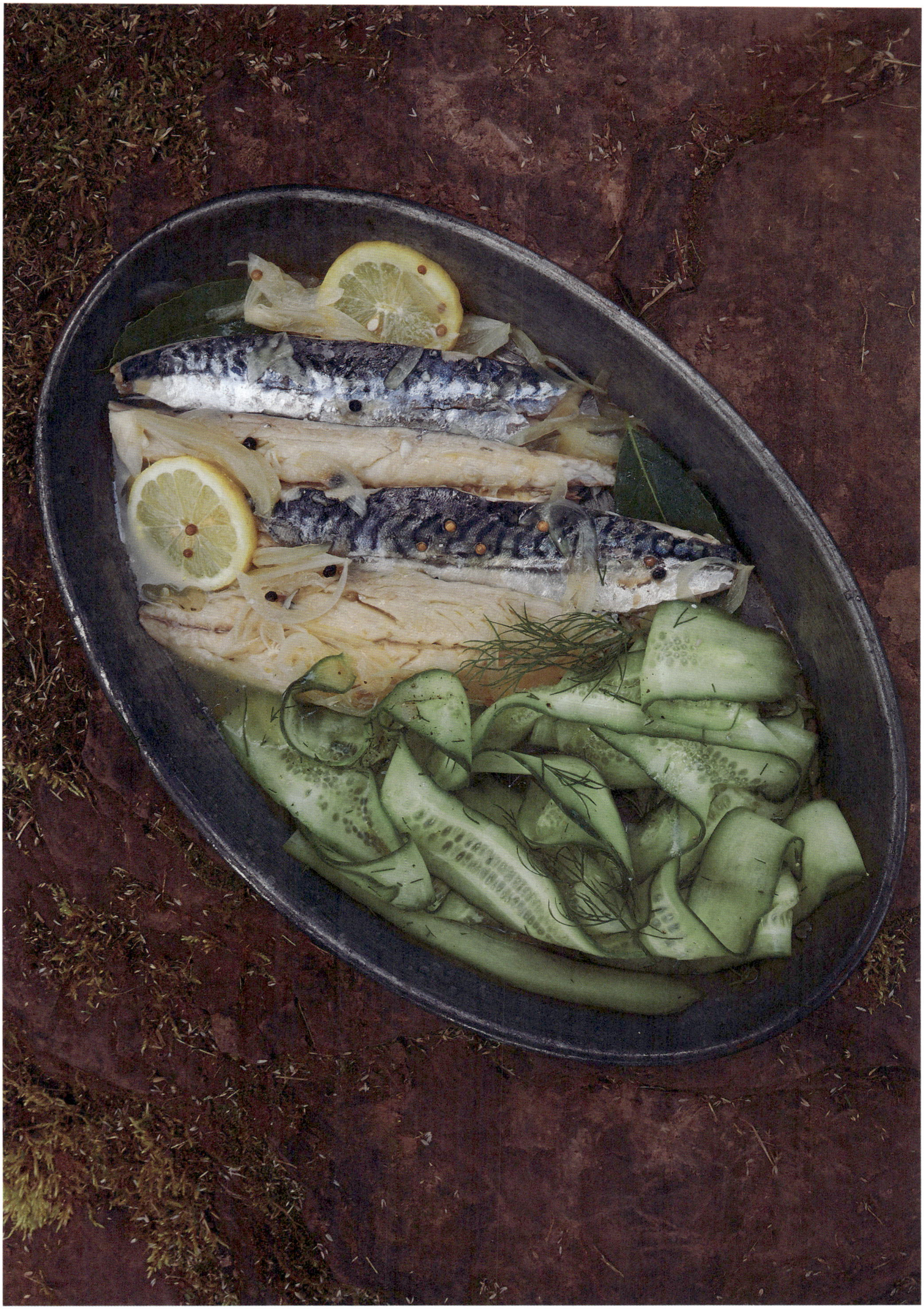

Barbecued chicken with sweetcorn and lime leaf relish

SERVES 4–6

1 large sprig of rosemary
1 small bunch of thyme
1 small bunch of oregano
4 garlic cloves
125ml olive oil
1 large chicken, jointed into 8
2 lemons
sea salt and black pepper

For the relish
10 fresh kaffir lime leaves, very finely shredded
50ml water
1 tablespoon sugar
4 large corn cobs
2 ripe but firm avocados
juice of 2 limes
½ red pepper, finely diced
½ green chilli, finely chopped
1 small red onion, finely diced
1 small bunch of coriander, roughly chopped
about 4 tablespoons olive oil

Cooking chicken over a wood fire can't be beaten. The smoky flavour and crispy golden skin is irresistible. Together with a brightly spangled fresh salsa, this dish makes a refreshing outdoor meal on a hot summer's evening. Joint a whole chicken into 8 pieces if you are willing and able; if not, then buy chicken pieces, but make sure they still have the skin on.

Try to select a light-green-skinned variety of avocado for the relish, as this kind tends to be less creamy and will hold its shape better.

Roughly chop the herbs and garlic and put them in a large, shallow dish. Add the olive oil and mix well. Then add the chicken pieces and squeeze the juice of the lemons over them. Add the empty lemon shells to the dish. Season the chicken pieces with salt and pepper and turn them until they are thoroughly coated in the marinade. Cover and leave to marinate in the fridge for at least 4 hours, turning them once to ensure that the chicken soaks up the flavours.

Meanwhile, prepare the relish. Place the lime leaves, water and sugar in a small saucepan and bring slowly to the boil, stirring to dissolve the sugar. Turn down the heat and simmer for about 10 minutes, until the liquid has reduced by half and the leaves are soft but still green. Remove from the heat and leave to cool.

Strip off the husks from the corn cobs. Cook the cobs in a large pan of boiling salted water for 8–10 minutes, until tender, then drain and refresh under cold running water. Stand each cob upright on a board and slice off the kernels.

Peel, stone and dice the avocados, then pour a little of the lime juice on to them to prevent browning. Mix the corn and avocado with the red pepper, chilli, onion and coriander, then pour the lime leaf mixture on top. Pour in the lime juice, then add some salt and pepper and enough olive oil to coat all the vegetables thoroughly. Taste and add more lime juice or olive oil if necessary.

Get a barbecue ready, then place the chicken on it. Cook, turning the meat frequently and brushing with the excess marinade from time to time. Test the chicken is done by inserting a sharp knife or skewer near the bone; the juices should run clear rather than pink. Depending on the heat of the barbecue, this could take up to 45 minutes. Serve with the relish.

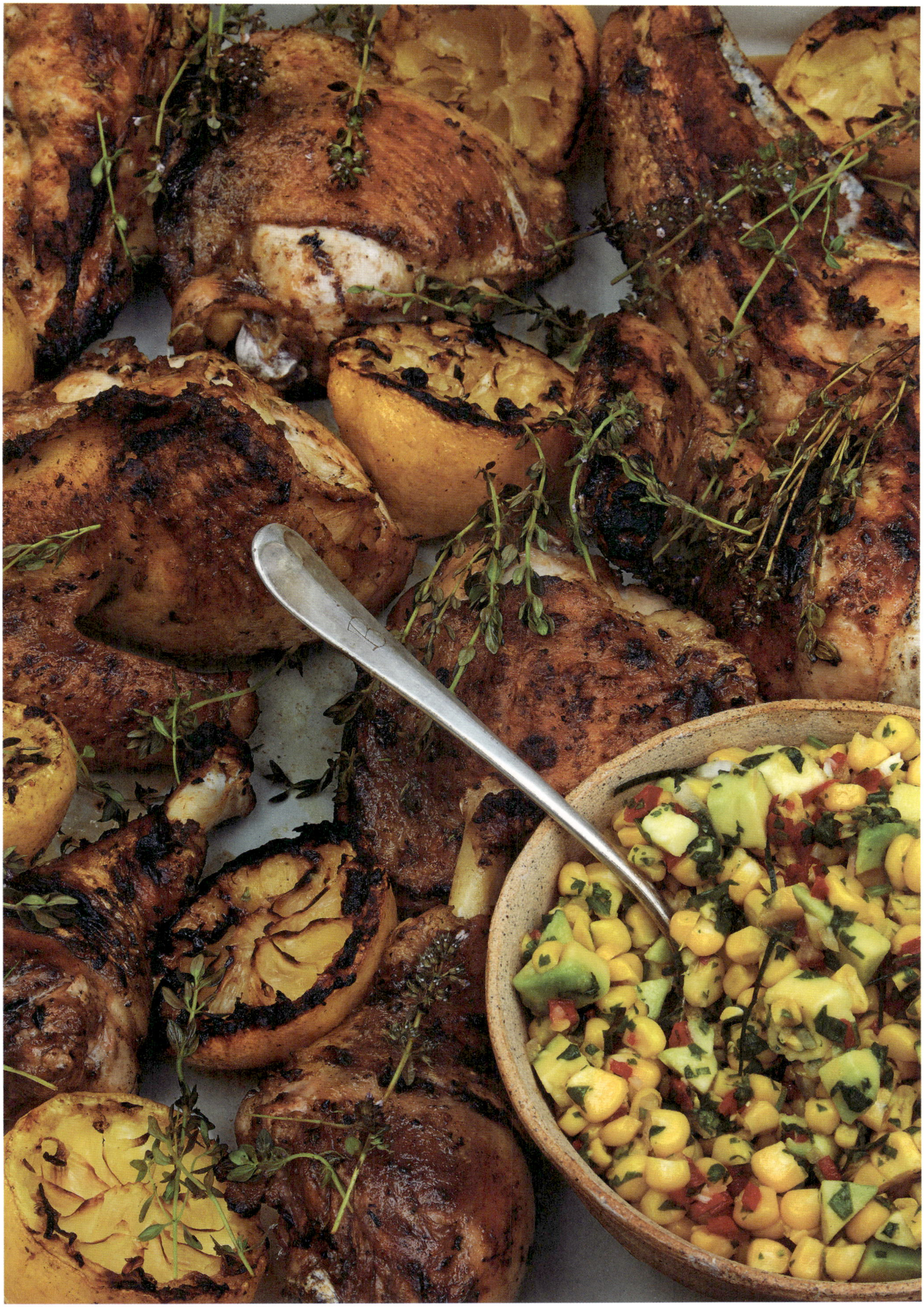

Lamb and vegetable kebabs

SERVES 4

750g shoulder of lamb, cut into 2–3cm cubes
2 large yellow or green peppers
4 small onions
3 courgettes
1 aubergine
sea salt and black pepper

For the marinade

500ml Greek-style yoghurt
2 tablespoons olive oil
3 garlic cloves, crushed
1 bunch of mint (and/or coriander), roughly chopped
1 teaspoon ground coriander
1 teaspoon ground cumin
1 teaspoon turmeric
juice and grated zest of 1 lime

For the yoghurt and cucumber dip

300ml Greek-style yoghurt
½ cucumber, cut into small cubes or grated
1 garlic clove, crushed
a small bunch of mint, chopped
1 teaspoon olive oil

These kebabs work best on a barbecue, but you can also cook them on a griddle pan in the kitchen – though it will be a rather smoky affair. This is a very adaptable recipe: the choice of meat and vegetables is up to you and you can even make vegetarian kebabs if you substitute halloumi for the meat.

If you are lucky enough to have apple, pear or cherry trees in your garden, collect reasonable-sized pieces of wood from them when pruning in the winter and store them in a dry place for at least a year. You can use them for a barbecue in the summer, as the wood burns beautifully and evenly.

First prepare the marinade. Mix the yoghurt and olive oil together in a shallow dish, then stir in all the remaining marinade ingredients. Add the cubed lamb and mix until it is well coated. Cover and leave to marinate in the fridge for at least 2 hours.

Cut the peppers into 3–4cm squares. Cut each onion into 6 wedges, leaving the trimmed root attached. Cut the courgettes into rounds 1cm thick. Do likewise with the aubergine, then cut each slice into quarters and steam them for 2–3 minutes. This helps the aubergine absorb the marinade better and prevents it becoming leathery.

Thread the meat and vegetables on to 8 wooden skewers, leaving plenty of room at either end for handling. Spoon the surplus marinade over the kebabs and leave for an hour or so to allow the vegetables to soften a little and soak up the flavours.

Meanwhile, make the yoghurt and cucumber dip. Spoon the yoghurt into a bowl and stir in the cucumber, garlic and mint. Season with salt and pepper, add the olive oil and set aside.

Place the kebabs on a hot barbecue and cook for about half an hour, turning frequently and brushing more marinade over them from time to time. When they are done, they should look golden yellow and slightly charred around the edges. Serve with the dip and some flatbreads or rice.

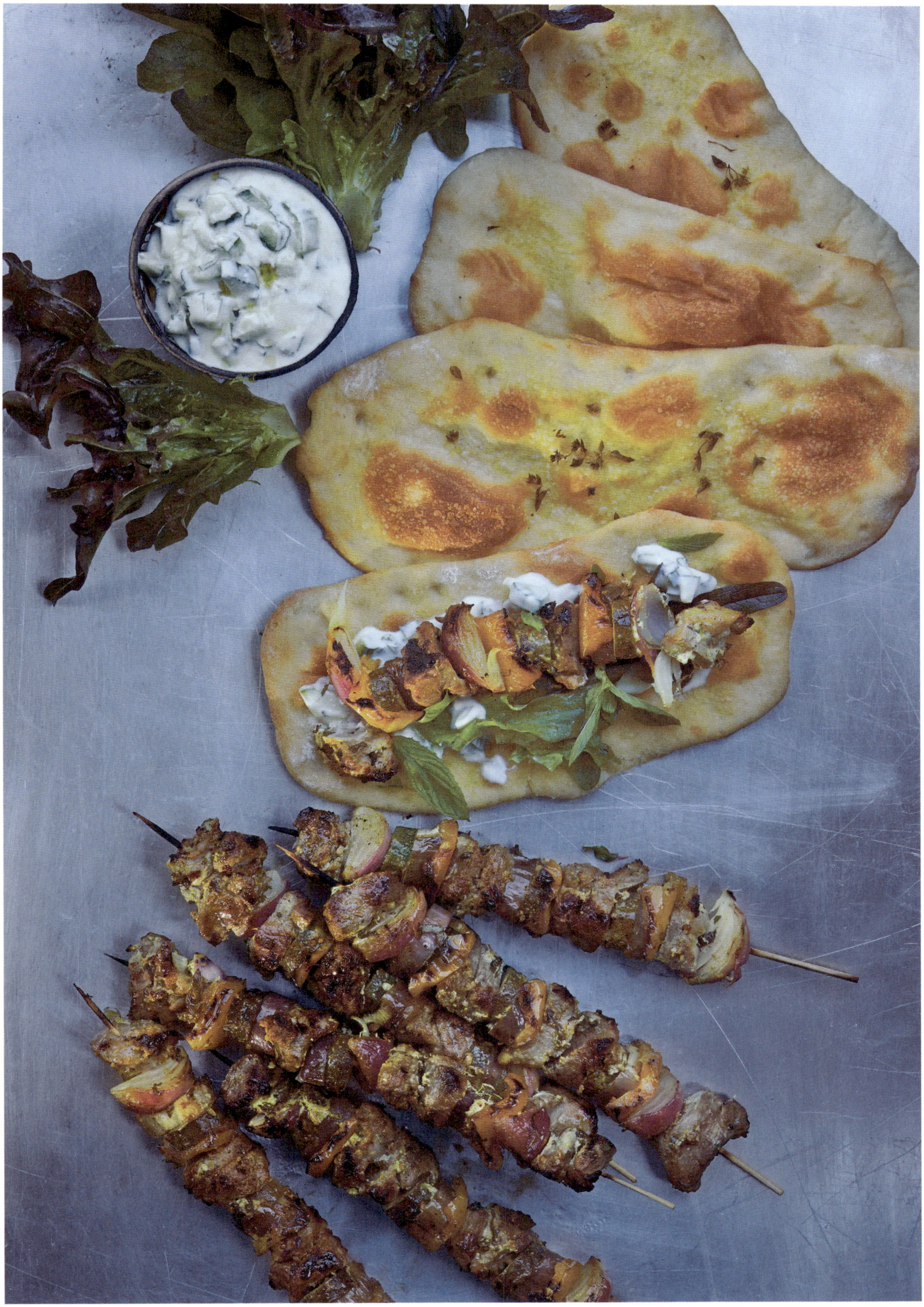

Fresh peas and baby carrots

SERVES 4 AS A SIDE DISH,
2 AS A LIGHT MEAL WITH
BREAD

a bunch of baby carrots
1kg peas in their pods, shelled
25g butter
1 tablespoon crème fraîche
1 tablespoon water
2 tablespoons chopped dill
juice of ½ lemon
sea salt and black pepper

Often people talk of spring carrots but this can be a little misleading. If you grow carrots outside, spring is the time to sow the seeds and it is not until the summer months that the orange roots appear.

We sometimes eat this dish as a meal in itself, using peas from a late-spring sowing. As a side dish it is particularly delicious with a roast chicken and new potatoes.

Wash and top and tail the carrots, but leave them whole. Put the carrots, shelled peas, butter, crème fraîche and water in a pan with some salt and pepper. Cover and cook over a moderate heat for 5 minutes. Remove the lid and continue to cook until the carrots are soft but still have some bite to them and the sauce has a light, creamy consistency. Stir in the dill and squeeze in the lemon juice. Adjust the seasoning if necessary and serve.

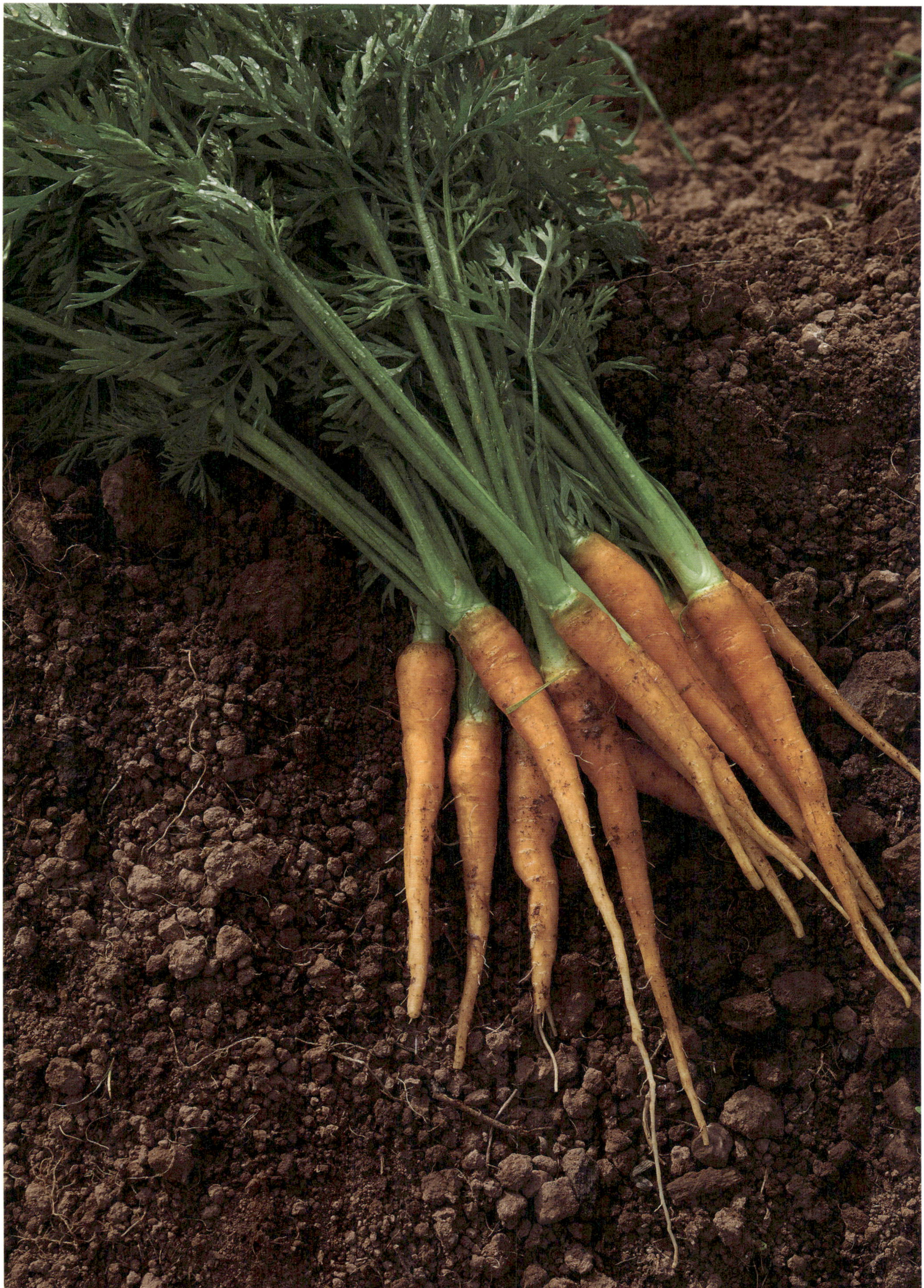

Working with the moon

'O swear not by the moon, th'inconstant moon,
That monthly changes in her circled orb'
SHAKESPEARE, *ROMEO AND JULIET* ACT 2, SCENE 2

THE MOON'S EFFECTS on water and tides, and on reproductive cycles, are well known. We've talked about the sun in our daily work (page 128); so, too, the moon brings its own influences in its sidereal journey around the earth.

In her four-week orbit, the moon spends two to four days passing in front of each constellation of the zodiac – the Fishes, Ram, Bull, Twins, Crab, Lion, Virgin, Scales, Scorpion, Archer, Goat and Water Carrier. Each of these has long been associated with one of the four primordial elements for life: earth, water, air and fire. For our crops, we reconcile these four elements with the four archetypal parts of all plants: root, leaf, flower and fruit. The root is connected to the earth element, the leaf to the water element, the flower is related to the air and light, and the fruit or seed of a plant to fire and warmth.

As biodynamic growers, we use the cycle of the moon to help us decide when, and on which plants, to carry out our cultivations.

We time our sowing, planting and hoeing according to which particular part of a plant we are interested in developing. For growing a root crop such as carrots, we carry out the necessary tasks when the moon is in an earth constellation (Goat, Bull or Virgin). We sow leaf crops, such as lettuce, celery and cabbage, and we transplant them and cultivate the soil around them when the moon is in a water constellation (Crab, Scorpion or Fishes). We tend to our flowers when the moon is in an air constellation (Twins, Scales or Water Carrier). If we want to encourage fruiting, for example in courgettes, peas or strawberries, we use a day when the moon is in a fire constellation (Ram, Lion or Archer).

By using the moon as a guide in our growing, we're attempting to stimulate the latent promise that each crop has to offer. Sometimes we have to compromise because of more immediate constraints of time and weather, but over the years we've noticed that the closer we work with these subtle rhythms of the cosmos*, the better the results.

*The Maria Thun Biodynamic Calendar, *which has been published annually for over 50 years, is an essential aid to us in this. It is a wonderful guide to the movements of the sun, moon and the planets as they pass the constellations of the zodiac and is invaluable to us in our daily work.*

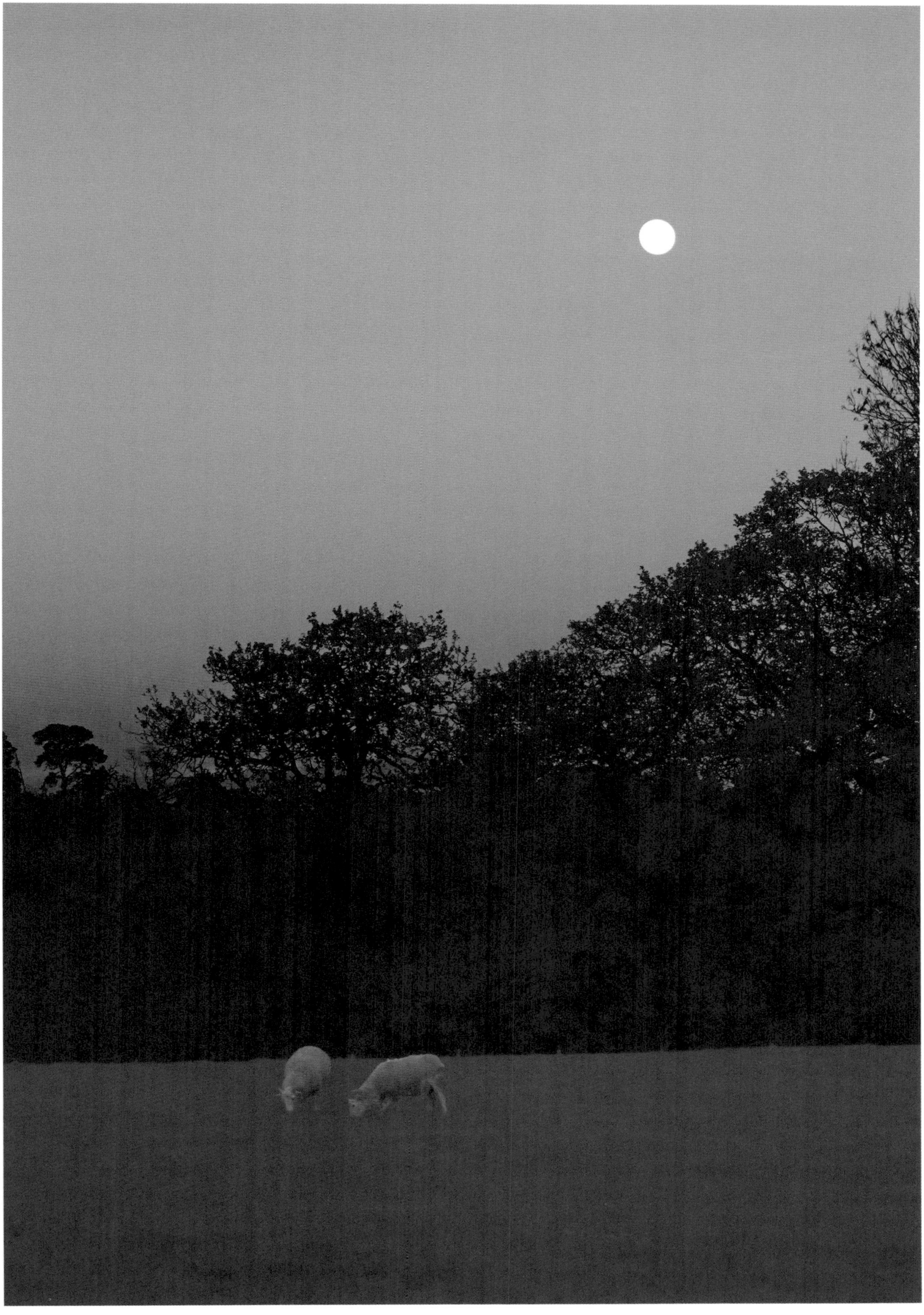

Peaches and cream

SERVES 4

4 large peaches

8 generous dessertspoons crème fraîche

caster sugar, for sprinkling

Peaches work fantastically well in this very easy pudding. Adding cream and sugar to a perfect fruit is often unnecessary and over-fussy. But this recipe is a marriage made in heaven. Later in the year you can make it with plums or greengages.

Heat the grill. Halve and stone the peaches, then place them in an ovenproof dish. Put a generous dessertspoon of crème fraîche on each peach half and add a sprinkling of caster sugar. Place under the hot grill and cook for 5 minutes. The cream will thicken, bubble and trickle down into the dish. Sprinkle more sugar on top and allow it to caramelise. Serve immediately. The peaches should be a little soft, but keep their shape and texture.

Blackcurrant pie

SERVES 4

750g blackcurrants, stalks removed
260g granulated sugar
2 teaspoons caster sugar

For the pastry
250g plain flour
a pinch of salt
250g chilled butter, cut into cubes
1 dessertspoon caster sugar
1 egg yolk
1½ tablespoons chilled water

Currants are among the prettiest of fruits while on the bush – beautiful enough to grow as an ornamental plant. Picking and preparing them can be a labour of love, but it's well worth it, given their wonderful flavour. Blackcurrants freeze really well; in fact, cooking them from frozen helps to release the juices from the skins.

Our blackcurrants are fairly tart, so we add a lot of sugar, but you can reduce the quantity if you prefer. This old-school pie is lovely eaten straight from the oven but we also like to serve it cold. The juices set, a little like jam. It is also delicious made with plums, damsons or greengages later in the summer, adjusting the sugar to the sweetness of the fruit you've used.

First make the pastry. Sift the flour and salt into a mixing bowl and add the butter. Cut it into the flour with a round-bladed knife until it is well coated in the flour, then rub it in with your fingertips until the mixture resembles breadcrumbs. Stir in the sugar. Beat the egg yolk with the chilled water, pour it into the flour mixture and mix to make a firm dough. Turn on to a lightly floured board and knead briefly until smooth, then put into a plastic bag or wrap in cling film and chill for at least 30 minutes.

Heat the oven to 190°C/Gas Mark 5 and place a baking sheet inside. Take the pastry out of the fridge and put aside about a third for the lid of the pie. Roll out the remaining pastry on a lightly floured surface to the thickness of a pound coin. Use to line a 24cm pie dish, then fill with the blackcurrants and sprinkle the granulated sugar evenly over the fruit. Roll out the remaining pastry. With a pastry brush, lightly dampen the edges of the pastry base with water. Place the lid on top, pressing the edges together gently, and trim off the excess. Make a few small holes in the centre to let the steam escape.

Brush the top of the pie with a little water and dust with the caster sugar for a twinkly finish. Place on the hot baking sheet in the oven and bake for approximately 30 minutes, until the pastry is an even golden colour. Serve hot or cold, with lashings of single or double cream.

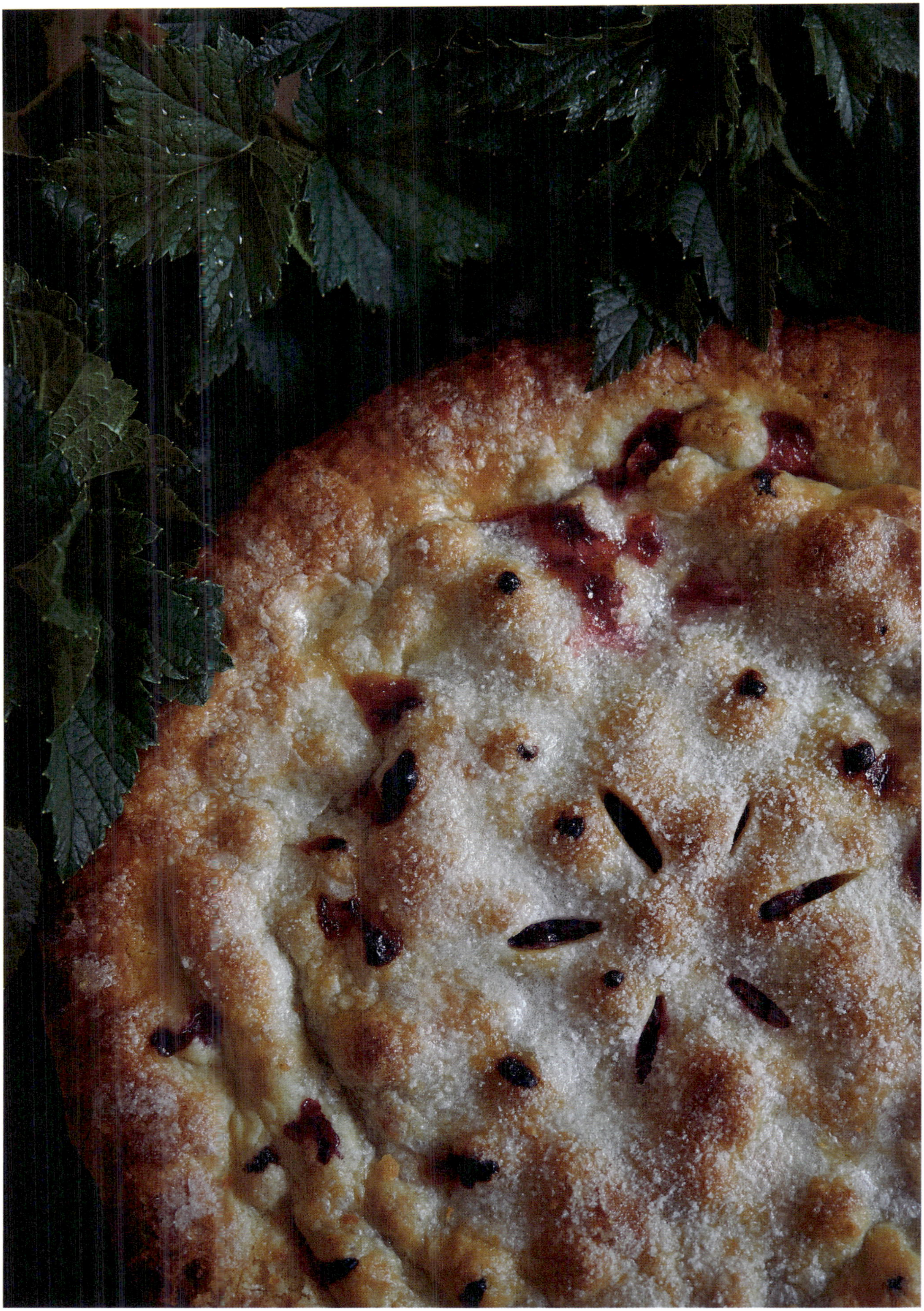

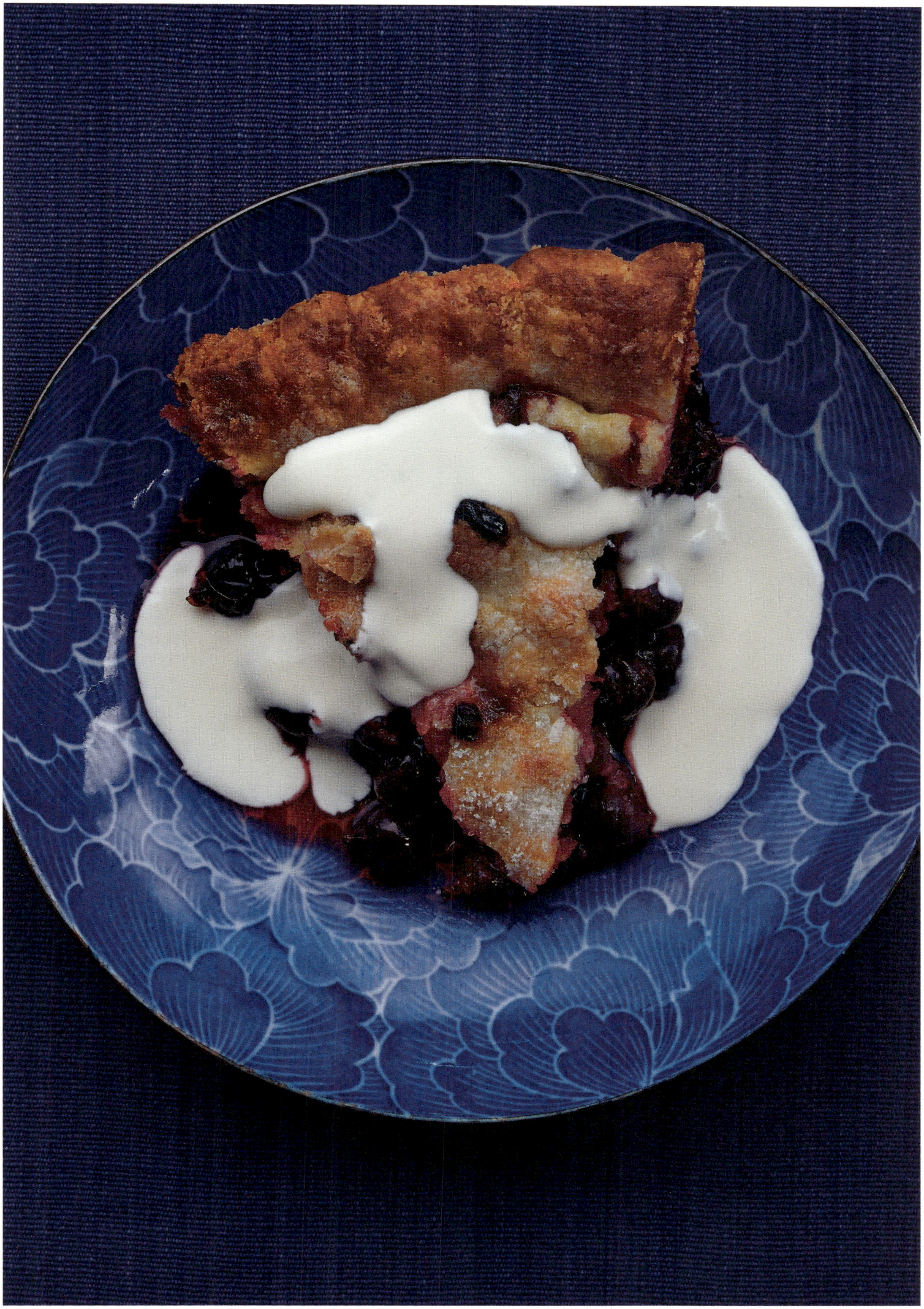

Peach Melba

SERVES 4

4 ripe white peaches

500g raspberries, plus a few extra to decorate, if liked

3 heaped tablespoons icing sugar, sifted

1 quantity of vanilla ice cream (follow the recipe for Jostaberry Ripple Ice Cream on page 190, but without the ripple)

This classic pudding rarely appears on menus today. It was invented at the Savoy Hotel in 1893 by the French chef Auguste Escoffier, in honour of the Australian soprano Nellie Melba. The sweet, cool flavours of vanilla ice cream, a perfect white peach and a tart raspberry sauce make an unbeatable combination. For the recipe photograph, we used marigold petals to decorate, their colour setting off the dish perfectly.

If the peaches are ripe you should be able to peel them without dipping in boiling water first. However, if you do have to use the water method to remove the skin, dip each whole peach into boiling water for a few seconds and then immerse it immediately in a bowl of chilled water to stop the cooking process.

Peel the peaches, cut each one in half and remove the stone. Cover and chill until you are ready to assemble the dessert. Purée the raspberries in a food processor or blender, then put them through a sieve to get rid of the pips. With a small whisk, beat in the icing sugar a little at a time to thicken and sweeten the purée.

To serve, scoop the ice cream into chilled pudding bowls, arrange the peach halves on the side and pour over the raspberry sauce, scattering over a few whole raspberries if you wish.

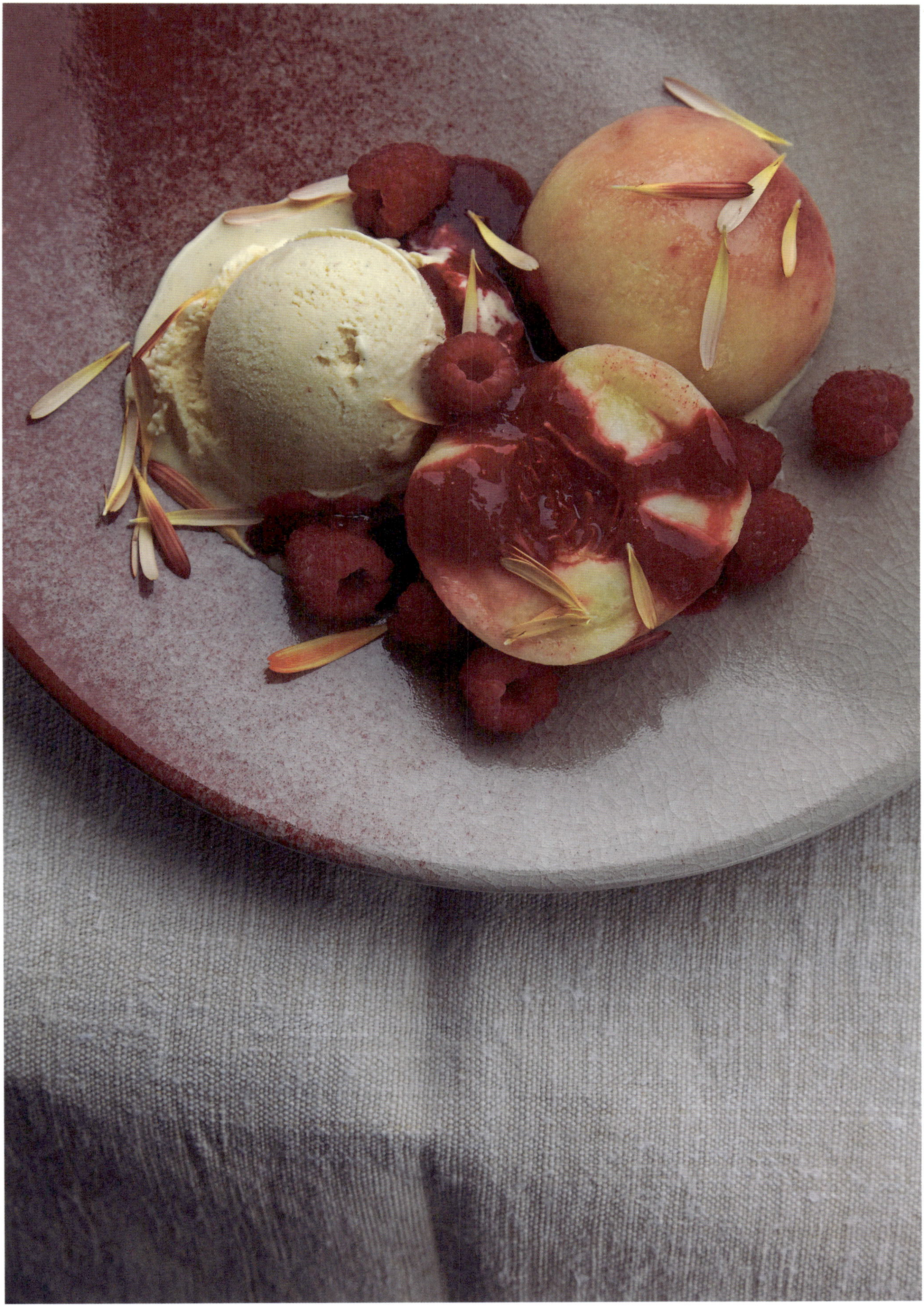

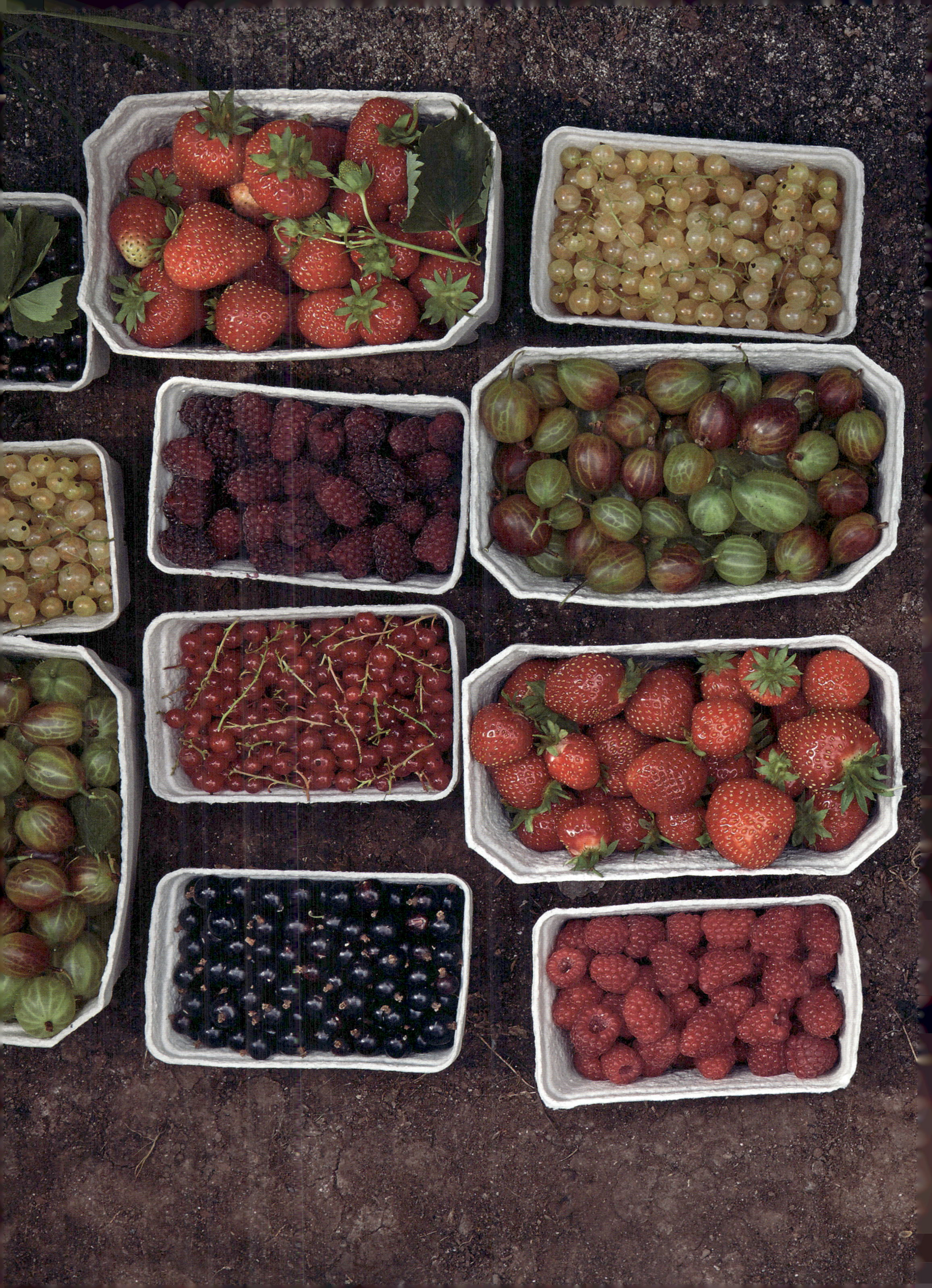

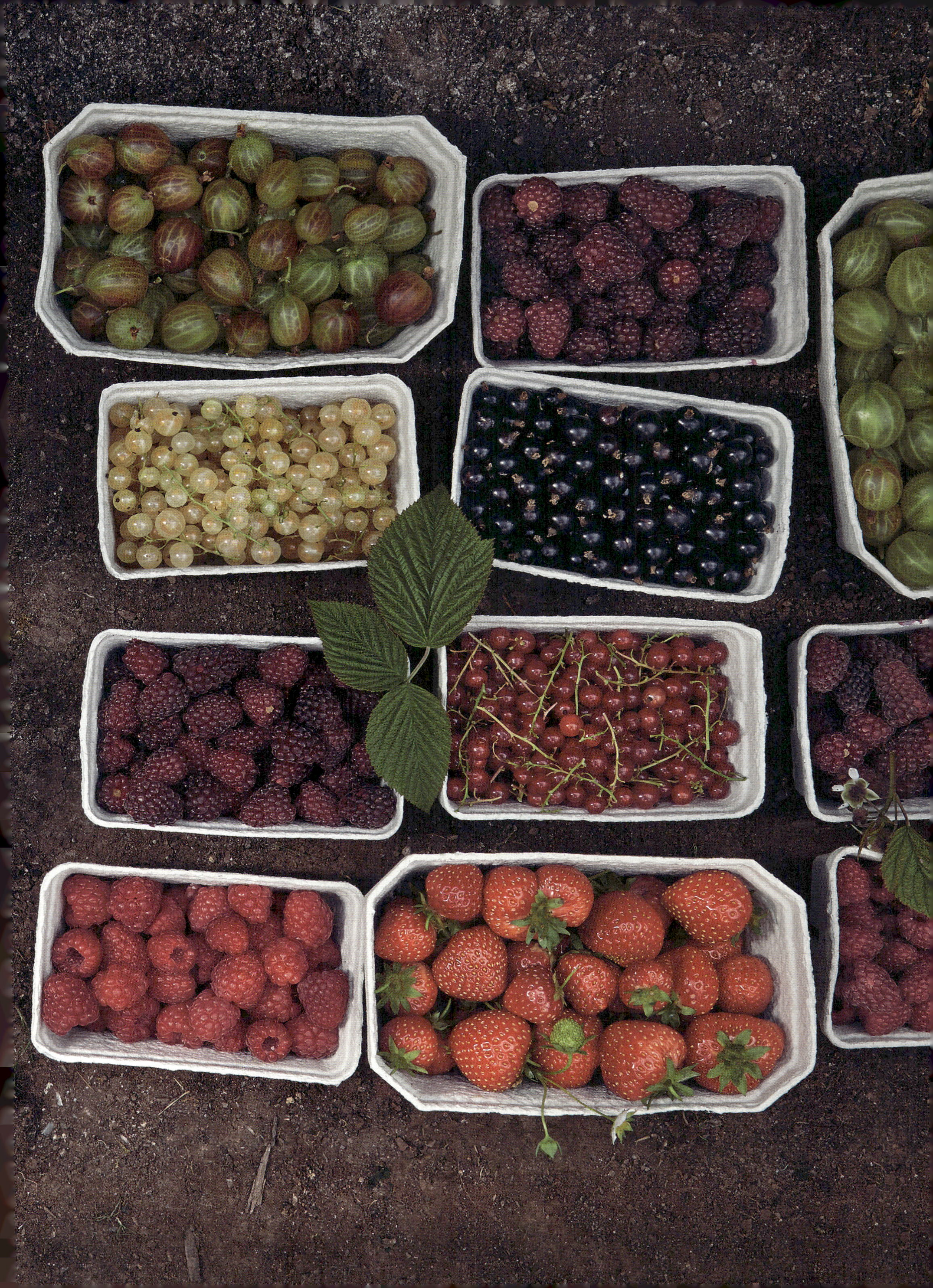

Summer fruit trifle

SERVES 8–10

For the jelly
1.5kg soft fruit (see right)
granulated sugar
5 gelatine leaves

For the génoise sponge cake
6 eggs
170g caster sugar
170g plain flour, sifted twice
75g unsalted butter, melted

For the custard
1 vanilla pod
600ml double cream
6 egg yolks
2 teaspoons cornflour
60g caster sugar

For the fruit fillings
300g blackcurrants, topped and tailed
1 dessertspoon granulated sugar
75ml kirsch (optional)
500g strawberries
500g raspberries

To finish the trifle
4 sprigs of redcurrants
4 sprigs of white currants
1 egg white
caster sugar
800ml double cream, stiffly whipped
a few edible flowers, such as violas, pansies or roses (optional)

Trifle is one of the great British puddings, but over the years it has lost its way, all too often turning out to be a nasty, synthetic-tasting dessert. This recipe, however, is an all-singing, all-dancing showstopper of a trifle. Yes, it is time-consuming to make – and you can, of course, cheat a little here and there, if you wish – but for a special occasion it will be a delight. For the jelly, you can use any soft summer fruit, such as raspberries, redcurrants, blackcurrants, loganberries, jostaberries or strawberries. It is a good idea to make the jelly the day before, leaving it in the fridge overnight, to ensure that it has set firmly and can take the weight of all the other ingredients.

First make the jelly. There's no need to remove the stalks from the fruit, just place it in a bowl. Cover tightly with foil and put the bowl in a roasting tin. Place them both in an oven preheated to 140°C/Gas Mark 1 and fill the roasting tin very full with hot water. Leave for about 1½ hours, until the fruit looks withered and all the juice has run out. You may want to mash the fruit lightly halfway through to speed things up a little.

Pour the mixture through a sieve set over a bowl and leave until all the juice has dripped through. Measure the juice and top it up with water if necessary to make 900ml. Pour into a saucepan, heat gently and sweeten to taste, stirring to dissolve the sugar. Currants will need about 2–3 tablespoons of sugar; raspberries or loganberries much less, possibly only a dessertspoon. Meanwhile, soak the gelatine leaves in cold water for 5 minutes, until soft and pliable, then gently squeeze out excess water. Remove the pan from the heat and drop the gelatine leaves into the juice. Stir until they dissolve; this should be fairly instant. Leave the juice to cool, then pour it into a 4-litre glass trifle bowl and cover with cling film. If you wish to make some jelly cubes for decoration, pour some of the juice into an ice-cube tray and put it in the fridge. Place the trifle bowl carefully in the fridge. The jelly will take 2–3 hours to set, but it is best left overnight.

Next make the cake. Lightly grease three 18cm sandwich cake tins and line the bases with a circle of baking parchment. Break the eggs into a large mixing bowl and add the sugar. Whisk with an electric hand mixer (or a balloon whisk and plenty of elbow grease) until the mixture is pale and mousselike; it should be thick enough to leave a ribbon trail on the surface when the whisk is lifted. Carefully fold in about half of the sifted flour with a large metal spoon. Pour the cool melted butter over the surface and fold it in, immediately followed by the remaining flour. It's important to do all this as quickly and lightly as possible, so you don't lose too much air.

Divide the mixture between the prepared cake tins and place in an oven preheated to 180°C/Gas Mark 4. Bake for 25–30 minutes, until the cakes are golden and beginning to shrink from the sides of the tins. Leave in the tins for 5 minutes, then turn out on to wire racks to cool.

continued overleaf

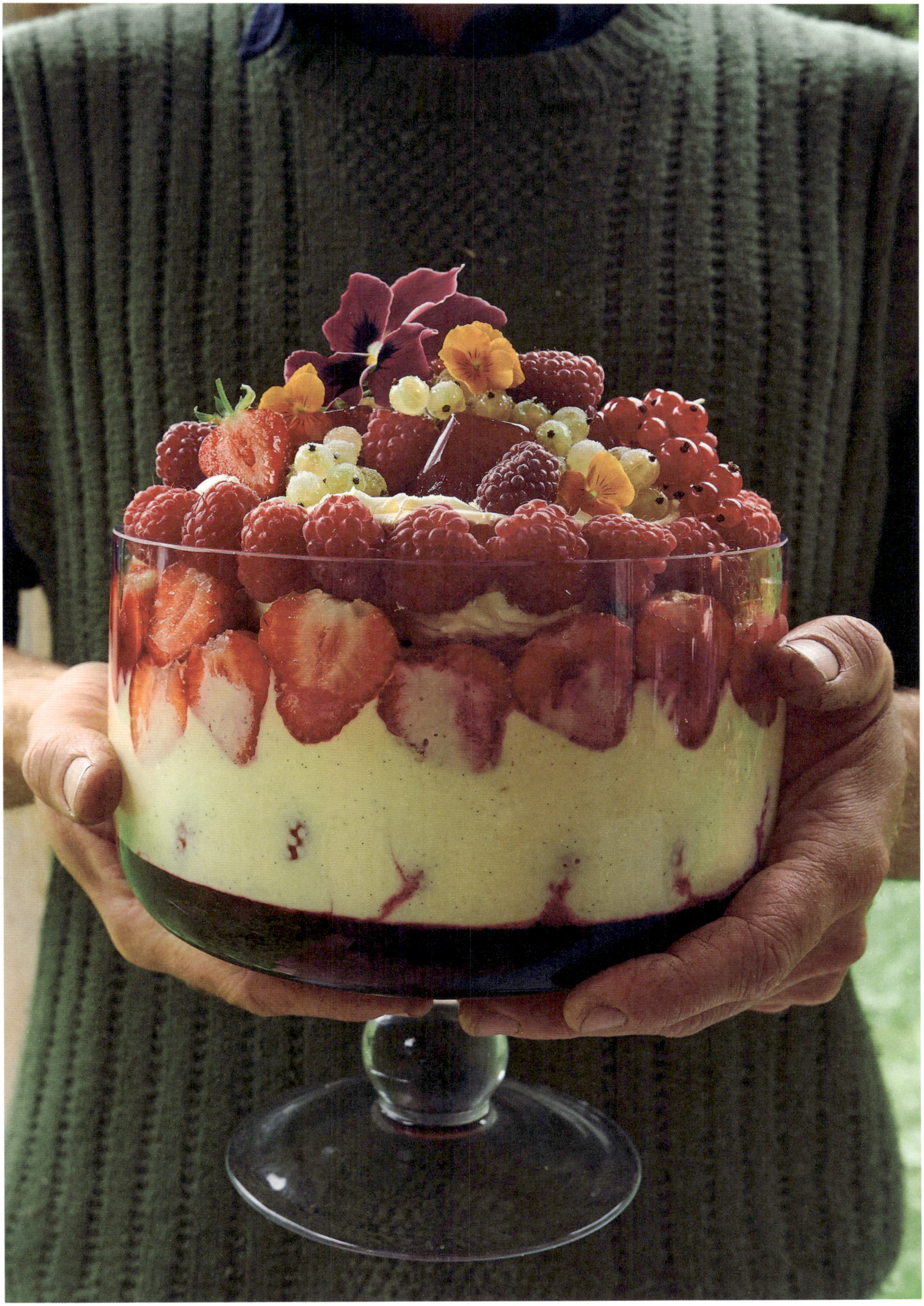

Now make the custard. Slit the vanilla pod open lengthways and scrape out the seeds. Pour the cream into a saucepan, add the vanilla pod and seeds and place on a low heat. Bring to just under a simmer, then remove from the heat. In a bowl, mix the egg yolks, cornflour and sugar together with a balloon whisk. Gradually pour the hot cream on to the egg mixture, whisking vigorously. Return the mixture to the pan and cook over a very low heat, whisking gently, for about 5 minutes, until thickened. Remove from the heat and strain through a fine sieve into a bowl. Press a sheet of cling film over the surface to prevent a skin forming and leave to cool.

Next prepare the fruit fillings. Put the blackcurrants in a saucepan with the sugar and bring to a simmer, stirring until the sugar has dissolved. They should resemble a sloppy jam, or compote. If you wish to make the trifle boozy, add the kirsch to the currants at the end of the cooking. Taste for sweetness and add a little more sugar, if necessary.

Cut the strawberries in half lengthways, saving a few for decoration. If the stalks are pretty on these, leave them on. Return them to the fridge until you are ready to assemble the trifle.

To frost the sprigs of currants for decorating the trifle, make sure they are completely dry. Lightly whisk the egg white with a fork for a minute, then take a small paintbrush and carefully paint the surface of each currant with egg white. As you finish each sprig, dip the fruit into a bowl of caster sugar, ensuring the currants are well coated. Place the glittering sprigs on a sheet of greaseproof paper and leave in a cool, airy spot to dry for half an hour.

Finally the time has come to assemble the trifle. Take the set jelly from the fridge. Spread the blackcurrant compote over the sponge cakes. Place the first sponge, currant-side up, on top of the jelly, trimming it to fit the bowl, if necessary. Spread half the custard over the sponge and then arrange some strawberries, cut side facing out, around the inside of the trifle bowl. Add the second layer of cake, spread it with the remaining custard and arrange the rest of the strawberries on top. Then add the final layer of cake and blackcurrant and top with some of the raspberries, leaving enough to fit round the edge of the bowl. Pile the whipped cream on top. Make a necklace of raspberries around the rim of the bowl, pushing them gently into the cream to stop them falling off. Decorate with the frosted currants, the reserved strawberries and some jelly cubes, if you made them. For extra prettiness, add the edible flowers. Serve slightly chilled.

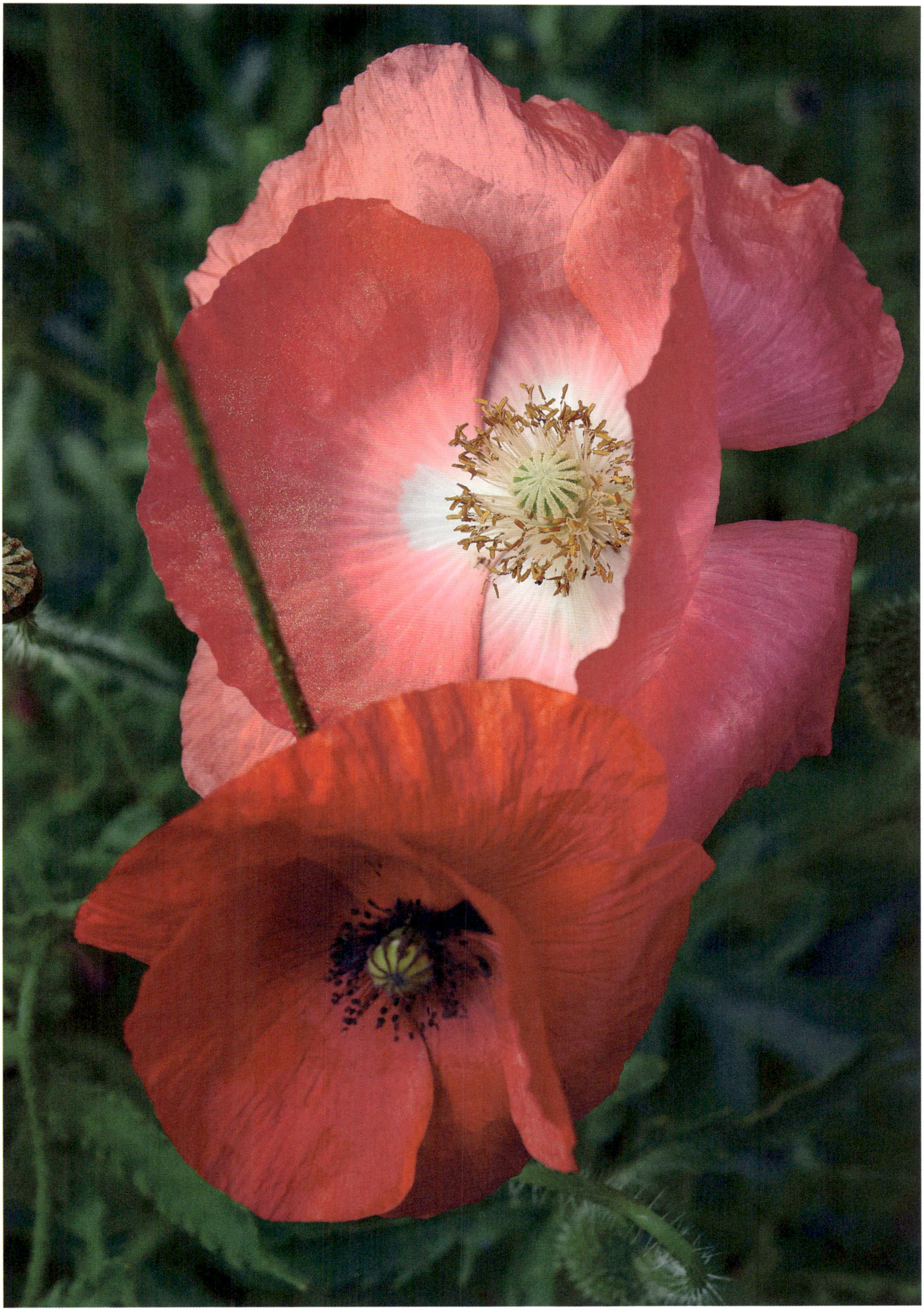

Jostaberry ripple ice cream

SERVES 6

For the vanilla ice cream
400ml milk
200ml double cream
1 vanilla pod
6 egg yolks, beaten
100g granulated sugar

For the ripple
400g jostaberries
200g granulated sugar

We can't remember how many times we have been asked what a jostaberry is. It is, in fact, a cross between a gooseberry and a blackcurrant – and the best of both. Jostaberries grow on a large bush with leaves and flowers similar to those of blackcurrant bushes, without the sharp needles of a gooseberry bush. The size of small marbles, with bright-green flesh and reddish-black skins, they have a flavour that swings more towards the blackcurrant. Their star attribute is not only their taste but their outstanding performance in the kitchen. When they are cooked for pies, fools and suchlike, their strong, concentrated flavour really shines. You could, of course, substitute blackcurrants in this recipe.

Put the milk and cream in a saucepan. Slit the vanilla pod open lengthways, scrape out the seeds and put the seeds and pod in the pan. Heat slowly, stirring occasionally, until it is just too hot to put your finger in; do not allow it to boil. Meanwhile, whisk the egg yolks and sugar together in a bowl. When the milk mixture is hot enough, pour it on to the eggs and sugar, whisking constantly. Return the mixture to the pan and heat gently, stirring, until it is thick enough to coat the back of the spoon. This can take up to 15 minutes. Remove from the heat and leave to cool, then chill for at least 2 hours.

For the ripple, put the berries and sugar in a pan, cover and cook gently, stirring occasionally to dissolve the sugar (there's no need to top and tail the fruit, as the sauce will be strained once cooked). Once the fruit has split its skins and the juices are flowing, remove from the heat. Allow it to cool a little, then blitz in a liquidiser or food processor. Strain through a sieve to remove the skin and pips, leaving the syrup to drip through until you are left with a dry pulp in the sieve. Cover the syrup and chill for a few hours.

Remove the vanilla pod from the custard and give it a good whisk to ensure it hasn't separated. Churn the custard in an ice-cream machine according to the manufacturer's instructions. When it is thick and almost frozen, pour the syrup into the machine and allow it to streak the ice cream as much or as little as you wish. Transfer to a plastic container and freeze. Soften slightly before serving.

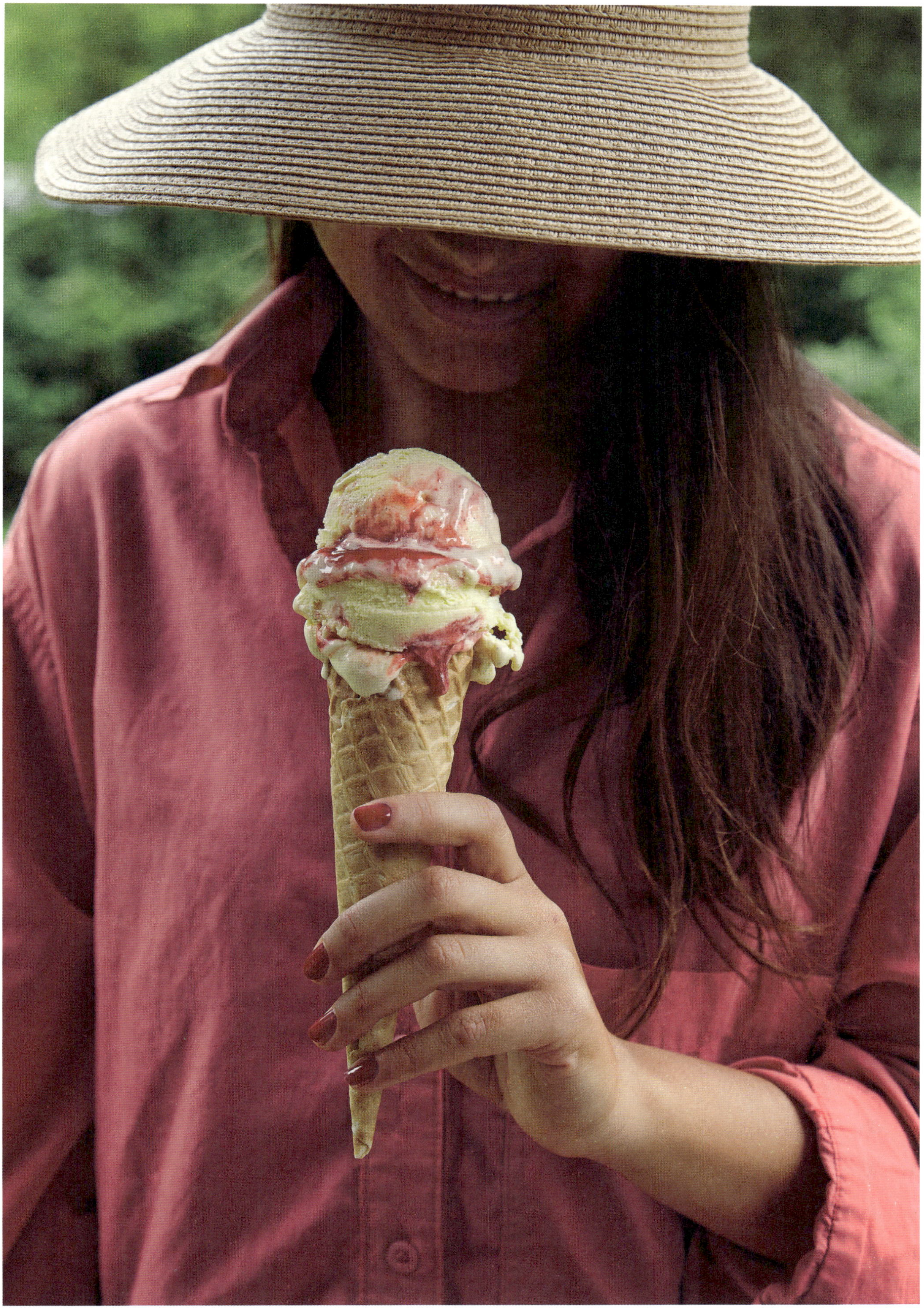

Rose angel cake with crystallised rose petals

85g plain flour
265g caster sugar
9 egg whites
a pinch of salt
1¼ teaspoons cream of tartar
½ capful of vanilla extract
3 drops of almond extract

For the crystallised rose petals
rose petals – as many or as few as you like
1 egg white
caster sugar for dusting

For the rosewater icing
80g icing sugar
2 dessertspoons rosewater
2 drops of pink food colouring

This cake has been in our family repertoire for years, made many times for a summer birthday party. It is as light as a feather, with a spongy, marshmallowy texture and looks beautiful decorated with baby-pink rosewater icing and rose petals. The cake is best made a day in advance as it needs to be left in the tin for at least 8 hours after baking. The rose petals also need preparing the day before you plan to serve the cake.

First pick your rose petals; a variety of sizes and colours is nice. Choose only perfect blooms and handle them carefully so as not to damage them. Lightly beat the egg white. If it is rather thick, add a tiny splash of water and beat briefly again. Using a small, delicate pastry brush or paintbrush, apply a very thin layer of egg white to the entire surface of each petal. Dust with caster sugar to form an even coating. Shake off any excess sugar. Lay the petals out on a tray lined with baking parchment and leave overnight in a warm, very dry place.

Heat the oven to 180°C/Gas Mark 4. Sift the flour and 150g of the caster sugar together 3 times, then set aside. Put the egg whites, salt and cream of tartar in a large bowl and whisk with an electric beater until foamy. Add the remaining caster sugar 2 tablespoons at a time, sprinkling it evenly over the mixture before whisking it in. Add the vanilla and almond extracts and continue to whisk until the mixture stands in stiff peaks. Using a large metal spoon, fold in the sifted flour and sugar a couple of tablespoons at a time, being careful not to over fold and knock out the air.

Transfer the mixture to an angel cake tin (don't grease the tin first), level the surface and draw a knife through it to break any bubbles. Bake for 35–45 minutes, until the cake is risen and light brown. Turn the tin over on to a wire rack and leave for at least 8 hours – overnight is ideal – then remove the cake from the tin.

For the icing, sift the icing sugar into a bowl and stir in the rosewater little by little, ensuring that the icing is not too thin. Add the colouring a drop at a time to achieve the desired shade. Spoon the icing in streams around the edge and top of the cake, allowing it to trickle down the sides.

Arrange the crystallised rose petals on top and, if you have plenty, apply them to the sides as well. Of course, you can eat the petals and, if you have chosen very scented roses, they will taste delightful.

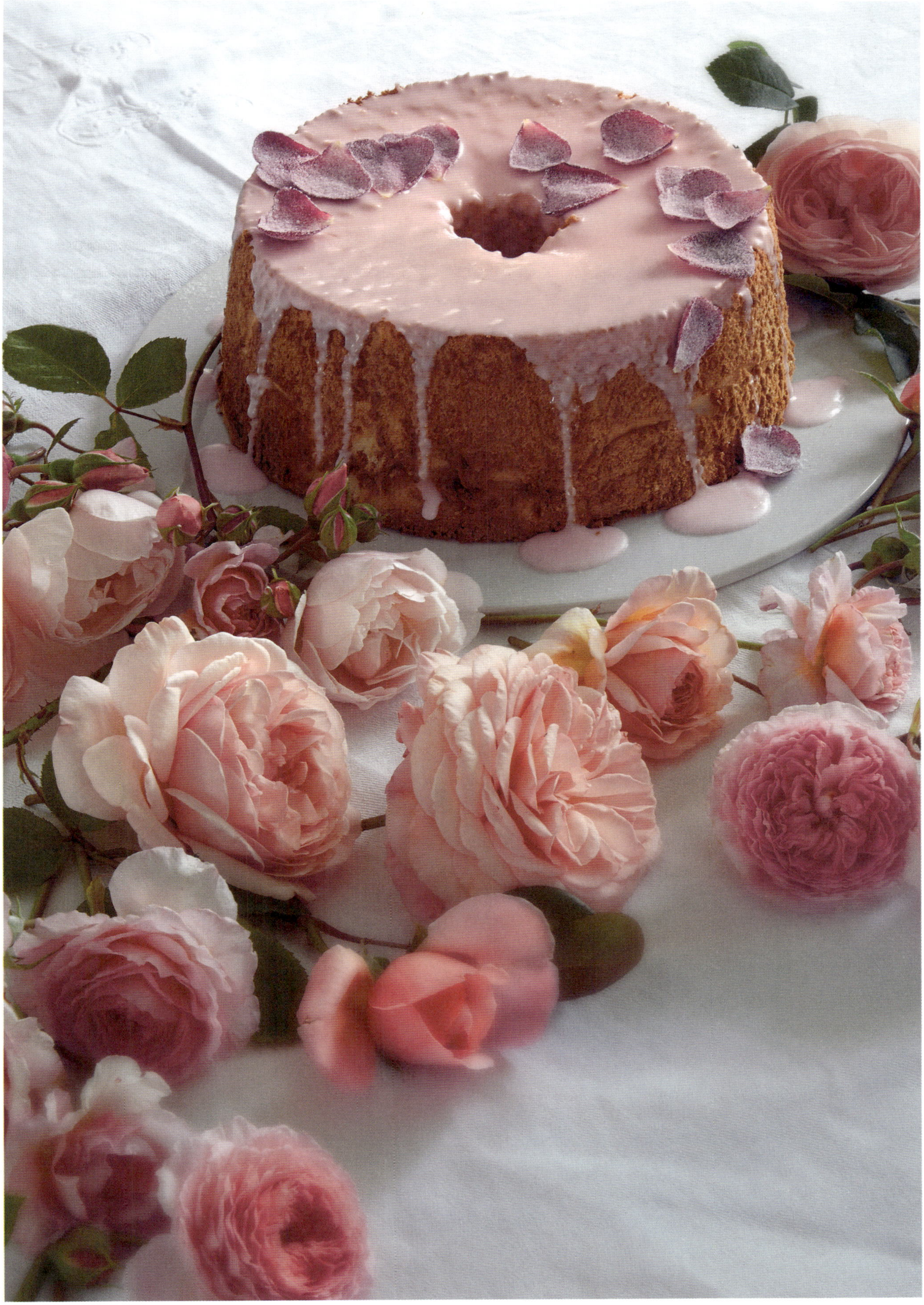

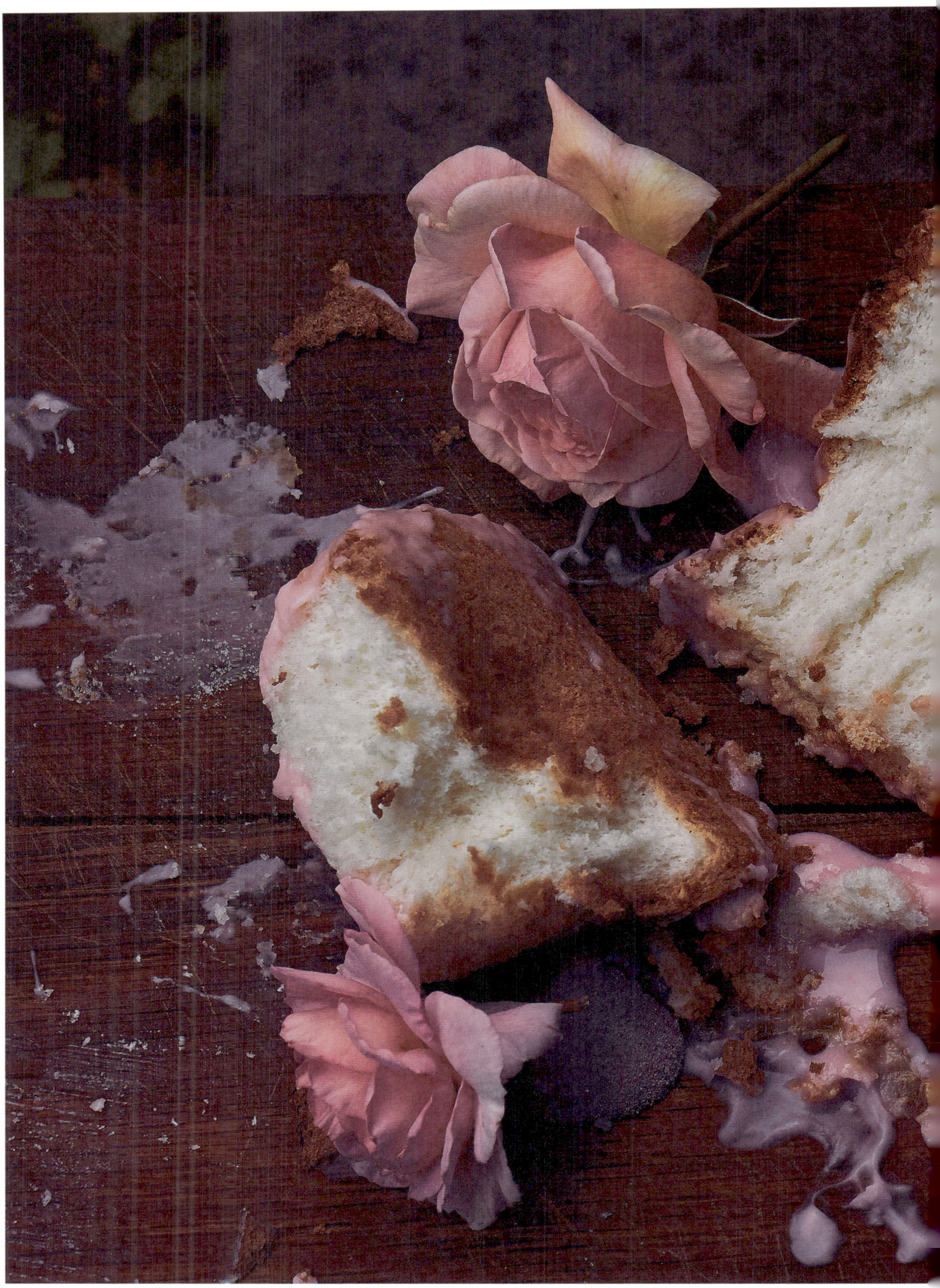

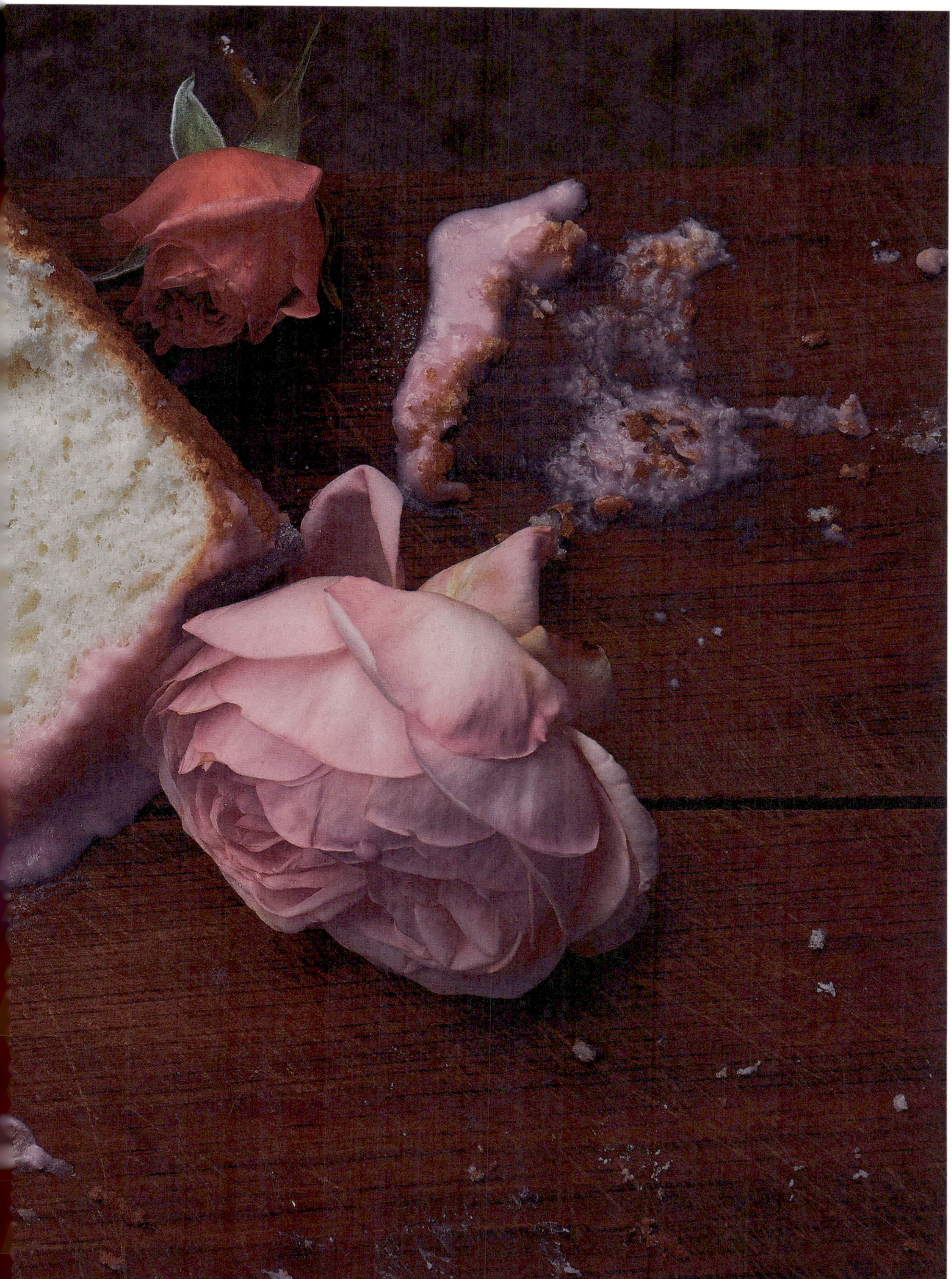

Fruit vinegar

MAKES 6 X 250ML BOTTLES

1kg berries
600ml cider vinegar
about 1.3kg granulated sugar

We started making our own berry vinegars during a glut some years ago, using the not-so-perfect-looking fruit that we couldn't take to the market. Favourites are raspberry, strawberry and loganberry or a mixture of these. Now fruit vinegars have become a staple in our kitchen and we find them extremely useful (see our suggestions below).

Always use the freshest fruit you can get hold of, but remember it doesn't matter what the fruit looks like, as you're going to mash it up for its juice. It is important that the fruit is dry, especially if you are using strawberries or raspberries, so try not to wash it. You can also use a mixture of elderberries and wild blackberries for a foraged, more savoury vinegar.

Put the berries into a large ceramic or glass bowl. Add the vinegar and gently crush the fruit with a potato masher or a large fork. Cover tightly and leave in a cool room for at least 5 days, stirring once each day.

Line a sieve with a piece of sterilised muslin, set it over a bowl and pour the fruit and vinegar into it. Tie the corners of the muslin together and suspend the bag over the bowl for 12 hours for the juice to drip through.

Measure the juice and allow 450g sugar for every 500ml. Put the juice and sugar into a large stainless steel saucepan, place over a low heat and slowly bring to the boil, stirring until the sugar is completely dissolved. Boil for 10 minutes, then remove from the heat and leave to cool. Pour into sterilised bottles (see page 251) and seal straightaway. It should keep for at least a year.

A few suggestions

Salad dressings – fruit vinegars suit the peppery and bitter salad leaves of winter and spring in particular. Wilted beetroot tops with goat's curd dressed in loganberry or raspberry vinegar makes a delicious warm salad.

Root vegetables – a good splash or two gives an uplifting sticky-sweet texture and flavour to a tray of roasting root vegetables (see page 40).

Marinades – add fruit vinegar for both flavour and viscosity; perfect for beautifully sticky ribs.

Gravy – use to deglaze the roasting tin when making gravy, or add a couple of tablespoons to a stew for a new flavour dimension.

Drinks – diluted with sparkling or still water, fruit vinegars make a refreshing, cleansing tonic.

Gooseberry and elderflower jam

MAKES 12 X 340G JARS

2kg gooseberries, topped and tailed
1 litre water
20 heads of elderflower
2kg granulated sugar

The best flavour combinations often come about when ingredients are at their prime, in full-blown season. The marriage of gooseberry and elderflower is no exception. This is one of our best-selling jams, and the tartness of the gooseberries with the heavily scented Muscat flavour of elderflower is glorious. We make this pretty pink jam in batches over a period of a few weeks; if the weather has been warm towards the end of the gooseberry season, the fruit can be sweeter than at the beginning. So if you are using a late-season variety, we suggest reducing the amount of sugar a little. Gooseberries have a high level of pectin so this is a quick jam to make, and a good set is pretty much guaranteed. On a dry day pick the elderflowers in the morning, choosing only the best and avoiding the ones with dying brown flowers. Shake them gently to remove any wildlife.

Place the gooseberries in a large pan and pour in the water. Tie the elderflowers into a piece of muslin. Place the elderflower bag on top of the gooseberries, then cover and stew gently over a low heat until the gooseberries are soft but still holding their shape.

Remove the bag of elderflowers but do not discard it. Add the sugar to the pan and stir gently until it dissolves. Replace the muslin bag and slowly bring the mixture to the boil. Cook at a rolling boil, uncovered, for 15 minutes, then test for setting point (see page 251). When the jam has reached setting point remove from the heat and allow it to rest for 10 minutes. Transfer to sterilised jars and seal straightaway. It should keep for a year.

Redcurrant jelly

MAKES 4 X 225G JARS

1kg redcurrants
400ml water
granulated sugar

Probably the best thing about growing redcurrants is how beautiful they look on the bush. They are the first of the currants to ripen, perfectly round opaque scarlet pearls, symmetrically arranged on delicate stalks. Birds are very attracted to these gems, so netting is essential.

The French like to eat redcurrant jelly with croissants, its tartness cutting through the sweet, buttery richness. It is also ideal to use as a glaze for a strawberry or raspberry tart or to fill jam tarts – a mixture of redcurrant jelly tarts and lemon curd tarts on a plate proves irresistible.

Place the redcurrants, stalks still attached, in a large pan, removing any leaves, damaged fruit or wildlife as you go. Add the water, cover and cook over a low heat for about 30 minutes, until the currants are very soft and the juice a very dark red. Line a sieve with a piece of sterilised muslin, set it over a bowl and pour the juice and fruit into it. To ensure that you have a crystal-clear jelly, do not push or squeeze the fruit through, tempting though it is, as any sediment will cloud the jelly and spoil its bright appearance. Tie the corners of the muslin together and suspend the bag over the bowl overnight or for at least 6 hours.

Strain the juice again through a sieve, only this time to remove any fruit flies that may have fallen in. Measure the juice and allow 400g sugar for every 600ml juice. Pour the juice into a saucepan and bring slowly to the boil. Add the sugar and stir until completely dissolved. Boil for 10 minutes, then test for setting point (see page 251). Remove from the heat, pour into sterilised jars (see page 251) and seal. It should keep for a year.

Variation

The jam tarts in the picture are filled with redcurrant jelly, gooseberry and elderflower jam (see page 197) and lemon curd (see page 121). Use the pastry recipe from the blackcurrant pie on page 179. Roll it out on a lightly floured surface to 3–4mm thick, cut out rounds with a pastry cutter or a glass and use to line bun tins. Spoon in the jam or lemon curd, filling the tarts no more than three-quarters full, otherwise they will bubble over in the oven and spoil the appearance. Bake at 180°C/Gas Mark 4 for 10–15 minutes, until the pastry is lightly coloured. Remove from the oven and leave to cool a little before lifting out on to a wire rack.

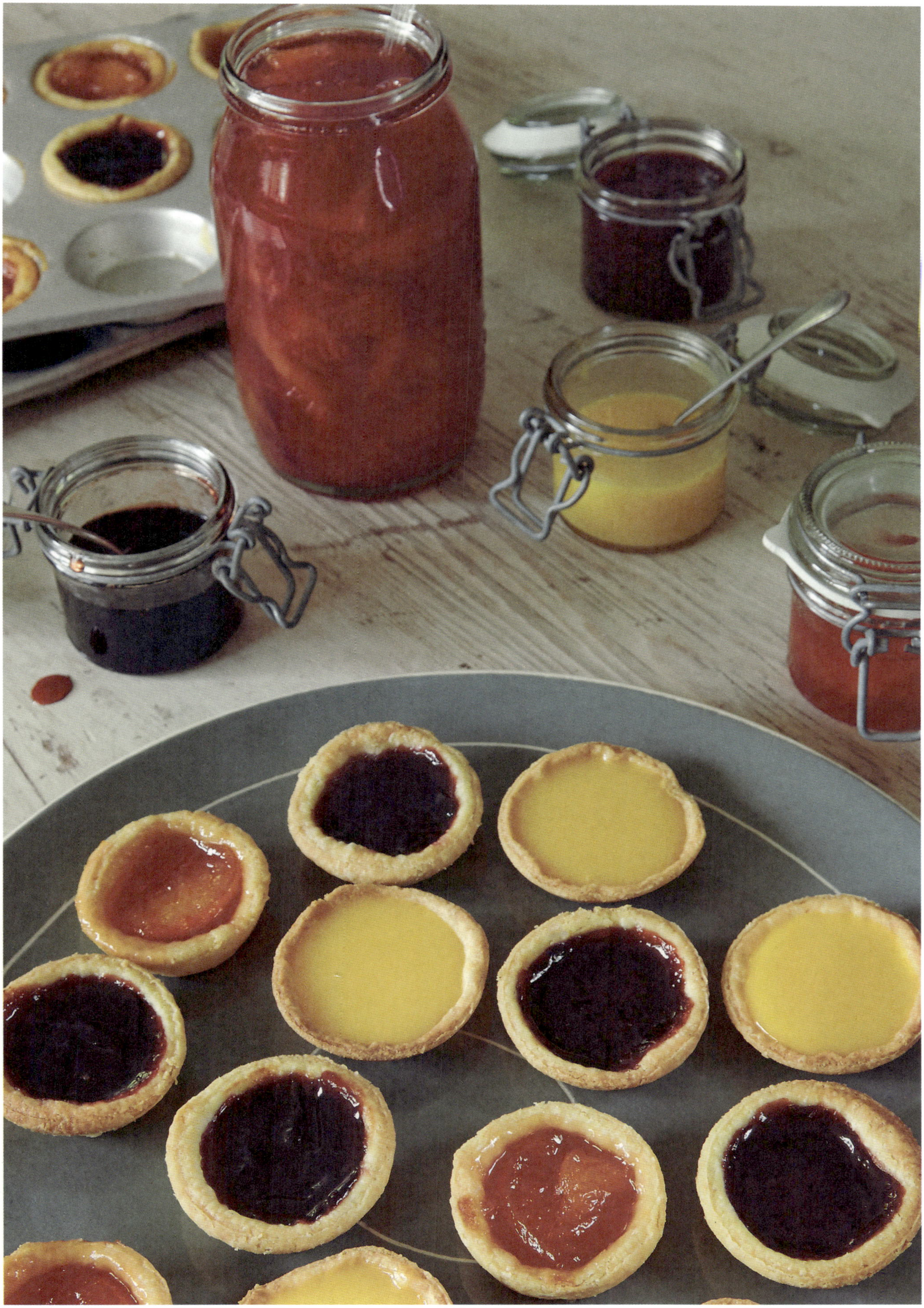

FIRE
Autumn

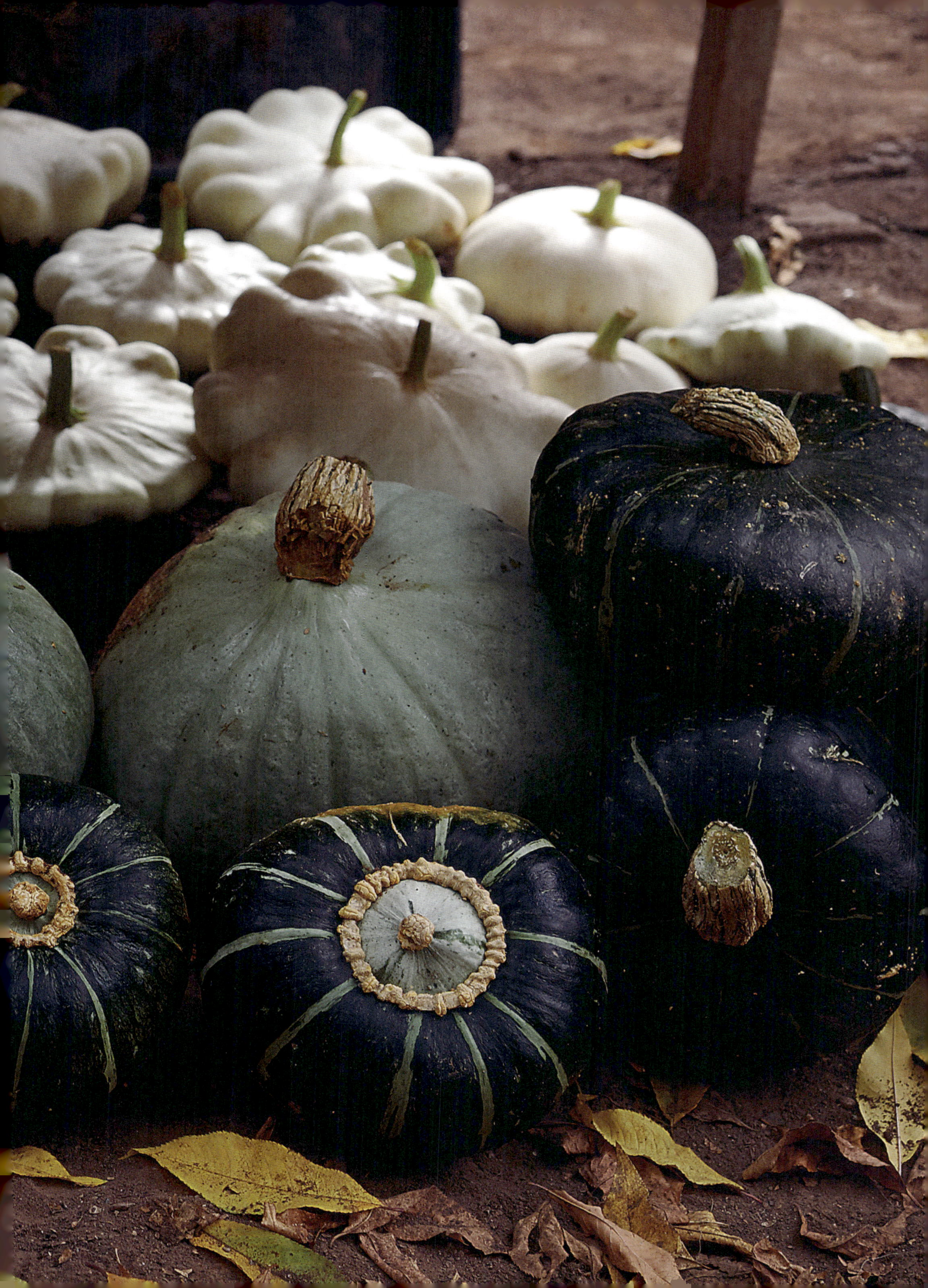

ON THE FARM the first sign of autumn spins us around and forces us to change direction. For the past six months, we have concentrated on nurturing and caring for the plants and animals, and adapting to their daily needs. We have spent every day immersed in the present. Autumn severs us from the immediacy of the plants, and the growth and warmth that carry us along with them. Now we must look ahead to the future; we feel the urgency of getting as much done as possible before the cold and wet slow everything down.

Animals, too, are busy preparing for what lies ahead. The hedgerows bustle with activity. Birds are feeding themselves up for migration. Field mice, squirrels and hedgehogs are gathering their winter stores. The sheep and cows are fattening and developing thicker coats. Sugar-seeking bees and wasps buzz around, eating the autumn raspberries and finding a taste for ripening apples, so harvesting and preserving these fruits is high on our list of priorities. The tang of vinegar and sugar hangs in the kitchen air as we go about making jams, jellies, syrups, chutneys and pickles.

Over the next couple of months, we will continue to sow, and to plant young salad leaves and other leaf crops in the greenhouse, but by the beginning of September planting outside has finished. The countless hours of weeding and cultivating that have filled the majority of each week, particularly since May, are coming to an end.

Each day the sun makes a slightly lower arc in the sky, its intense golden light casting longer shadows. With less warmth and daylight, the outward

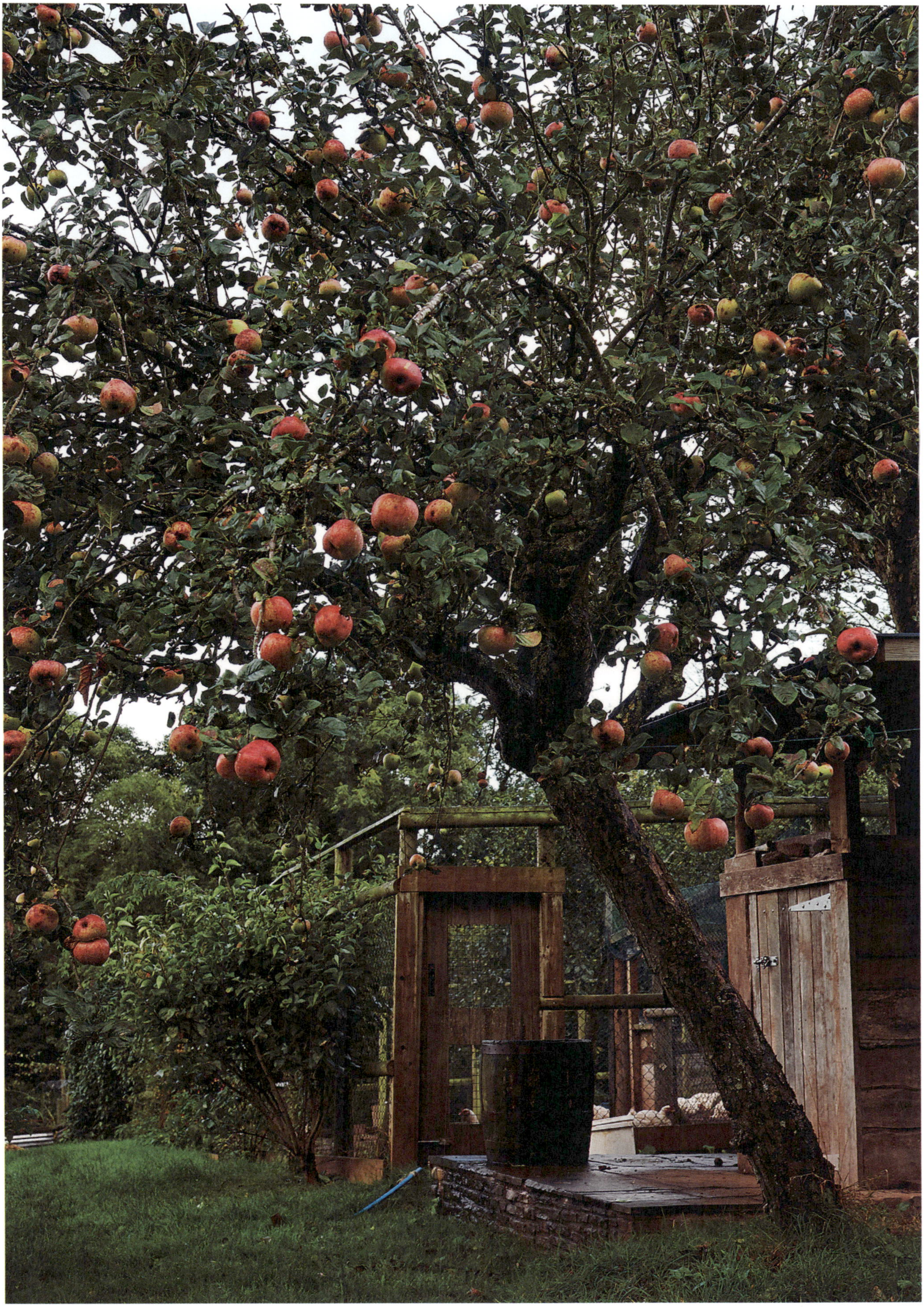

growth of the plants slows down. Now their activity turns inwards. The heads of cabbages begin to fill and all the leaf and root crops start to develop their depth of flavour and colour. The flowers that have produced so generously since spring are gracefully diminishing their display and the fruiting processes take their curtain call.

We feel very much a part of the ebb and flow of the seasons, the breathing out in spring and summer and the breathing in of autumn and winter. Autumn is a time for initiative. At Michaelmas, in late September, we celebrate this strong inner renewal and we conquer our exhaustion.

Now the radicchio and endive planted in the middle of August are at their best, with exquisite leaves and pleasingly bitter flavours that are particularly good with a raspberry vinegar dressing. The arrival of the winter squash brings inspiration for purées, roasts and risottos. Walking along the rows of growing cauliflowers, we are thrilled when we come across the first heads of creamy curds, as if we have never seen them before. The leeks have beautiful blue-green leaves and pure white shafts: at this moment in the year they look perfect, although their flavour intensifies with time and is usually at its best from mid-October.

Fewer daylight hours for outdoor work mean there is now more time for the kitchen. We relish the last tastes of the summer vegetables and fruit, but now it's the turn of the new textures, colours and flavours of the autumn harvest to stimulate our senses. For us this is the most exciting time of the year with the greatest variety of delicious food to cook and eat.

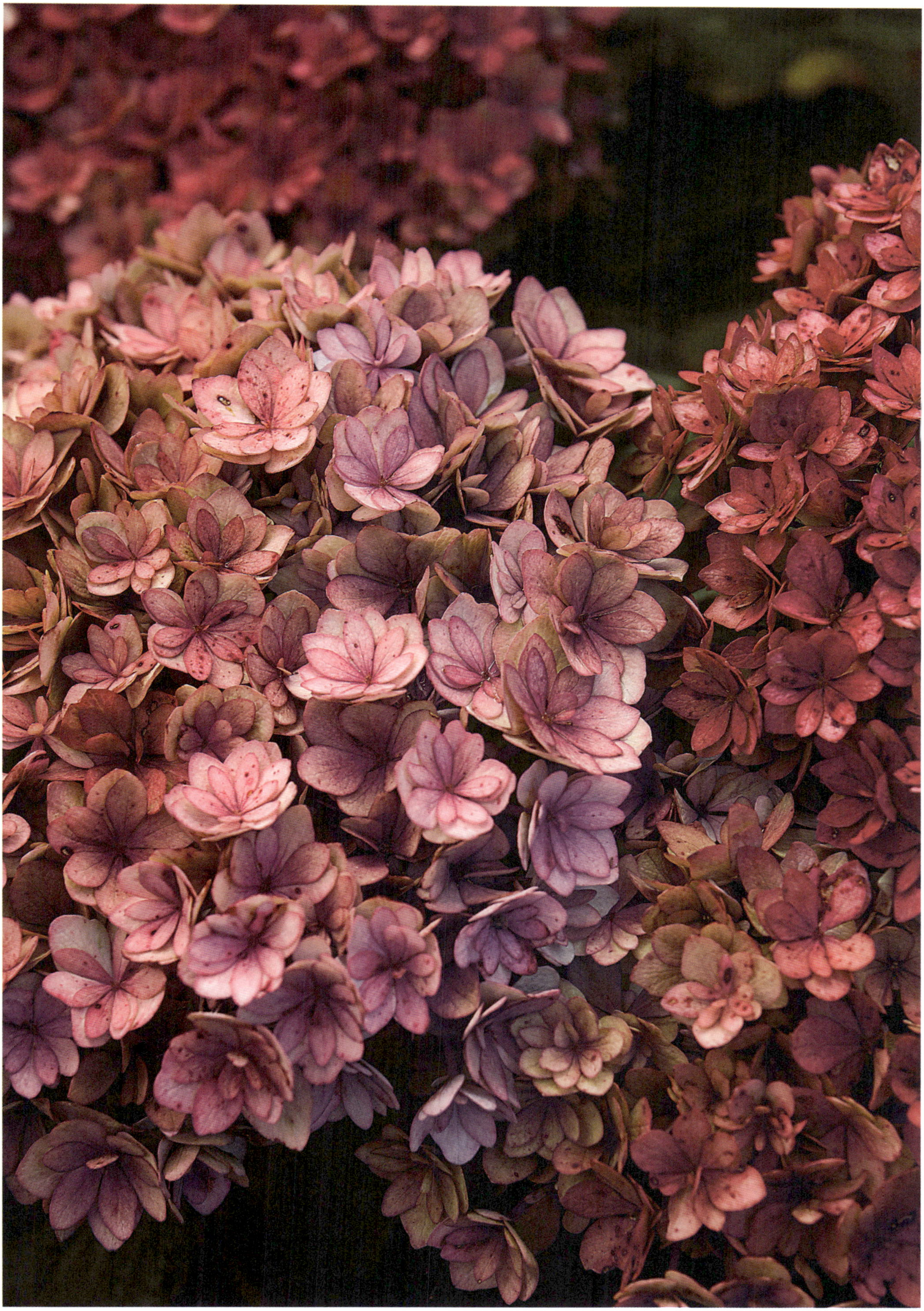

Tomato, red lentil and orange soup

SERVES 6–8

4 tablespoons olive oil

1 onion, roughly chopped

1 celery stick, plus its leaves, roughly chopped

2 carrots, chopped

1 garlic clove, crushed

2 bay leaves

2kg beefsteak tomatoes, or other ripe, juicy tomatoes, roughly chopped

250g red lentils

500ml water

3 finger-length strips of orange zest

sea salt and black pepper

The inclusion of red lentils not only gives this soup great texture and body, it also takes the edge off the acidity that can sometimes be unpleasant in a tomato soup. You can use very ripe tomatoes here, ones that are perhaps too ripe for eating fresh, and they will give a more intense flavour. We like to serve the soup topped with sprouted seeds, but a sprinkling of parsley will do just as well.

Heat the oil in a large pan and stir in the onion, celery, carrots, garlic and bay leaves. Cover and cook gently for about 15 minutes, until soft. Add the chopped tomatoes, mix well and season with salt and pepper. Cook, covered, over a medium heat for about 20 minutes, until the tomatoes have broken down and released their juices. Add the lentils, water and orange zest and bring to the boil. Reduce the heat and simmer, covered, for 40 minutes, stirring occasionally to prevent the lentils sticking to the bottom of the pan. When the soup is done, the lentils should be very soft and beginning to break up a little.

Allow the soup to cool slightly, then pass it through a mouli-légumes, if you have one. Alternatively, blitz the soup in a food processor and then pass it through a nylon sieve. The tough tomato skins will be left behind and the soup will have a lovely texture and glossy appearance. Reheat gently, adding a little water if the soup is too thick, and season to taste.

Sweetcorn, chilli, lime and potato soup

SERVES 4

3 tablespoons toasted sesame oil
1 small red onion, finely chopped
2 garlic cloves, finely chopped
30g fresh ginger, finely chopped
1 lemongrass stalk, finely chopped
1 green chilli, finely chopped
4 fresh lime leaves, finely chopped
1.5 litres chicken stock
4 corn cobs, husks removed
500g waxy potatoes, peeled and cut into 1cm cubes
juice of 1 lime
1 tablespoon fish sauce
1 bunch of coriander, chopped
sea salt and black pepper

Sweetcorn can be tricky to grow in the UK, as it depends so much on the presence of the sun to turn the starchy kernels sweet — something that can never really be relied upon on these islands. If we have had a warm summer that has in turn rolled into a warm, bright autumn, you can be sure that sweetcorn will be plentiful and of great quality. It will be cheap at the markets and this is the right moment to make this wonderfully fresh, clean-tasting humdinger of a soup.

Heat the sesame oil in a good-sized pan, add the onion, garlic, ginger, lemongrass, chilli and lime leaves and fry gently for about a minute to release their fragrance. Pour the chicken stock into the pan. Strip the corn nuggets from the cobs with a sharp knife and put them in the pot, adding the stripped cobs as well, as they will give flavour and texture to the soup. Add the potatoes and bring to the boil. Season with salt and pepper, then simmer for about 15 minutes, until the potatoes are cooked, but not falling apart.

Remove from the heat and discard the cobs. Stir in the lime juice, fish sauce and coriander and serve immediately.

Baked squash with celery and herb cream

SERVES 2 HUNGRY PEOPLE

a 1–2kg squash, such as Uchiki Kuri, Buttercup or Blue Ballet

about 300ml crème fraîche (you need enough to fill the squash by three-quarters)

juice of ½ lemon

3 sprigs of celery leaves or 1 lovage leaf

2 sprigs of rosemary, thyme or sage

1 knob of butter

1 garlic clove, finely chopped

a little grated nutmeg or ½ cinnamon stick

150g good melting cheese, such as Comté, Gruyère or Cheddar, grated

sea salt and black pepper

To garnish (optional)

3 tablespoons olive oil

4–5 sage leaves

This recipe was devised on one of the rare occasions that we had a major power cut, with three young children needing to be fed and only the wood burner for warmth and cooking. We wrapped the squash in foil and tucked them into the edges of the wood burner, away from the flames. The children dipped cubes of bread into the cheesy, fondue-style filling. It became a popular supper dish in less chaotic times, too.

Our favourite squashes to use for this recipe are Uchiki Kuri (also known as onion squash), Buttercup and Blue Ballet. All have dense, strongly flavoured flesh that soaks up flavours and fat without becoming mushy and marrow-like. The skin of the squash retains its beautiful, vibrant colour and is thin enough not to need peeling. We think it is the best part.

You can also serve this dish as a starter, using individual smaller squashes. The photo shows Sweet Dumpling – a very pretty striped and dimpled squash that is ideal for this.

Heat the oven to 200°C/Gas Mark 6. Cut the top off the squash to make a lid and set aside. Scoop out the seeds and a little of the flesh so that you are left with a clean squash bowl. To stop the squash toppling over, it is a good idea to make a base for it to sit on: take a roughly 30cm square piece of foil, squeeze it together and shape it into a 'bracelet'. Put it in a roasting tin and place the squash on top. Fill the squash three-quarters full with crème fraîche and then add the lemon juice, herb sprigs, butter, garlic and grated nutmeg or the cinnamon stick. Season with salt and pepper.

Place the lid back on the squash. Cover with foil and bake for at least an hour. The cooking time will vary, depending on the size of your squash. It is done when a sharp knife slides through the flesh with no resistance.

Remove the herb sprigs and sprinkle in the grated cheese. Place the squash back in the oven, without the foil, for about 10 minutes, until it has browned and the cheese is nice and gooey.

The fried sage garnish is optional, but it looks and tastes great. Heat the olive oil in a small frying pan and add the sage leaves, making sure they are completely dry if you have washed them. Fry for about 30 seconds, until crisp, then remove and place on kitchen paper to drain. Sprinkle the leaves on top of the squash filling.

The easiest way to serve this is to spoon out the creamy contents on to each person's plate and then cut chunks off the squash horizontally, working your way down. Serve with toasted sourdough bread.

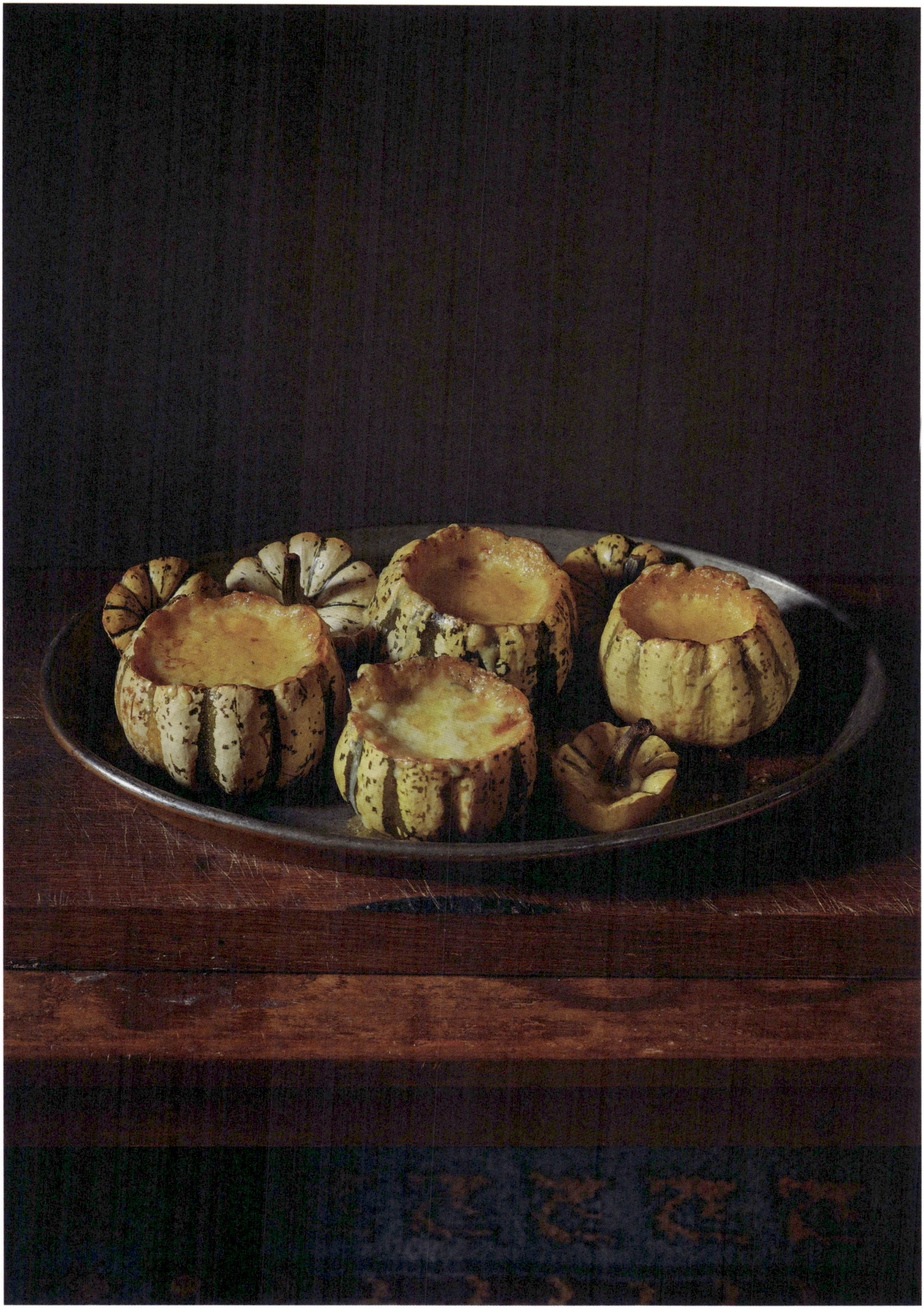

Red Florence onion Tatin

SERVES 4

8 Red Florence onions (or banana shallots or ordinary red onions)
75g butter
3 sprigs of thyme
2 dessertspoons Fruit Vinegar (see page 196)
sea salt and black pepper

For the cheese pastry
170g plain flour
a pinch of cayenne pepper
a pinch of sea salt
115g chilled butter, diced
115g cheese (half Cheddar, half Parmesan), grated
1 egg yolk
1 tablespoon cold water

We grow a lot of Red Florence onions. They are not only outstandingly beautiful, with their pink-crimson colour and pleasing shape, but they are also the perfect onion for summer and autumn – strong enough for cooking, yet sweet enough to serve raw when finely sliced or diced in salads. These onions are not storing onions and should be used fresh.

You can also make this tart with beetroot, choosing small beets and cutting them in half. The initial cooking time (between 30 and 40 minutes, depending on their size) is, of course, longer than for the onions, but bear in mind that a bit of crunch in the beetroot is nice.

First make the pastry. Sift the flour, cayenne and salt into a bowl, add the butter and cut it into the flour with a round-bladed knife. Once the butter is well coated in the flour, rub it in with your fingertips until the mixture resembles breadcrumbs. Stir in the grated cheese with a knife. Mix the egg yolk and water together and add them to the dry ingredients, mixing with the knife until everything comes together to form a dough. Knead briefly until smooth, then wrap in cling film and chill for at least half an hour.

Peel the onions, cut them in half or into quarters, depending on size, then trim the base so that the pieces remain intact. Melt the butter over a moderate heat in a 24cm Tatin tin, if you have one; if not, a 24cm ovenproof frying pan will do, providing it is at least 4cm deep. Arrange the onions cut-side down in the tin, packing them in tightly as they will shrink with cooking. Fry over a low heat so they soften rather than colour at first, then increase the heat a little and continue to cook until the onions are browned underneath; this can take about 20 minutes in total. Carefully turn the onions over, adding more butter if necessary, then add the thyme and some salt and pepper. Pour over the raspberry vinegar, turn the heat down and cover the tin with a lid or a sheet of foil to allow the heat to build and the onions to cook thoroughly. Cook for about 20 minutes, until the onions are golden and caramelised, then remove the lid or foil and allow to cool a little.

Heat the oven to 190°C/Gas Mark 5. On a lightly floured work surface, roll out the pastry to a circle about 8cm bigger than the diameter of your Tatin tin or frying pan. Cover the onions with the pastry, tucking it down the side of the tin. This does not have to be too tidy, as it will not show. Bake for about 25 minutes, until the pastry is golden brown.

Remove from the oven and leave to settle for about 5 minutes. Run a knife around the edge of the Tatin to loosen it, then place a serving plate on top of the tin and turn them both over to turn out the Tatin. Serve hot or cold, with a green salad.

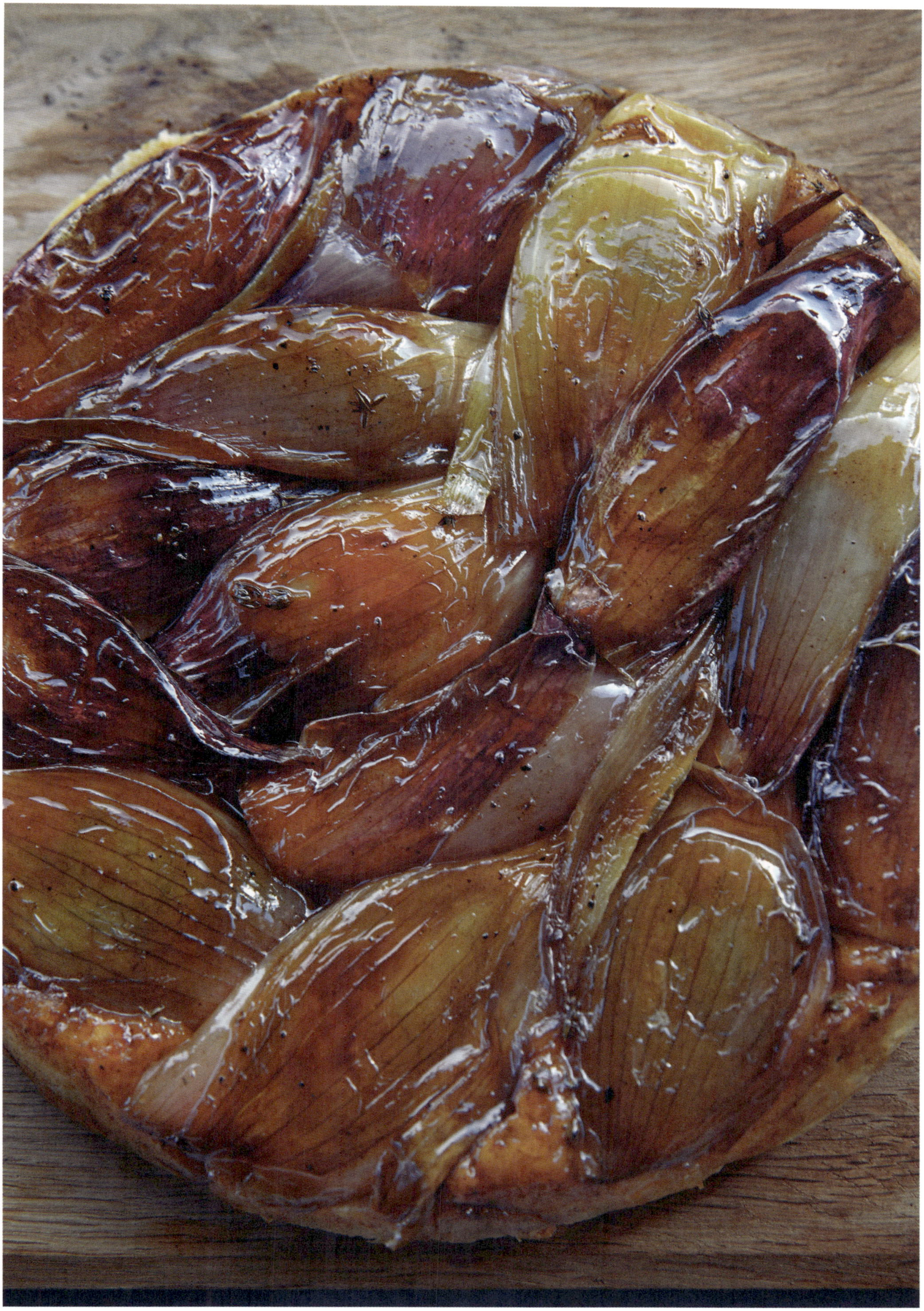

Building fertility and making compost

IN SEVERAL LOCATIONS around the farm, we've set up a series of bays through which we move compost as it progressively breaks down. Often, while we're turning a heap from one bay to the next, the conversation turns to this richly theorised subject, and we contemplate why we're collecting what's often called waste, and how it is transformed into something of great value to us in building the fertility of the soil.

Humus is naturally created from fallen leaves and other plant and animal matter that has gradually broken down and become incorporated into the ground, accumulating over time. When we make compost, we're participating in this wondrous cycle of life, death and renewal; gathering materials that were recently very much alive, putting them together, and trying to retain this life potential through the process of decay. The basis of all our growing is what we return to the soil; we're always building out of what has gone before.

Once we've assembled a good assortment of items, we begin to construct a heap. We use vegetable trimmings, fruit peelings and eggshells from the kitchen, and from outside we gather all kinds of plant matter: grass cuttings, wood ash, hedge clippings, ditch clearings, leaves, and soil scrapings from the yard, animal manure and straw from the animals' bedding. We build up the heap in alternate layers of brown rotting material (such as the manure from the poultry houses) or some soil, followed by a layer of green waste (grass cuttings and vegetable trimmings). In dry periods we add some water, to moisten everything and help with the breakdown.

We also have mineral powders to hand, to sprinkle between the layers if anything smells unpleasant. These are calcium- and silica-rich rock dusts, which we refer to as 'salt and pepper', and they always appear to help set things on the right track towards a healthy decomposition. The addition of small quantities of the biodynamic compost preparations greatly enhances this process. We make these from yarrow, chamomile, stinging nettle, oak bark, dandelion and valerian, all of which we find growing on the farm.

It's helpful to us to consider the compost heap as a living organism, composed of matter, moisture, air and warmth. When we build one anew, we cover it in a thin layer of earth that acts as a kind of skin, to protect and contain it. The freshly built heap resembles a large burial mound. On returning a couple of months later, to turn it, we find the number of worms at work within has vastly increased.

For us, it usually takes between six and nine months for the original waste materials to fully transform into a fine, dark, sweet-smelling compost. In a nutshell, we're trying to use everything available to us, and handle it in such a way that the substances that we return to the soil are infused with a stronger tendency towards life.

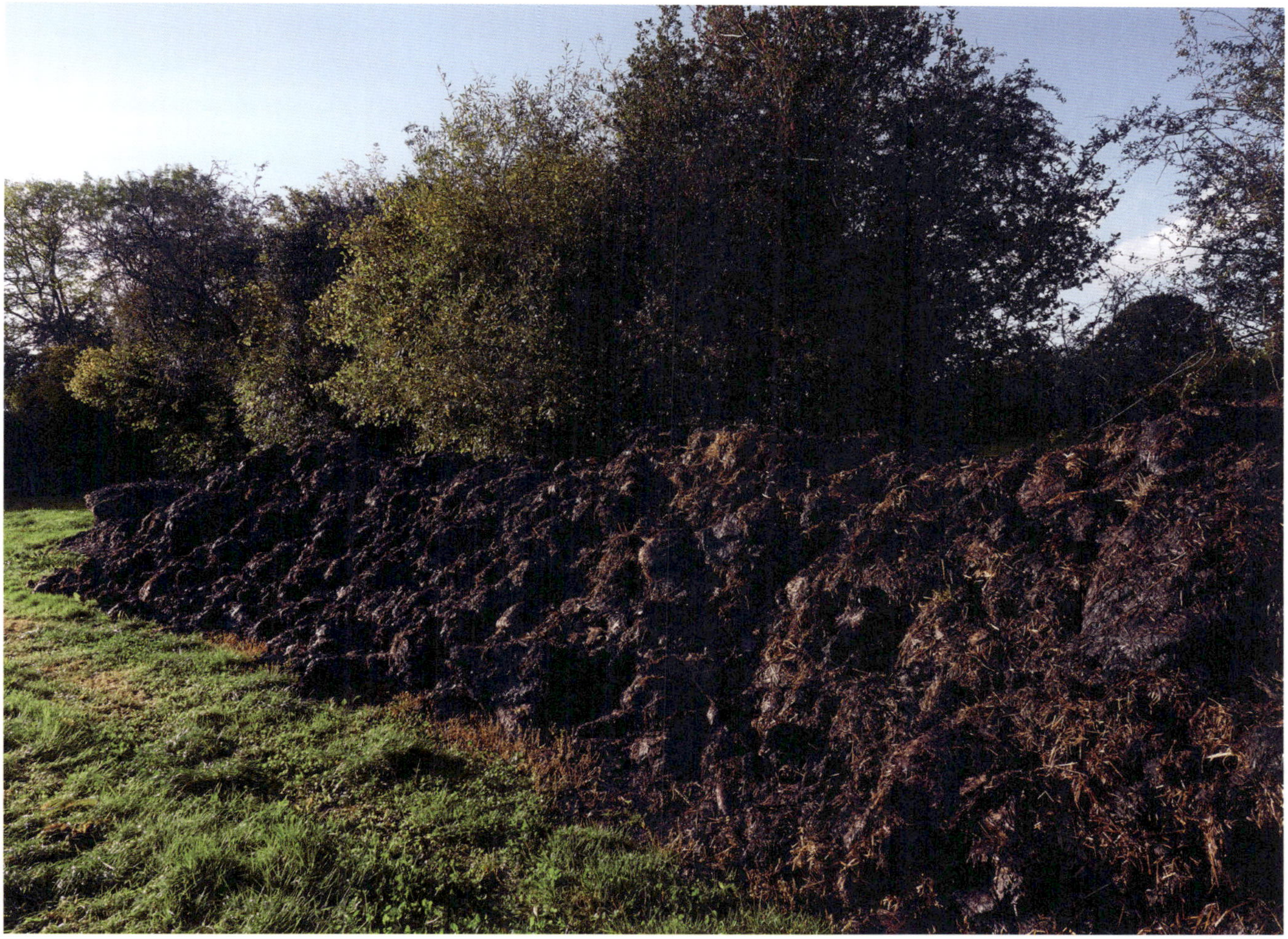

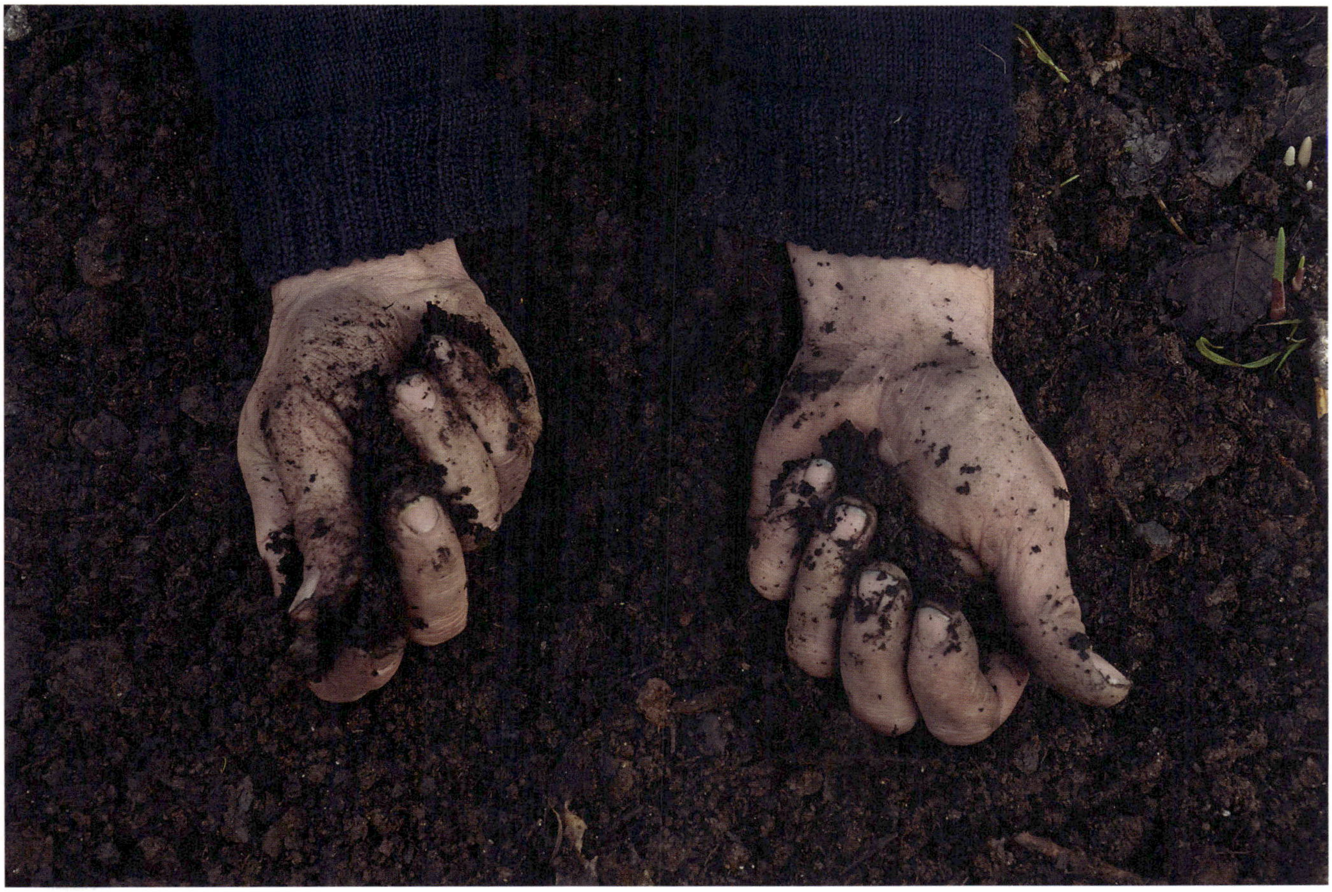

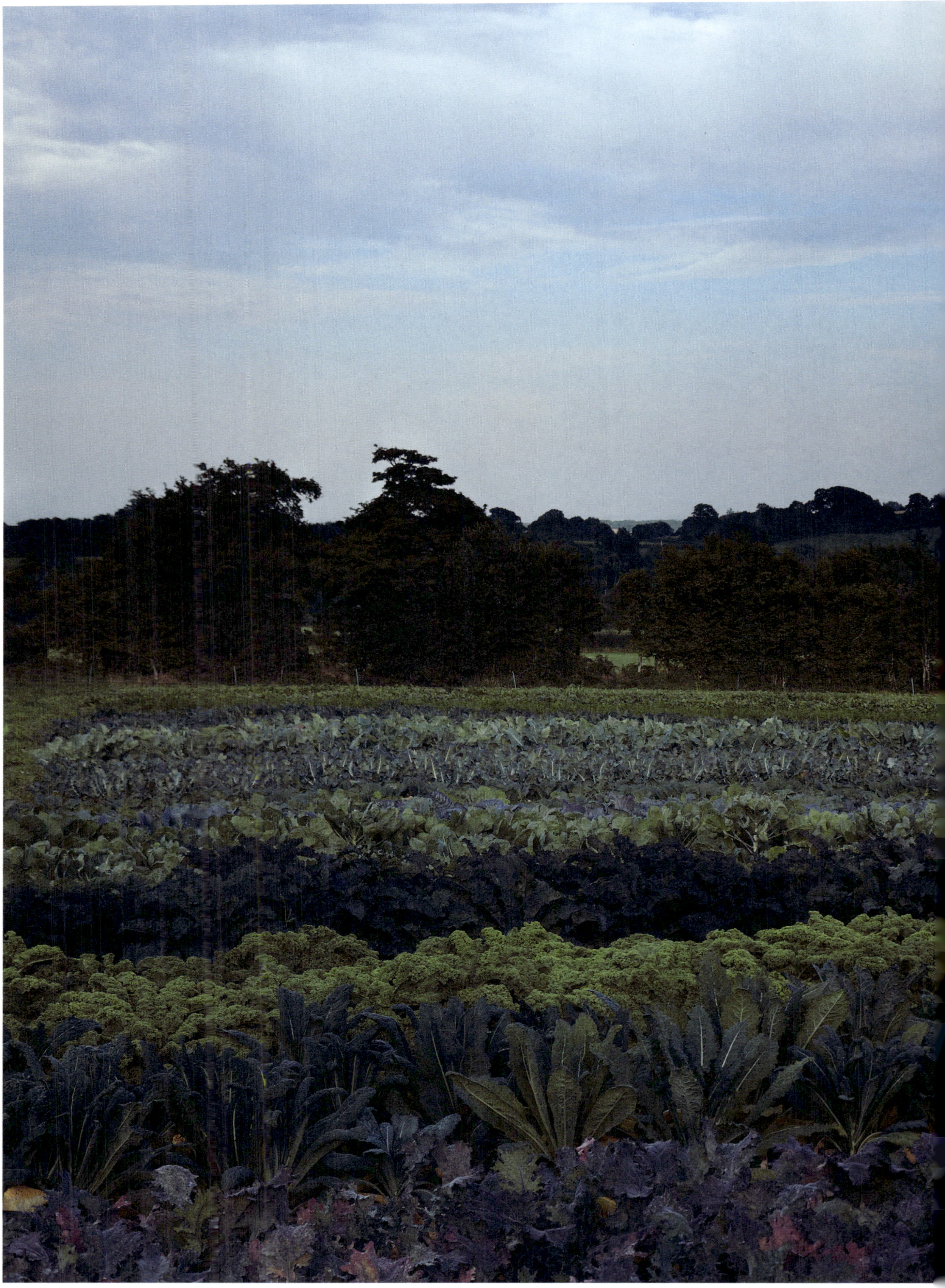

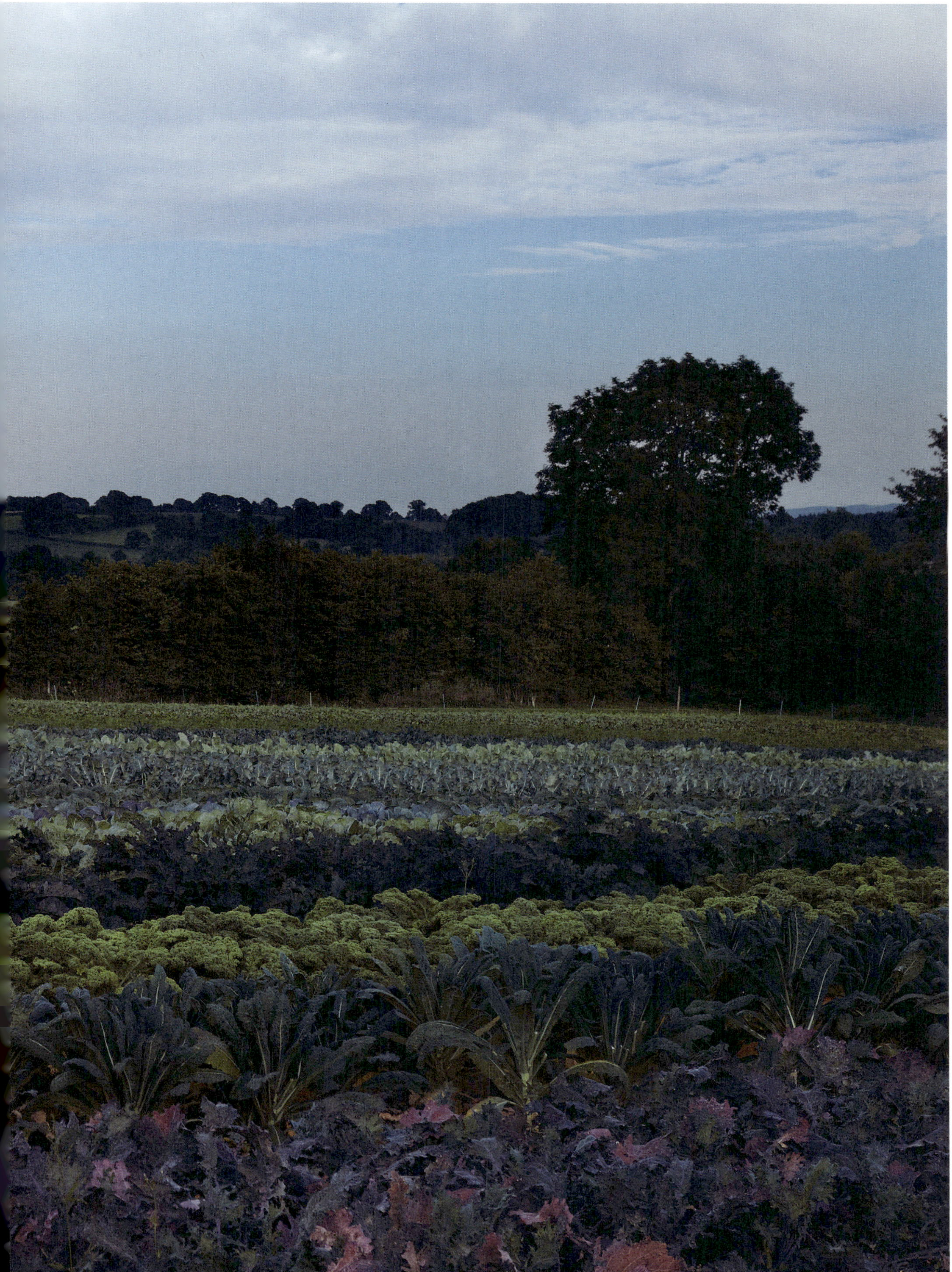

Fennel, celery, aubergine, lentil and feta salad

SERVES 4

1 large aubergine
175g Puy lentils
1 bay leaf
100ml olive oil
1 small red onion, finely chopped
1 garlic clove, crushed
juice and grated zest of 2 lemons
2 celery sticks, thinly sliced
1 fennel bulb, cut into bite-sized slivers
30g fresh ginger, finely chopped
1 garlic clove, finely chopped
2 teaspoons ground cumin
1 bunch of parsley, chopped
150g feta cheese
sea salt and black pepper

Puy lentils, with their meaty texture and taste, work best in this salad. You can serve it warm, but it improves if left to cool, as all the flavours combine and infuse the oil. Be sure to make plenty; this salad is great for a packed lunch.

Cut the aubergine into roughly 2cm chunks and place in a colander. Sprinkle a generous pinch of salt over them and then leave them be for about 30 minutes. Salt draws out moisture, and this is useful for extracting some of the bitterness aubergines can have.

Give the lentils a good rinse, then put them in a pan with the bay leaf, cover with plenty of water and bring to the boil. Reduce the heat and simmer for about 20 minutes, until they are tender but still have a little bite to them. Strain through a sieve and set aside.

Pour half the olive oil into a large bowl, add the red onion, crushed garlic and lemon juice and zest and season lightly with salt and pepper. Add the celery and fennel, mixing to coat them well in the dressing.

Put a large, heavy-based frying pan over a high heat and add the remaining oil. Pat the aubergine pieces dry with paper towel, then add to the hot oil and fry until they are starting to char around the edges. Stir in the ginger, finely chopped garlic and ground cumin and cook for a minute or two longer. Add the lentils and heat through for a few moments. Season with a little salt and pepper, then add the mixture to the fennel and celery. Turn with a spoon to make sure everything is well coated, then leave to cool.

Just before serving, add the chopped parsley and crumble in the feta cheese. Gently fold everything together.

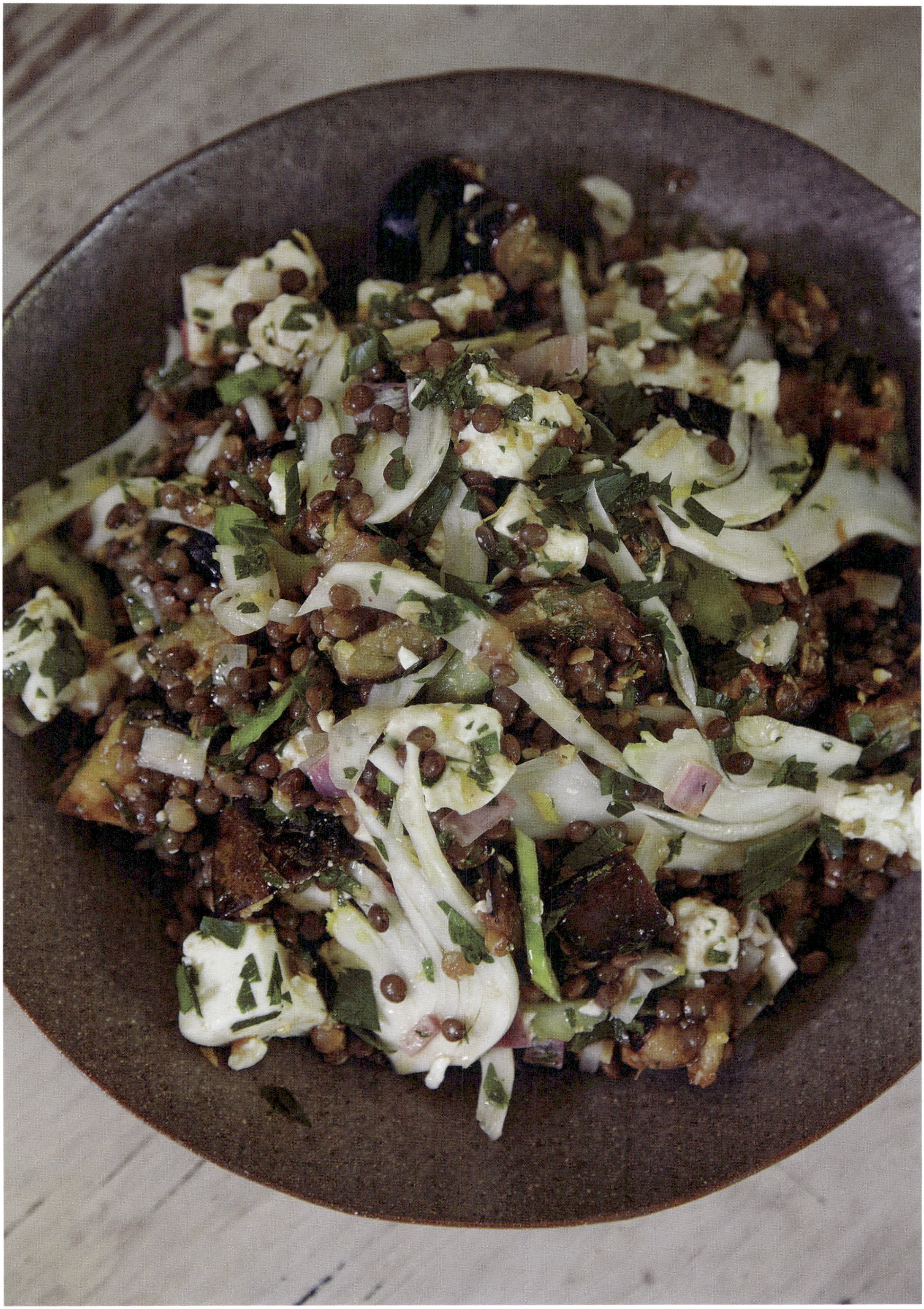

Yellow French bean salad

SERVES 4

6 tablespoons olive oil

1 onion, chopped

700g yellow French beans, trimmed

700g tomatoes, roughly chopped

2 tablespoons chopped flat-leaf parsley

12 basil leaves, torn

sea salt and black pepper

This is lovely served cold and the taste improves with time, so we advise preparing it a few hours before you plan to eat. It can also be enjoyed as a hot main course, accompanied by bread and butter and a green salad. You could use green beans instead, but the waxy, buttery texture of the yellow beans really suits this dish.

Heat the oil in a heavy-based pan, add the onion and cook over a low heat until translucent and soft. Add the beans and toss them through the oil, allowing them to absorb its flavour. Stir in the tomatoes and some salt and pepper. Cover the pan and simmer over a low heat for 30–40 minutes, until the beans are soft and waxy; the cooking time may vary according to the age and size of the beans. The sauce should be glossy. If it is too thick, add a little water; if too thin, take off the lid, raise the heat and cook for a few minutes longer, until reduced and thickened. Scatter over the parsley and basil and adjust the seasoning if necessary.

Baked radicchio and Parma ham

SERVES 2

1 large or 2 small heads of radicchio
12–16 slices of Parma ham
250ml double cream
50g Parmesan cheese, finely grated
juice of 1 lemon
sea salt and black pepper

We grow many varieties of radicchio here at Fern Verrow, having been seduced by seed catalogues from around the world selling beautiful, exotic-looking varieties. We sow the seeds in the greenhouse in early August and plant the seedlings out in the fields as soon as they are large enough. The sumptuous red tones of radicchio look at home with the colours of autumn, the cooler days and nights deepening the crimson streaks. It is a pleasure to harvest these beautiful plants, and an even greater pleasure to eat them. The candy-striped radicchio is often eaten raw in salads. However, it is extremely delicious cooked: here, its faint bitterness is sublime with the saltiness of Parma ham.

Heat the oven to 200°C/Gas Mark 6. Cut the radicchio into 6 wedges, if you are using a large one, or into quarters if you have 2 small ones, leaving a little of the base attached to each wedge so that they stay intact. Place a ridged griddle pan over a moderate heat. As it begins to get hot, brush a little oil on to the ridges. Once the griddle is hot, add the radicchio wedges and cook for 2–3 minutes on each side, until coloured.

Wrap 2 slices of Parma ham around each wedge and place in a shallow baking dish. Mix the cream with half the grated Parmesan and some seasoning, then pour it evenly over the radicchio wedges. Add the lemon juice, cover with foil and bake for 15 minutes. Remove the foil, baste the radicchio with the sauce and sprinkle the remaining Parmesan over the top. Continue to cook for 5–10 minutes, until the radicchio is tender and the sauce is bubbling.

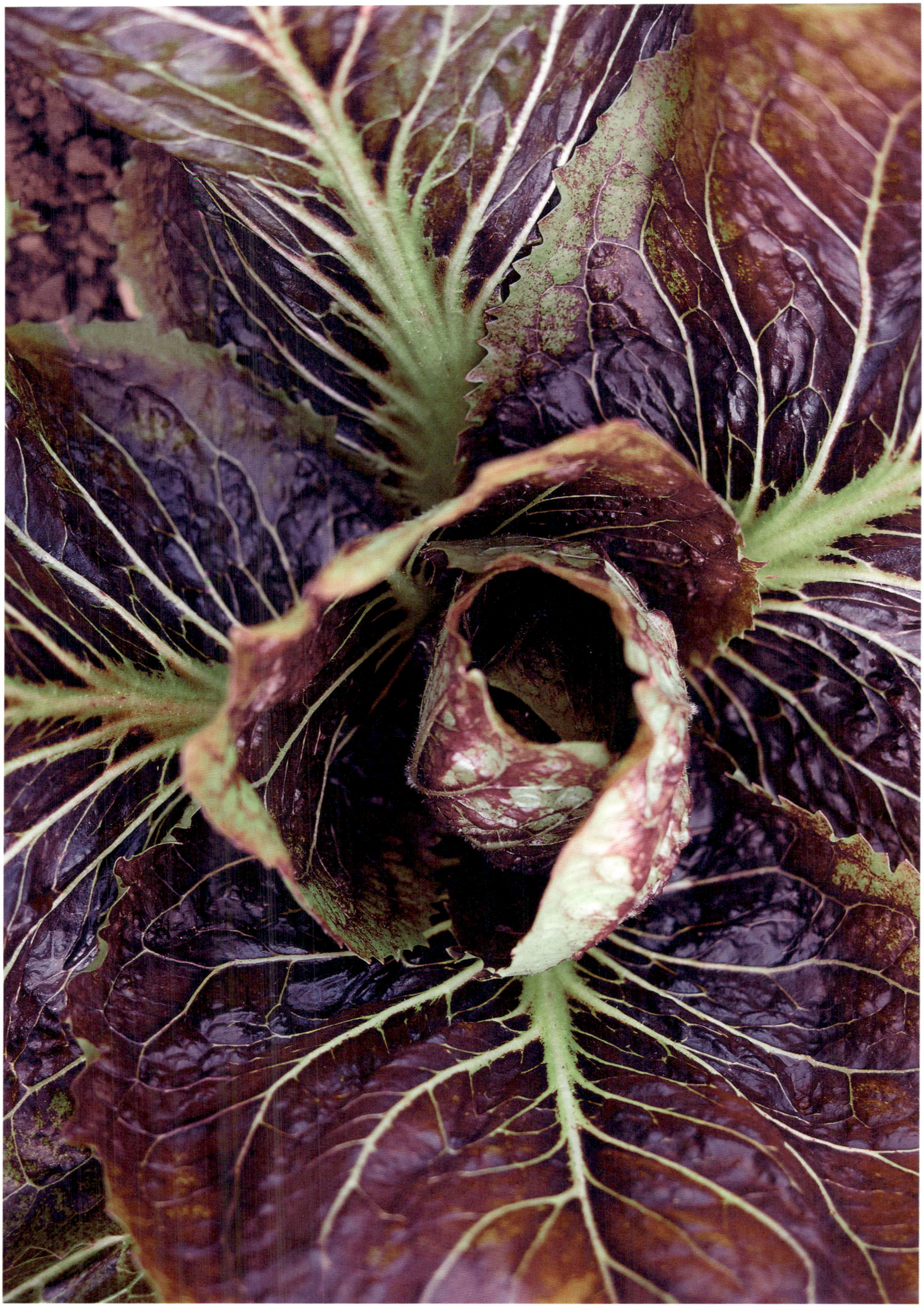

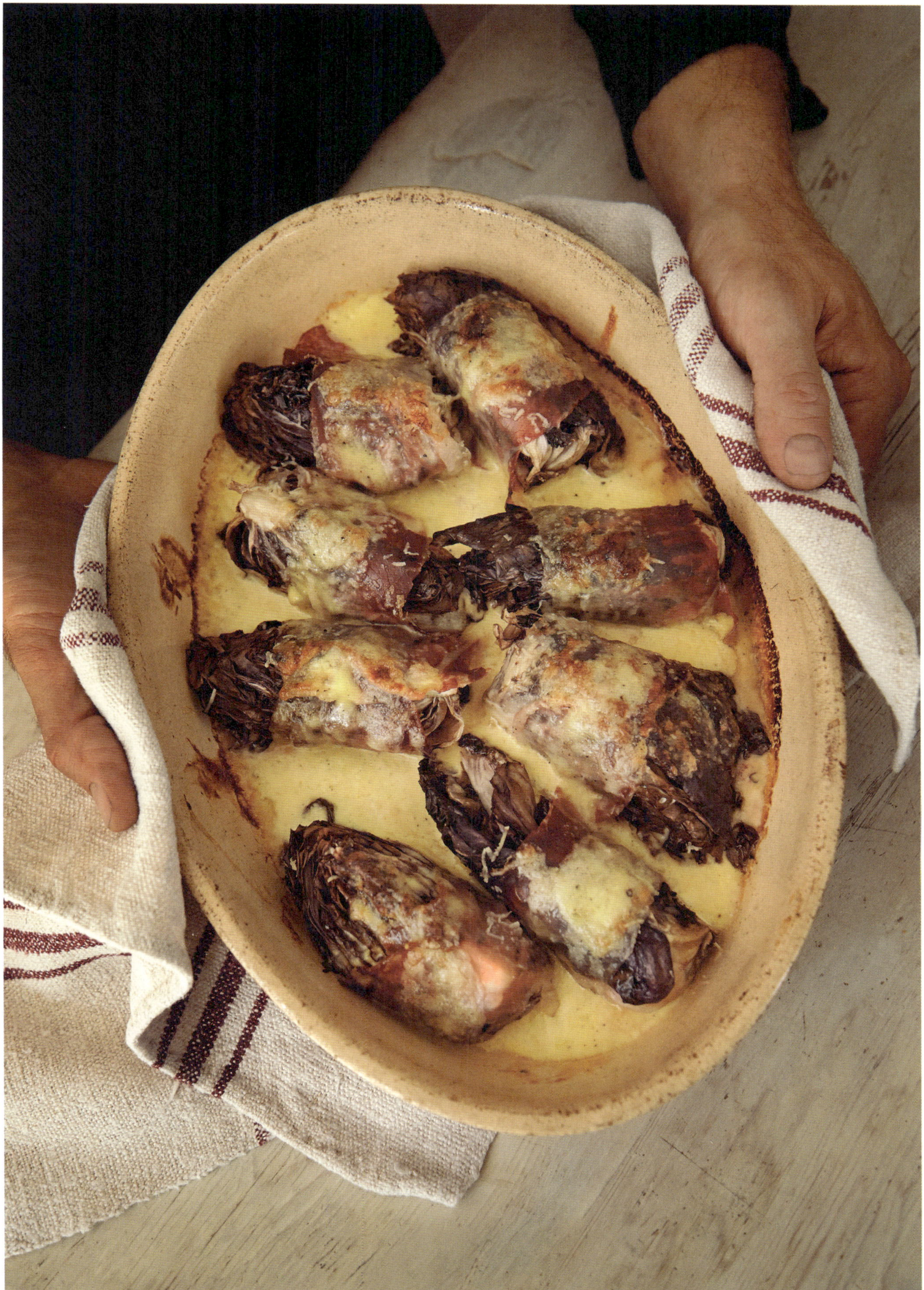

Aubergines baked with tomato, garlic and parsley

SERVES 4

2 large aubergines, weighing about 650g in total
2 large pinches of sea salt
2 tablespoons olive oil

For the tomato sauce

2 tablespoons olive oil
1 onion, finely chopped
4 garlic cloves, finely chopped
1kg tomatoes, roughly chopped
3 heaped tablespoons chopped parsley
sea salt and black pepper

For the topping

50g dried breadcrumbs
1 tablespoon chopped parsley
1 garlic clove, finely chopped
1 tablespoon olive oil

We often eat this dish the day after baking, serving it cold for lunch with some bread or a baked potato. The smokiness of the chargrilled aubergine works perfectly with the rich tomato sauce.

Slice the aubergines lengthways into tongues about 5mm thick. Arrange the slices in a single layer on a baking tray (you may need two), sprinkle the salt on top and leave for at least 30 minutes.

Meanwhile, prepare the tomato sauce. Heat the olive oil in a wide pan, add the onion and cook over a moderate heat for a few minutes. Add the garlic and cook for about 5 minutes, until the garlic and onion have softened. Stir in the tomatoes. Turn down the heat, cover the pan and cook over a gentle heat for about 10 minutes, until the tomatoes start to soften and release their juices. Remove the lid and stir in a generous seasoning of salt and pepper. Simmer gently, stirring occasionally, until the sauce is thick and not at all watery. This should take 30–40 minutes, depending on the juiciness of the tomatoes.

While the tomato sauce is reducing, cook the aubergines. Using kitchen paper, gently pat the moisture off the aubergine slices. Place a griddle over a high heat. Once it is very hot, take a slice of aubergine, brush one side with olive oil and place it oil-side down on the griddle. Repeat this process until the griddle is full. Cook for 2–3 minutes, then brush the tops with oil and turn. Cook for about 2 minutes, until golden brown and slightly charred. Repeat with the remaining aubergine slices.

Heat the oven to 200°C/Gas Mark 6. Stir the chopped parsley into the tomato sauce. Fill an ovenproof baking dish with the tomato sauce and aubergine slices in alternate layers, beginning and ending with the sauce. Place in the oven and bake for 30 minutes. For the topping, mix the breadcrumbs, parsley and garlic together and sprinkle the mixture over the bake. Trickle the olive oil on top and return to the oven for 10 minutes or until the breadcrumbs are toasted.

Ruby chard, tomato and lime curry

SERVES 2

500g ruby chard

2 tablespoons toasted sesame oil

2 Red Florence onions (or large shallots), cut into quarters

200g medium-sized tomatoes, cut into quarters

a walnut-sized piece of fresh ginger, finely chopped

2 garlic cloves, finely sliced

1 red chilli, deseeded and finely chopped

1 tablespoon garam masala

250ml water

2 dessertspoons thick yoghurt

1 large handful of coriander, roughly chopped

juice of 1 large lime

sea salt

With its dark, pine-forest-green leaves and vibrant scarlet veins and stems, ruby chard is one of the most decorative vegetables to grow. It can be used in place of spinach in many recipes. This refreshing curry makes a quick and easy supper dish. Serve with rice or flatbreads.

Roll up the chard and shred it into thick strips and set aside. You can include the stems, providing they are not tough. Pour the sesame oil into a large, heavy-based pan and place over a high heat. Add the onions and tomatoes and stir-fry until they are starting to get a few burned edges but are still quite raw. Add the chard a large handful at a time, so it will fit in the pan – it should wilt quickly in the heat. Add a good sprinkling of salt, plus the ginger, garlic, chilli and garam masala. It is very important to cook the curry over a high heat, or it will become mushy and stewed. Keep the chard on the move so that it doesn't get dry or burned, but be careful not to break the tomatoes up too much. Add more oil, if necessary, to keep everything well lubricated.

Pour in the water, cover and leave to simmer over a very gentle heat for about 20 minutes, until the chard is tender. Swirl in the yoghurt, sprinkle over lots of roughly cut coriander and the lime juice. Serve straightaway.

Beetroot and cream cheese tart

SERVES 6–8

750g evenly sized beetroot
280g cream cheese
140ml crème fraîche or double cream
15g fresh horseradish, finely grated
sea salt and black pepper

For the shortcrust pastry
150g plain flour
75g wholemeal flour
a pinch of salt
140g chilled butter, diced
2–3 tablespoons chilled water

The important thing to watch out for here is the consistency of the filling. If it is too wet, the pastry will be soggy; too dry and the texture can be a little cloying. Get it right and this is a delicious and beautiful tart. It's quite rich, so serve with a green salad.

Steam or boil the unpeeled beetroot until tender; this may take an hour or so, depending on size. Peel the beetroot when cool enough to handle, then purée in a food processor until smooth. Transfer the purée to a sieve set over a bowl and leave to drain for a couple of hours.

Meanwhile, make the pastry. Sift the flours together with a generous pinch of salt. Add the butter and cut it into the flour with a round-bladed knife until it is well coated. Rub it into the flour with your fingertips until it resembles fine breadcrumbs. Stir in 2 tablespoons of chilled water with the knife and press the dough together with your fingers, adding more water if necessary to give a firm dough. Knead briefly until smooth, then wrap in cling film and chill for at least 30 minutes.

Roll the pastry out on a lightly floured surface to 3–4mm thick and use to line a 25cm loose-bottomed tart tin, trimming off the excess. Allow to rest in the fridge again for 20 minutes. Heat the oven to 200°C/Gas Mark 6.

Line the pastry case with a sheet of baking parchment and fill with baking beans or rice. Bake blind for 12–15 minutes, until the pastry is dry to the touch. Remove the paper and beans or rice, then return the pastry case to the oven and cook for 5 minutes, until lightly coloured. Allow to cool for a few minutes before adding the filling.

Mix together the cream cheese, cream, grated horseradish and some seasoning, then fold in the beetroot purée. The mixture should be moist and easily spreadable – roughly the consistency of whipped cream. If it is a little dry, add some of the drained beetroot juice. Spread the mixture into the pastry case and bake at 190°C/Gas Mark 5 for about 20 minutes, until the filling is lightly coloured but still moist. Serve warm.

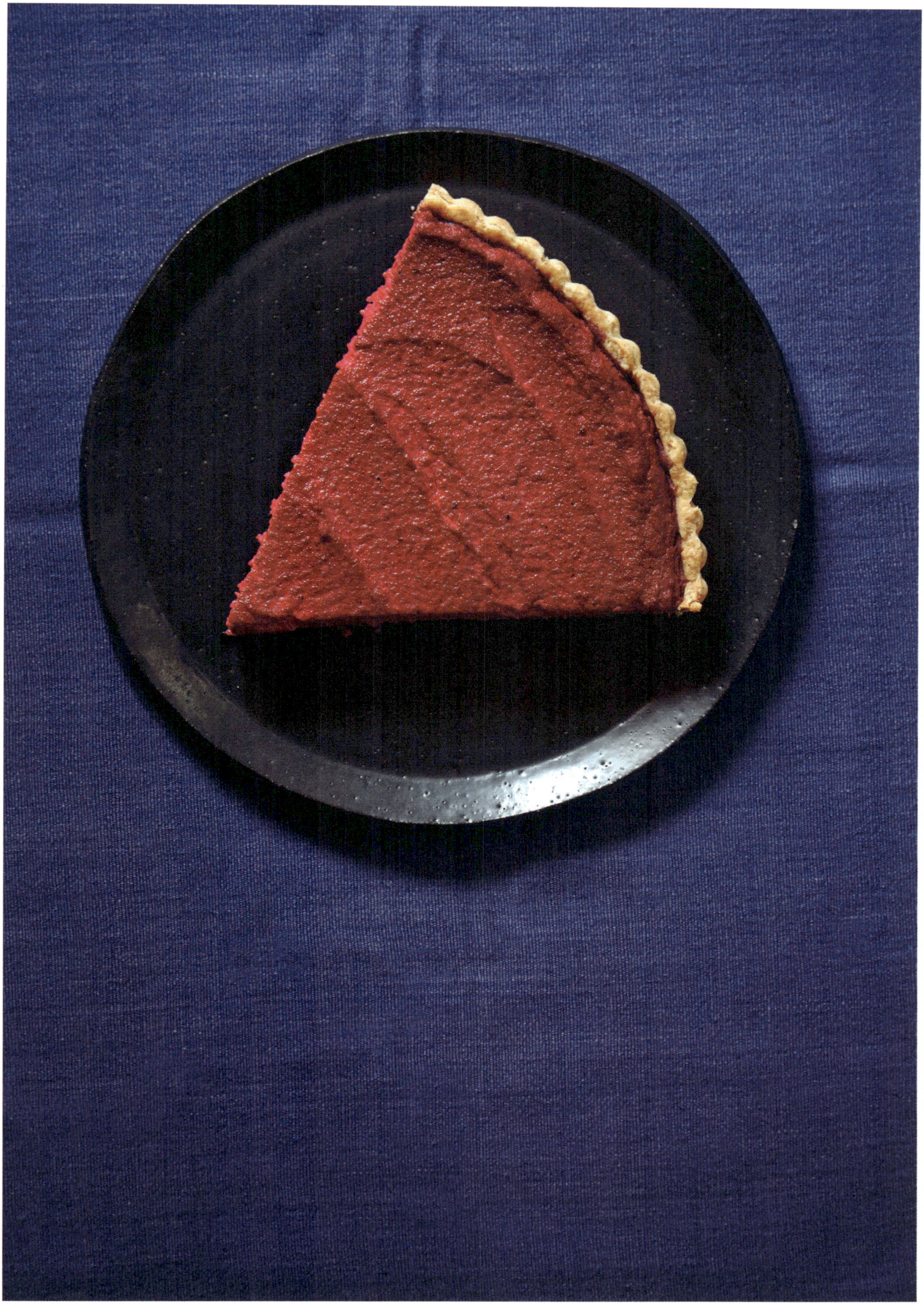

Our animals

FERN VERROW WOULD not be the same without its animals. Each creature brings its individual character and personality deep into the farm organism, contributing to the spirit of the place. The animals' wellbeing is paramount to us, and our approach to raising them for meat is considered and respectful. We aim to offer them as good a life as possible, giving them natural environments in which they can fully express their instincts. By providing them with proper food, plenty of space to roam, graze and scratch around, clean and comfortable housing, and our help when they need it, we believe we are fulfilling our responsibility to them.

Cows

Cows are central players in a biodynamic approach to agriculture. The cow's complex digestive system means that its precious manure – 'farmer's gold' – is more valuable to us as a soil-improver than that of any other animal. We have a small herd of Hereford cattle; handsome animals with coats the colour of Hereford soil, they are a curious and friendly breed. So that we can feed them exclusively on our own grass and hay, we stock a maximum of five animals at any time. This means that each year one cow will produce a calf and one adult will be slaughtered for meat.

The cows are rotated through the grazing fields from March. During the summer months, they methodically munch their way through the golden buttercup meadows, flicking their long tails at the annoying flies. In early December, we bring them into the cow barn for the winter, where they enjoy the best view on the farm. We visit them every day, often with vegetables or fruit as a treat. The way they eagerly poke out their drooling sandpaper tongues to curl around an apple makes them look rather comical.

As we break open a new bale of hay, the aroma reminds us of the distant summer days. We scratch the cows' heads while inhaling their pleasant, sweet-smelling breath. We value their quiet wisdom and calming influence.

Sheep

With 'golden hoof and a silver mouth', as the old saying goes, our sheep help to maintain and improve the pastures by nibbling the grass. They provide us with wool when we shear them in early summer and with meat when the grass-fattened lambs are ready for sale in late autumn. Early in November we put our ewes to the ram – or tup, as he is called in these parts. Six to eight weeks before they are due to lamb, the ewes help us to clear the vegetable fields, eagerly stripping the plants and bringing huge entertainment with their smudged 'lipstick' after they have gorged on a few beds of beetroot.

Our greatest connection with the sheep is during lambing time in early spring, when the flock unites in motherhood and their maternal instincts come to the fore. Later in the year, when the young lambs are playing together in the pastures, their 'Harrier jump jet' leaps epitomise the joys of spring.

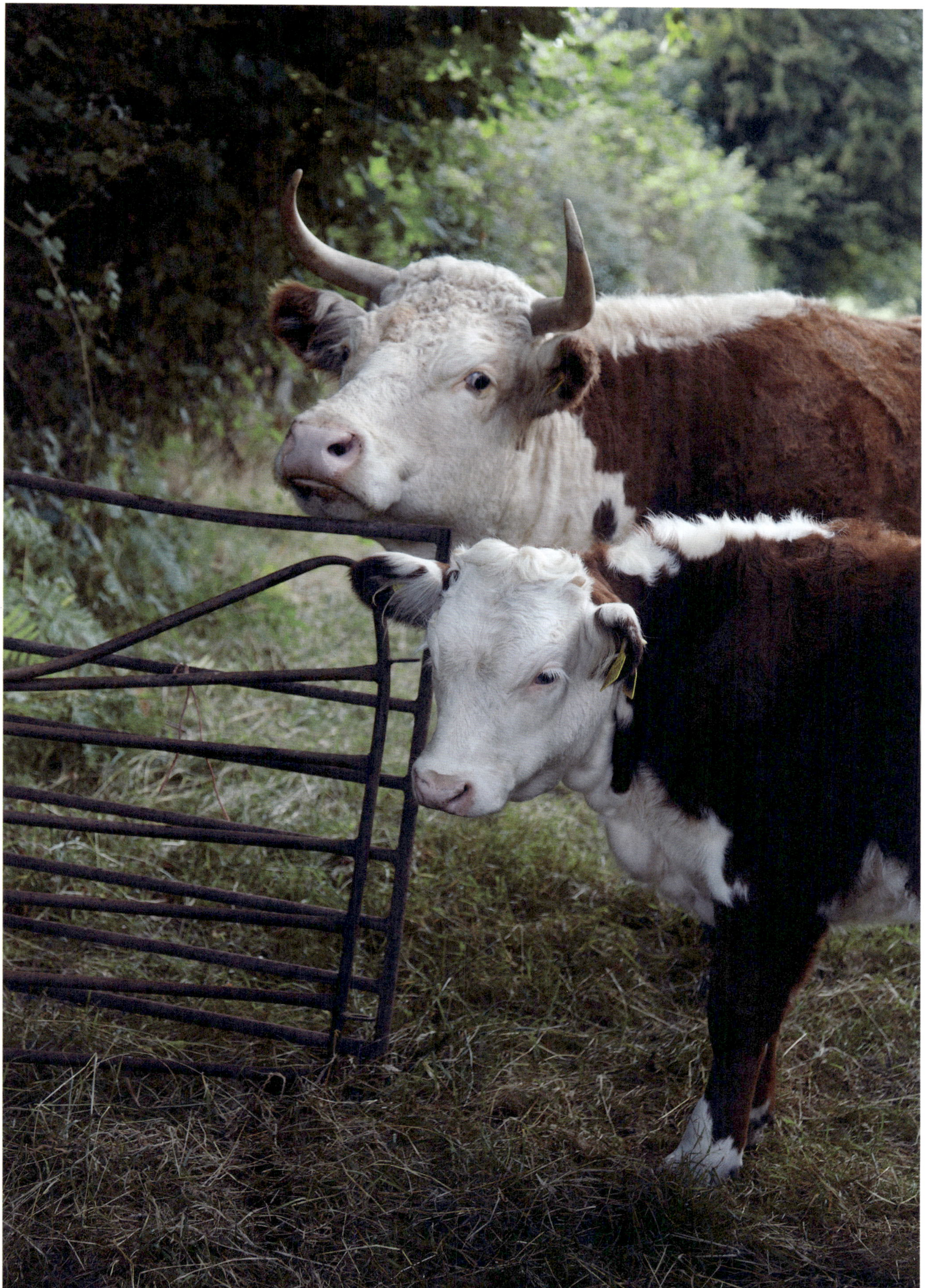

Flighty and suspicious when young, as the sheep grow older they seem to become more placid and willing to follow our call. The bond we build with them as their carers is life-affirming and reminds us of why we farm.

Pigs

Our ginger-bristled Tamworth pigs are probably the most intelligent of all the farm animals. Their gestation is three months, three weeks and three days, and our sows have sometimes had litters of up to a dozen piglets. In the first few weeks of life, the piglets are adorable, with soft, smooth hair, fat, pink bellies and wrinkly, squashed faces. By the time we come to wean them at ten weeks old, they are noisy troublemakers, with voracious appetites for food and mischief, often behaving like a crowd of football hooligans.

The pigs spend the summer in the outdoor pigpens, where we feed them grain and vegetables. During the cold and wet winter months, we house them in the pig barn. In the springtime we put them to good use as an alternative to ploughing. They will eat any weeds and vegetable remains and – with their strong necks and inquisitive snouts – they give the soil a thorough working, opening it up and turning it over. Some go off to the butcher at between six and nine months old for pork joints, and the others at one year for bacon, ham and sausages. They are very useful, consuming damaged or excess crops, and never turning their snouts up at any food that comes their way.

Ducks, geese and chickens

The poultry field is like a school playground. The quacking of the ducks sounds like raucous laughter at smutty jokes. These comical birds, waddling from side to side on their little legs while on land, become so graceful on water. The geese, full of bravado, are actually cowardly at heart. They have a distinct pecking order, and the gander never fails to turn at us and hiss a final passing shot as we close the door of their house at dusk. In the morning they hear our approach and rush out like a cork from a bottle, showing off to each other and anyone else they think might be watching.

As for the chickens, they are in their own world, always busy, scratching and pecking the ground or ruffling their feathers in dust baths. They are so pretty and their colourful plumage is reflected in the subtle tints of their eggs. The handsome cockerels, with their multicoloured tail-feathers, strut about in a proprietary manner, dominating the females in their overtly masculine, competitive way. We feel quite sorry for the chickens in wet weather, when their less-waterproofed feathers go lank and shabby. On the really wet days, they shelter underneath their houses, looking like people at a bus stop who have forgotten their umbrellas.

Turkeys

Of all the poultry, the turkeys are our favourites – we see beauty in their quirkiness. They are always genteel, never rushing around, but obliging, kindly and trusting. They are with us from late May until Christmas, when they become the centrepieces of our customers' festive tables. Our attempts to allow the hen-turkeys to raise their fragile young have been thwarted over the years by marauding magpies and hawks. Nowadays, we intervene and incubate the eggs, then protect the young during the first vulnerable weeks, reintroducing them to the flock at 12 weeks old. As well as their diet of grain, the growing turkeys enjoy pecking at surplus fruit and bruised windfalls as they range over the meadows and orchard.

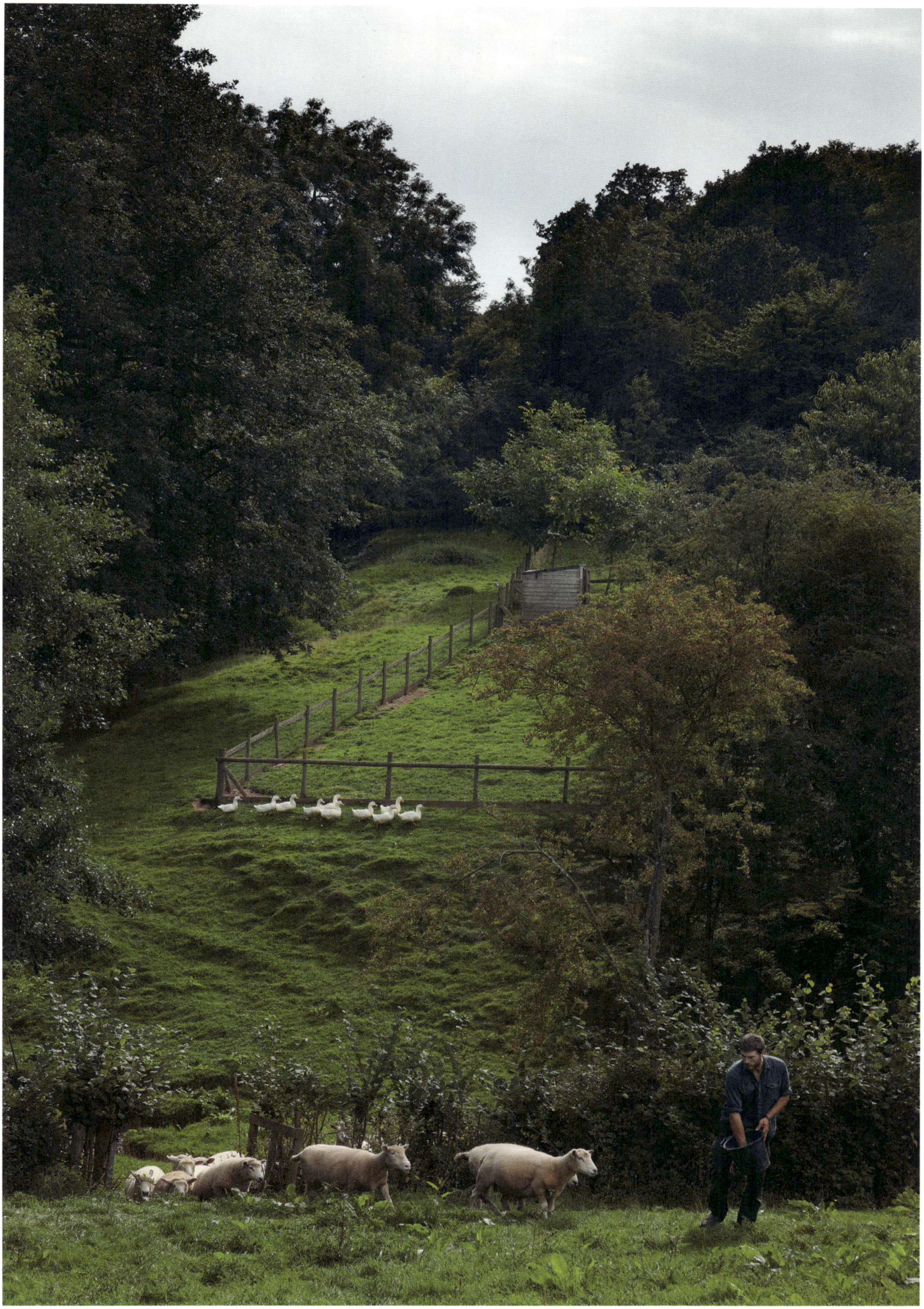

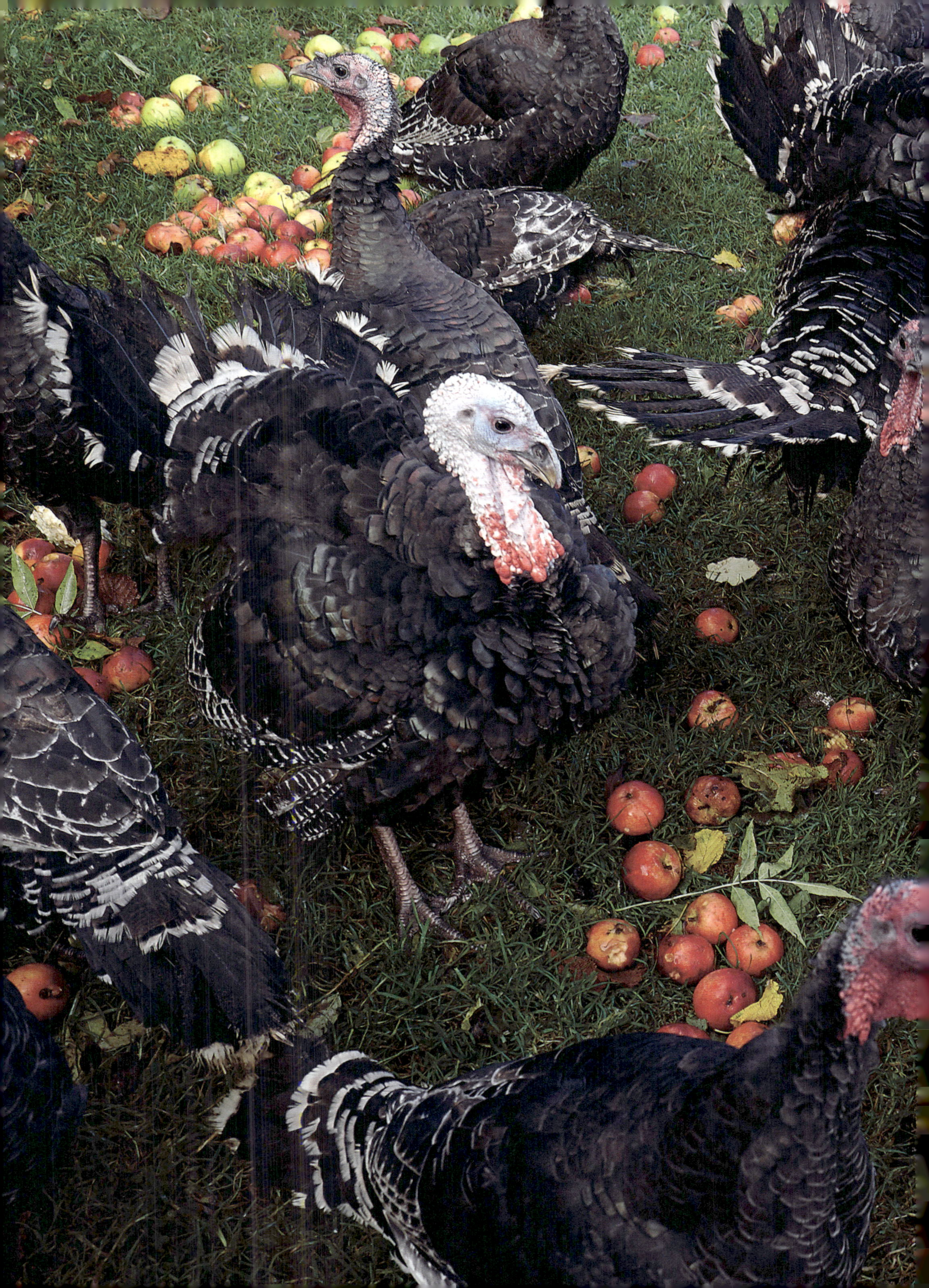

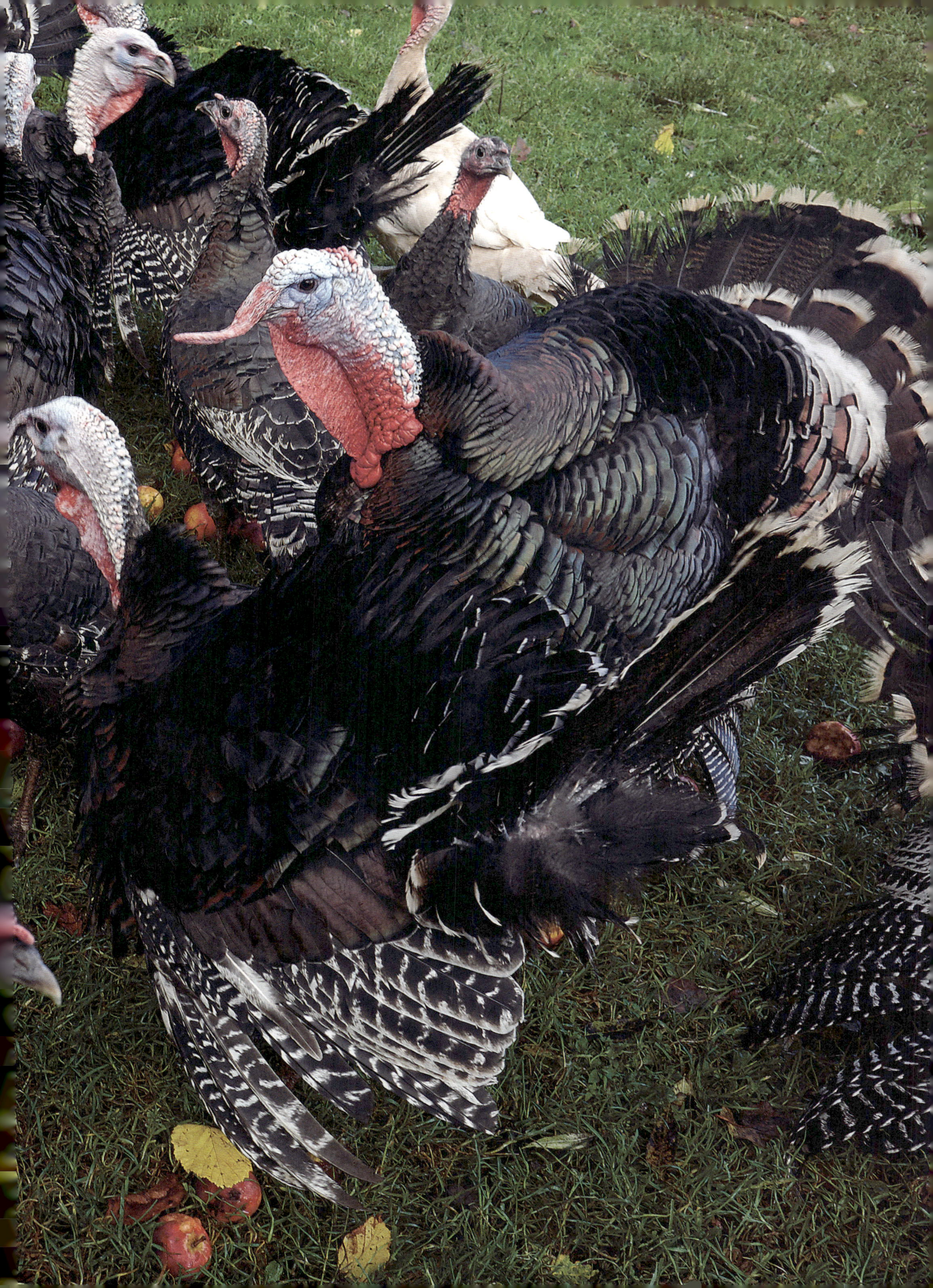

Cod rarebit with Swiss chard

SERVES 4

500g Swiss chard
60g butter
juice of ½ lemon
4 x 200g pieces of cod fillet, skinned
a little flour, seasoned with salt and pepper, for coating
2 tablespoons olive oil
sea salt and black pepper

For the rarebit
25g butter
25g plain flour
100ml stout
150g mature Cheshire cheese or any other strong hard cheese, grated
1 teaspoon Dijon mustard
1 teaspoon Worcestershire sauce
1 egg yolk

This dish fits into the comfort-food category for us. It takes a lot to beat a beautiful piece of cod. With a strong, cheesy topping and a helping of Swiss chard, it makes a sustaining meal on a chilly night. You could also serve the rarebit on toast with a layer of finely sliced onion underneath – a regular Sunday-evening supper in our house.

First prepare the rarebit. Melt the butter in a small pan over a low heat, then stir in the flour and cook for a couple of minutes, being careful that it doesn't burn. Pour in the stout a little at a time, stirring constantly, until the mixture becomes thick and smooth. Add the grated cheese, mustard and Worcestershire sauce and stir over a low heat until all the cheese has melted. Remove from the heat and beat in the egg yolk. The texture should be thick and gloopy. Set aside.

Prepare the chard by separating the thick stalks from the leaves. Shred the leaves and cut the stalks into chunks. Melt 40g of the butter in a frying pan over a medium heat. Add the chard stalks and cook gently for 3 minutes, until they are starting to soften. Add the shredded leaves, toss them in the butter to ensure that they are well coated, then reduce the heat and cover the pan. Cook for just a few minutes, until the stalks are tender and the leaves have just wilted. Season and add the lemon juice. Keep warm while you cook the fish.

Lightly coat each piece of cod in the seasoned flour. Heat the olive oil in a large frying pan over a high heat. Once it is hot but not smoking, add the remaining butter. Place the cod in the oil and foaming butter and cook for about 2 minutes, until lightly coloured underneath. Turn the fillets and cook for a further 2 minutes, until just cooked through. Lift the cod out of the pan and place in a heatproof dish that will fit under the grill. Spoon a generous amount of rarebit on top of each piece of fish. Place under a hot grill and cook until the rarebit is bubbling and browned. Depending on the grill, this will take only a minute or two.

Divide the chard between 4 warmed plates. Put the cod on top and serve straightaway.

Leek, potato and mint stovetop

SERVES 4

50g butter

2 tablespoons olive oil

700g potatoes, peeled and cut into 1cm cubes

1 garlic clove, finely chopped

500g leeks, cut into 1cm dice

300ml crème fraîche or double cream

juice of 1 lemon

2 tablespoons water

3 sprigs of mint

freshly grated Parmesan cheese, to serve (optional)

sea salt and black pepper

This is a great one-pot supper dish that can be eaten on its own or with lamb chops or sausages. Most varieties of potato work well here, but the floury texture of Cara or Desiree is particularly good.

Heat the butter and oil together in a wide, heavy-based pan over a moderate heat. When the butter is gently sizzling, add the potatoes and cook for a few minutes, making sure that they are well coated in the fat. Stir in the garlic and leeks and cook for a couple of minutes, until the leeks begin to wilt. Season with salt and pepper. Add the cream, lemon juice, water and mint, place the lid on the pan and turn the heat down very low. Stir occasionally to ensure the mixture doesn't catch. Allow to steam away for about half an hour, until the potatoes are cooked. The mixture should be creamy and saucelike.

Remove the mint sprigs and grate some Parmesan on top, if you like. Serve piping hot.

Borlotti bean, chorizo and tomato stew

SERVES 4

1 tablespoon olive oil

200g chorizo, cut into chunks

75g smoked bacon, diced

1 green pepper, roughly chopped

3 large Red Florence onions (or banana shallots), cut into quarters

2 garlic cloves, finely sliced

2 teaspoons hot smoked paprika

150ml red wine

600g tomatoes, chopped

3 saffron strands

1 sprig of rosemary, chopped

1 sprig of thyme, chopped

500g fresh or canned borlotti beans

sea salt

chopped parsley, to serve

We are often asked which is our favourite vegetable to grow. Borlotti beans have to be in the top three. Their growing season is a long one, from sowing in March/April to harvesting in September/early October. Harvesting the beans from the pods requires patience, and you mustn't be tempted to pick them early. The flat pods start off a pale green colour, then gradually the red streaks begin to show through. As time moves on, the green fades to a cream buff colour and the streaks intensify to a bright cherry red. It's a truly beautiful vegetable – so beautiful that it could be grown as an ornamental plant, although that would be rather a waste. As soon as the beans are so swollen that the pod looks as if it will burst, you can split it open and cook the freckled beans within.

If fresh borlotti beans are unavailable, canned or dried will do just as well in this recipe. Dried beans will need soaking and cooking first. Serve with thick slices of bread or with baked potatoes and a green salad.

Heat the oven to 180°C/Gas Mark 4. Heat the olive oil in a flameproof casserole over a high heat. Add the chorizo, bacon, green pepper and onions and fry for a few minutes, until browned. Don't worry if they burn a little; this all adds to the slightly smoky flavour of the stew. Stir in the garlic and paprika and cook for 1 minute. Splash in the wine and cook for a couple of minutes, until it has evaporated a little. Stir in the tomatoes, saffron, rosemary and thyme. Season with salt, tasting it first, as the chorizo and bacon may make the stew salty enough. Bring to a simmer, then cover and place in the oven. Cook for 1 hour, then stir in the beans, adding half a glass of water if the stew looks too thick. Continue to cook for another hour or until the beans are tender but still have a little bite. Serve with a sprinkling of parsley on top.

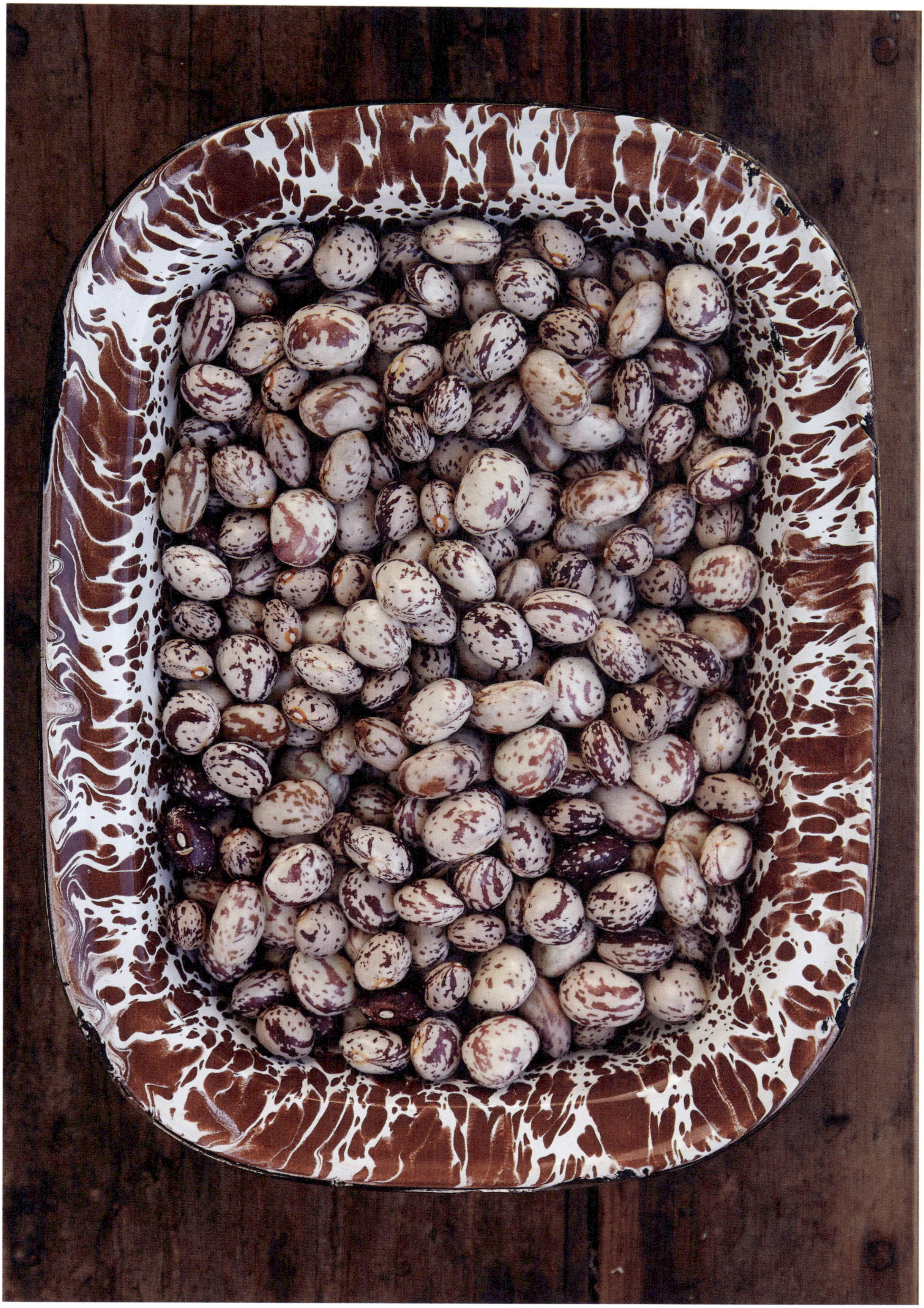

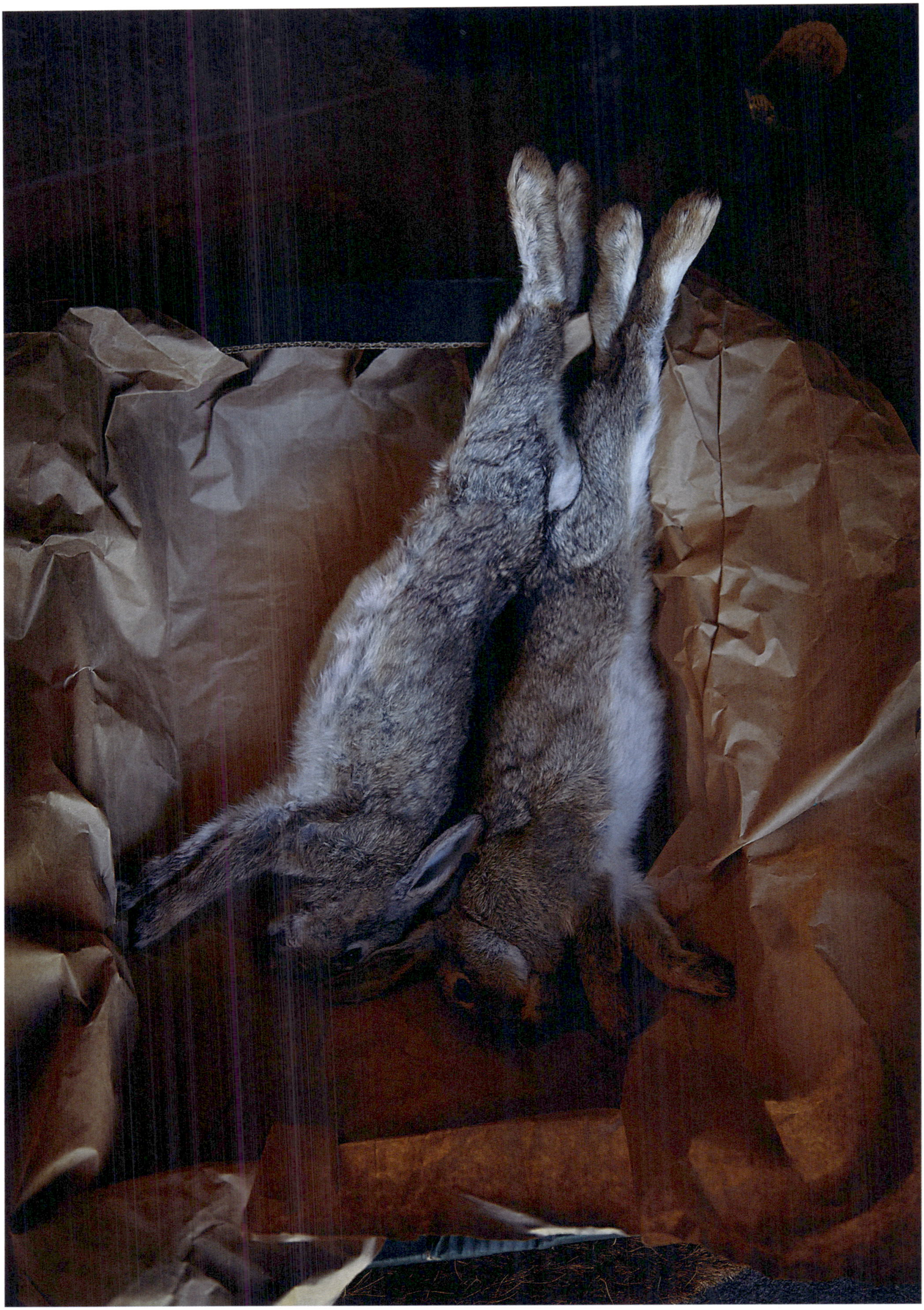

Braised rabbit with juniper berries

SERVES 4

1 rabbit, jointed

60g plain flour, seasoned with salt and pepper

3 tablespoons olive oil

30g butter

2 onions, finely sliced

1 small bunch of thyme, chopped

10g juniper berries, roughly crushed

150ml white wine

250ml chicken stock

3 tablespoons crème fraîche or double cream

1 bunch of parsley, leaves finely chopped, stalks chopped and kept separate

sea salt and black pepper

We have a bit of a love/hate relationship with these shy, cotton-tailed little creatures. During the summer months the young rabbits can become a big nuisance for us. Their numbers often get out of control and our crops are devastated by them. We are sympathetic and respectful that our fields are also the home of many creatures, so we reach a compromise and try to keep things balanced. This means that in the autumn we have a few rabbits for our table. The meat is one of our favourites, and wild rabbit tastes far superior to farmed. Rabbit is very lean, so it is important not to cook it too fast or it may become tough.

This dish is good served with wide-ribboned pasta or sautéed potatoes.

Coat the rabbit joints lightly in the seasoned flour. Heat the olive oil over a moderate heat in a wide, heavy-based pan, then add the rabbit and quickly brown on both sides. Remove the rabbit from the pan and set aside. Melt the butter in the pan, add the onions and fry until soft and just beginning to colour. Stir in the thyme and juniper berries. Pour in the wine and allow it to sizzle and reduce for a minute. Return the rabbit pieces to the pan and pour in the stock. Stir in the cream, sprinkle in the parsley stalks and some salt and pepper and turn up the heat. When the stock begins to bubble, reduce the heat to a simmer. Cook, uncovered, for 30–40 minutes, basting and turning the rabbit occasionally. The sauce should be a nice coating consistency. Adjust the seasoning, if necessary, and serve sprinkled with the parsley leaves.

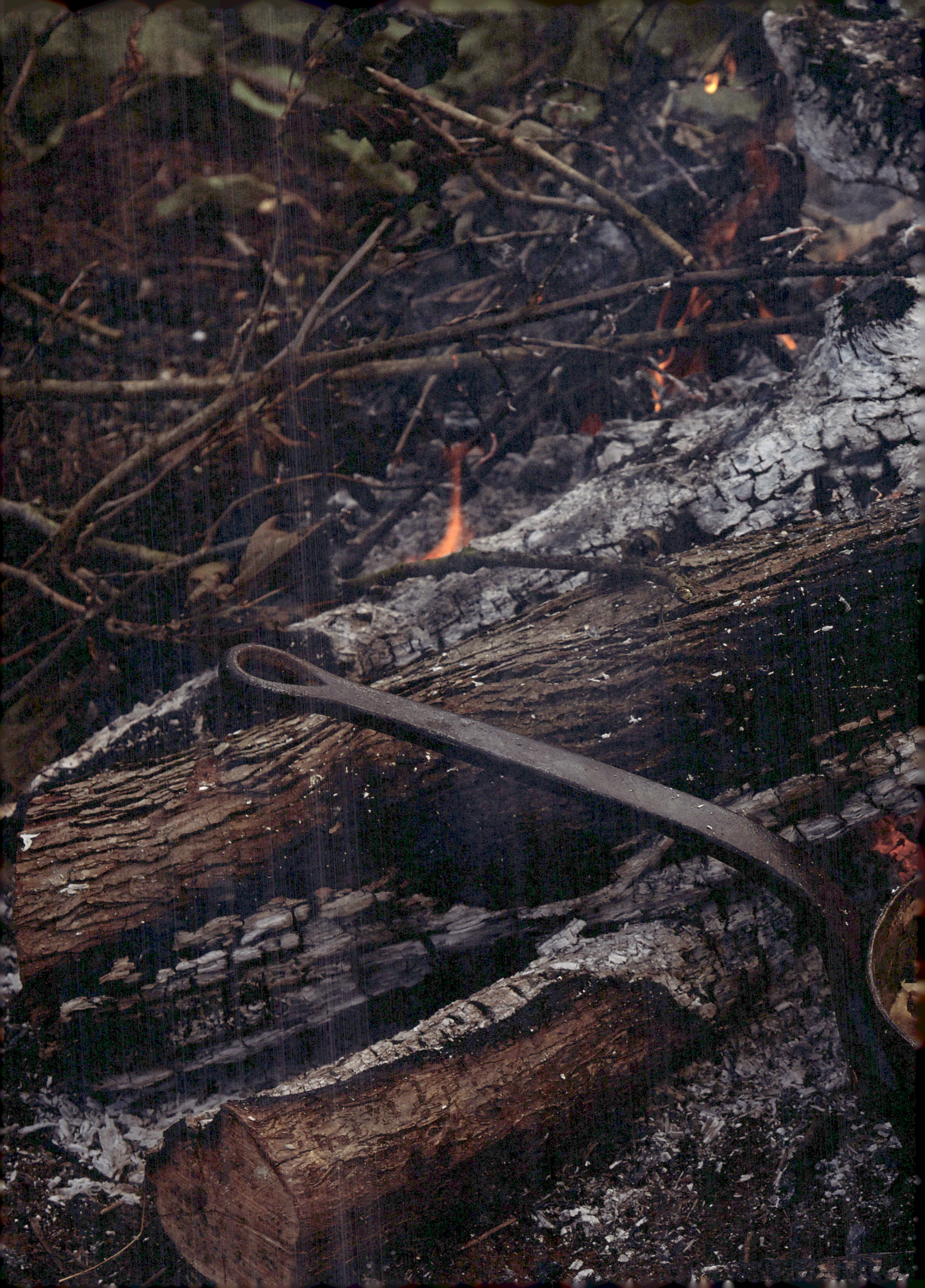

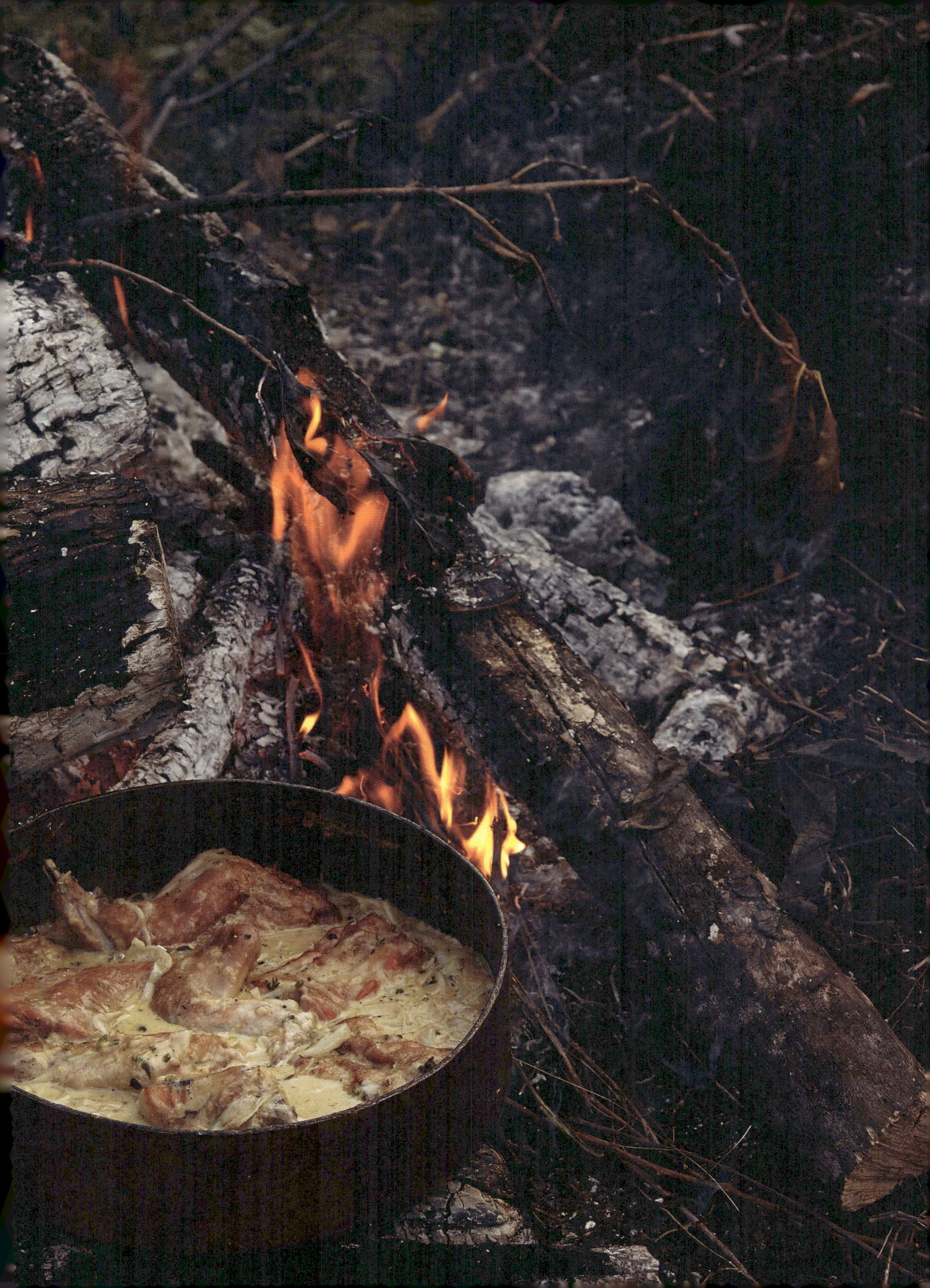

Rabbit and peanut kebabs

SERVES 4

600g rabbit meat, cut into roughly 2cm chunks

24 dried apricots

2 red peppers, cut into 3cm squares

4 small onions, peeled and cut into quarters

a little sesame oil, for brushing

Buttered Onion Rice (see page 38), to serve

For the marinade

3 heaped tablespoons smooth, unsalted peanut butter

2 garlic cloves, crushed

1 lemongrass stalk, finely chopped

20g fresh ginger, peeled and finely chopped

1 green chilli, finely chopped

1 tablespoon fish sauce

1 tablespoon toasted sesame oil

juice and grated zest of 1 lime

For the yoghurt, lime and coriander sauce

300ml thick full-fat yoghurt

½ teaspoon ground coriander

juice and grated zest of 1 lime

a sprig of fresh coriander, chopped

2 teaspoons olive oil

sea salt and black pepper

It is best to cook these kebabs on a cast-iron griddle to give them a smoky flavour and chargrilled appearance, but you can do them under the grill if necessary – or on a barbecue, of course. The ingredients below are just a suggestion. You could also try whole cherry tomatoes, whole button mushrooms or prunes – whatever will fit on to a skewer and not fall off during cooking. If rabbit is tricky to find, then chicken will do very well as a replacement.

Serve with rice, or take everything off the skewers after cooking and serve in pitta bread with some finely shredded white cabbage or lettuce and the yoghurt, lime and coriander sauce.

Put all the ingredients for the marinade into a large dish and mix well. It should be thick and sticky. Add the rabbit chunks and stir until they are completely coated. If the mixture is too thick and coating the meat evenly proves a challenge, add a little more sesame oil or lime juice. Cover and leave to marinate for at least 2 hours.

Put the dried apricots into a bowl, pour over boiling water and leave to soak for an hour.

To make the sauce, put the yoghurt into a bowl and stir in the ground coriander, lime juice and zest, together with some seasoning. Sprinkle the coriander leaves on the top and swirl over the olive oil.

Thread the rabbit, vegetables and apricots alternately on to 8 wooden skewers, ensuring there is plenty of room at each end for turning. Place a griddle pan over a high heat and, when it is hot, brush it with a little sesame oil. Place the kebabs on the hot griddle and cook for 15–20 minutes. There will be plenty of smoke, so turn the skewers often to prevent the peanut butter burning. Remove from the griddle and serve the skewers on the rice, accompanied by the yoghurt, lime and coriander sauce.

Roast chicken stuffed with couscous, preserved bergamot lemons and saffron

SERVES 6

1 large chicken, weighing about 2kg

75g butter, at room temperature

½ lemon

a selection of vegetables (such as 2 onions, 3 carrots, 2 fennel bulbs and 2 celery stalks), cut into quarters

sea salt and black pepper

For the couscous stuffing

100g couscous

150ml boiling water

15g butter

1 small onion or 1 large shallot, finely chopped

1 garlic clove, finely chopped

3 Preserved Bergamot Lemon quarters (see page 45) or ½ bought preserved lemon

1 small handful of marjoram or thyme leaves, chopped

3 good pinches of saffron, soaked in an eggcup of warm water for a few minutes

Roast chicken does not always have to be kept for Sunday. This hearty slow-roast is reasonably quick to prepare (you can always make the stuffing beforehand) and has lovely clean, fragrant flavours.

We often use a cockerel for this dish. Cockerels tend to have less breast meat than the hens, but they do have rugby-player-style large legs, where the meat is dark, more gamey and deliciously sticky, which suits this recipe very well. They are not easily available, but if you can get hold of one you're in for a treat.

If your chicken came with a plastic bag full of its offal (neck, liver, heart and gizzard), you can put the offal in the tin with the vegetables for added flavour, then discard it.

Take the chicken out of the fridge a good 2 hours before cooking, if you can. Don't worry if this is not possible. Heat the oven to 200°C/Gas Mark 6.

Put the couscous in a large bowl. Pour the boiling water over it, stir, then cover with cling film or a tea towel. Leave for 10 minutes, until the couscous has absorbed the water. Fluff it up with a fork.

If your chicken has ample fat at the opening of the cavity, remove it and add to a frying pan with the 15g butter. Melt over a moderate heat, then add the onion and garlic and cook gently until they are soft but not browned. To prepare the preserved lemon, remove and discard the flesh and pith, then finely chop the skin. If the lemons have been preserved in a lot of salt, you may need to rinse them first. Stir the cooked onion and garlic, chopped preserved lemon, marjoram or thyme, a quarter of the saffron threads and all the saffron liquid into the couscous. Season generously.

Stuff the cavity of the bird with the couscous mixture, packing it in fairly loosely. Push the lemon half into the opening of the cavity. Beat the remaining saffron into the butter and rub it all over the skin of the bird. Sprinkle with a good pinch of salt.

Place the chicken in a roasting tin, put it in the oven and roast for about 15 minutes, until the skin is nicely browned. Reduce the temperature to 180°C/Gas Mark 4. Arrange the vegetables around the chicken, turning them to coat them in the fat, and return to the oven. Cook for about an hour and a half, basting the bird regularly to keep it moist. To check if the chicken is cooked, insert a skewer into the fattest part of the leg, near the bone; the juices should come out clear.

Remove the chicken from the oven and leave to rest for about 10 minutes, then remove the lemon half and spoon out the couscous before carving. Serve with the vegetables and the juices from the pan. It's very good with a little salad of nasturtium leaves and flowers, whose spicy freshness will complement the rich flavours.

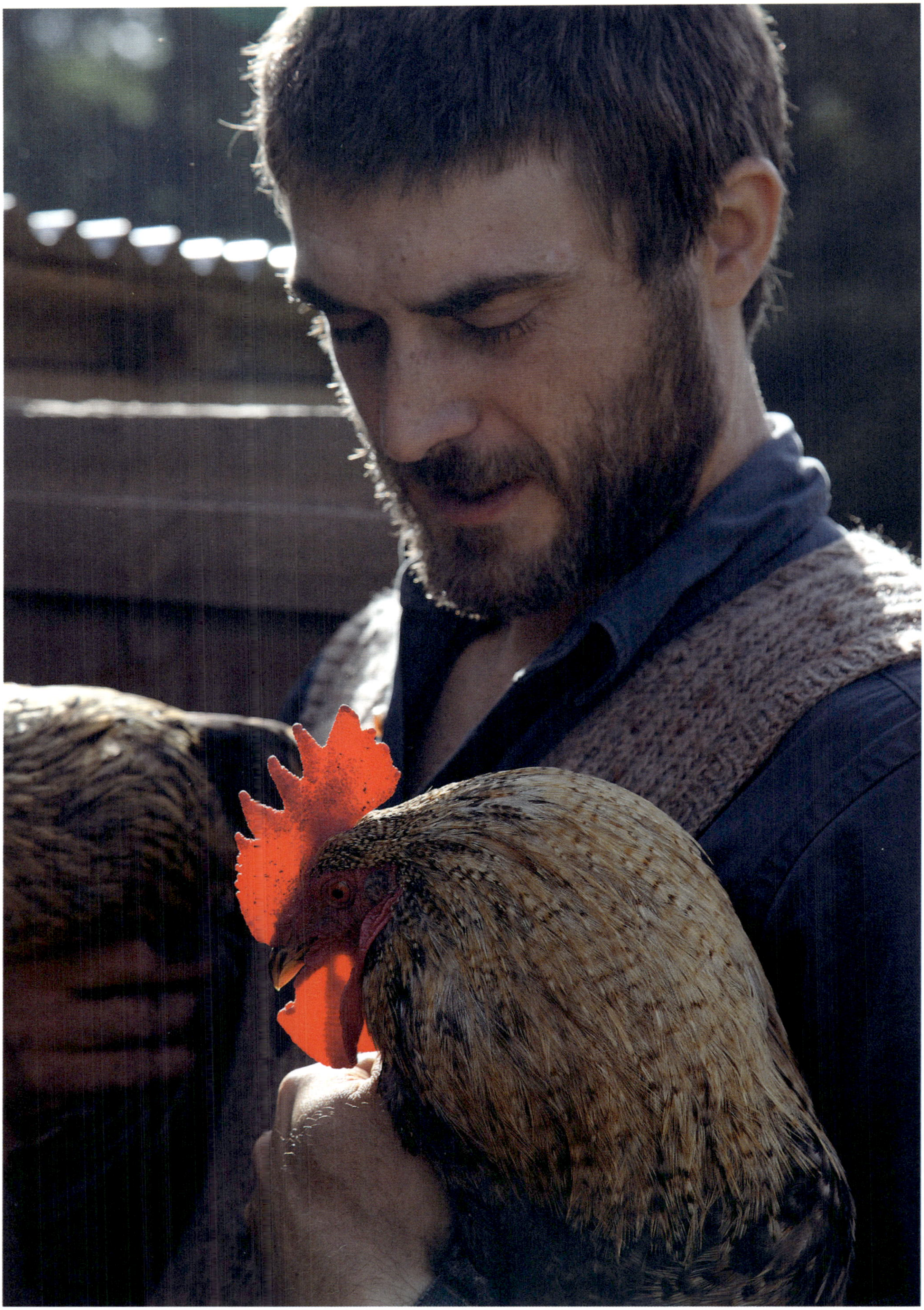

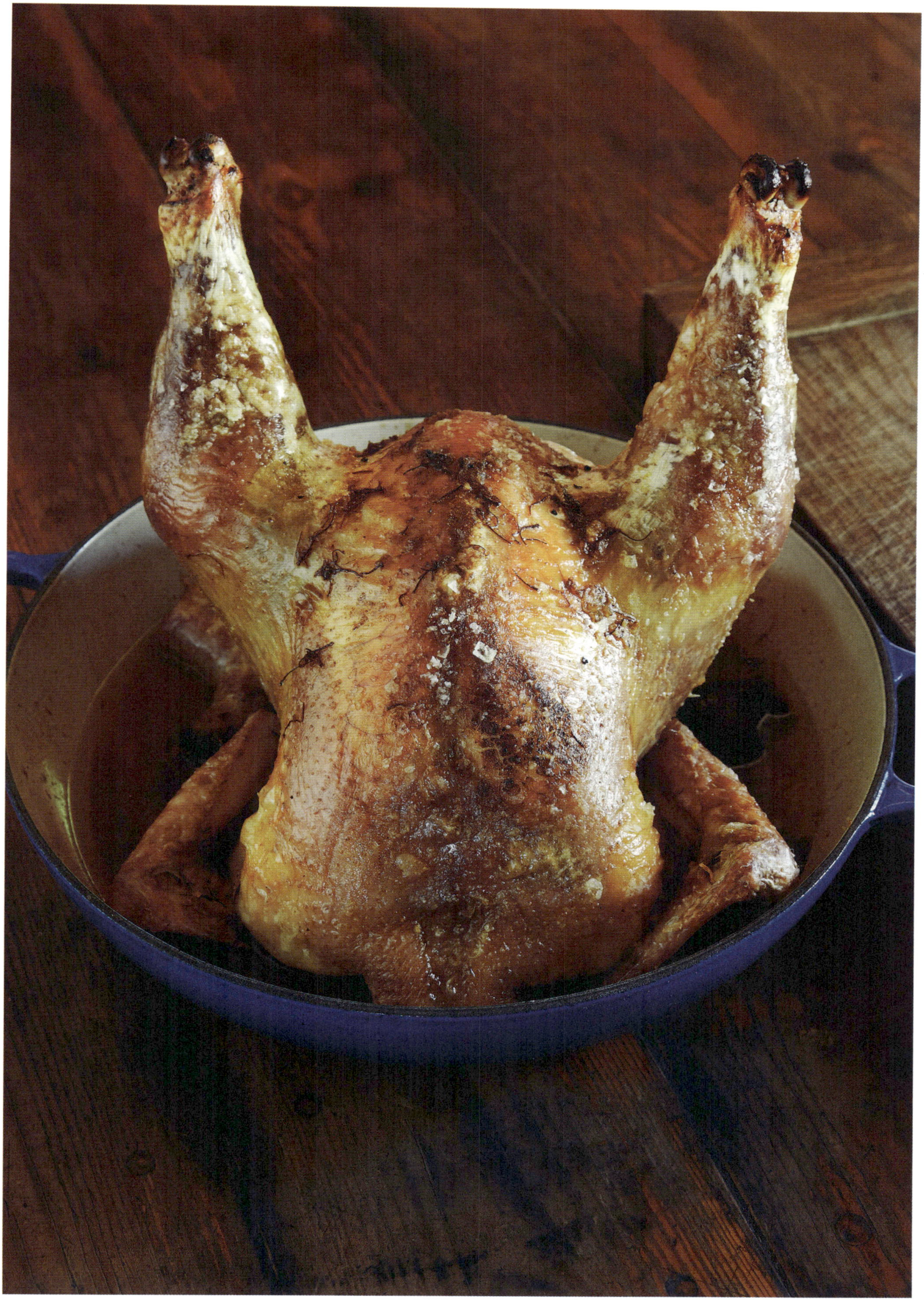

Baked apples with caramel pecans and maple syrup ice cream

SERVES 4

4 cooking apples
20g unsalted butter
50g granulated sugar
2 tablespoons water
50g pecan nuts

For the maple syrup ice cream
400ml double cream
400ml milk
6 egg yolks
200ml maple syrup

Baked apples are such a traditional autumn pudding. This one has its arms outstretched across the Atlantic, with the addition of pecan nuts and maple syrup. Bramleys are the most readily available cooking apples these days. If you find other varieties, perhaps at a farmers' market, do try them for this dish. We can highly recommend the wonderfully named Reverend Wilks, Lord Derby and Grenadier.

First make the ice cream. Pour the cream and milk into a saucepan and heat gently to a simmer, but do not let it boil. Meanwhile, beat the egg yolks together in a bowl. Gradually pour the hot milk and cream on to the yolks, beating constantly. Return this custard to the saucepan and add the maple syrup. Cook over a gentle heat for about 10 minutes, stirring constantly with a wooden spoon, until the mixture is thick enough to coat the back of the spoon lightly. Cover and leave to cool. Chill for at least 2 hours, then give the custard a good whisk to ensure it hasn't separated. Churn in an ice-cream machine according to the manufacturer's instructions, then transfer to the freezer.

Heat the oven to 200°C/Gas Mark 6. Core the apples, leaving them whole. Score lightly around the belly of each one with a sharp knife. Place the apples on a baking tray, cut the butter into quarters and drop a piece into each apple cavity. Bake for 30–45 minutes, until the apples are soft but still retain their shape.

Meanwhile, caramelise the pecans. Prepare a very lightly oiled baking sheet. Put the sugar and water in a small, heavy-based saucepan and place over a moderate heat until the sugar has dissolved, stirring occasionally. Once the sugar has fully dissolved, add the pecans and continue to cook until the syrup becomes golden brown. To test that the caramel has reached the right stage, tilt the saucepan and check that the layer on the bottom of the pan is a rich, dark golden brown. Be careful not to allow it to burn. Pour the praline quickly on to the oiled baking sheet and leave to cool. Once it is cold and hard, break it into small pieces, either in a food processor or by putting it into a sealed plastic bag and bashing with a rolling pin.

To assemble the pudding, place the baked apples in individual bowls and sprinkle the pecan praline inside and on top of them. Add a scoop of ice cream to each one.

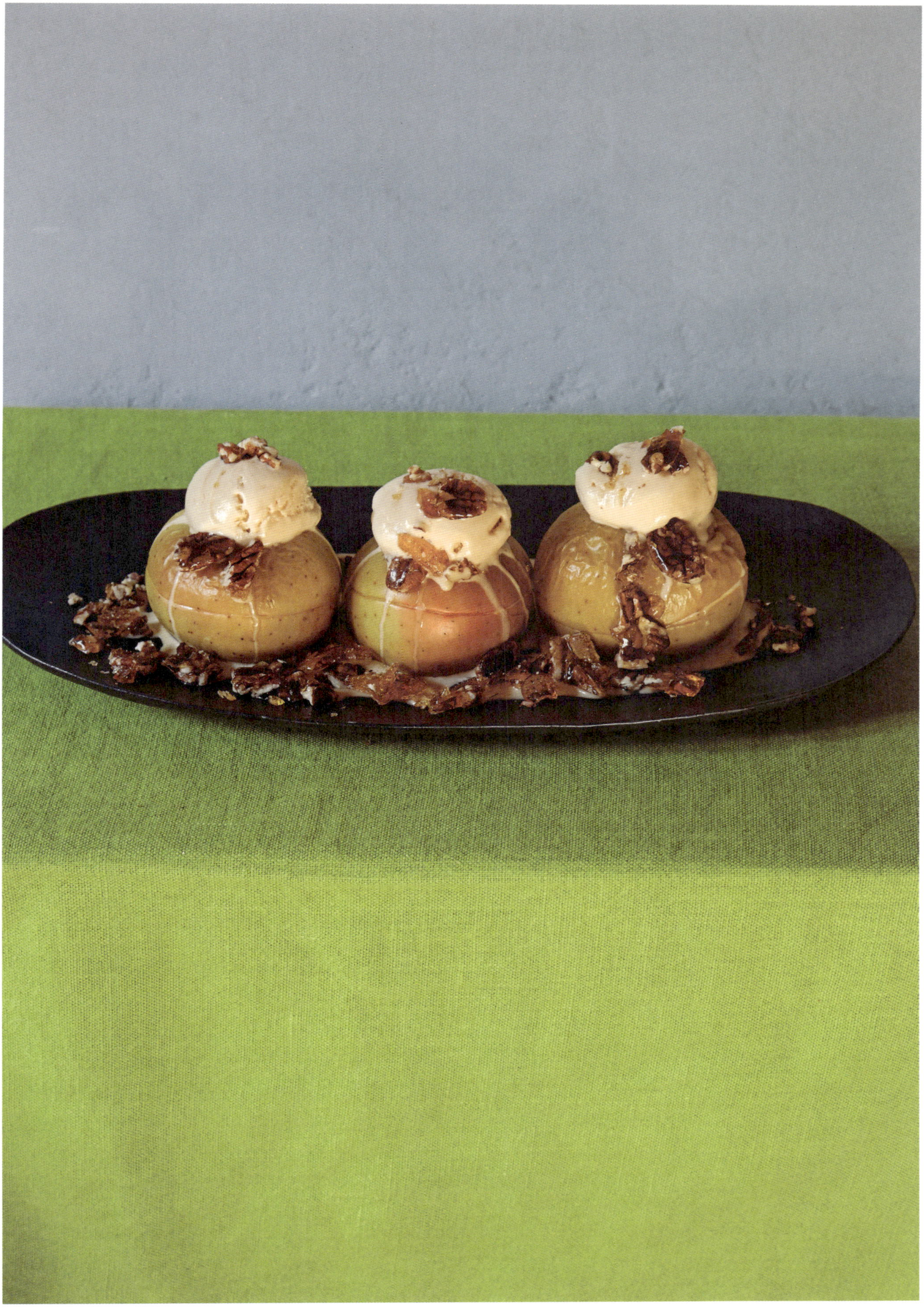

Quince and ginger upside-down cake

SERVES 6–8

140g self-raising flour
¼ teaspoon salt
1 teaspoon ground ginger
½ teaspoon ground cinnamon
¼ teaspoon ground nutmeg
115g demerara sugar
90g butter
115g black treacle
1 egg, lightly beaten
75ml milk

For the quince
2 large or 3 small quinces
50g unsalted butter
125g caster sugar
1 vanilla pod, slit open lengthways
1 lemon

We have three or four quince trees at Fern Verrow. They are all a good age now and, providing there isn't a late frost in April or early May (which sadly happens from time to time), we are blessed with an abundant crop of quinces each year. A funny-looking, gnarly, pear-like thing, covered in a downy coat, the quince, in our eyes, is a very beautiful fruit. Quinces are rarely smooth, unmarked and perfect looking, but don't be put off by this. Just watch out for any with soft brown spots, which may lead to rot, and use these first. Quinces are not for eating raw. When they are cooked, their colour changes from white to a delightful topaz pink.

The fragrance of quince is amazing. One customer buys our quinces to have in a bowl in his house solely to scent the room.

Heat the oven to 180°C/Gas Mark 4. Peel the quinces with a potato peeler or a sharp knife. Cut them into sixths, if large, or quarters, if small, and take out the cores. Be careful, as they are rock hard and quite tricky to cut.

Put the butter and caster sugar in a 21cm Tatin tin or ovenproof frying pan and melt over a gentle heat. Arrange the quince pieces in the tin, cut-side up, so that they are tightly packed in a single layer. Place the vanilla pod on top, along with 2 or 3 wide strips of lemon zest. Squeeze the juice of the lemon over the fruit. Cover with foil and place in the oven. Bake for about 30 minutes, until the fruit is tender, basting regularly to ensure that each piece is coated with the butter and sugar. Remove from the oven, take off the foil and discard the lemon zest and vanilla pod.

While the quinces are in the oven, make the ginger cake. Sift the flour, salt and spices into a bowl and stir in the demerara sugar. Put the butter and treacle into a pan and stir over a gentle heat until melted. Stir into the dry ingredients, along with the beaten egg. Beat with a wooden spoon until smooth, then mix in the milk.

Pour the cake mixture over the quinces and bake for about 40 minutes at 160°C/Gas Mark 3, until the cake is firm to the touch and slightly cracked on top. Allow the cake to cool a little in the tin, then run a knife around the side to loosen it, place a large plate on top and flip them both over to turn out the cake. Serve warm or cold. There may be some excess syrup from the quinces; just spoon this over the top of each serving.

AUTUMN

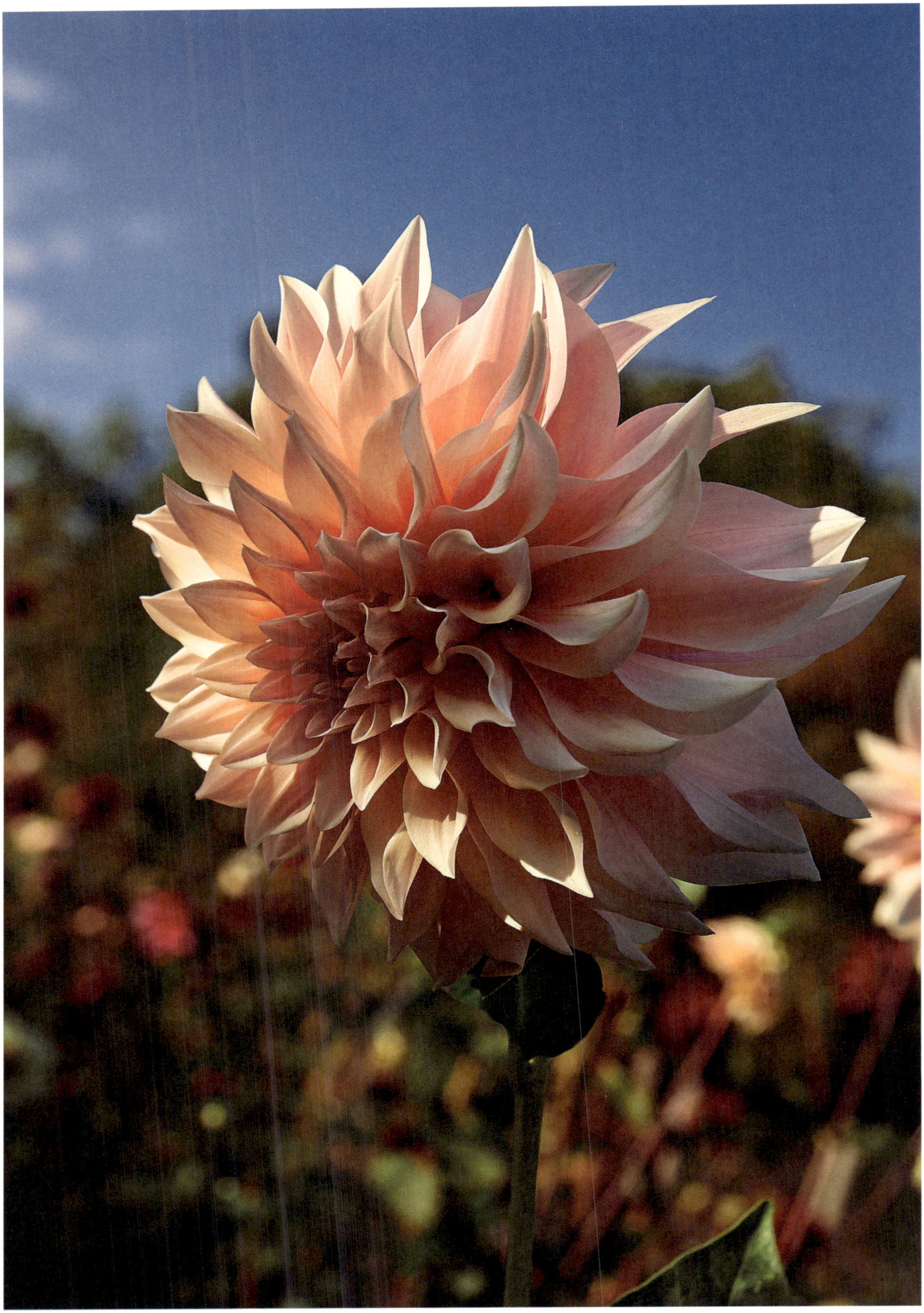

Steamed greengage pudding

SERVES 6

25g butter
750g greengages
75g caster sugar
grated zest of ½ lemon

For the pastry
250g self-raising flour
a pinch of sea salt
125g suet
about 125ml water

Out of all the varieties of the plum family, the greengage is our favourite. A very pretty plum, its skin is almost translucent, sage green in colour with a mother-of-pearl sheen. The gage tends not to be as sweet as other plums. However, used in cooking, the bright flavour of a greengage is outstanding, particularly when matched with a little sugar and custard — sweet, sour and creamy, one of the very best combinations.

Use the butter to grease a 1.2-litre pudding basin. To make the pastry, sift the flour into a mixing bowl, add the salt and suet and mix together lightly with your hands. Stir in enough water to make a soft but not sticky dough. Cut off about a third of the pastry and set aside. On a lightly floured surface, roll out the remaining pastry into a round and use to line the buttered pudding basin, trimming off the excess. Cut the greengages in half and remove the stones. Fill the pastry-lined bowl with the fruit, incorporating the sugar and zest as you go. Roll out the remaining pastry and use to cover the pudding, trimming off the excess and pinching the edges together to seal.

Cover the pudding with a piece of well-buttered baking parchment and then a piece of foil, both with 2cm pleats in the centre to allow room for the pudding to rise. Tie a piece of string firmly around the lip of the basin to hold the paper and foil in place, leaving a long loop of string to act as a handle. Steam the pudding in a steamer for 3 hours, topping up the water as necessary. If you don't have a steamer, place it in a large saucepan and add enough boiling water from the kettle to come three-quarters of the way up the side of the basin. Cover and simmer for 3 hours, checking the water level regularly and topping it up with boiling water as necessary.

Remove the pudding from the steamer or pan, take off the foil and baking parchment and turn it out on to a large plate. Serve immediately, with custard and extra sugar if desired.

Preserving fruit and vegetables

PRESERVING BRINGS BACK strong childhood memories, full of nostalgia. The parade-ground lines in Granny Winnie's larder, with its ranks of bottled greengages and raspberries, jars of jam and chutneys, were a sight to be seen. High tea at her house always had an air of formality and importance. She was a stern lady who liked children to have good manners, especially at the table. Her teas were a credit to her cooking and reflected her desire that everything should be done properly.

A large oak table was laid with matching bone china cups and saucers with a pretty strawberry flower print, shiny silver forks and spoons and bone-handled knives. Sometimes we had boiled eggs with the thinnest of thin slices of beautifully buttered brown bread, flanked by modest slabs of home-cooked ham. But it was the chutneys, pickles and jams that we waited for: a rainbow of summer and autumn colours tidily presented in that same matching china, each dish with its own spoon.

Preserving for us always carries a sense of occasion. The memory of precision and care, and the capturing of a moment in a jar, is one we hold in high esteem. Our kitchen shelves hold many preserving books, old and new. A favourite is a wartime leaflet where many of the recipes suggest using wild fruits, such as elderberry, rosehips and rowan berries. Other books have scribbled notes in the margins, yellowed scraps of paper in familiar handwriting, revealing secret ingredients and techniques.

When it comes to making preserves we always try to allow the fresh ingredients to do the talking. In chutneys, keep a crunch to the texture and add warmth by using spices to lift and add tang. In jams and cordials, let the fruit shine with its natural sweetness and perfume. Following the seasons and capturing the essence of that season is a joy and tremendously satisfying and rewarding.

Every year provides us with seasonal gluts and bounties. If you want to do plenty of preserving keep an eye out at markets and buy ingredients while they are very fresh and cheap: Seville oranges and European lemons in January and February for marmalade and preserved lemons (pages 56–57 and 45); rhubarb in March for cordial (page 130); gooseberries and elderflowers in late May; the soft fruits in the height of summer; and runner beans and onions in late August.

While some forms of preserving require technical processes and precision, in fact jams, jellies, chutneys and pickles are not difficult to make. A good bit of housekeeping, common sense and quality ingredients are all that are needed for a successful preserve.

Equipment

Here is our list of essentials

preserving pan or other wide, large, heavy-based stainless steel pan

accurate weighing scales

sugar thermometer

jam funnel (this saves on waste and washing up)

2 large wooden spoons (one for sugar, one for vinegar and spice)

ladle

nylon sieve

2 or 3 muslin squares in different sizes for holding spices and 1 large one to act as a Jelly bag

a few clean tea towels

jars and lids (you can buy these online relatively cheaply)

General rules for making jams and jellies

Use good-quality fresh ingredients. Try not to wash soft fruit unless absolutely necessary: just pick over for any mouldy fruit or bugs. For other fruits, rinse and dry carefully with kitchen paper or a clean tea towel.

Always add sugar to the warm liquid and do not allow jam or jelly to boil until all the sugar has dissolved, as this can lead to crystallisation later. Once the jam or jelly has reached boiling point, keep the heat at a steady, gentle boil, stirring only occasionally to check for catching. Do not over-stir as this will break up the fruit and spoil the appearance of the jam.

A jam needs to contain at least 60 per cent sugar in order for it to keep. Jam should be kept in a cool, dark place and be consumed within six months. You can make 'fridge jams' with less sugar, but once the jar is open, you will need to keep it in the fridge and eat within two months.

Setting point

Pectin, a gelling agent which occurs naturally in many fruit, is the key to obtaining the perfect set. Generally speaking, the more sour and less ripe the fruit, the more pectin is present. Fruits that are low in pectin, such as strawberries, need the addition of lemon juice (the acid present will draw out the pectin), or use jam sugar, which has added pectin, to assure a perfect set. The red, white and black currants are very high in pectin and set beautifully. White currants are particularly good as a clear base for herb or flower jellies.

The setting point for most jams and jellies is 104.5°C. Fruits with high pectin content, such as gooseberries and currants, will set at a couple of degrees lower. We recommend getting a sugar thermometer, which is not too expensive and the accuracy is very helpful for the success of jam making.

If you don't have a sugar thermometer then use the wrinkle test. Put a dry saucer in the fridge to chill for at least 10 minutes. Then, remove the saucer from the fridge and drop a teaspoon of the jam or jelly on to the cold saucer. Place it back in the fridge, then after 5 minutes run your finger through the centre of the jam. If the jam or jelly is set it will wrinkle and the 2 halves will stay apart.

Sterilising jars and bottles

This is imperative when doing any kind of preserving. Place clean, dry jars into a low oven for at least 15 minutes immediately before you intend to fill them with your jam. Boil the lids in water for 5 minutes, drain, and place them on a clean tea towel to dry. Place the hot jars on a wooden surface or a cloth before ladling the hot preserve into them.

continued on page 254

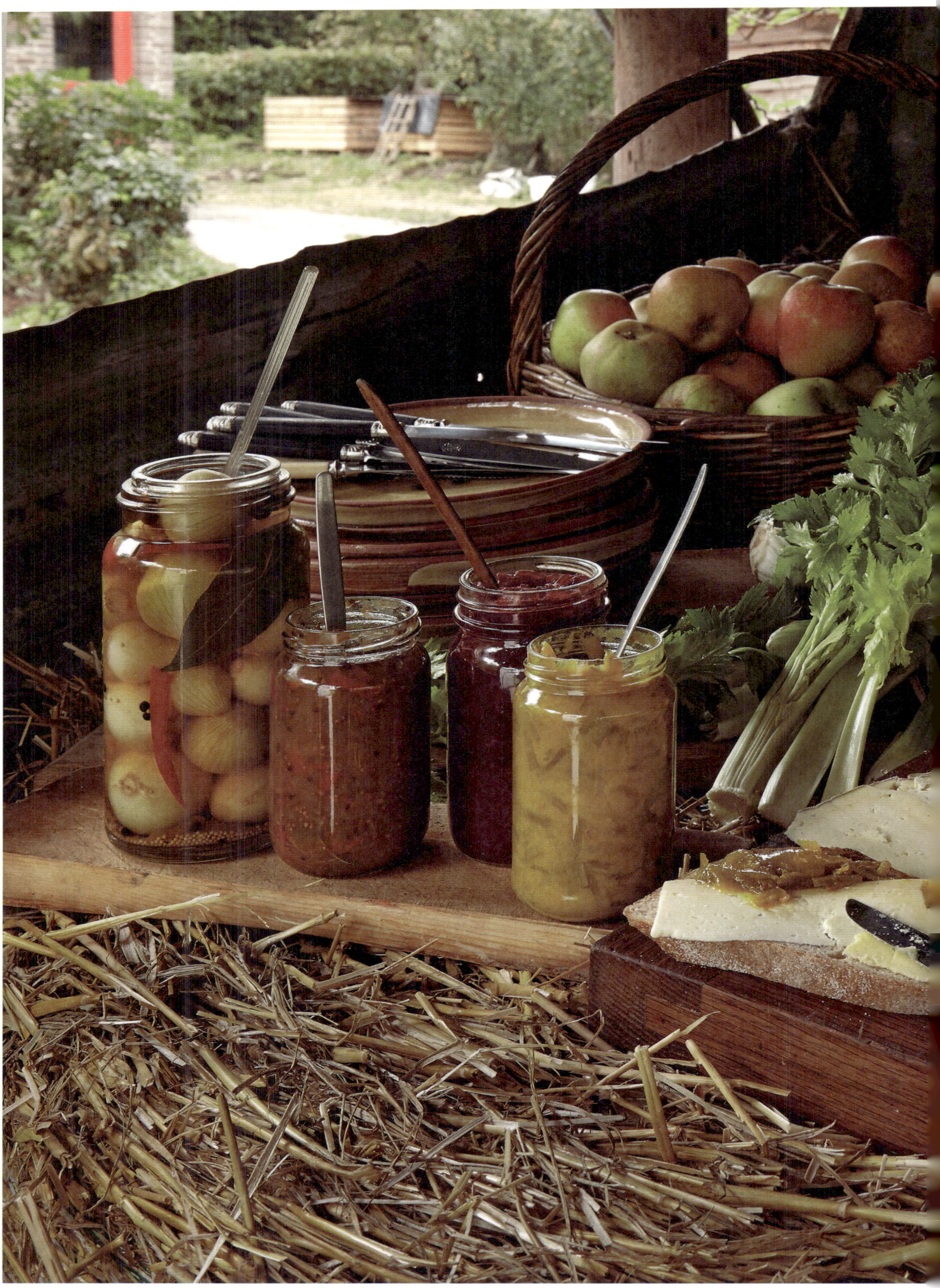

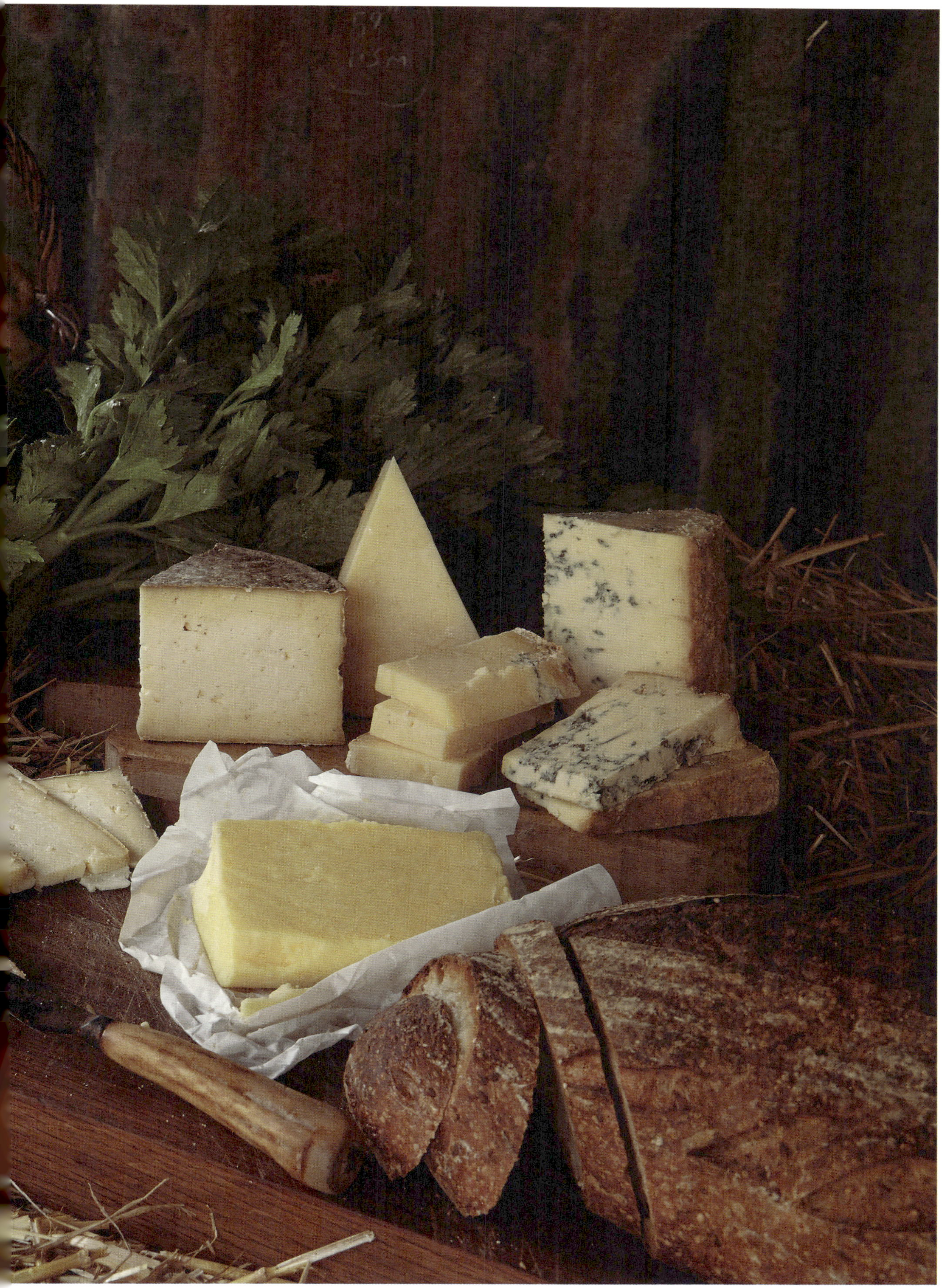

If the jam has whole fruit in it, allow the jam to cool and thicken in the pan for 10–15 minutes before putting it into the hot jars, as this will stop the fruit floating to the top. Skim jam or jelly at the end of cooking only, as it is important only once jarring it up; otherwise it is unnecessary and wasteful.

Screw on the still-hot sterilised lids immediately to seal the jars, then leave the bottled jam undisturbed overnight to cool and set beautifully. Label and date the jars, and store in a cool, dry space.

Jars and lids

We have talked about the importance of precision when preserving. Using the correct jar and lid for each type of preserve is essential, too.

For both jams and chutneys, use a lid with a plasticised seal. This is particularly important when you make vinegar-based preserves – without a plastic seal, over time, the lid will corrode, ruining the chutney. You can reuse jars that you may have at home but we recommend buying new lids.

For making fruit gins we use large (2-litre or 3-litre) Le Parfait jars, which have swing-top lids and reusable thick rubber seals.

When making cordials use bottles that have screw-top or swing-top lids, as these can easily be sterilised. If you wish to use cork stoppers then new ones are essential.

For bottling fruit, such as the raspberries on page 259, screw-band Kilner or Mason jars work best. These are made of thicker glass than regular jam jars and can withstand the high temperatures of the sterilising process. They come with rubber-lined discs to seal the jar and, with the screw band, form the necessary vacuum to ensure preservation.

Tips for making chutneys

It is the combination of salt, vinegar and the cooking process that makes good-keeping chutney. When making a new chutney it is important not to get carried away with your flavours, or you could end up wasting time, ingredients and fuel on something you will never eat. Think through the flavour combinations and keep things simple at first.

Cut vegetables and fruit into bite-sized pieces – 'first date' pieces, as we call them. Use good-quality vinegar: we recommend organic cider vinegar. Generally speaking, cook chutneys slowly, so that all the spices and other flavours blend together to taste rich and full.

Cordials, fruit gins and vinegars

All of these are so simple to make and have a luxurious quality about them. Cheap to produce, cordials can be used throughout the year. On hot days on the farm we have made ice lollies with them, mixing one part cordial to three parts water. Cold, refreshing and sweet, they help us to pick up our hoes with renewed enthusiasm and get those carrots weeded.

Beetroot and horseradish chutney

MAKES 5 X 450G JARS

1.5kg beetroot
500g onions, chopped
1 litre cider vinegar
500g cooking apples, peeled, cored and chopped
500g rhubarb, cut into small chunks
3 tablespoons grated fresh horseradish
1 teaspoon sea salt
750g granulated sugar

The addition of a little rhubarb to this chutney is fantastic, giving it an original texture and flavour. We tend to use the older stalks – too stringy and tough for a crumble, they're a thrifty use of end-of-season rhubarb.

This chutney disappears very quickly in our house. We often eat it as a side vegetable with cold beef for lunch.

Wash the beetroot well, put them in a saucepan, cover with water and bring to the boil. Simmer until tender, then drain and leave for a few minutes until cool enough to handle.

While the beetroot are cooking, put the onions in a preserving pan with 200ml of the vinegar and cook gently until soft. Add the apples and rhubarb and continue to cook gently, stirring occasionally, until the apples and rhubarb begin to fall apart and become pulpy.

Peel the beetroot and grate them either with the grating attachment of a food processor or with a cheese grater on the largest hole. Add the grated beetroot to the pan along with the horseradish, salt and remaining vinegar. Bring back to a simmer, add the sugar and stir until dissolved. Continue to cook for 30–40 minutes, until thick, stirring occasionally to prevent the chutney catching and burning. To check that it is the right consistency, run a wooden spoon across the base of the pan; the mixture should briefly split before it comes back together again.

Allow the chutney to cool a little, then transfer to sterilised jars (see page 251) and seal. Although you can eat the chutney immediately, the flavour matures and improves after a week. Use within a year.

The sheep enjoy eating beetroot, too.

Blackberry and elderberry condiment

MAKES 8 X 225G JARS

1kg crab apples or cooking apples
500g blackberries
500g elderberries
4 small dried red chillies
1 litre water
golden granulated sugar

When we moved from London to Fern Verrow in the autumn of 1996, we spent the first few weeks living the urban fantasy of gathering from the hedges and trees growing around our newly acquired acres. We returned to the kitchen with our bounty rather pleased with ourselves, and feeling that we were the luckiest people in the world. We made this jelly for the first time that year and have always made sure to have it in our store cupboard ever since.

This is not a jelly to spread on a piece of toast, but to use as a flavouring in a stew or a braised meat dish. The warmth of the dried chillies gives a stew a lift, while the berries add depth of flavour and colour to the gravy.

Roughly chop the apples, leaving the skin on and keeping the pips. Place them in a large, heavy-based pan and add the berries, chillies and water. Cover and bring slowly to a simmer. Cook for 30–45 minutes, until the fruit is quite mushy and all the juices have run. Allow to cool a little. Line a sieve with a piece of sterilised muslin, set it over a bowl and pour the fruit and their juices into it. Tie the corners of the muslin together and suspend the bag over the bowl for at least 6 hours (overnight is best) so the juice can drip through. Remember, as with most jelly-making, do not squeeze the bag or you will cloud the jelly and lose its sparkle.

Measure the juice and allow 400g sugar for every 600ml. Pour the juice into a pan, bring to the boil, then add the sugar and stir until dissolved. Boil for about 10 minutes, until it reaches setting point (see page 251). Ladle into sterilised jars (see page 251) and seal. Use within a year.

Runner bean chutney

MAKES 4 X 450G JARS

1kg runner beans, stringed and cut into thin strips about 3cm long
4 onions, sliced
680g demerara sugar
600ml malt vinegar
45g English mustard powder
1½ teaspoons ground turmeric
45g cornflour

We put our hands in the air and admit that this gem of a chutney is not our recipe. There is a rather yellowed handwritten piece of paper in our preserving file that must be at least 25 years old. It comes from Granny Whitby, another queen of preserving (and pastry-making).

Tip the runner beans and onions into a preserving pan full of boiling salted water and cook until just tender. Drain, then return to the pan. Add the sugar and half the vinegar and bring to the boil, stirring to dissolve the sugar. Turn the heat down to a simmer and cook for 15 minutes. Meanwhile, mix the remaining vinegar with the mustard powder, turmeric and cornflour to make a smooth paste. Stir this into the beans and onions and simmer for a further 15 minutes, until thick, stirring occasionally to prevent the mixture catching and burning.

Allow the chutney to cool a little, then transfer to sterilised jars (see page 251) and seal. You can eat the chutney immediately, although the flavour does improve after a couple of weeks. Use within a year.

Spicy green tomato chutney

MAKES 6 X 450G JARS

1kg green tomatoes, cut into 2cm chunks
750g cooking apples, peeled, cored and cut into 2cm chunks
375g onions, thinly sliced
1 large red pepper, cut into thin strips 3cm long
400ml cider vinegar
1 teaspoon sea salt
juice and grated zest of 1 large lime
1 tablespoon yellow mustard seeds
1 tablespoon brown mustard seeds
1 red chilli, deseeded and finely chopped
350g granulated sugar

For the spice bag

1 tablespoon coriander seeds
1 teaspoon peppercorns
1 teaspoon allspice berries
1 teaspoon cloves
½ cinnamon stick
a knuckle of fresh ginger

We grow a lot of tomatoes. As the sun's warmth lessens towards the end of September and the time comes to pull the plants out of our greenhouse, we inevitably have a few unripe green ones. We must admit that we have never been big fans of green tomato chutney – usually a rather dull-looking jar that gets left on the shelf. One year, though, we decided to experiment and make an exciting, fresh, spicy chutney with our unripe tomatoes. The recipe below is what we came up with, and it has proved to be one of our bestsellers. We based it on a fresh green tomato relish often used in Indian cooking.

Place the tomatoes, apples, onions and red pepper in a preserving pan with the vinegar and salt. Slowly bring to a simmer and cook for 20 minutes, stirring occasionally. Add the lime juice and zest, mustard seeds and chilli, then add the sugar and stir until dissolved.

To make the spice bag, place all the spices in a clean piece of muslin and tie into a ball. Add to the pan and simmer for about 30 minutes, until most of the liquid has evaporated and the chutney is thick, stirring frequently to prevent it catching and burning. To check that the chutney is the right consistency, run a wooden spoon across the base of the pan; the mixture should briefly split before it comes back together again.

Remove the pan from the heat and take out the spice bag. Let the chutney cool a little, then transfer it to sterilised jars (see page 251) and seal. Use within a year.

Fruit gins

Being keen on a nice tipple, we have experimented over the years with fruit gins. We mostly enjoy them at Christmas with our family. We have also been known to have a quick nip on particularly cold afternoons in December while cleaning cratefuls of muddy, wet leeks in the yard. It gets the job done more quickly, putting ourselves in better spirits!

Damsons are among our favourite stone fruit, both for cooking and for making gin. These wild, peacock-blue plums are also cultivated now, for good reason. The fruit has such a unique deep, concentrated flavour that we always look forward to it reappearing in our kitchen each autumn.

Most people are familiar with the delightful sloe gin. Sloes are inky-blue wild plums from the blackthorn tree and are ready to harvest from about mid-October.

You can use the method below for all stone fruit, such as sloes, damsons and plums. Pick the fruit on a dry day, choosing ripe but undamaged specimens. Any damaged fruit might spoil the flavour and appearance of the gin. Prick each one with a large needle to release the juices. This takes a little time, of course, but it's a very pleasant activity while sitting around the kitchen table having a natter.

Pack a sterilised large jar such as a Le Parfait (see page 254) with the fruit until the jar is two-thirds full. Pour caster sugar on top of the fruit, to just below the rim. Then carefully pour the gin, which will trickle down between the fruit. Continue pouring until the jar is full to the brim. Close the lid, seal with the clip and turn the jar upside down a few times to disperse the sugar.

Store in a cool, dry place, repeating the turning process every couple of days until the sugar has dissolved. The gin will be ready to use after 3–4 months. You can strain the liquor into sterilised bottles before use, although this is not essential. The fruit can be eaten either in small glasses or spooned over ice cream.

Soft-fruit gins

At the height of summer we have made gins using soft fruit. Raspberry and strawberry are especially good, while blackcurrants can also be transformed into a special-tasting gin. The method is the same as above. Again, choose unblemished fruit that you have picked on a dry day. Avoid washing it; just remove the stalks and carefully pick over the fruit. There's no need to prick the berries. For flavour and attractiveness, you can also add a raspberry or blackcurrant leaf to the jar, especially if making the gin to give as a present.

Gin fizz

This recipe is a great festive drink and well loved in our family. We use 3 parts fruit gin to 1 part lemon juice and 3 parts soda water. Place several ice cubes into a cocktail shaker or jug. Pour over the gin and lemon juice and give them a vigorous shake or stir. Strain into ice-filled glasses and top up with soda water.

Raspberries in syrup

about 300g freshly picked raspberries per jar (this quantity is a guide only)

granulated sugar

Making jams and chutneys is not the only way to preserve fruit and vegetables. Bottling that essence of summer, particularly with soft fruit, is a wonderfully satisfying activity. We preserve our excess raspberries and other soft fruits in sugar syrup. We line up the twinkly, jewelled jars in our kitchen like ornaments. Seeing them on a winter's day makes us feel good and reminds us that warmer weather will return, while opening a jar of these precious jewels never fails in the oooh and ahhh department.

As with all preserving, the freshness and quality of the ingredients is key to success here, in terms of both taste and keeping qualities. Bottling is an exercise in precision, but does not involve lengthy preparation. You will need a large, deep pan in which to simmer the filled jars. An accurate thermometer is essential.

It's best to pick the raspberries directly into 500ml screw-top Kilner jars to reduce the risk of bruising. If you cannot pack them directly into jars, then arrange them in a single layer as you pick them. If you like, add 50ml brandy to each jar with the sugar syrup to make this a more grown-up preserve.

Pack as many clean but unwashed ripe, perfect raspberries as you can into 500ml screw-top Kilner jars. Do not squash the berries or they will break, which will spoil their appearance. A chopstick or long-handled teaspoon will help.

We usually use a light sugar syrup for raspberries, so the result is not too sweet. If we have had a wet, chilly summer and the fruit is less sweet, we will make a heavier syrup. For each jar, pour 150ml water into a pan and add 25g sugar for a light syrup, 45g sugar for a medium one and 60g sugar for a heavy syrup. Place over a low heat and let the sugar dissolve slowly, stirring occasionally with a metal spoon. Once the sugar has dissolved, turn up the heat and boil for 1 minute. Then let the syrup cool until it measures 60°C on a thermometer. Pour it into each jar of raspberries, filling them to the brim. Place a sterilised seal on top. Fasten the screw band but release it a quarter turn to allow steam to escape.

Place the jars in a large, deep pan and fill it with warm water so the jars are completely covered. Put it over a moderate heat and slowly bring to simmering point (88°C) over a period of half an hour. Maintain this temperature for 2 minutes, checking the thermometer throughout.

Lift the jars from the water on to a thick cloth or wooden board. Tap each jar to remove any bubbles and then tighten the seals fully. Leave the jars undisturbed for 24 hours. Don't worry if the fruit appears to be floating; if you have packed the jars well, the raspberries will plump up as they absorb the syrup and sink to the bottom. Ideally store the filled jars in a cool, dark place; however, they are so very beautiful that we store them on the kitchen shelves where we can warm our eyes on them. They will keep for a year.

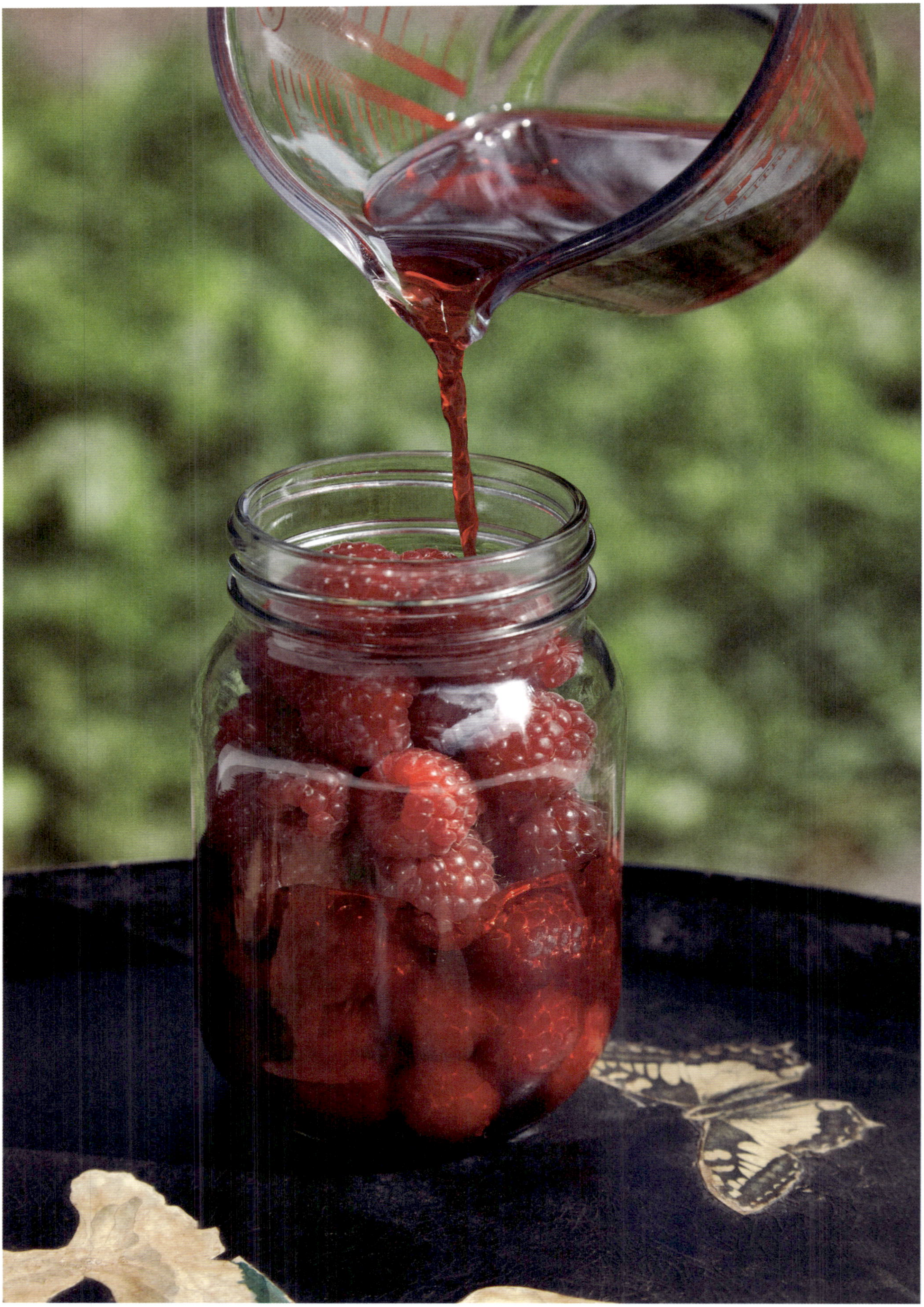

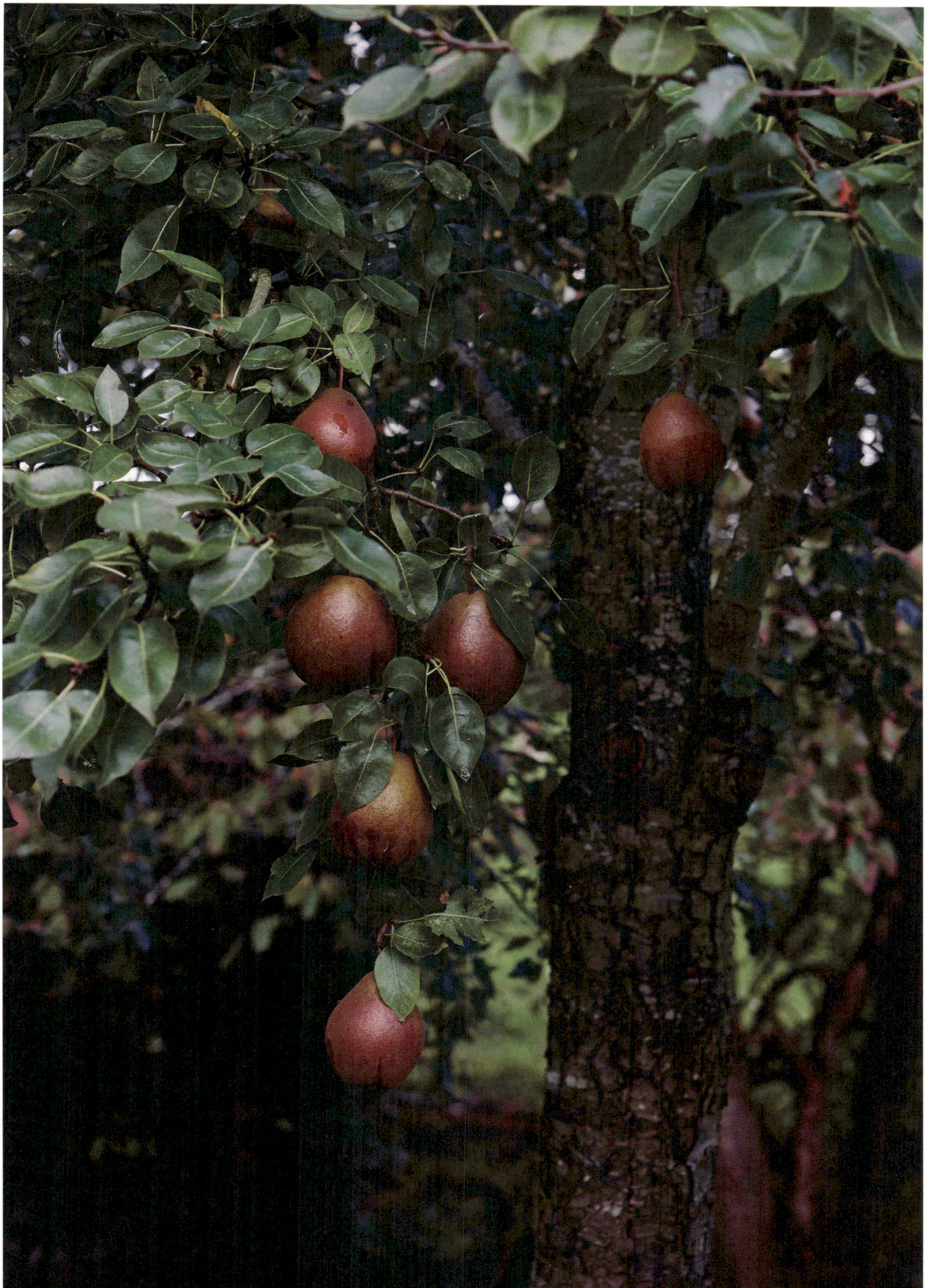

Reflecting on the year

How each the Whole its substance gives,
Each in the other works and lives!
See heavenly forces rising and descending,
Their golden urns reciprocally lending:
On wings that winnow sweet blessing
From heaven through the earth they're pressing,
To fill the All with harmonies caressing.
  GOETHE, *FAUST*, PART ONE*

*From the translation of Faust, Part One *by Bayard Taylor, revised and edited by Stuart Atkins (Collier Books, New York, 1962)*

NO TWO SEASONS are ever the same – this is part of the beauty of working the land and living with the elements. Late autumn is a special time: both an ending and a beginning. We've reached a point of culmination and there's a feeling that things are drawing to a conclusion. Our cultivations of the soil have come to a close as the ground becomes wetter and colder. Now we make preparations for the forthcoming year's production: applying compost and leaf mould to the perennial flowers and herbs, and manure to the fruit plants and bushes; ensuring everything is in its place, bedded down and ready for the winter.

We feel a relief as the days draw in. There's a real sense of our consciousness waking up from a summer dream. There's clarity, as we assess which crops have performed well and outshone the others, and which have struggled and sometimes failed. We make notes of successes and mistakes to inform our planning through the winter. Our memories of the whole growing cycle are still very vivid as we think back over the year.

This time brings an increasing hunger for information and knowledge, to follow up on what we've learned from the past season. Our bodies have been fully engaged, driving ever forward in the physical, practical work. Now it is time to use our mental capacities more actively, to build a bridge out of everything that's happened. We need to take care of the future. We chew over the thoughts that we will cultivate and refine through the winter and then put into practice next spring and summer.

Our relationship with the farm continues to feed us; the work never ceases, our lives are played out on this plot of land. We set out with certain intentions years ago, but these have become much more. Through the work we find the answers to our questions. The more involved we are, the more we get back. The deep bond we've forged with this place has shown us where to look for beauty, even in the hardest times. Our endurance and capacity increase as our intimate knowledge of the land grows: a reciprocal partnership between the soil, the plants, the animals and ourselves. The gifts of the year have come full circle, transforming the past into the seeds of the future.

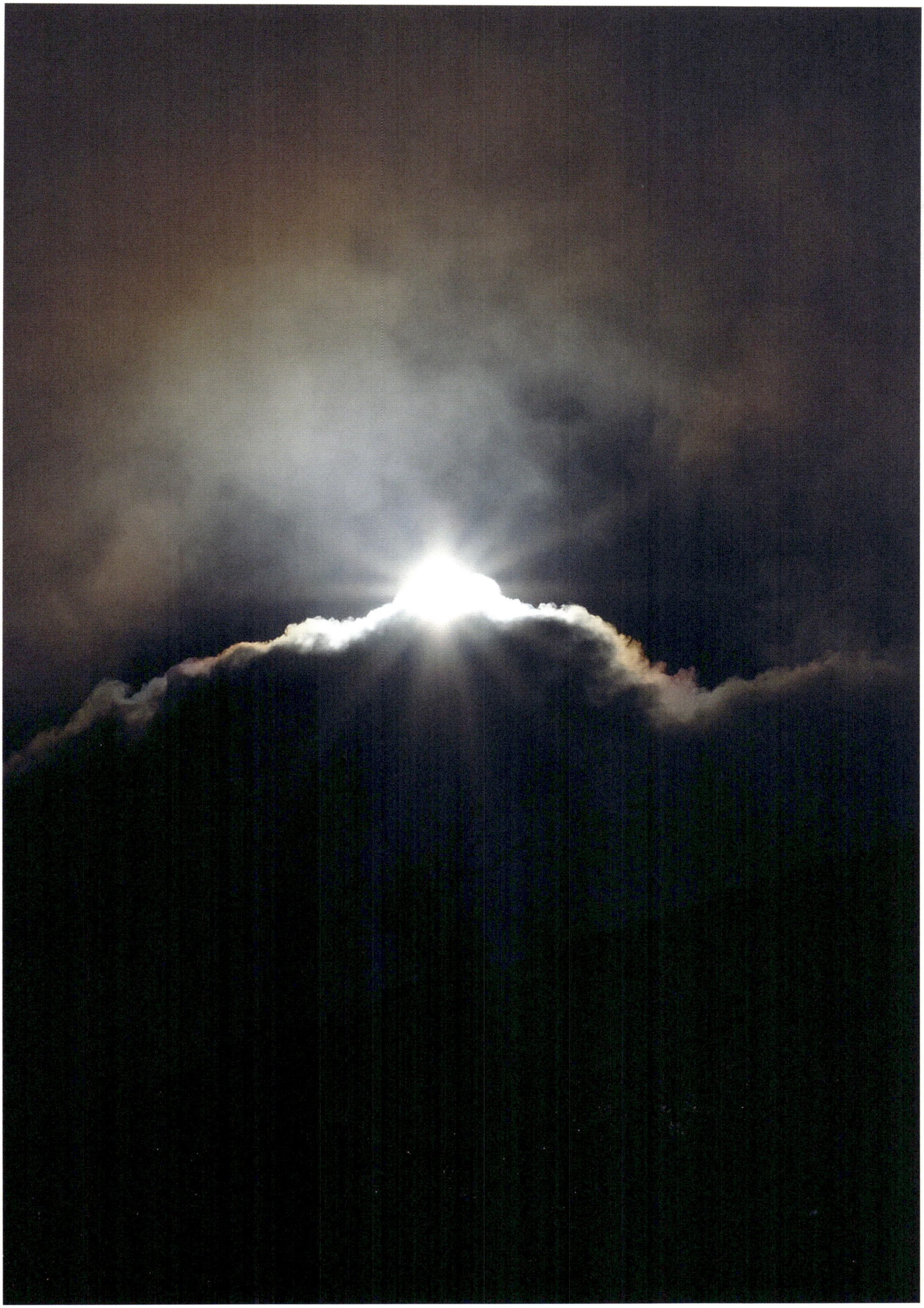

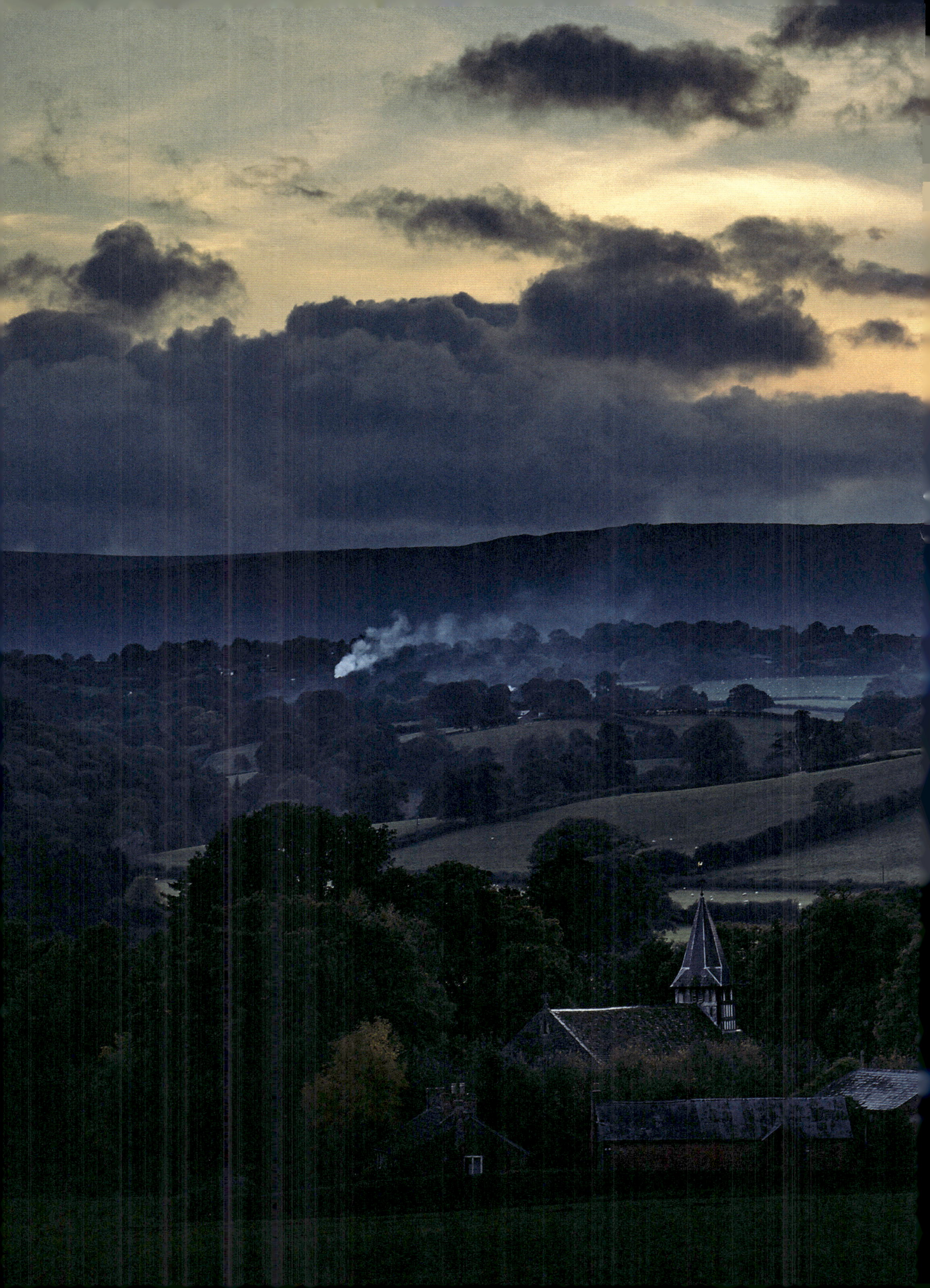

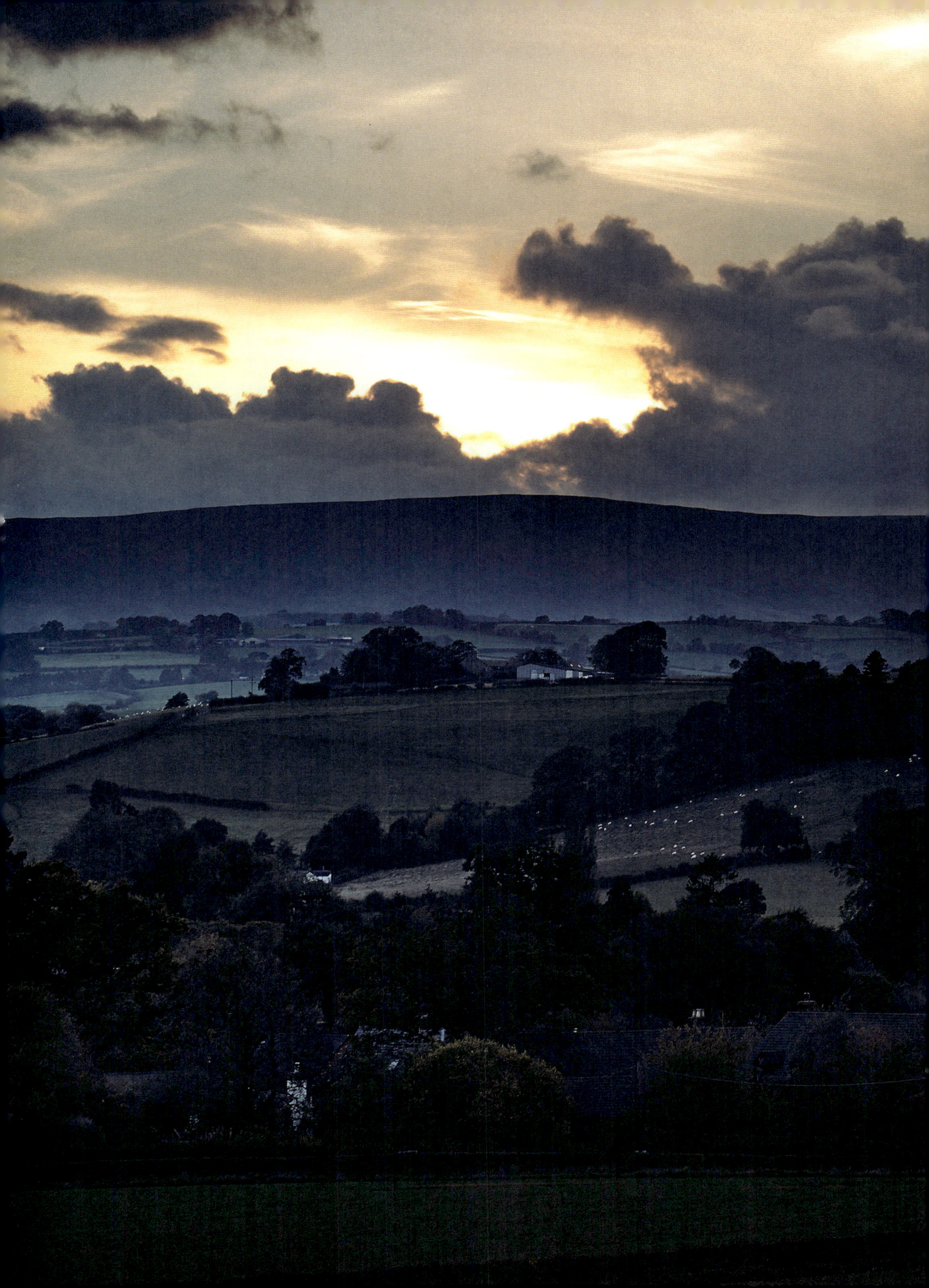

Index

A

animals 74–6, 140, 226–8, 255
   poultry 114, 128, 138, 140, 228
apples
   apple and lemon crumble with a nutty topping 52
   baked apples with caramel pecans and maple syrup ice cream 244
artichokes, Jerusalem *see* Jerusalem artichokes
asparagus 82
   barbecued asparagus with sheep's cheese and lemon 82
   fried duck egg with asparagus, sage and parmesan 116
   spring fritters with wild garlic mayonnaise 88
astronomy 176
aubergines
   aubergines baked with tomato, garlic and parsley 222
   fennel, celery, aubergine, lentil and feta salad 216
avocadoes 170

B

barbecues 170, 172
beans
   borlotti bean, chorizo and tomato stew 234
   broad bean hummus 142
   broad beans in parsley sauce on fried bread 148
   runner bean chutney 257
   yellow French bean salad 218
beef
   beef stew with parsley dumplings 36
   cottage pie 44
   summer vegetable lasagne 162–3
bees 140
beet leaves
   spring garden sandwiches 98
beetroot 255
   beetroot and cream cheese tart 224
   beetroot and horseradish chutney 255
biodynamic farming methods 8, 166–7, 176
   biodynamic preparations 70, 105, 166–7
   compost preparations 93, 166, 212
   field sprays 105, 166–7
   horn preparations 12, 166–7
biscuits
   parsnip and hazelnut oat biscuits 54
blackberries
   blackberry and elderberry condiment 256
   fruit vinegar 196
blackcurrants
   blackcurrant pie 179
borage 152, 155
   spring fritters with wild garlic mayonnaise 88
borlotti beans
   borlotti bean, chorizo and tomato stew 234

bread
   spring garden sandwiches 98
   bread sauce 63
broad beans 148
   broad bean hummus 142
   broad beans in parsley sauce on fried bread 148
Brussels sprouts
   braised Brussels sprouts with chestnuts 64
buckwheat
   buckwheat galettes filled with spinach béchamel 106
butter
   herb butters 96
   spring garden sandwiches 98
buttercream 134

C

cabbage 84
   braised red cabbage with apple 64
   spicy stuffed Savoy cabbage leaves 33
cabbage flowers 152, 156
cakes
   baked cheesecake with rhubarb compote 126
   carrot and almond cake 55
   elderflower cake 134
   quince and ginger upside down cake 246
   rose angel cake with crystallised rose petals 192
   for trifle 186
carrots 174
   carrot and almond cake 55
   fresh peas and baby carrots 174
cauliflower
   cauliflower salad with Dijon mustard and parsley dressing 111
   spring fritters with wild garlic mayonnaise 88
celery
   fennel, celery, aubergine, lentil and feta salad 216
   spring fritters with wild garlic mayonnaise 88
chamomile 92, 212
chard
   cod rarebit with Swiss chard 232
   ruby chard, tomato and lime curry 223
   spring garden sandwiches 98
cheese
   baked cheesecake with rhubarb compote 126
   beetroot and cream cheese tart 224
cheese pastry 210
   fennel, celery, aubergine, lentil and feta salad 216
   halloumi and vegetable kebabs 172
   tomatoes on toast with herbed goat's cheese 144
   Tondo courgettes stuffed with peas, marjoram and goat's curd 163
chervil, in herb butter 96

chestnuts
   braised Brussels sprouts with chestnuts 64
   herb and chestnut stuffing 62
chicken
   barbecued chicken with sweetcorn and lime leaf 170
   roast chicken stuffed with couscous, preserved bergamot lemons and saffron 241
   side dishes with 28
chickens 114, 138, 140, 228
chicory
   braised chicory and bacon 28
chive flowers 155
   in herb butter 96
   spring garden sandwiches 98
chives 155
   in herb butter 96
   pasta with green sauce 100
   spring garden sandwiches 98
chlorophyll 84
Christmas 58, 60, 66, 70, 228
   Christmas pudding, sour cherry 66
chutneys 250, 254
   beetroot and horseradish chutney 255
   blackberry and elderberry condiment 256
   runner bean chutney 257
   spicy green tomato chutney 257
cicely *see* sweet cicely
cockerel
   roast chicken stuffed with couscous, preserved bergamot lemons and saffron 241
cockerels 138, 228
cocktails 130, 155, 258
cod
   cod rarebit with Swiss chard 232
comfrey
   spring fritters with wild garlic mayonnaise 88
compost 212
   see also biodynamic preparations
constellations 176
cordials 155, 254
   elderflower cordial 132
   rhubarb cordial 130
coriander, in herb butter 96
cornflowers 156
courgette flowers 150, 156
   lemon and courgette flower risotto 149
courgettes
   courgettes in saffron and basil butter 150
   spring fritters with wild garlic mayonnaise 88
   Tondo courgettes stuffed with peas, marjoram and goat's curd 163
couscous
   preserved lemon, prune, quince and couscous stuffing 62
   roast chicken stuffed with couscous, preserved bergamot lemons and saffron 241

cows 76, 140, 226
cowslips 156
cress
  spring garden sandwiches 98
cucumber
  soused mackerel with cucumber and dill 168
  yoghurt and cucumber dip for kebabs 172
curries
  ruby chard, tomato and lime curry 223
custards
  blood orange jelly with stem ginger custard 50
  rhubarb and custard fool 124
  for trifle 186–8
cycles 128, 176, 202–204, 212

D
damsons 258
dandelions 86, 152, 212
  spring fritters with wild garlic mayonnaise 88
desserts
  apple and lemon crumble with a nutty topping 52
  baked apples with caramel pecans and maple syrup ice cream 244
  baked cheesecake with rhubarb compote 126
  blackcurrant pie 179
  blood orange jelly with stem ginger custard 50
  jostaberry ripple ice cream 190
  peach melba 182
  peaches and cream 178
  rhubarb and custard fool 124
  sour cherry Christmas pudding 66
  steamed greengage pudding 249
  summer fruit trifle 186–8
drinks
  fruit vinegar 196
  see also cocktails, cordials and teas
drying herbs 90
duck eggs 116
ducks 140, 228
dumplings, parsley 36

E
eggs 114
  chive, sorrel and ramson frittata 118
  fried duck egg with asparagus, sage and parmesan 116
  goose eggs 121
  spring garden sandwiches 98
elderberries
  blackberry and elderberry condiment 256
  fruit vinegar 196
elderflowers 93
  elderflower cake 134
  elderflower cordial 132
  gooseberry and elderflower jam 197
elements 12, 176
Epiphany 70

equipment
  mandolines 168
  mouli-légumes 206
  for preserving 250, 254
Erbe, Hugo 70

F
fennel 92
  baked fish with fennel and saffron 168
  fennel, celery, aubergine, lentil and feta salad 216
  spring fritters with wild garlic mayonnaise 88
Fern Verrow 8, 104–105
  map 6–7
  water supply 8, 104–105
fertilising 105, 166–7, 212
  see also compost
field sprays 105, 166–7
fish
  baked fish with fennel and saffron 168
  baked trout in a new-season herb crust with beurre blanc 120
  cod rarebit with Swiss chard 232
  roast hake with spinach, bacon and Puy lentils 26
  sauces for 101
  soused mackerel with cucumber and dill 168
flowers 86, 152–6
  see also courgette flowers
fool
  rhubarb and custard fool 124
foraging 86, 156
French beans
  yellow French bean salad 218
frittata
  chive, sorrel and ramson frittata 118
fritters
  spring fritters with wild garlic mayonnaise 88
fruit 138
  summer fruit trifle 186–8
  see also individual fruits
fruit gins 258
fruit vinegars 86, 196

G
galettes
  buckwheat galettes filled with spinach béchamel 106
game animals/birds see rabbit and pigeon
garlic mustard see jack-by-the-hedge
garlic, wild see wild garlic
geese 140, 228
ginger 33
  blood orange jelly with stem ginger custard 50
  in chamomile tea 90, 92
gins, fruit 258
gold, frankincense and myrrh 70
goose
  roast goose 58, 60

goose eggs 121
gooseberries
  gooseberry and elderflower jam 197
  gooseberry sauce 62
gravy 60
  apple gravy 32
  fruit vinegars and 196
greengages 249
  steamed greengage pudding 249
ground elder
  spring fritters with wild garlic mayonnaise 88

H
hake
  roast hake with spinach, bacon and Puy lentils 26
halloumi
  halloumi and vegetable kebabs 172
ham
  baked radicchio and Parma ham 219
  hawthorn leaves 86
hay 140
herbs 90–93, 96
  drying 90
  herb butters 96
  pasta with green sauce 100
  spring garden sandwiches 98
  storing 90
  wild 86
  see also individual herbs
honey 92, 140
horn preparations 166–7
hummus, broad bean 142

I
ice cream
  jostaberry ripple ice cream 190
  maple syrup ice cream 244
ice lollies 254
icing 134
infusions 90–93

J
jack-by-the-hedge (garlic mustard) 86
  pasta with green sauce 100
  spring garden sandwiches 98
jam tarts 198
jams/jellies 250–54
  blackberry and elderberry condiment 256
  caramel Seville orange marmalade 56–7
  gooseberry and elderflower jam 197
  redcurrant jelly 198
jelly
  blood orange jelly with stem ginger custard 50
  rose petals in 156
  for trifle 186
Jerusalem artichokes
  Jerusalem artichoke and parsley soup 24
jostaberries 190
  jostaberry ripple ice cream 190

K

kale 84
    seared wood pigeon with crispy kale, swede and hazelnuts 42
kale flowers 152, 156
kebabs
    lamb and vegetable kebabs 172
    rabbit and peanut kebabs 240
kippers
    kippers with marmalade 57

L

lamb
    lamb and vegetable kebabs 172
lambing 74–6, 226
lasagne
    summer vegetable lasagne 162–3
lavender 154
leeks
    leek, potato and mint stovetop 233
    stir-fried leeks with lime juice and lime leaves 46
lemon balm 92
    tea with elderflower 93
    tea with mint 92
lemon thyme 92
lemons
    goose egg lemon curd 121
    lemonade, borage flowers in 155
    pink lemonade 130
    preserved bergamot lemons 45
lentils
    fennel, celery, aubergine, lentil and feta salad 216
    roast hake with spinach, bacon and Puy lentils 26
    tomato, red lentil and orange soup 206
lettuce
    braised lettuce with peas, spring onion and mint 81
    butterhead lettuce with crème fraîche and parsley dressing 108
    spring garden sandwiches 98
lime (linden) flowers 92
lime leaves
    barbecued chicken with sweetcorn and lime leaf 170
    sweetcorn, chilli, lime and potato soup 207
loganberries
    fruit vinegar 196
lovage
    lovage and potato soup 80
    pasta with green sauce 100
    spring fritters with wild garlic mayonnaise 88

M

mackerel
    soused mackerel with cucumber and dill 168
mallow 152
manure 105, 166
Maria Thun Biodynamic Calendar 176
marigolds 155
marinades 172, 196, 240
marmalade
    caramel Seville orange marmalade 56–7
    kippers with marmalade 57
mayonnaise
    wild garlic mayonnaise 88
meditation 149
mint 90, 92
    in herb butter 96
    pasta with green sauce 100
    tea with elderflower 93
moon, working with 176

N

nasturtiums 154
nettles 93, 212
    nettle soup 78
    spring fritters with wild garlic mayonnaise 88

O

oak bark 212
onions
    Red Florence onion tatin 210
oranges
    blood orange jelly with stem ginger custard 50
    caramel Seville orange marmalade 56–7
    in herb butter 96
organic farming 8
    see also biodynamic farming methods

P

pak choi
    pak choi and spring onion stir-fry 110
pancakes
    buckwheat galettes filled with spinach béchamel 106
pansies 155
parsley
    beef stew with parsley dumplings 36
    broad beans in parsley sauce on fried bread 148
    in herb butter 96
    Jerusalem artichoke and parsley soup 24
    pasta with green sauce 100
    spring garden sandwiches 98
parsnips
    parsnip and hazelnut oat biscuits 54
pasta dishes
    pasta with green sauce 100
    summer vegetable lasagne 162–3
pastry
    savoury 210, 224
    sweet 179
peaches
    peach melba 182
    peaches and cream 178
peas 81, 147
    braised lettuce with peas, spring onion and mint 81
    fresh pea and mint soup 147
    fresh peas and baby carrots 174
    using pods for stock 81, 147
pectin 251
Phillips, Roger, *Wild Food* 86
pigeon
    seared wood pigeon with crispy kale, swede and hazelnuts 42
pigs 228
pizza
    pizza with summer vegetable toppings 158–60
ploughing 30
plums 258
    steamed greengage pudding 249
pork
    paprika pork tenderloin with fennel seeds and buttered onion rice 38
    pork chops with apple gravy 32
    spicy stuffed savoy cabbage leaves 33
pot marigolds 155
potatoes
    leek, potato and mint stovetop 233
    lovage and potato soup 80
    roast potatoes 63
    sweetcorn, chilli, lime and potato soup 207
poultry
    cooking *see* chicken *and* goose
    stuffings for 60, 62, 241
    see also animals
preserves and preserving 250–54
    bottled fruit 259
    caramel Seville orange marmalade 56–7
    crystallised flowers 155, 156, 192
    fruit vinegars 196
    goose egg lemon curd 121
    herbs 90, 96
    preserved bergamot lemons 45
    see also chutneys, cordials *and* jams/jellies
primroses 156
pumpkins 54

Q

quartz 105, 167
quinces 246
    quince and ginger upside down cake 246

R

rabbit
    braised rabbit with juniper berries 237
    rabbit and peanut kebabs 240
radicchio
    baked radicchio and Parma ham 249
radishes
    spring garden sandwiches 98
    ramsons *see* wild garlic
rarebit
    cod rarebit with Swiss chard 232
raspberries
    raspberries in syrup 259
    raspberry vinegar 196

red cabbage
  braised red cabbage with apple 64
red onions
  Red Florence onion tatin 210
redcurrants
  redcurrant jelly 198
rhubarb 124
  baked cheesecake with rhubarb compote 126
  beetroot and horseradish chutney 255
  rhubarb cordial 130
  rhubarb and custard fool 124
rice
  buttered onion rice 38, 240
  jasmine rice, pak choi and spring onion stir-fry with 110
  lemon and courgette flower risotto 149
rocket 156
rose petals 152, 156
  rose angel cake with crystallised rose petals 192
rosemary
  pasta with green sauce 100
ruby chard *see* chard
runner beans
  runner bean chutney 257

S
sage 93
  pasta with green sauce 100
  spring fritters with wild garlic mayonnaise 88
salads
  butterhead lettuce with crème fraîche and parsley dressing 108
  cauliflower salad with Dijon mustard and parsley dressing 111
  dressings for 86, 108, 196
  fennel, celery, aubergine, lentil and feta salad 216
  flowers in 154, 156
  wild ingredients for 84–6
  yellow French bean salad 218
sandwiches 98
sauces
  beurre blanc 120
  bread sauce 63
  creamed sorrel and spinach sauce 101
  gooseberry sauce 62
  green sauce for pasta 100
  see also custards *and* gravy
sea bass
  baked fish with fennel and saffron 168
seeds 74
setting point for jams/jellies 251
shallots 210
sheep 74–6, 140, 226–8, 255
silica *see* quartz
sloe gin 258
soil 30
sorrel
  chive, sorrel and ramson frittata 118
  creamed sorrel and spinach sauce 101
  spring fritters with wild garlic mayonnaise 88

soups
  Golden Ball turnip soup 22
  Jerusalem artichoke and parsley soup 24
  lovage and potato soup 80
  nettle soup 78
  sweetcorn, chilli, lime and potato soup 207
  tomato, red lentil and orange soup 206
  winter vegetable and pearl barley broth 22
spaghetti
  pasta with green sauce 100
spinach
  buckwheat galettes filled with spinach béchamel 106
  creamed sorrel and spinach sauce 101
sprays 105, 166–7
spring onions
  pak choi and spring onion stir-fry 110
  spring fritters with wild garlic mayonnaise 88
spring garden sandwiches 98
sprouts *see* Brussels sprouts
squash
  baked squash with celery and herb cream 208
  squash flowers 156
Steiner, Rudolf 8, 74, 166
sterilising jars/bottles 251
stews
  beef stew with parsley dumplings 36
  borlotti bean, chorizo and tomato stew 234
  reheating 36
stinging nettles *see* nettles
stock
  pea pods for 81, 147
  sweetcorn cobs for 107
strawberries
  fruit vinegar 196
stuffings
  couscous, preserved bergamot lemons and saffron 241
  herb and chestnut stuffing 62
  preserved lemon, prune, quince and couscous stuffing 62
summer savory 142
sun, working with 128
swede
  seared wood pigeon with crispy kale, swede and hazelnuts 42
  swede and nutmeg purée 64
sweet cicely 90, 92
  in herb butter 96
sweet violets *see* violets
sweetcorn
  barbecued chicken with sweetcorn and lime leaf 170
  cobs for stock 207
sweetcorn, chilli, lime and potato soup 207
Swiss chard *see* chard

T
tarragon, in herb butter 96

tarts
  beetroot and cream cheese tart 224
  jam tarts 198
  Red Florence onion tatin 210
teas 90–93
Three Kings Preparation 70
Thun, Maria 176
thyme 92
  pasta with green sauce 100
timing 176
tomatoes 144
  spicy green tomato chutney 257
  tomato, red lentil and orange soup 206
  tomato sauce for aubergines baked with tomato, garlic and parsley 222
  tomatoes on toast with herbed goat's cheese 144
trifle
  summer fruit trifle 186–8
trout
  baked trout in a new-season herb crust with beurre blanc 120
turkeys 114, 228
turnips
  Golden Ball turnip soup 22

V
valerian 93, 212
vegetable dishes
  roasted root vegetables with a fruit vinegar glaze 40
  summer vegetable lasagne 162–3
  winter vegetable and pearl barley broth 22
  see also individual vegetables
vinegar 86
violets 152, 155

W
water
  and biodynamic preparations 70, 104, 105
  supply and distribution 104–105
  vortex in 104, 105
watering 140
whitecurrant
  whitecurrant jelly 156
Wild Food (Phillips) 86
wild garlic
  chive, sorrel and ramson frittata 118
  pasta with green sauce 100
  spring fritters with wild garlic mayonnaise 88
wild plants 84–6, 156
  for preserves 250
  spring fritters with wild garlic mayonnaise 88
  see also nettles

Y
yarrow 212

Z
zodiac 176

Acknowledgements

Thank you to Caroline Harris and Clive Wilson for coming up with the idea and guiding us through the process of writing this book; Judy Barratt and Jane Middleton for their patience and attention to detail; Claire Ptak for her cooking, styling and exceptional baking skills; Joe Woodhouse and Kit Hodgson for helping out so generously in the kitchen.

Thanks also to Lawrence Morton for his good taste and friendship; Lindsay Sekulowicz for drawing the map so beautifully; Richard Taylor for his skill and fine company.

Our gratitude to Anne Furniss, Sarah Lavelle and Helen Lewis at Quadrille Publishing for the opportunity to make this book.

With very special thanks to Tessa Traeger for her magic and generosity of spirit. And to Patricia Thompson for all her time and support – we couldn't have done it without her.

To Nigel Slater for his kindness, and wonderful writing; to Allan Jenkins for the many years of advice and encouragement.

To Anna Hodgson (www.anna-hodgson.com) for lending us her gorgeous bowls and plates; Kaori Tatebayashi (www.kaoriceramics.com) for her beautiful ceramics; David Herbert (www.itstartedwithajug.com) for letting us rootle through his cupboards and borrow so many things.

Also thanks to Allegra McEvedy, Lucas Hollweg, Caroline Howell, Jessica Le Gros, Susan Hitch, Leanne MacMillan, Richard Thornton Smith, Peter Dixon, Tristan Hill and Columb Thompson for all their help and advice – and of course to our many faithful customers who have supported us all these years.

Special thanks to our families: Jess, Jack, Bill and Maya for putting up with us and our farming; Richard and Rosie Astley for always being on our team and being so encouraging and supportive.

To everyone who has worked with us at Fern Verrow.

Finally, our heartfelt thanks to the pioneering work of Rudolf Steiner and to all the farmers, gardeners, scientists and researchers who have helped in developing biodynamics.

Further reading

Spiritual Foundations for the Renewal of Agriculture Rudolf Steiner (Biodynamic Farming & Gardening Association, Inc., Pennsylvania, U.S.A; Trans. 1993). The seminal course of lectures given by Rudolf Steiner in 1924 that began the biodynamic movement.

The Maria Thun Biodynamic Calendar Compiled by Matthias Thun (Floris Books). An annual lunar calendar that has proved indispensable for our work.

Gardening for Life, the Biodynamic Way Maria Thun (Hawthorn Press, 1999). A practical introduction to the art of gardening, sowing, planting, harvesting.

Biodynamic Agriculture Willy Schilthuis (Floris Books, 2003). A concise introduction to the principles and practice of biodynamic agriculture.

Cosmos, Earth and Nutrition, the Biodynamic Approach to Agriculture Richard Thornton Smith (Sophia Books, 2009). Marries a scientific approach with a spiritual approach.

Culture and Horticulture Wolf D. Storl (Biodynamic Literature, 1999). A very readable philosophy of gardening.

Biodynamic Farming Practice Friedrich Sattler and Eckard von Wistinghausen (Biodynamic Agricultural Association, 1992). The definitive manual of biodynamic farming.

Soil, Soul, Society, a Trinity of our Times Satish Kumar (Ivy Press, 2013). An affirmative, ecological treatise presenting a moral imperative for our time.

Principles of Biodynamic Spray and Compost Preparations Manfred Klett (Floris Books, 2006). A series of talks given by an experienced practitioner providing a fascinating overview of agriculture and the philosophy behind the preparations.

Agriculture for the Future: Biodynamic Agriculture Today Ueli Hurter (Perfect Paperbacks, 2014). This celebration of biodynamic agriculture provides an overview of the key ideas and their development since Steiner's 'Agriculture Lectures' ninety years ago.

Websites

To purchase biodynamic books and for information on training, conferences and so on, visit the website of the Biodynamic Association: www.biodynamic.org.uk

For other national biodynamic associations: www.sektion-landwirtschaft.org

Biodynamic agricultural products are marketed under the Demeter brand trademark: www.demeter.net

You can find more information on biodynamic products at: http://www.biodynamic.org.uk/certification

HARRY ASTLEY AND JANE SCOTTER are approaching their twentieth year at Fern Verrow, the Herefordshire farm celebrated for its extraordinary fruit and vegetables. Harry and Jane's biodynamic approach demonstrates an unparalleled affinity with nature that yields beautiful and delicious results.

Jane was trained at Le Cordon Bleu Cookery School in London before becoming co-owner of Neal's Yard Dairy. In 1996 she bought Fern Verrow. Harry trained at Pru Leith's School of Food and Wine. He spent seven years as a chef, first in London and then in Sydney before joining Jane at Fern Verrow as her apprentice in biodynamic agriculture. Harry and Jane are now partners, both in business and in life.

Publishing Director: Sarah Lavelle
Editorial Director: Anne Furniss
Creative Director: Helen Lewis
Design: Lawrence Morton
Photographer: Tessa Traeger
Food Stylist: Claire Peak
Recipe editor: Jane Middleton
Map: Lindsay Sekulowicz
Production: Vincent Smith, Emily Noto

Produced by Harris + Wilson

Colour Reproduction by Colourscan PTY, Singapore

First published in 2015 by Quadrille
Text © Jane Scotter and Harry Astley 2015
Photography © Tessa Traeger 2015
Quadrille is an imprint of Hardie Grant
www.hardiegrant.com.au
Quadrille, 52–54 Southwark Street, London SE1 1UN

ISBN 978 184949 5462

The moral rights of Jane Scotter and Harry Astley to be identified as the authors of this work have been asserted by them in accordance with the Copyright, Designs and Patents Act 1988.

All rights reserved. No part of this publication may be reproduced, stored in a retrieval system or transmitted in any form by any means, electronic, electrostatic, magnetic tape, mechanical, photocopying, recording or otherwise, without the prior written permission of the Publisher.

British Library Cataloguing-in-Publication Data. A catalogue record for this book is available from the British Library.

Printed and bound in China by C&C Offset Printing Ltd

www.cooked.com

10 9 8 7 6 5 4 3 2 1